UNITED NATIONS CONFERENCE ON TRADE AND DEVELOPMENT
Geneva

THE LEAST DEVELOPED COUNTRIES
REPORT 2007

Prepared by the UNCTAD secretariat

UNITED NATIONS
New York and Geneva, 2007

Note

Symbols of United Nations documents are composed of capital letters with figures. Mention of such a symbol indicates a reference to a United Nations document.

The designations employed and the presentation of the material in this publication do not imply the expression of any opinion whatsoever on the part of the Secretariat of the United Nations concerning the legal status of any country, territory, city or area, or of its authorities, or concerning the delimitation of its frontiers or boundaries.

Material in this publication may be freely quoted or reprinted, but full acknowledgement is requested. A copy of the publication containing the quotation or reprint should be sent to the UNCTAD secretariat at: Palais des Nations, CH-1211 Geneva 10, Switzerland.

The Overview from this Report can also be found on the Internet, in all six UN languages,
at the following address:
http://www.unctad.org

UNCTAD/LDC/2007

UNITED NATIONS PUBLICATION
Sales No. E.07.II.D.8

ISBN 978-92-1-112717-1
ISSN 0257-7550

What are the Least Developed Countries?

Fifty countries are currently designated by the United Nations as "least developed countries" (LDCs): Afghanistan, Angola, Bangladesh, Benin, Bhutan, Burkina Faso, Burundi, Cambodia, Cape Verde, Central African Republic, Chad, Comoros, Democratic Republic of the Congo, Djibouti, Equatorial Guinea, Eritrea, Ethiopia, Gambia, Guinea, Guinea-Bissau, Haiti, Kiribati, Lao People's Democratic Republic, Lesotho, Liberia, Madagascar, Malawi, Maldives, Mali, Mauritania, Mozambique, Myanmar, Nepal, Niger, Rwanda, Samoa, Sao Tome and Principe, Senegal, Sierra Leone, Solomon Islands, Somalia, Sudan, Timor–Leste, Togo, Tuvalu, Uganda, United Republic of Tanzania, Vanuatu, Yemen and Zambia. The list of LDCs is reviewed every three years by the Economic and Social Council (ECOSOC) in the light of recommendations by the Committee for Development Policy (CDP).

The following criteria were used by the CDP in the 2006 review of the list of LDCs:

(a) A "low-income" criterion, based on the *gross national income (GNI) per capita* (a 3-year average, 2002–2004), with thresholds of $750 for cases of addition to the list, and $900 for cases of graduation from LDC status;

(b) A "human assets" criterion, involving a composite index (the *Human Assets Index*) based on indicators of (i) nutrition (percentage of the population undernourished); (ii) health (child mortality rate); (iii) school enrolment (gross secondary school enrolment rate); and (iv) literacy (adult literacy rate); and

(c) An "economic vulnerability" criterion, involving a composite index (the *Economic Vulnerability Index*) based on indicators of (i) natural shocks (index of instability of agricultural production; share of population displaced by natural disasters); (ii) trade shocks (index of instability of exports of goods and services; (iii) exposure to shocks (share of agriculture, forestry and fisheries in GDP; merchandise export concentration index); (iv) economic smallness (population in logarithm); and (v) economic remoteness (index of remoteness).

For all three criteria, different thresholds are used for addition to, and graduation from, the list of LDCs. A country will qualify to be added to the list if it meets the three criteria and does not have a population greater than 75 million. A country will qualify for graduation from LDC status if it has met graduation thresholds under at least two of the three criteria in at least two consecutive reviews of the list. After a recommendation to graduate a country has been made by the CDP and endorsed by ECOSOC and the General Assembly, the graduating country will be granted a three-year grace period before actual graduation takes place. In accordance with General Assembly resolution 59/209, this standard grace period is expected to enable the relevant country and its development partners to agree on a "smooth transition" strategy, so that the loss of LDC-specific concessions at the end of the grace period does not disturb the socioeconomic progress of the country.

Acknowledgements

The Least Developed Countries Report 2007 was prepared by a team consisting of Charles Gore (team leader), Lisa Borgatti, Michael Herrmann, Ivanka Hoppenbrouwer-Rodriguez, Zeljka Kozul-Wright, Madasamyraja Rajalingam, Rolf Traeger and Stefanie West. Penélope Pacheco-López worked with the team until 28 February 2007, and Agnès Collardeau-Angleys participated in the final stage of preparation of the Report from 9 May 2007. The work was carried out under the overall supervision of Habib Ouane, Director, Division for Africa, Least Developed Countries and Special Programmes within UNCTAD.

Two ad hoc expert group meetings were organized as part of the preparations for the Report. The first, "New Policy Mechanisms to Enhance the Role of Knowledge in Developing Productive Capacities in the LDCs", was held in Geneva on 2 and 3 October 2006. It brought together specialists in the fields of innovation and technology for development, knowledge ecology and intellectual property. The participants in the meeting were as follows: Martin Bell, Ermias Biadgleng, Mario Cimoli (ECLAC), Eduardo Escobedo, Dominique Foray, Carlo Pietrobelli, Francisco Sercovich, François Vellas and Larry Westphal, as well as colleagues from other Divisions of UNCTAD — Kiyoshi Adachi, Victor Konde and Simonetta Zarrilli. The second expert group meeting, "Expert Review of the Least Developed Countries Report 2007", was held in Geneva on 10 March 2007. It brought together the following experts on the same themes: Martin Bell, Dominique Foray, Padmashree Gehl Sampath, Jorge Katz, Richard Nelson, Carlo Pietrobelli, Rajah Rasiah, Francisco Sercovich and Tony Thirlwall. Both meetings discussed background papers prepared by Charles Gore, Zeljka Kozul-Wright and Rolf Traeger.

Background papers or specific inputs for the Report were commissioned from Martin Bell, Carlos Correa, Sara Farley, Dominique Foray, Tadashi Ito, Christopher Manning, Carlo Pietrobelli, Rajah Rasiah, Padmashree Gehl Sampath, François Vellas, Sam Wangwe and Alex Warren-Rodriguez.

We are grateful for comments on earlier drafts of specific chapters received from Martin Bell, Sara Farley, Richard Nelson, Ruth Okediji and from UNCTAD colleagues — Kiyoshi Adachi, Joerg Mayer, Christoph Spennemann and Taffere Tesfachew. The staff of the Central Statistics Branch of the Division on Globalization and Development Strategies of UNCTAD also supported the work.

Secretarial support was provided at different times by Mounia Atiki, Sylvie Guy, Paulette Lacroix, Regina Ogunyinka, Stefanie West and Cora Yance Roberts. Diego Oyarzun-Reyes designed the cover, based on www.worldmapper.org, whose permission to reproduce the cartograms is gratefully acknowledged. The text was edited by Graham Grayston. The overall layout, graphics and desktop publishing were done by Madasamyraja Rajalingam.

The financial support of donors to the UNCTAD LDC Trust Fund, particularly the Governments of Norway and Finland, is gratefully acknowledged.

Contents

List of Boxes

List of Charts

Box Charts

List of Tables

Box Tables

Explanatory Notes

The term "dollars" ($) refers to United States dollars unless otherwise stated. The term "billion" signifies 1,000 million.

Annual rates of growth and changes refer to compound rates. Exports are valued f.o.b. (free on board) and imports c.i.f. (cost, insurance, freight) unless otherwise specified.

Use of a dash (–) between dates representing years, e.g. 1981–1990, signifies the full period involved, including the initial and final years. An oblique stroke (/) between two years, e.g. 1991/92, signifies a fiscal or crop year.

The term "least developed country" (LDC) refers, throughout this report, to a country included in the United Nations list of least developed countries.

In the tables:

Two dots (..) indicate that the data are not available, or are not separately reported.

One dot (.) indicates that the data are not applicable.

A hyphen (-) indicates that the amount is nil or negligible.

Details and percentages do not necessarily add up to totals, because of rounding.

Abbreviations

ACP	Africa, Caribbean and Pacific
AfT	Aid for Trade
AGOA	African Growth and Opportunity Act
ALDC	Division for Africa, Least Developed Countries and Special Programmes
API	active pharmaceutical ingredient
ARIPO	African Regional Intellectual Property Organization
ASEAN	Association of Southeast Asian Nations
BIT	bilateral investment treaty
CEO	chief executive officer
CGIAR	Consultative Group for International Agricultural Research
CORFO	Chilean Economic Development Agency
CIPR	Commission for Intellectual Property Rights
DFID	Department for International Development (United Kingdom)
DTIS	Diagnostic Trade Integration Studies
ECLAC	Economic Commission for Latin America and the Caribbean
ECOSOC	Economic and Social Council
EU	European Union
EUCD	European Union Copyright Directive
FAO	Food and Agriculture Organization of the United Nations
FDI	foreign direct investment
FTA	free trade agreement
FTE	full-time equivalent
GATS	General Agreement on Trade in Services
GATT	General Agreement on Tariffs and Trade
GDP	gross domestic product
GFCF	gross fixed capital formation
GMO	genetically modified organism
GSP	Generalized System of Preferences
GVC	global value chain
ICT	information and communication technology
ICTSD	International Centre for Trade and Sustainable Development
IF	Integrated Framework
IFAD	International Fund for Agricultural Development
IMF	International Monetary Fund
IOM	International Organization for Migration
IP	intellectual property
IPP	intellectual property protection
IPR	intellectual property right
LDC	least developed country
MFA	Multifibre Arrangement
NARS	national agricultural research system
NEPAD	New Partnership for Africa's Development
NERICA	New Rice for Africa
NGO	non-governmental organization
NIS	national innovation system
OAPI	Organisation Africaine de la Propriété Intellectuelle (African Intellectual Property Organization)
ODA	official development assistance

ODC	other developing country
OECD	Organisation for Economic Co-operation and Development
PRSP	poverty reduction strategy paper
R&D	research and development
RMG	ready-made garment
RQAN	Return of Qualified African Nationals
S&T	science and technology
SAP	structural adjustment programme
SITC	Standard International Trade Classification
SMEs	small and medium-sized enterprises
STI	science, technology and innovation
TNC	transnational corporation
TPM	technology protection measure
TRIMs	Agreement on Trade-Related Investment Measures
TRIPS	Agreement on Trade-Related Aspects of Intellectual Property Rights
UNDP	United Nations Development Programme
UNESCO	United Nations Educational, Scientific and Cultural Organization
UNCTAD	United Nations Conference on Trade and Development
UNDESA	United Nations Department of Economic and Social Affairs
UNIDO	United Nations Industrial Development Organization
UNU-MERIT	United Nations University – Maastricht Economic and Social Research and Training Centre on Innovation and Technology
WHO	World Health Organization
WIPO	World Intellectual Property Organization
WTO	World Trade Organization

OVERVIEW

"Where is the wisdom we have lost in knowledge?
Where is the knowledge we have lost in information?"

T.S. Eliot, *The Rock*

The Changing Challenge of Development

Since the year 2000, UNCTAD's *Least Developed Countries Report* has argued that there are two possible future scenarios for the 767 million people who now live in the poorest countries in the world.

At the one extreme, the LDCs will remain trapped at a low level of economic development. By 2015, they will be the major locus of extreme dollar-a-day poverty in the global economy. They will continue to fall behind other developing countries and be obliged to call on the international community for aid to tackle humanitarian crises and for peace-keeping missions to deal with recurrent conflicts. They will also be epicentres of the global refugee population, incubators of global health crises and major sources of international migrant workers, who leave their countries, sometimes dramatically risk their lives, for the sake of earning a living because their life-chances are simply too restricted at home.

At the other extreme, it is possible to envisage a progressive transition in which sustained and accelerated economic growth is achieved through the development of productive capacities, and that with the associated expansion of productive employment opportunities, there will be substantial poverty reduction. In that scenario, foreign aid supports development rather than "fire fighting" complex humanitarian emergencies. Moreover, dependence on development aid is reduced as economic growth is more and more sustained by domestic resources mobilization and the LDCs are no longer marginalized from beneficial international private capital flows.

This Report is a contribution to promoting the second scenario. It focuses on how LDC Governments and their development partners can promote technological progress in LDCs as part of their efforts to develop domestic productive capacities.

If one focuses on the problems associated with the first scenario, that may seem to be an irrelevant luxury. Some might also argue that existing policies are already adequate. In the past few years the economic growth performance of the LDCs as a group has indeed much improved. However, from the *LDC Report 2006* it is apparent that a significant number of LDCs still have slow growth and the poverty-reducing effects of the form of GDP growth that is occurring are weak. The recent growth spurt which some LDCs have experienced is also very fragile as it depends in particular on high commodity prices and, for a number of LDCs, high levels of aid and also FDI to exploit natural resources. Experience indicates that such growth spurts can easily be followed by growth collapses unless windfall resources are properly invested.

Sustained economic growth and substantial poverty reduction in the least developed countries require the development of the latter's productive capacities in such a way that the working-age population becomes more and more fully and productively employed. This was discussed at length in the *LDC Report 2006*. National productive capacities develop through the interrelated processes of capital accumulation and technological progress, which in turn lead to structural change. Promoting technological progress is thus vital for achieving a positive scenario in the LDCs. The basic challenge of development is to increase the knowledge intensity of their economies.

The overall argument of this Report is that unless the LDCs adopt policies to stimulate technological catch-up with the rest of the world, they will continue to fall behind other countries technologically and face deepening marginalization in the global economy. Moreover, the focus of those policies should be on proactive technological learning by domestic enterprises rather than on conventionally understood technological transfer, and on commercial innovation rather than on pure scientific research. Since the 1990s most LDCs have undertaken rapid and deep trade and investment liberalization. Liberalization without technological learning will result, in the end, in increased marginalization.

The Approach of this Report

Effective national and international policies to promote technological progress in LDCs require a good understanding of how technological change occurs. This Report builds on the commonly accepted insight that processes of technological change in rich countries, where firms are innovating by pushing the knowledge frontier further, are fundamentally different from such processes in developing countries, where innovation primarily takes place through enterprises learning to master, adapt and improve technologies that already exist in more technologically advanced countries. Policies to promote technological development should be different in technologically leader countries from those in follower countries, including LDCs. The central issue is not acquisition of the capability to invent products and processes. Rather, policies to promote technological change in LDCs, as in all developing countries, should be geared to achieving catch-up with more technologically advanced countries. That is, they are concerned with learning about and learning to master ways of doing things that are used in more technologically advanced countries.

From that perspective some might argue that innovation is irrelevant to the LDCs. But this view is based on a definition of innovation *sensu stricto*, as occurring only when enterprises introduce for the very first time, products or production processes that are new to the world. It can hardly be expected that an LDC is already knocking at the frontiers of technological breakthroughs. Whilst this strict definition has wide currency, it is now common to recognize that creative technological innovation also occurs when products and processes that are new to a country or an individual enterprise are commercially introduced, whether or not they are new to the world. With this broader view, innovation is a critical aspect of technological catch-up even though it does not depend on inventions which are new to the world. Innovation also occurs when a firm introduces a product or process to a country for the first time. It occurs when other firms imitate this pioneering firm. Moreover, it occurs when the initial or follower firms make minor improvements and adaptations to improve a product or production process, leading to productivity improvements. In short, innovation occurs through "creative imitation", as well as in the more conventional sense of the commercialization of inventions.

In the context of technological catch-up, the process of innovation within a country depends critically on its links with the rest of the world. However, there are divergent views on how technological acquisition occurs.

According to one extreme view, technological acquisition in follower countries depends on the transfer of technology. In that process, access to foreign technology is equivalent to its effective use. Such access can be maximized through openness to trade and foreign investment, coupled with investment in education and perhaps increasing access to the Internet and stimulating competition between international telecom providers.

A basic problem with this view is that it largely treats knowledge in static terms, as a commodity with almost instantaneous transformative properties that can be transferred from one context to another quickly and with little cost. From that perspective, technology is seen as a blueprint which can be acquired off the shelf by any producer seeking to transform a particular combination of inputs dictated by a given factor endowment. At its most simplistic level, that perspective assumes that knowledge is like any other commodity, without geography or history. Information, knowledge and learning are all collapsed into one simple input into the universal productive process. In this approach, there is almost no discussion of how information is converted into knowledge or how learning occurs in practice — indeed, learning is not really understood or elucidated in any meaningful way. The complex dynamics of knowledge accumulation are essentially excluded from the picture altogether. This conception of knowledge ignores the fundamentally dynamic character and plural aspects shaping knowledge production and generation, as knowledge is perceived as socially disembodied and universally transferable. That perspective essentially ignores the components and processes that shape the production and generation of knowledge.

In practice, it is clear that the assimilation and the absorption of foreign technology involve costs and risks, and that success depends on technological effort — investments in technological change — of various kinds, and the development of competences and capabilities at the enterprise level.

For agriculture, the type of technological effort that is required reflects the fact that a key feature of agricultural technology is its high degree of sensitivity to the physical environment (circumstantial sensitivity). The strong interaction between the environment and biological material makes the productivity of agricultural techniques, which are largely embodied in reproducible material inputs, highly dependent on local soil, climatic and ecological characteristics. This means that there are considerable limits to the agricultural development which can occur simply through the importation of seeds, plants, animals and machinery (agricultural technology) that are new to the country. What is required is experimental agricultural research stations to conduct tests and, beyond that, indigenous research and development capacity to undertake the inventive adaptation of prototype technology which exists abroad — for example, local breeding of plant and animal varieties to meet local ecological conditions. Without such inventive adaptation capabilities, knowledge and techniques from elsewhere are locally of limited use.

For industry and services, such circumstantial sensitivity is less important, but nevertheless technological effort is required because technology is not simply technological means (such as machinery and equipment) and technological information (such as instructions and blueprints), but also technological understanding (know-how). The latter is tacit and depends on learning through training, experience and watching. Tacit knowledge is important because various adaptations are required in establishing and operating new facilities. These may capitalize on local knowledge of various kinds. The development of firm-level capabilities and support systems is vital for successful assimilation of foreign technology.

The capabilities which are required in agriculture, industry and services are both core competences and dynamic capabilities. The former refer to the knowledge, skills and information to operate established facilities or use existing agricultural land, including production management, quality control, repair and maintenance of physical capital, and marketing. In contrast, dynamic capabilities refer to the ability to build and reconfigure competences to increase productivity, competitiveness and profitability and to address a changing external environment in terms of supply and demand conditions. The latter "technological capabilities" are particularly important for the process of innovation. The effective absorption (or assimilation) of foreign technologies depends on the development of such dynamic technological capabilities.

R&D can be part of those capabilities, but only a part. Design and engineering capabilities are particularly important for establishing new facilities and upgrading them. Moreover, technological capabilities are best understood not simply in the narrow sense of mastering "physical" technologies which are associated with machinery and equipment, the properties of materials, and the knowledge possessed by engineers and scientists. Beyond this, production processes involve various complex organizational processes related to the organization of work, management, control and coordination, and the valorization of output requires logistic and marketing skills. All these can be understood as part of "technological learning" in a broad sense.

The enterprise (firm or farm) is the locus of innovation and technological learning. But firms and farms are embedded within a broader set of institutions which play a major role in these processes. In advanced countries, national innovation systems have been established to promote R&D and link it more effectively to processes of innovation. In LDCs, what matters in particular are the *domestic knowledge systems* which enable (or constrain) the creation, accumulation, use and sharing of knowledge. Those systems should support effective acquisition, diffusion and improvement of foreign technologies. In short, there is a need to increase the absorptive capacity (or assimilation capacity) of domestic firms and the domestic knowledge systems in which they are embedded.

Key Issues Addressed in the Report

The subject of knowledge, technological learning and innovation is a large one, and this Report is the first to address the issue in the context of the least developed countries. It focuses on five issues:

- The extent to which the development of technological capabilities is occurring in LDCs through international market linkages, particularly through international trade, FDI and licensing;
- The way in which science, technology and innovation (STI) issues are currently treated within LDCs, particularly in the Poverty Reduction Strategy Papers (PRSPs), and how STI policies geared towards technological catch-up could be integrated into the development strategies of LDCs;
- Current controversies about how stringent IPR regimes affect technological development processes in LDCs and policy options for improving their learning environment;
- The extent of loss of skilled human resources through emigration and policy options for dealing with that issue; and
- How ODA is supporting technological learning and innovation in the LDCs and ways to improve it.

The rest of this overview summarizes the major findings and recommendations of the Report in each of those areas.

Building Technological Capabilities through International Market Linkages

The level of development of technological capabilities in LDCs is very weak. Indicators to show this are scarce and not wholly appropriate. But examination of where LDCs stand on some of the key indices reveals a dismal performance from an international comparative perspective:

- UNDP Technological Achievement Index (TAI) classifies countries as leaders, potential leaders, dynamic adopters and marginalized countries, and all the LDCs for which there are data are in the last category.

- Work conducted within the RAND Corporation has classified countries into scientifically advanced, scientifically proficient, scientifically developing and scientifically lagging countries, and of the 33 LDCs in the sample all except Benin are in the scientifically lagging category.

- LDCs are ranked at the bottom of UNCTAD's Innovation Capability Index. Moreover, for half the LDCs their "innovation capability", relative to the rest of the world, was worse in 2001 than in 1995.

The domestic knowledge systems in the LDCs are very weak and the level of technological capabilities of domestic enterprises is very low. Initiating a sustainable process of knowledge accumulation that could accelerate the development of productive capacities in the LDCs is not a simple task, but it is not an impossible one either. A strategy for catch-up needs to focus on the building of an endogenous knowledge base, but also facilitate the transfer and effective absorption of foreign technology. Informal knowledge systems in LDCs and in informal sectors in other countries include creative repair, reprocessing and recycling of artefacts, including in some cases complex technologies. In addition, traditional knowledge plays a crucial role in various sectors, including agriculture, health and creative industries. The design of policies aimed at upgrading technological capabilities in LDCs should not ignore but develop the potential offered by existing local innovation and integrate it with transferred technologies. However, learning through international linkages is vital. A fundamental issue for LDCs is how to access the international knowledge pool, master foreign technologies and thus benefit from international technology diffusion.

This Report examines the extent to which the diffusion of foreign technology is now occurring in LDCs through international trade and FDI, and has a number of key findings.

IMPORTS OF CAPITAL GOODS

By far the most important source of technological innovation in LDCs, as perceived by firms themselves, is new machinery or equipment. Most of the machinery and equipment operated in LDCs is imported, and therefore imports of capital goods, and their effective use, are overall the main source of innovation for firms in LDCs.

Total capital goods imports by LDCs have lost momentum over the last 25 years. While expanding in nominal terms, they have either been stagnant or risen only marginally when compared with macroeconomic variables or the population. While the technological effort of acquiring foreign embodied technology was comparable in LDCs and other developing countries (ODCs) in the 1980s, the gap has widened greatly since that time. In 2000–2005 LDC capital goods imports corresponded to 6 per cent of GDP, only half the level for ODCs.

In the LDCs, imports of capital goods have been hampered by their premature de-industrialization process, the slow progression of the investment rate, the composition of their fixed capital formation (with a low share of machinery and equipment) and balance-of-payments restrictions. The sluggishness of those imports means that domestic firms are upgrading their processes and products only marginally. Importing relatively few capital goods implies that LDC firms are forgoing the potential technological learning and adaptive innovation associated with a greater volume of imports of technology embodied in those goods, in contrast to what ODC firms are doing.

The composition of LDCs' capital goods imports to a large extent mirrors changes in those countries' productive structure, trade specialization, FDI patterns and overall level of technological development. African LDCs were the group of countries that imported mining and metal-crushing machinery most intensively in 2000–2005, as compared with all groups of developing countries. At the same time Asian LDCs were the group with the relatively highest imports of textile machinery. As a group LDCs imported relatively little agricultural machinery and ICT capital goods. This indicates, on the one hand, the low level of technological development of those countries' agriculture and, on the other hand, the still incipient penetration by the recent wave of ICT and ICT-based innovation.

EXPORTS AND THE ROLE OF GLOBAL VALUE CHAINS

LDC firms can develop their technological capabilities through the market linkages they develop with their downstream customers, including in particular the foreign ones. Integration into global value chains (GVCs) often represents one of the very few options for LDC firms and suppliers to secure access to international markets and innovative technologies, and to learn by exporting. However, the upgrading process is fraught with difficulties and obstacles, which are particularly great for LDC firms.

International value chains are increasingly driven by buyers and downstream lead firms. The latter have the power to set the standards (technical, quality, environmental) that must be met in order to participate in the chain. Chain leaders, however, rarely help producers to upgrade their technological capabilities so that they are able to fulfil those requirements. Barriers to integrate GVCs are therefore becoming higher.

Although LDCs had increased their specialization in several value chains since the mid-1990s, they did not manage to significantly upgrade their specialization within those chains. The analysis of 24 selected value chains that are relevant for LDC exports reveals that the LDCs have achieved upgrading in only nine of them. By contrast, their exports were downgraded in 12 value chains. The latter represent 52 per cent of total merchandise exports, but the former account for just 18 per cent. In most cases LDCs have increased their specialization in relatively basic products at a low stage of processing. Those export patterns indicate that little technological upgrading has taken place recently among LDC firms, irrespective of their participation in GVCs.

FOREIGN DIRECT INVESTMENT

It is generally contended that the arrival of TNCs leads to technological upgrading of domestic firms through technological spillovers via imitation, competition, training, labour mobility, backward and forward linkages, and exports (which entail exposure to the technology frontier). Those spillover effects have the potential to increase the productivity of other firms. However, the materialization of the potential positive impacts of FDI on knowledge accumulation in host countries hinges on a large number of conditions, including their structural characteristics, the type of insertion of TNCs in host economies, their job-generating impact, and the direct consequence of their entry for domestic firms.

FDI inflows into LDCs have increased markedly since the early 1990s. Between 2000 and 2005 they were on average three times higher than during the preceding 10 years. LDCs accounted for 3.5 per cent of total developing country inflows during that period and for 2.7 per cent of the total FDI stock of developing countries in 2005. Since the 1990s the FDI intensity of LDCs has accelerated considerably, so that FDI inflows as a share of both GDP and gross fixed capital formation doubled between the 1990s and 2000–2005. During the early years of the 21st century LDCs largely surpassed other developing countries in those respects.

There is little evidence of a significant contribution by FDI to technological capability accumulation in LDCs. This is not due to those countries' insufficient "opening" to foreign investors, given the policy changes that they have enacted since the 1980s and the substantial growth of FDI penetration since the 1990s. Rather, its limited contribution is due to the type of integration of TNCs into host countries' economies, the sectoral composition of FDI, the priorities of policies enacted by LDCs and the low absorptive capacity of those countries.

In African LDCs typically the mineral extraction activities of TNCs are capital-intensive, have little impact on employment, are highly concentrated geographically, have high import content and result in exports of their output as unprocessed raw materials. Most of those operations are wholly owned by foreign investors (rather than joint ventures) and a large share of their foreign exchange earnings is retained abroad. Those operations tend to operate as enclaves since they are weakly integrated into domestic economies, as they have few forward and backward linkages in host economies. Some of the main channels for potential knowledge circulation between TNCs and domestic firms are largely absent, namely linkages, joint ventures and labour turnover.

In Asian LDCs the rapid growth in garment-related FDI inflows, employment and exports has not been accompanied by a corresponding development of firms' technological capabilities. The Governments of these countries have not enacted an effective policy to develop garment manufacturing and foster its anchoring in the domestic economy, although the industry plays a major role in those economies. Their policy actions have been limited to liberalizing foreign investment regulation, promoting private enterprise, coordinating investment approvals, customs facilitation and basic infrastructure provision in exporting processing zones to stimulate the growth of the different segments of activities in the value chains. Indeed, none of these economies has even imposed training levies on firms to stimulate upgrading. The lack of embedding in the domestic economy and of technological learning in the garment industry means that garment manufacturing in LDCs remains dependent on preferential market access conditions and is therefore vulnerable to their disappearance.

LICENSING

The use of licensing as a channel for accessing the international knowledge pool (through imports of disembodied technology) is directly related to the income level and technological sophistication of economies. Licensing should therefore be less relevant to LDCs than to other developing countries as a channel for foreign technology diffusion, and this is borne out by evidence. Licensing activity in LDCs is much lower than in ODCs: licence payments as a share of GDP in the former was just 6 per cent of the level of the latter in 2000–2005. Moreover, while ODCs have increased their effort to acquire foreign technology through licensing since the mid-1990s, in relative terms this has been stagnant in the LDCs.

To summarize this analysis of international linkages, technological assimilation and absorption in LDCs through market mechanisms are taking place only to a very limited degree, as reflected in the weak development of technological capabilities and productive capacities. For some channels, notably capital goods imports, the scale of interaction in relation to GDP is much too low. For other channels, notably FDI and exports, the scale of interaction is actually high, but the learning effects of those channels are low. Thus, the growing integration of LDCs into international trade and investment flows since the 1980s has not prevented their marginalization from technology flows.

The learning associated with international transactions does not occur automatically. There is, for example, no "fixed quotient" of learning that arrives in developing countries with every "unit" of exports or FDI. Consequently, measures to increase the volume of exports or FDI inflows do not guarantee any increase in learning. Instead, the learning intensity of such transactions is variable, and the key policy issue is to raise that learning intensity — that is, to increase the magnitude of knowledge and skill acquired "per unit" of exports, imports or inward FDI. It is on the learning potential of international linkages that policy — at national, regional and international levels — should focus.

National Policies to Promote Technological Learning and Innovation

Analysis of recent PRSPs in a sample of LDCs shows a striking paradox. Although LDC Governments are concerned with promoting sustained economic growth as a basis for poverty reduction, the treatment of technological change as a source of economic growth in PRSPs is generally weak. Only four out of the sample of 11 recent PRSPs which were systematically analysed include science and/or technology as a priority policy for poverty reduction. But all mention the importance of agricultural research and extension. However, there is only a marginal concern for how to learn through international linkages. Moreover, only three countries note the need to expand business services to support the technological upgrading efforts of local firms.

The limited attention to technological change reflects the marginalization of technology policies within structural adjustment programmes, which have been particularly intensely implemented within the LDCs, the omission of technology issues from the PRSP approach, and the failure to embed PRSPs, which are essentially three-year public expenditure plans within broader development strategies which include actions to promote technological progress. But it is paradoxical because promoting technological change is recognized as a key source of economic growth. It is at the heart of efforts by the OECD to promote growth in member countries. Moreover, it is becoming a central component of development strategies in more and more developing countries.

The broad revival of interest in policies to promote technological change, partly inspired by the East Asian success, is indicative of wide dissatisfaction with current policies. There is a desire to find a new, post-Washington Consensus policy model, as well as the intuition that it is in this area — promoting technological change — that it is possible to find more effective policies to promote growth and poverty reduction. If LDCs do not participate in this policy trend they will be increasingly marginalized in the global economy, where competition increasingly depends on knowledge rather than on natural-resource-based static comparative advantage. Moreover, accelerated and sustained growth depends on diversification out of economic activities subject to diminishing returns into activities with increasing returns, which generally are knowledge-based.

New policy directions

As argued in earlier LDC Reports with respect to international trade, LDC Governments should elaborate development strategies which include a strategic vision for national economic development and the way to achieve that vision. Technology issues should be included in the development strategy through the integration of an STI policy as part of the development strategy. The priority actions within PRSPs can be derived from those development strategies.

Successful developing countries have adopted policies to promote technological learning and innovation which are geared towards achieving technological catch-up with more advanced countries. There is no reason why LDC Governments should not adopt a similar orientation. However, policies to promote technological learning and innovation in LDCs need to be appropriate to their level of technological development, economic structure and the capabilities of their Governments and business sector.

Technological catch-up in LDCs will require the co-evolution of improvement in physical infrastructure, human capital and financial systems, together with improved technological capabilities within enterprises and more effective knowledge systems supporting the supply of knowledge and linkages between creators and users of knowledge. It will also require a pro-growth macroeconomic framework which can ensure adequate resources for sustained technological learning and innovation, as well as a pro-investment climate which stimulates demand for investment.

Improving physical infrastructure, human capital and financial systems is absolutely vital because many LDCs are right at the start of the catch-up process and have major deficiencies in each of those areas. Without an improvement in these foundations for development, it is difficult to see how technological change will occur. But it is important that LDC Governments and their development partners go beyond these foundations. In that regard, it is possible to identify six major strategic priorities for LDCs at the start and the early stages of catch-up:

- Increasing agricultural productivity in basic staples, in particular by promoting a Green Revolution;
- Promoting the formation and growth of domestic business firms;
- Increasing the absorptive capacity of domestic knowledge systems;
- Leveraging more learning from international trade and FDI;
- Fostering diversification through agricultural growth linkages and natural-resource-based production clusters; and
- Upgrading export activities.

Those priorities should be promoted through a systems rather than a linear model of the innovation process. This requires measures which go beyond those that are traditionally identified with S&T policies, particularly supporting scientific research, expanding universities and setting up research institutes. It should include measures to stimulate the supply side of technology development, but also measures to stimulate the demand for technology development, measures to lubricate the links between supply and demand, and measures that address framework conditions. They should influence all the interrelated factors that affect the ability and propensity of enterprises (both firms and farms) to innovate.

The relevant STI policy tools thus include explicit measures which are concerned with S&T human resource development, public S&T infrastructure and policies to affect technology imports. But beyond this they include a number of implicit measures — for example, public physical infrastructure investment; financial and fiscal policies which increase the incentive for investment and innovation; trade policy and competition policy; public enterprises and public procurement; and regulation, notably in relation to intellectual property rights and other innovation incentive mechanisms. There is above all a need for improved coherence between macro- and microeconomic objectives. Excessive pursuit of macroeconomic stabilization objectives can undermine the development of conditions necessary for productive investment and innovation.

In the past the instruments of STI policy were articulated through an old-style industrial policy which involved protection and subsidies for selected sectors. Those instruments should now be articulated within the framework of a new industrial policy which is based on a mixed, market-based model, with private entrepreneurship and government working closely together in order to create strategic complementarities between public and private sector investment. Within the new industrial policy, the State should act as a facilitator of learning and entrepreneurial experimentation. The private sector is the main agent of change. However, the relevant institutions and cost structures are not given but need to be discovered. The State should facilitate this process and play a catalytic role in stimulating market forces; and it should perform a coordinating function based on an agreed strategic vision of country-level priorities for technological development. There are significant private sector risks in undertaking pioneer investments which involve setting up activities that are new to a country. Moreover, there are significant spillover effects which are beneficial to the country but which the private entrepreneur cannot capture. This implies the need for a partnership and synergies with the public sector to socialize risks and promote positive externalities. The State stimulates and coordinates private investment through market-based incentives aimed at reducing risks and sharing benefits.

STI GOVERNANCE

There are many who would argue that the types of STI policies described above can work hypothetically, but they are inappropriate for LDCs because State capacities are simply too weak. But the PRSPs in which the LDCs are currently engaged are as complicated as the type of STI policies envisaged here. There are major deficiencies in governmental capacity in LDCs, particularly with regard to long-neglected STI issues. However, the problem of State capacity needs to be seen in dynamic rather than static terms. Just as firms learn over time by doing, Governments also learn by doing. The key to developing State capacity in relation to STI issues is therefore to develop such capacity through policy practice. Policy space is required in order to pursue independent and experimental policies in line with countries' development objectives.

Government bureaucracy must not only be competent and independent. An important lesson from successful catch-up experiences is that the Government does not act as an omniscient central planner, but formulates and implements policy through a network of institutions which link government to business. The establishment of intermediary government–business institutions should be a priority in the good governance of technological learning and innovation. A basic condition for success is that policies to promote technological learning and innovation do not favour or protect special interest groups, or support particular firms ("cronyism").

Finally, good governance of technological learning and innovation is likely to require organizational restructuring within the State apparatus itself owing to the cross-sectoral nature of technological learning and innovation. Some countries have started to establish ministries of science and technology to take a lead on S&T issues. But the mere establishment of such a ministry can be counterproductive, as it can lead to an overemphasis on science and an underemphasis on innovation at the enterprise level. The appropriate organizational structure for integrating technological development issues into policy processes needs careful consideration.

Intellectual Property Rights and Other Incentive Mechanisms for Innovation

A number of difficult issues arise with respect to the role of IPRs in the LDCs. Economists have found it notoriously hard to measure the costs and benefits of IPRs, particularly at different stages of development. It seems clear, however, that IPRs do not automatically lead to learning and innovation, and may even jeopardize the latter in an LDC context.

In that regard, important lessons for LDCs' learning strategies can be drawn from the successful development experiences of countries that have achieved catch-up, such as a number of East Asian countries. In the first, *initiation* stage of their technological development, the basic conditions for patents to operate as incentives for innovations, namely large R&D investments and capacity for reverse engineering and low-cost production, do not exist. In the second, *internalization* stage, local firms can learn through imitation under a flexible IPR regime; technology owners face a growing risk of imitation and tensions between domestic and foreign firms increase. It is only in the third, *generation* stage that local innovative firms in the most dynamic sectors aim at a more stringent IPR regime to protect greater R&D investments and accumulate IPRs as a defensive strategy, as well as to improve their bargaining position vis-à-vis competitors.

In the light of that, IPRs are unlikely to play a significant role in promoting local learning and innovation in the initiation stage, the point in the catch-up process where most LDCs are now located. Moreover, technology transfer through licensing is unlikely to provide great benefits for LDCs. Even if under certain conditions IPRs were to positively encourage technology transfer through licensing, LDCs are unlikely to become significant recipients of licensed technology. The low technical capacity of local enterprises constrains their ability to license in technology, while the low GDP per capita in LDCs is not likely to stimulate potential transferors to engage in such arrangements. IPRs, particularly patents, promote innovation only where profitable markets exist and where firms possess the required capital, human resources and managerial capabilities. Similarly, licensing is out of reach for firms without a certain level of absorptive capacity, particularly in countries with low GDP. As firms' capability increases, patents may increasingly perform their incentive, transactional and signalling functions and the information contained in patent applications may be more useful for planning and undertaking innovative activities.

CASE STUDY OF BANGLADESH

The case study of Bangladesh, which is one of the most advanced LDCs in terms of its technological development, confirmed those theoretical and historical observations. The study, which is the first on IPRs in least developed countries and was commissioned specially for this Report, focused on three sectors: agro-processing, textiles and garments, and pharmaceuticals. It showed that innovative capacity within local firms remains very low across all three sectors. Moreover, irrespective of the presence of intellectual property rights, in the local context those rights do not play a role either as a direct incentive for innovation or as an indirect incentive enabling knowledge spillovers (through various technology transfer mechanisms such as licensing, imports of equipment or government–firm technology transfer). Currently, intellectual property rights are benefiting mostly the TNCs operating in the local market, as the local firms are not sufficiently specialized to protect their innovations under the current IPR regime, which in any case may not be appropriate for the types of incremental innovations in which most firms engage. For the large majority of local firms there was no observable positive impact of intellectual property rights on licensing, technology transfer or technology sourcing through foreign subsidiaries. The only important sources of innovation at the firm level are the firms' own innovation efforts and innovation through imitation/copying.

Although the study found that intellectual property rights do not contribute to new product/process development in any of the three sectors, domestic entrepreneurs had serious concerns regarding the impact of intellectual property rights on their inputs, such as seed availability and seed price. Larger firms tended to view IPRs differently and in a more benevolent light than the smaller firms, as a tool through which they could protect their products and secure benefits. Others, which regarded IPRs as detrimental to innovation, based their assessment largely on the indirect impact of IPRs on increasing prices of seeds and other inputs. In the textiles and ready-made garment sector, most of the firms interviewed were of the view that IPRs did not play any role as an inducement for innovation, because they simply assembled the final output according to precisely given, buyer-determined specifications, since they did not possess any indigenous design-related capabilities. The firms in the pharmaceutical sector were very concerned that since foreign firms can obtain patents on their products in the country, this might adversely affect their efforts to venture into reverse engineering of active pharmaceutical ingredients. The patents on pharmaceutical products (approximately 50 per cent of the 182 granted in 2006) are not on local innovations, and this point to the presence of other reasons for patenting, such as strategic use, monopoly profits and prevention of parallel imports.

It will be important conduct more studies of this type. But many experts in the area of IPRs now argue that "one size does not fit all', implying that the design and implementation of IPR policies need to consider the impact of varying levels of development and countries' initial conditions. IPR protection has historically followed rather than anticipated economic and technological development. There is thus a significant movement towards thinking about how to add a development dimension to IPR regimes. As the Secretary-General of the United Nations, Mr. Ban Ki-moon, put it, when speaking at the opening of ECOSOC's session on 16 April 2007, "The rules of intellectual property rights need to be reformed, so as to strengthen technological progress and to ensure that the poor have better access to new technologies and products".

LDCs in the multilateral framework

The current IPR regimes can be adapted in order to provide a more supportive multilateral governance regime that is needed to ensure that low-income countries are assisted in building their knowledge base and technological and productive capacities. There are two major types of improvements that can be made: (i) fine-tuning and calibrating of norms and standards, namely, improved adaptation, in line with needs and specific initial conditions; and (ii) enhancing TRIPS flexibilities. Simultaneously, LDCs, in collaboration with their development partners, should explore the full panoply of non-IP options available to enhance incentives for innovation in an LDC context.

Developing countries are entitled under the TRIPS Agreement to the same minimum standards of protection applicable to developed countries, subject only to transitional periods. The same treatment was granted to the LDCs; only longer transitional periods, renewable upon request, were permitted. In many cases, TRIPS-plus regulations in bilateral and regional agreements impose on LDCs even higher standards and greater obligations than on other WTO members. However, a differential approach for LDCs was recognized by the TRIPS Agreement (Article 66.1), and this is reflected in the lack of LDC obligations for IP protection under the Agreement, so that LDCs can develop "a sound and viable technological base" (Preamble to the TRIPS Agreement). Until 2013, LDCs still have the opportunity to undertake an imitative path of technological development, as developed countries had in the past (and until 2016, in the case of pharmaceutical products and processes). However, such a window of opportunity may close in a period shorter than that enjoyed by the majority of developed countries, and although LDCs may have the freedom to imitate, foreign markets will be closed to their products, as higher standards of IPR protection have almost become universal. As interactive learning is a time-consuming, cumulative and historical process involving many agents, the major recommendation of this Report is that the transitional period for LDCs should not be subject to an arbitrarily predetermined deadline, but become only enforceable once those countries have achieved "a sound and viable technological base".

Furthermore, Article 66.2 requires the granting of incentives to promote transfer of technology to LDCs by developed countries. Those incentives should be accorded to enterprises and institutions that specifically aim at facilitating the transfer of technology to LDC enterprises (such as through tax breaks and subsidies). This obligation cannot be met merely through cooperation provided by public agencies. It is also recommended that the concept of "transfer of technology", for the purposes of compliance with Article 66.2, be elucidated by the WTO, so as to make it clear that developed countries' Governments should provide firm-based incentives for the transfer of IPRs and non-IPR-protected technology, and that "technology" should be understood as manufacturing methods, formulae, designs, basic and detailed engineering — that is, knowledge that may be effectively applied to upgrade the technological capacity of LDC recipients, rather than merely transfer of general training and technical assistance or scientific cooperation.

With regard to technical assistance, it is recommended that the supply of technical assistance by WIPO and other organizations be inter alia unbiased and development-focused, and clearly inform LDCs about all the flexibilities allowed by the TRIPS Agreement. The content and forms of delivery of IPR-related technical assistance should be defined by the recipient Government, in accordance with its own priorities and development objectives and in full consultation with other stakeholders, including public-interest-oriented NGOs. Moreover, independent studies should be carried out, assessing the economic impact of IPR regimes on the development of productive capacities in LDCs, with the assistance and cooperation of all relevant partners, including those from the wider international community, for example UNCTAD and public-interest oriented NGOs.

The LDCs that are currently in the process of accession to the WTO should not be required to provide accelerated and TRIPS-plus protection, and should be granted the same transitional periods as for other LDC members. Additionally, it is recommended that LDCs use to the fullest extent possible the flexibilities allowed by the TRIPS Agreement (such as parallel imports, compulsory licences, permissible exceptions to exclusive rights and fair dealing), and seek to avoid the erosion of such flexibilities through FTAs, BITs or bilateral trade and investment agreements, or in the context of accession to the WTO. Moreover, it is recommended that the inclusion of IPRs as "covered investments" be reviewed in any bilateral or regional agreement.

Furthermore, the international community should reconsider the development dimension of the TRIPS Agreement, with a view to meeting the need for a balanced approach and pro-development IPR regime, especially with regard to LDCs, and particularly concerning LDC-specific standards relating to novelty, the nature of inventions, terms of protection and calibrated disclosure. For example, the full use of exceptions and limitations should be granted to LDCs, especially in research and fair use. In order to reverse the trend for imposing TRIPS-plus requirements, it is recommended that IPR provisions be excluded from any future FTAs and BITs. In drafting national legislation, LDCs would be well advised to develop their own guidelines in patent offices with respect to patentability criteria, — that is, to examine applications carefully rather than simply copy international standards. With a view to increasing their bargaining position in multilateral forums, the LDCs are advised to pool LDC-based resources and knowledge in the search for economies of scale and collective efficiency solutions in all IPR-related institutional arrangements.

As regards alternative non-proprietary mechanisms for knowledge governance, the LDCs, in collaboration with the international community, should explore the panoply of existing mechanisms that are being successfully used in many other countries in order to stimulate learning and knowledge governance — for example, patent buy-outs, price discrimination mechanisms, public–private partnerships, subsidizing research (directly and indirectly) via grants, tax credits, fiscal measures to support R&D and other types of innovative activities, developing prizes, government-based advanced market commitments, open source collective mechanisms, information and knowledge commons, joint research initiatives of various kinds, local as well as regional technology-sharing consortia, joint research ventures, licensing agreements with technology transfer clauses and compensatory liability regimes. Moreover, improving linkages between S&T institutions and the enterprise sector is highly recommended. In order to encourage institutional diversity for enhanced knowledge ecology (the institutional framework that enables access to and production and use of, knowledge for learning and innovation), a plurality of options should be explored with a view to accelerating technological learning and innovation.

In conclusion, the main challenge that policymakers in LDCs need to address is how to devise supportive policy frameworks to enhance learning and to consider the plurality of options available with a view to better managing and benefiting from the LDCs' own as well as already available knowledge resources. Establishing proprietary IPR systems and creating property rights are but one, among various responses, to a more generic and fundamental problem, which is how to create and improve LDCs' knowledge ecology. This challenge goes beyond fine-tuning the existing intellectual property rights regime.

International Migration of Skilled Labour

BRAIN DRAIN AND BRAIN GAIN

The cross-border movement of persons possessing a particular type of knowledge is a means of international technology diffusion. Countries may either gain or lose from the permanent (or long-term) international migration of skilled persons. International migration of skilled persons in principle contributes to building the recipient countries' skills endowment, while entailing a loss in the origin country's stock of human capital (at least immediately). Those two processes are commonly referred to as "brain gain" and "brain drain" respectively. The most important issue for countries' long-term development is the net effect of migratory flows.

LDCs have a low skill endowment. Therefore, the international migration of skilled persons from and to those countries can have a strong impact on their human capital stock. The human capital endowment of an economy is a fundamental determinant of its long-term growth performance, its absorptive capacity and its performance in technological learning. It is also a requirement for the effective working of trade, FDI, licensing and other channels as means of technology diffusion. In LDCs the major migratory flow of qualified professionals is that of skilled people settling mainly in developed countries.

On the other hand, if emigrants are unemployed before leaving the country, the immediate loss for the latter is less great. Moreover, the costs of emigration can in principle be (partly) offset by other developments, including higher enrolment in tertiary education, an increase in remittances and the eventual brain gain through the return of emigrants, brain circulation by means of temporary return, and creation of business and knowledge linkages between emigrants and home countries (leading to technology flows, investment, etc.). These increased flows in knowledge, investment and trade are more likely to occur in the case of industries producing tradable products than those producing non-tradables. Many of those positive effects, however, occur only once countries have reached a certain level of development and income growth. That implies the existence of considerably improved economic conditions in home countries, which provide incentives for temporary or permanent return of emigrants and for the establishment of stronger knowledge and economic flows. Moreover, an improved domestic environment entails lower out-migration pressure. That situation is obviously not the one prevailing in LDCs. Those countries are therefore the most likely to suffer from brain drain, rather than benefiting from brain circulation, brain gain or the other positive effects possibly associated with emigration.

CAUSES OF INTERNATIONAL MIGRATION

International migration of skilled persons is driven by both supply pressures in home countries and demand forces in destination countries. In countries of origin, the main reasons for emigration of qualified persons are limited employment possibilities, poor working conditions and/or weak career paths, slow economic growth and political instability, as well as the low level of pay and the huge and widening gap between earnings in LDCs and those in developed countries for the same careers (in some cases amounting to 20 times in PPP terms).

At the same time, demand pressure for greater deployment of skilled migrants from developing countries (including LDCs) has grown in industrialized countries, despite their rapidly rising numbers of tertiary graduates. Opportunities for work among professionally qualified immigrants in developed countries have greatly increased since the 1990s. While skill shortages have been experienced across the board in many increasingly technologically advanced developed countries, three sets of factors have been especially important in influencing renewed demand for skilled manpower. First, the ageing of developed country populations, especially in Europe and later in Japan, has contributed to slow growth in labour supply and increased demand for skill-intensive non-tradable services, particularly in health and aged care. Second, the information technology revolution has greatly increased the demand for skilled manpower in the production of computer software and the demand for computer and ICT engineers. Third, shortages of lower- to middle-level skilled manpower — technicians, electricians, plumbers, nurses and teachers — have been especially marked, as developed country workers shun difficult blue-collar and related jobs, and the output of those countries' educational institutions has failed to keep pace with demand. The major labour-importing economies, particularly the United States, the EU and its member States, Canada and Australia, have reacted to increasing shortages of skilled manpower by implementing more open policies to attract qualified immigration.

DEVELOPMENTS IN LDCS

Three main features of skilled emigration from LDCs since the 1990s stand out:

- Emigration rates were generally high among tertiary-educated persons by international standards, with an unweighted mean for LDCs of 21 per cent in 2000. That was much higher than for all lower-middle-income and low-income countries, whose skilled emigration rate was below 8 per cent (weighted).

- There was considerable variation in the total rates of emigration among tertiary–educated persons by and within country groups among the LDCs. They were close to 25 per cent (unweighted) in the island LDCs, West Africa and East Africa, and lowest in the generally more populated Asian LDCs (6 per cent), with Central Africa falling in between (14 per cent). Apart from in island LDCs, out-migration rates were especially high in countries that had experienced political instability in the 1980s and 1990s (Sudan, Liberia, Mozambique, Somalia and Eritrea) and in some of the poorest countries (e.g. Sierra Leone). By contrast, emigration rates were lowest in all the more populous Asian countries (especially Nepal, Myanmar and Bangladesh) and in some of the larger countries (Democratic Republic of the Congo, Sudan, Niger and Malawi).

- Out-migration among tertiary-educated persons from LDCs to OECD countries has accelerated over the last 15 years. The unweighted mean emigration rate rose from 16 per cent in 1990 to 21 per cent 10 years later. That intensification of emigration among skilled persons was much stronger than among all emigrants from LDCs.

Emigration of highly educated persons with more than basic tertiary training tends to be much greater than for the tertiary-educated population as a whole. It is estimated that as many as 30–50 per cent of the developing world's population trained in science and technology (including those from LDCs) live in the developed world. This has a direct impact on those countries' skills base, their absorptive capacity and their technological catch-up possibilities.

POLICY RECOMMENDATIONS

It is not possible to halt the emigration of qualified persons from LDCs to developed countries. Therefore, policies in both sending and receiving countries should be targeted at reducing the flows that are shown to be most detrimental to national development, and at increasing the benefits deriving from all types of skilled out-migration. Those policies should be implemented by destination countries and origin countries, and at the international level.

The main policy actions to be considered in destination countries are as follows:

- Favouring the temporary entrance of qualified professionals from LDCs, rather than permanent immigration;

- Establishing development assistance programmes that help LDCs to retain their professionals (e.g. in academia or in the health sector) through better pay, redesign of career paths and better working conditions;

- Creating programmes of assistance for skilled emigrants returning to their home countries, which support their professional reinsertion and their gainful employment by making use of their skills; and

- Refraining from recruiting LDC professionals in those careers where it is clear that emigration has negative consequences for home countries.

Home countries have three basic lines of policy alternatives for dealing with the emigration of skilled persons:

- Retention. Preventing immigration requires that professionals be offered more job opportunities, better working conditions and career paths. This depends on general economic conditions, but targeted government initiatives in sectors such as education, research and health can have an immediate impact.

- Return. LDCs gain more from the permanent return of skilled emigrants than from short-term stays. However, policies to that end are more difficult to devise and implement. Therefore, in the short run they should focus more on the short-term return of emigrants. This can involve teachers and professors giving crash courses, engineers providing specific inputs in sectors relevant to their field of expertise, doctors returning to assist with specific health-care campaigns, and so forth. Such programmes can eventually lead to permanent return.

- Diaspora. Countries of origin can benefit from diaspora professionals by maintaining contact with them and attracting them to specific activities and projects. This requires that databases of emigrated skilled persons be established and maintained, so as to engage them in those activities and projects.

International action by donors, international organizations and/or developing countries themselves should concentrate on:

- Supporting LDCs in attracting back emigrants on both a permanent and a temporary basis by establishing target programmes;

- Providing assistance to LDCs in enhancing the gains from diaspora links; and

- Establishing regional initiatives that facilitate temporary movement of professionals so as to enable LDCs to benefit from brain circulation.

Knowledge Aid

The justification for foreign aid is usually articulated within a framework which stresses the limited ability of most LDCs to mobilize the domestic financial resources needed to meet a range of pressing economic, social and political objectives. But equally important, and actually even more fundamental, aid can help to build up the knowledge resources and knowledge systems of LDCs. This is particularly important for the LDCs because their level of technological development is so low and technological learning through international market linkages is currently weak. Aid can play an important role in developing a minimum threshold level of competences and learning capacities which will enable LDCs to rectify that situation. Indeed, the provision of more knowledge aid, if directed towards the right areas and appropriate modalities, may be the key to aid effectiveness.

There is no agreed definition of knowledge aid. Since the 1990s, there have been an increasing number of knowledge-based activities designed to increase aid effectiveness by strengthening the knowledge base of the donors themselves — for example, through internal reforms to increase intra-organizational knowledge-sharing, better knowledge management and IT system development. But in the present Report, knowledge aid is defined as aid that supports knowledge accumulation within partner countries. Knowledge aid is provided in two ways: either through supplier-executed services, where, for example, donors provide consultants who advise on, or design and develop, projects, programmes and strategies; or through strengthening the knowledge resources and knowledge systems of the partners themselves, a process which may be called partner learning. In either case, those activities might be designed to increase knowledge resources for institutional, regulatory and policy development, or to support the development of productive capacities through technological learning. Aid to build science, technology and innovation capacity is a particular form of knowledge aid. Aid for STI should support (i) the development of productive capacities through building up domestic knowledge resources and domestic knowledge systems, and (ii) the development of governmental capacities to design and implement STI policies.

It is very difficult to quantify the scale of aid for STI to LDCs. But the available evidence indicates that this is a low priority in LDCs. Reported aid disbursements for research and the development of advanced and/or specific human skills (including agricultural education and extension), constituted only 3 per cent of total aid disbursements during the period 2003–2005, with 90 per cent allocated to building human skills, particularly higher education. Reported aid disbursements for agricultural research to all LDCs were equal to only $22 million per year during 2003–2005 and LDCs received only $62 million for vocational training, $12 million per year for agricultural education and training and $9 million per year for agricultural extension. The non-agricultural sector was also neglected, with disbursements for the development of advanced technical and managerial skills constituting only $18 million per year, while disbursements for what is described in the reporting system as "technological research and development" — which covers industrial standards, quality management, metrology, testing, accreditation and certification — received only $5 million per year during 2003–2005.

It may be argued that those low levels of reported aid reflect the weak treatment of STI issues in PRSPs. But in practice, for the one STI area that is emphasized in the PRSPs, namely agricultural research and extension, aid commitments to LDCs have actually fallen rather than risen since the late 1990s. Donor priorities are starkly evident in the fact that annual technical cooperation commitments to improve governance (in the widest sense) in 2003–2005 were $1.3 billion, which may be compared with annual aid commitments for agricultural extension during the same period of $12 million. Of course, improving governance is vital. However, it will be impossible to achieve this sustainably unless LDC governments strengthen their fiscal base through the development of the productive base of their economies.

A qualitative survey of the types of STI projects and programmes which are being supported in LDCs found that there needs to be stronger coordination between STI human resource capacity projects and sector development projects, and that projects and programmes need to be more integrated, rather than disjointed, and embedded within a systemic approach. Only one project that sought to develop STI policy capacity in LDCs was identified. Similarly, global linkage initiatives, such as scientific networks and business-to-business matchmaking schemes, tend to exclude LDCs. Furthermore, the provision of global and regional public goods in the form of scientific research is not sufficiently responsive to LDCs' research needs.

STRENGTHENING AID FOR SCIENCE, TECHNOLOGY AND INNOVATION

There are a number of new initiatives by donors to elaborate a coherent strategic perspective on aid for STI, including by the International Development Research Centre (IDRC) of Canada, the United Kingdom's Department for International Development (DFID), the Swedish International Development Agency (SIDA), the African Development Bank and the World Bank. It is important that the role of STI in LDCs is not neglected in those initiatives. However, beyond that, the Report makes a number of specific recommendations, which are set out below.

Firstly, there is a need for a rapid increase in ODA for agricultural R&D for the LDCs. Although agriculture is the major livelihood in the LDCs, the current agricultural research intensity — expenditure on agricultural research as a share of agricultural GDP — is only 0.47 per cent. That compares with 1.7 per cent in other developing countries. The LDC agricultural research intensity is far below the 1.5 to 2 per cent recommended by some international agencies. Moreover, the low level reflects a serious decline in the agricultural research intensity in the LDCs since the late 1980s, when the figure stood at 1.2 per cent.

Secondly, the effectiveness of ODA for non-agricultural technological learning and innovation has been severely compromised because donors typically do not support this activity. Although agriculture is still the major source of employment and livelihood in the LDCs, the employment transition which they are undergoing means that this position is not tenable if development partners wish to reduce poverty sustainably and substantially. There are, however, difficult issues regarding how aid should be used to support technological learning and innovation outside agriculture. One important recommendation is that donor-supported physical infrastructure projects should all include components use the construction process to develop domestic design and engineering capabilities. In addition, there is a need for public support for enterprise-based technological learning, which should be in the form of grants or soft loans for investment in the relevant types of knowledge assets. Such support should be undertaken as a cost-sharing public–private partnership for creating public goods, particularly in relation to the development of design and engineering skills through enterprise-based practice. These STI capacity-building activities could be particularly useful if they are linked to value chain development schemes, FDI linkage development and the facilitation of South–South cooperation.

Thirdly, LDC development partners have expressed strong support for "Aid for Trade" and there is widespread support for scaling up this kind of aid. Experiences show that technological learning and innovation are central to successful cases of trade development. However, technological learning and innovation have been conspicuously absent from past efforts to provide Aid for Trade for LDCs through the Integrated Framework and are neglected within current attempts to define the scope of the subject. It is recommended that aid for technological learning and innovation for tradable sectors be a key component of Aid for Trade, and LDC development partners should adopt best practices which are evident from successful cases of trade development, such as palm oil in Malaysia and Nile perch in Uganda. In that regard, technological development should be seen as an integral part of the definition of "supply-side capacities", as it was in the Monterrey Consensus.

Finally, there has been some discussion of ways in which trade preferences for LDCs could be enhanced not simply by extending their depth and coverage but also by linking them to supply-side support, for example through complementary measures to encourage FDI. From the point of view of technological assimilation, it is clear that trade preferences, in particular in relation to garments, have successfully stimulated the initial implementation of manufacturing activities within some LDCs. However, they do not explicitly facilitate the diffusion of best practices to domestic firms within a country and do not encourage technological upgrading. Against this background, it is worth examining whether trade preferences can be supplemented with some kind of technology fund that seeks to leverage the technological learning effects of the productive activities that are stimulated through such preferences, in particular through diffusion of best practices and encouragement of upgrading. In the current context, as transitional arrangements associated with the ending of the Agreement on Clothing and Textiles come to an end, this is likely to be particularly important in order to ensure the sustainability of existing activities in a number of countries. Work should be done on the possible design of such a fund.

*   *   *

This Report does not provide all the answers to the issues which it raises. It is intended to provoke fresh thinking about development strategies and poverty reduction in the LDCs by both LDC Governments and their development partners. There is at the present time a search for alternatives to the current development paradigm, and the role of knowledge in development is critical for the formulation of new approaches. The LDCs should not refrain from exploring new paths of knowledge-based development through technological learning and innovation. We hope that this Report will open up avenues for further policy-oriented research and policy innovation. Our common goal is to ensure that a positive future scenario for the LDCs prevails.

There is a choice.

Dr. Supachai Panitchpakdi
Secretary-General of UNCTAD

Introduction: Why Technological Learning and Innovation Matter for LDCs

A. Introduction

This Report explores how national and international policies can promote more effective technological learning and innovation in the least developed countries (LDCs). It extends and deepens the analysis in *The Least Developed Countries Report 2006*.

The *Least Developed Countries Report 2006* advanced three major propositions:

- First, sustained economic growth and substantial poverty reduction in the LDCs require the development of their productive capacities in such a way that the population of working age becomes more and more fully and productively employed.

- Second, productive capacities develop through three closely interrelated processes — capital accumulation, technological progress and structural change.

- Third, the development of productive capacities, and the associated expansion of productive employment opportunities, should be at the heart of national and international policies to promote sustained economic growth and poverty reduction in the LDCs.·

The present Report extends and deepens the earlier analysis by focusing on policies to promote technological progress with a view to achieving sustained and accelerated economic growth and substantial poverty reduction.

The basic argument of the Report is that unless the LDCs adopt policies to stimulate technological catch-up with the rest of the world, they will continue to fall behind other countries technologically and face deepening marginalization in the global economy. Moreover, the focus of those policies should be on proactive technological learning by domestic enterprises rather than on conventionally understood technological transfer, and on commercial innovation rather than on pure scientific research.

Unless the LDCs adopt policies to stimulate technological catch-up with the rest of the world, they will continue to fall behind other countries technologically and face deepening marginalization in the global economy.

B. Technological development in LDCs in a comparative international perspective

The level of technological development in the LDCs is very low. This is apparent in various indices that measure the technological capabilities and knowledge assets of countries. There are a growing number of such indices (Archibugi and Coco, 2004, 2005). For LDCs, the data are incomplete. However, examination of where LDCs are ranked with regard to some of the key indices commonly used for country-level comparisons reveals a uniform picture — most of the LDCs are at the bottom of the rankings:

- The UNDP Technological Achievement Index (TAI) classifies countries as leaders, potential leaders, dynamic adopters and marginalized countries. All the LDCs for which there are data are in the last category (UNDP, 2001).

- LDCs are near the bottom of the rankings of the UNIDO Competitive Industrial Performance Index and, apart from Bangladesh and Nepal, their rankings have been falling (UNIDO, 2002: 46).

- An analysis undertaken by the RAND Corporation classifies countries into scientifically advanced, scientifically proficient, scientifically developing and scientifically lagging countries, and of the 33 LDCs in the sample all except Benin are in the scientifically lagging category (Wagner et al., 2001).

- LDCs are ranked at the bottom of UNCTAD's Innovation Capability Index. Moreover, for half the LDCs, their "innovation capability", relative to the

The level of technological development in the LDCs is very low.

Chart 1. Where LDCs stand on UNCTAD's Innovation Capability Index

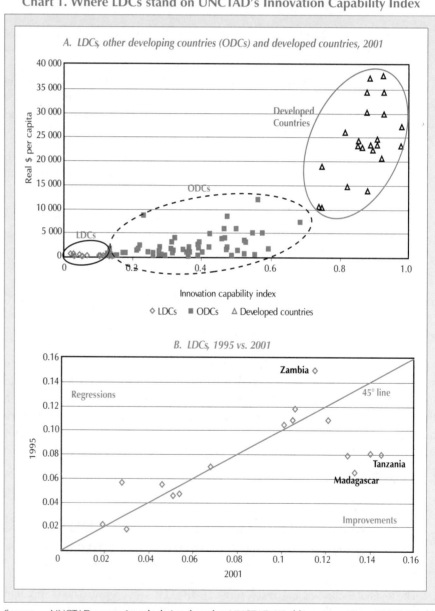

Source: UNCTAD secretariat calculations based on UNCTAD, *World Investment Report 2005*; World Bank, *World Development Indicators 2006*, CD-ROM.

Note: LDCs include: Angola, Bangladesh, Benin, Djibouti, Ethiopia, Eritrea, Haiti, Madagascar, Malawi, Mauritania, Mozambique, Senegal, Uganda, United Republic of Tanzania, Yemen and Zambia.

rest of the world, was worse in 2001 than in 1995, as shown in charts 1a and 1b (UNCTAD, 2005).

It should be noted that there are limitations to the relevance of those indicators in an LDC context (James, 2006). For example, industrial R&D is much more important for technological progress in advanced countries than in LDCs. Furthermore, none of the indices actually tells us how technological advances are embodied in countries' productive systems. However, whatever way it is measured, there is a strong sense that there is a major technological gap between the developed and the developing world, and particularly the LDCs, and this gap has grown over the years as a result of rapid technological advances in the developed countries and the relatively slow advances in most developing countries, and particularly the LDCs (Patel, 1995).

There is a major technological gap between the developed and the developing world, and particularly the LDCs, and this gap has grown over the years.

Charts 2a and 2b provide a more disaggregated picture, which compares the performance of LDCs, other developing countries and developed countries with

Chart 2. Selected Knowledge Assessment Methodology indicators for the LDCs, other developing countries (ODCs) and high-income countries: Technological and ICT capabilities

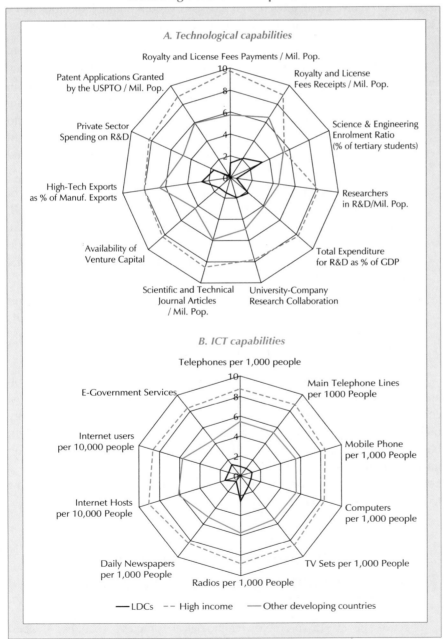

Source: Knell (2006), based on World Bank, Knowledge Assessment Methodology database 2006.

regard to a number of different indicators. The charts illustrate the vast difference in performance between the LDCs and other country groups. The widest disparity is in the number of researchers per million population and patent applications granted by the United States Patent Office per million. The charts also indicate that the LDCs have inadequate access not only to information and communication technology (ICT) infrastructure such as computers and the Internet, but also to more simple forms of communication such as radios, televisions, newspapers and telephones.

Table 1 shows a further disaggregation of the position of individual LDCs with regard to the basic physical infrastructure needed to support technological development, human capital and research and development (R&D). Some island countries are doing much better than other LDCs. But both African and Asian LDCs seriously lag behind other developing countries on those indicators. Notable in this regard are the very low levels of basic human capital and physical infrastructure.

It is unfortunately impossible to construct a picture of long-term changes in technological development. However, discussion in *The Least Developed Countries Report 2006* showed that, judged on the basis of various output indicators, many LDCs are locked into primary commodity sectors and low-skill activities. Thus:

> *The Least Developed Countries Report 2006 showed that many LDCs are locked into primary commodity sectors and low-skill activities.*

- The share of manufacturing value added in total GDP was only 11 per cent in 2000–2003, and almost 40 per cent of the total manufacturing value added of the LDCs as a group was located in one country, Bangladesh. Over the 10 year period between 1990–1993 and 2000–2003, the share of manufacturing in total value added declined in 19 out of 36 LDCs and stagnated in another two. During the 1990s, the share of medium- and high-technology manufactures in total manufacturing value added also declined in half the LDCs for which data are available.

- Primary commodity exports accounted for approximately 70 per cent of LDC merchandise exports during the period 2000–2003. During that period, processed minerals and metals constituted a lower share of total mineral and metals exports than 20 years earlier (down from 35 to 28 per cent) and processed agricultural goods constituted a lower share of total agricultural goods exports (down from 23 to 18 per cent).

- Low-technology, medium-technology and high-technology manufactures exports from the LDCs are expanding much more slowly than such exports from other developing countries. Their share in total merchandise exports was only 4 per cent during 2000–2003, the same share as 20 years earlier.

> *In open economies, international competitiveness depends on their having up-to-date technology, even in primary production.*

During the last 20 years, most LDCs have undertaken deep trade liberalization and they now have open trade regimes (UNCTAD 2004: 179–187). International competitiveness depends on their having up-to-date technology, even in primary production. In open economies this is not simply a matter of export development but is also necessary for competing in the national market. Trade liberalization means that policies to promote technological progress have now become a necessity for the future economic viability of the LDCs. The challenge now is how to increase the knowledge intensity of their economies.

> *Policies to promote technological progress have now become a necessity for the future economic viability of the LDCs.*

C. The importance of innovation and technological learning for LDCs

Effective policy to promote technological progress requires a good understanding of how technological change occurs. For poor developing countries,

Table 1. Selected S&T-related indicators for LDCs, other developing countries (ODCs) and high-income OECD countries, latest years available

Countries	R&D		Human capital					Physical infrastructure		
	R&D (% of GDP)	Researchers in R&D (per million people)	Scientific and technical journal articles	School enroll-ment, tertiary (% of age group)	Tertiary students in science, engineering (% total tertiary)	Literacy rate, adult total (% of people ages 15 and above)	Average years of schooling	Fixed line and mobile phone sub-scribers (per 1,000 people)	Internet users (per 1000 people)	Electricity consump-tion p.c. (kwh)
	2003[a]	1990-2003[b]	1999[c]	2004[a]	1999-2004[b]	2004	2000	2004[a]	2004[a]	2003
Afghanistan	..	..	0.0	1.1	..	28.1	..	22.7	0.9	..
Angola	..	..	3.0	0.8	18.0	67.4	2.4	54.0	11.1	178.0
Bangladesh	0.6	..	177.0	6.5	13.0	..	4.2	37.0	2.2	145.0
Benin	..	..	20.0	3.0	25.0	34.7	2.3	38.2	12.2	82.0
Bhutan	..	..	1.0	..	..	..	..	52.9	22.3	218.0
Burkina Faso	0.2	17.0	23.0	1.5	..	21.8	0.9	37.4	4.1	32.0
Burundi	..	..	3.0	2.3	10.0	59.3	2.0	12.5	3.4	23.0
Cambodia	..	..	5.0	2.9	19.0	73.6	..	39.5	3.0	9.0
Cape Verde	..	127.0	1.0	5.6	106.0	..	..	281.1	50.5	100.0
Central African Republic	..	..	4.0	1.8	..	48.6	2.9	17.6	2.3	35.0
Chad	..	..	2.0	0.8	..	25.7	..	14.4	6.4	11.0
Comoros	..	..	0.0	2.3	11.0	..	..	26.5	13.6	32.0
Dem. Rep. of the Congo	..	..	6.0	1.3	..	67.2	..	37.0	..	86.0
Djibouti	..	..	0.0	1.6	22.0	..	..	43.4	11.6	455.0
Equatorial Guinea	..	..	1.0	2.6	..	87.0	..	106.2	10.2	..
Eritrea	..	..	2.0	1.1	37.0	..	..	14.0	11.8	62.0
Ethiopia	..	..	93.0	2.5	19.0	..	1.9	7.8	1.6	33.0
Gambia	..	..	17.0	1.2	21.0	..	..	99.0	33.2	101.0
Guinea	..	251.0	2.0	2.2	34.0	29.5	..	15.3	5.0	89.0
Guinea-Bissau	..	..	6.0	0.4	..	..	..	7.9	16.9	45.0
Haiti	..	..	1.0	..	..	..	3.6	64.2	59.5	61.0
Kiribati	..	..	0.0	..	..	..	..	52.5	20.4	..
Lao People's Dem. Rep.	..	..	2.0	5.9	11.0	68.7	..	48.2	3.6	135.0
Lesotho	0.0	42.0	1.0	2.8	6.0	82.2	..	109.1	23.9	..
Liberia	..	..	1.0	15.5	..	..	..	2.8	0.3	..
Madagascar	0.1	15.0	..	2.5	20.0	70.7	3.7	19.5	5.0	50.0
Malawi	..	..	36.0	0.4	33.0	64.1	4.3	25.0	3.7	77.0
Maldives	..	..	3.0	0.2	..	96.3	..	450.7	59.2	..
Mali	..	..	11.0	2.1	..	19.0	1.1	36.2	3.8	38.0
Mauritania	..	..	2.0	3.5	10.0	51.2	..	134.5	4.7	60.0
Mozambique	0.6	..	14.0	1.2	24.0	..	2.4	26.9	7.1	399.0
Myanmar	0.1	..	10.0	11.3	42.0	89.9	4.4	10.3	1.3	126.0
Nepal	0.7	59.0	39.0	5.6	..	48.6	3.3	21.8	6.6	91.0
Niger	..	..	21.0	0.8	..	28.7	1.0	12.8	1.8	40.0
Rwanda	..	..	4.0	2.7	..	64.9	..	18.2	4.3	39.0
Samoa	..	..	3.0	7.5	14.0	..	..	130.4	32.7	613.0
Sao Tome and Principe	..	..	0.0	1.0	..	..	..	78.9	130.8	102.0
Senegal	..	..	62.0	4.9	..	39.3	2.6	72.4	42.3	192.0
Sierra Leone	..	..	3.0	2.1	8.0	35.1	3.6	27.2	1.9	49.0
Solomon Islands	..	..	6.0	..	..	..	..	17.0	6.4	69.0
Somalia	..	..	0.0	..	..	..	..	87.9	25.1	..
Sudan	0.3	263.0	43.0	6.1	..	60.9	2.9	58.5	32.1	101.0
Timor-Leste	..	..	..	10.2	..	..	..	..	..	301.0
Togo	..	..	11.0	3.6	..	53.2	..	48.1	36.9	91.0
Uganda	0.8	24.0	91.0	3.4	..	66.8	3.3	44.4	7.2	59.0
United Rep. of Tanzania	..	..	87.0	1.2	..	69.4	3.5	32.2	8.9	78.0
Vanuatu	..	..	3.0	5.0	..	74.0	..	83.3	36.2	..
Yemen	..	..	10.0	9.4	..	..	..	92.0	8.9	212.0
Zambia	0.0	51.0	26.0	2.3	..	68.0	6.1	33.7	20.1	631.0
LDC	0.3	94.3	18.2	3.5	24.0	56.5	3.0	58.4	17.4	130.5
African LDCs	0.3	94.7	24.2	2.7	20.0	52.8	2.8	42.4	13.1	115.2
Asian LDCs	0.5	59.0[d]	30.5	6.1	21.3	61.8	4.0	40.6	6.1	133.7
Island LDCs	..	127.0[e]	2.0	4.5	43.7	85.2	..	140.0	43.7	202.8
ODCs	0.8	313.0	628.8	23.0	21.5	86.1	7.1	425.5	97.6	527.5
High income OECD	2.4	3 728.1	532 308.0	68.7	24.7	92.2[f]	11.4	1 321.0	562.7	9 654.4

Source: UNCTAD secretariat calculations based on UNDP, *Human Development Report 2006*; World Bank, *World Development Indicators 2006*, CD-ROM; and Cohen and Soto, 2001.

a Or latest available; b Data refers to the most recent year available during the period specified; c 2001 for Bangladesh, Ethiopia, Senegal, Uganda and United Republic of Tanzania; d Data refers to Bangladesh only; e Data refers to Cape Verde only; f Based on data for Italy and Switzerland.

technological change occurs primarily through learning — that is, the acquisition, diffusion and upgrading of technologies that already exist in more technologically advanced countries — and not by pushing the global knowledge frontier further. In short, the key to technological progress in the LDCs is technological catch-up through learning rather than undertaking R&D to invent products and processes which are totally new to the world.

From that perspective some might argue that innovation is irrelevant to the LDCs. But that view is based on a definition of innovation *sensu stricto*, as occurring only when enterprises introduce for the very first time products or production processes which are new to the world. An LDC can hardly be expected to be already knocking at the frontiers of technological breakthroughs. Whilst this strict definition has wide currency, it is now common to recognize that creative technological innovation also occurs when products and processes that are new to a country or to an individual enterprise are commercially introduced, whether or not they are new to the world (OECD, 2005). This Report adopts this broader definition of innovation. With this broader view, innovation is a critical aspect of technological catch-up even though it does not depend on inventions which are new to the world. Innovation also occurs when a firm introduces a product or process to a country for the first time. It occurs when other firms imitate this pioneering firm. Moreover, it occurs when the initial or follower firms make minor improvements and adaptations to improve a product or production process, which lead to productivity improvements. In short, innovation occurs through "creative imitation", as well as in the more conventional sense of the commercialization of inventions.

In the context of technological catch-up, innovation depends critically on the linkages of a country with the rest of the world. However, there are divergent views on how technological development in follower countries occurs.

In one extreme view, technological acquisition in follower countries depends solely on the transfer of technology. In that process, access to foreign technology is equivalent to its effective use. Such access can be maximized through openness to trade and foreign investment, coupled with investment in education and perhaps increasing access to the Internet and stimulating competition between international telecom providers.

A basic problem with that view is that it largely treats knowledge in static terms, as a commodity with almost instantaneous transformative properties that can be transferred from one context to another quickly and with little cost. From that perspective, technology is seen as a blueprint which can be acquired off-the-shelf by any producer seeking to put together a particular combination of inputs dictated by a given factor endowment. That perspective assumes that knowledge is like any other commodity, without geography or history. Information, knowledge and learning are all collapsed into one simple input into the universal productive process. In that approach, there is almost no discussion of how information is converted into knowledge or how learning occurs in practice; indeed, learning is not really understood or elucidated in any meaningful way. The complex dynamics of knowledge accumulation are essentially excluded from the picture altogether. This conception of knowledge ignores the fundamentally dynamic character and plural aspects shaping knowledge production and generation, as knowledge is perceived as socially disembodied and universally transferable. That perspective essentially ignores the components and processes that shape the production and generation of knowledge.

In practice, it is clear that the assimilation and the absorption of foreign technology involve costs and risks, and that success depends on technological

Creative technological innovation also occurs when products and processes that are new to a country or to an individual enterprise are commercially introduced, whether or not they are new to the world.

The assimilation and the absorption of foreign technology involve costs and risks, and that success depends on technological effort of various kinds, and the development of competences and capabilities at the enterprise level.

effort — investments in technological change — of various kinds, and the development of competences and capabilities at the enterprise level. This applies to both firms and farms.

For agriculture, the type of technological effort that is required reflects the fact that a key feature of agricultural technology is its high degree of sensitivity to the physical environment (circumstantial sensitivity). The strong interaction between the environment and biological material makes the productivity of agricultural techniques, which are largely embodied in reproducible material inputs, highly dependent on local soil, climatic and ecological characteristics (Hayami and Ruttan, 1985; Evenson and Westphal, 1995).

For industry and services, such circumstantial sensitivity is less important, but nevertheless technological effort is required because technology is not simply technological means (such as machinery and equipment) and technological information (such as instructions and blueprints), but also technological understanding (know-how). The latter is tacit and depends on learning through training and experience. The whole process is complex because firms work in an environment of uncertainty with imperfect knowledge; time, effort and costly investment are required in order to learn to use technology efficiently; and learning is cumulative and path-dependent.

Technology is not simply technological means (such as machinery and equipment) and technological information (such as instructions and blueprints), but also technological understanding (know-how). The latter is tacit and depends on learning through training and experience.

The idea of tacit knowledge is particularly important. It is based on the fact that knowledge is formed gradually, over time, through repetition, and recurrent interaction, is situated in systems of ongoing practices and routines, and is a product of social, cultural and economic and political conditions. While codified knowledge is partly transferable and universal, tacit knowledge is embedded in social and cultural practices — that is, it is context-specific. Tacit knowledge that represents the outcome of learning and experience is deeply rooted in the context of social interaction, practices, routines, ideas, values and emotions. In short, "it does not travel well" (Nonaka, Ryoko and Boysière, 2001: 7). Knowledge can be acquired only through some form of participation in practice; and it is transformed by the process of circulation itself. Knowledge is thus conceived as a social learning process, which is situated in social institutions; hence it is socially and culturally embedded, and context-specific. The process of acquiring and transforming knowledge is neither linear nor timeless, nor is it costless. Knowledge itself is neither bounded nor fixed (Nelson and Winter, 1982).

Against that background, technological learning is critical for innovation in LDCs.[1] It is the development of the capabilities to use and improve technologies, and encompasses:

While codified knowledge is partly transferable and universal, tacit knowledge is embedded in social and cultural practices — that is, it is context-specific.

- Core competences, which are the routine knowledge, skills and information needed for operating established facilities or using existing agricultural land, including production management, quality control, and repair and maintenance of physical capital and marketing; and

- Dynamic capabilities, which refer to the ability to build and reconfigure competences to increase productivity, competitiveness and profitability and to address a changing external environment in terms of supply and demand conditions.

The latter are particularly important for the process of innovation. The effective absorption (or assimilation) of foreign technologies depends on the development of such dynamic technological capabilities.

R&D can be part of those capabilities but it is not the only one. Design and engineering capabilities are particularly important for establishing new facilities and upgrading them. Moreover, technological capabilities are best understood not simply in the narrow sense of mastering "physical" technologies which are associated with machinery and equipment, the properties of materials and the knowledge possessed by engineers and scientists. Beyond this, production processes involve various complex organizational processes related to the organization of work, management, control and coordination, and the valorization of output requires logistic and marketing skills. All of those can be understood as part of "technological learning" in a broad sense.

The enterprise (firm or farm) is the locus of innovation and technological learning. But firms and farms are embedded within a broader set of institutions which play a major role in those processes. In advanced countries, national innovation systems have been established to promote R&D and link it more effectively to processes of innovation (OECD, 1997). In LDCs, what matter in particular are the domestic knowledge systems which enable (or constrain) the creation, accumulation, use and sharing of knowledge (UNCTAD, 2006). Those systems should support effective acquisition, diffusion and improvement of foreign technologies. In short, there is a need to increase the absorptive capacity (or assimilation capacity) of domestic enterprises and of the domestic knowledge systems in which firms and forms are embedded.[2]

The enterprise (firm or farm) is the locus of innovation and technological learning. But firms and farms are embedded within domestic knowledge systems which enable (or constrain) the creation, accumulation, use and sharing of knowledge.

D. Technological progress and poverty reduction

There is wide agreement that technological progress is a critical source of economic growth.[3] Technological change increases the productivity of land, labour and capital, reducing costs of production and improving the quality of outputs. It is through innovation, in the broad sense used here, that diversification and structural transformation occur. Knowledge and creativity are also becoming more and more important for competitiveness. They are now widely hailed as the key engines driving growth in the new millennium.

Through its effects on economic growth, technological progress should have long-term positive effects in reducing the incidence of poverty. However, if economic growth is based solely on labour-saving technological progress, there will be a strong tendency for jobless growth. Skill-biased technological change, which increases demand for skilled labour only, will also be a cause of growing income inequality.

Promoting technological progress should not be seen as something that is different from promoting poverty reduction. The achievement of inclusive development (or pro-poor growth) depends on technological choices and technological development trajectories.

The poverty-reducing impact of growth can be increased if more labour-using technologies are adopted. Poverty reduction will occur if all opportunities for labour-using technology are exploited, and if the negative employment effects of technological change in some sectors are offset by positive effects in other growing parts of the economy. If technological progress leads to a reduction of the demand for labour in some sectors, this will not necessarily worsen unemployment, underemployment and poverty if technological progress is at the same time leading to the introduction of new growing sectors into which the labour which is released from the declining sectors can be absorbed.

Promoting technological progress should thus not be seen as something that is different from promoting poverty reduction. The achievement of inclusive development (or pro-poor growth) depends on technological choices and technological development trajectories.[4]

E. Organization of the Report

The Report examines various aspects of the policy challenge of promoting technological learning and innovation in the LDCs. Chapter 1 discusses the extent to which technological learning and innovation are currently taking place through international market linkages, and in particular international trade, FDI and licensing. Chapter 2 focuses on national policies to promote technological learning and innovation. It discusses the way in which science, technology and innovation (STI) issues are currently treated in the LDCs, focusing on their Poverty Reduction Strategy Papers (PRSPs), and explores how the idea of technological catch-up can be applied within an LDC context. Chapter 3 explores the current controversies about how stringent IPR regimes affect technological development processes in LDCs, and policy options for improving incentives for innovation and learning. Chapter 4 looks at the loss of skilled human resources through emigration and at policy options for dealing with that issue. Chapter 5 examines how ODA is supporting technological learning and innovation in the LDCs and ways to make it more effective.

This Report is intended to provoke fresh thinking about development strategies and poverty reduction in the LDCs by both LDC Governments and their development partners.

The Report does not provide all the answers to the issues which it raises. It is intended to provoke fresh thinking about development strategies and poverty reduction in the LDCs by both LDC Governments and their development partners. There is at the present time a search for alternatives to the current development paradigm, and the role of knowledge in development is critical for the formulation of new approaches. The Report should open up policy dialogue and avenues for policy innovation and further policy-oriented research.

Notes

1. The notion of technological learning has been most applied extensively to the development of technological capabilities for manufacturing in developing countries (see Lall, 1992; UNIDO, 2002; UNIDO, 2006). But it is also relevant for agriculture (Omamo and Lynam, 2003; Lele and Ekboir, 2004) and services. In the present Report it encompasses both firms and farms, and includes services as well as industrial activities.
2. The idea of "absorptive capability" derives from Abramovitz (1986), who speaks of the "social capability" for technological advance during catch-up. Cohen and Levinthal (1989: 569) define "absorptive capacity" as "the firm's ability to identify, assimilate and exploit knowledge from the environment", whilst Rogers (2004: 578) defines "absorptive capability" as "the capability to access, learn and absorb relevant overseas technology". For analyses of East Asian development success in terms of the ability of countries to assimilate and absorb foreign technology, see Nelson and Pack (1999) and Kim (1995).
3. For a review of different perspectives on technological change and economic growth, see Nelson and Winter (1982), Nelson (1998) and Verspagen (2004). The importance of innovation for structural change and economic growth is argued in Ocampo (2005). Like the *LDC Report 2006*, this Report is based on evolutionary and structuralist approaches to economic growth.
4. For a discussion on bridging the gap between policies for technological change and policies for poverty reduction, see Mackintosh, Chataway and Wuyts (2007).

References

Abramovitz, M. (1986). Catching up, forging ahead and falling behind. *Journal of Economic History*, 46 (2): 385–406.

Archibugi, D. and Coco, A. (2004). A new indicator of technological capabilities for developed and developing countries. *World Development*, 32 (4): 629–654.

Archibugi, D. and Coco, A. (2005). Measuring technological capabilities at the country level: A survey and a menu for choice. *Research Policy*, 34 (2): 175–194.

Cohen, D. and Soto, M. (2001). Growth and human capital: good data, good results. Discussion Paper No. 3025, Centre for Economic Policy Research, London.

Cohen, W.M. and Levinthal, D.A. (1989). Innovation and learning: The two faces of R&D. *Economic Journal*, 99: 569–596.

Evenson, R. and Westphal, L.E. (1995). Technological change and technology strategy. Chapter 37 in Behrman, J. and Srinivasan, T.N. (eds.), *Handbook of Development Economics*. Vol. III, Elsevier, St. Louis, MO.

Hayami, Y. and V.W. Ruttan (1985). *Agricultural Development: An International Perspective*. Johns Hopkins University Press, Baltimore and London.

James, J. (2006). An institutional critique of recent attempts to measure technological capabilities across countries. Journal of Economic Issues, 40 (3): 743–766.

Kim, L. (1995). Absorptive capacity and industrial growth: A conceptual framework and Korea's experience. Chapter 12 in Kim, L., *Learning and Innovation in Economic Development*, Edward Elgar, Cheltenham, UK and Northampton, Mass.

Knell, M. (2006). Uneven technological accumulation and growth in the least developed countries. Study prepared for UNCTAD as a background paper for *The Least Developed Countries Report 2006*, UNCTAD, Geneva.

Lall, S. (1992). Technological capabilities and industrialization. *World Development*, 20 (2): 165–186.

Lele, U. and Ekboir, J. (2004). Technological generation, adaptation, adoption and impact: towards a framework for understanding and increasing research impact. Working Paper, World Bank, Washington, DC.

Mackintosh, M., Chataway, J. and Wuyts, M. (2007). Promoting innovation, productivity and industrial growth and reducing poverty: Bridging the policy gap. Special Issue of *The European Journal of Development Research*, 19 (1).

Nelson, R.R. (1998). The agenda for growth theory: A different point of view. *Cambridge Journal of Economics*, 22: 497–520.

Nelson, R. R. and Pack, H. (1999). The Asian growth miracle and modern economic growth. *Economic Journal*, 109: 416–436.

Nelson, R.R. and Winter, S. (1982). *An Evolutionary Theory of Economic Change*. Harvard University Press, Cambridge, Mass.

Nonaka, I. Ryoko, T. and Boysiere, P. (2001). A theory of organizational knowledge creation: Understanding the dynamic process of creating knowledge. In Dierkes, M., Antal A., Child, J. and Nanaka, I. (eds.), *Handbook of Organizaitonal learning and Knowledge*, Oxford University Press, Oxford, UK.

Ocampo, J.A. (2005). The quest for dynamic efficiency: Structural dynamics and economic growth in developing countries. In Ocampo, J.A. (ed.), *Beyond Reforms: Structural Dynamics and Macroeconomic Vulnerability*. Latin American Development Forum Series, United Nations Economic Commission for Latin America and the Caribbean (ECLAC), Washington, DC.

OECD (1997). National Innovation Systems. Organization for Economic Co-operation and Development, Paris.

OECD (2005). Oslo Manual: Guidelines for Collecting and Interpreting Innovation Data. Organization for Economic Co-operation and Development, Paris.

Omamo, S.W. and Lynam, J.K. (2003). Agricultural science and technology policy in Africa. *Research Policy* 32: 1681–1694.

Patel, S. (1995). *Technological Transformation in the Third World: Volume 5: The Historic Process*. Ashgate, London.

Rogers, M. (2004). Absorptive capability and economic growth: how do countries catch-up? *Cambridge Journal of Economics*, 28: 577–596.

UNCTAD (2004). *The Least Developed Countries Report 2004: Linking International Trade to Poverty Reduction*. United Nations publication, sales no. E.00.II.D.21, Geneva and New York.

UNCTAD (2005). *World Investment Report 2005: Transnational Corporations and the Internationalization of R&D*. United Nations publication, sales no. E.05.II.D.10.

UNCTAD (2006). *The Least Developed Countries Report 2006: Developing Productive Capacities*. United Nations publication, sales no. E.06.II.D.9, Geneva and New York.

UNDP (2001). *Human Development Report 2001: Making New Technologies Work for Human Development*. United Nations Development Programme, New York.

UNIDO (2002). *Competing through Innovation and Learning*. United Nations Industrial Development Organization, Vienna.

UNIDO (2006). *Industrial Development Report 2005: Capability Building for Catching-up: Historical, Empirical and Policy Dimensions*, United Nations Industrial Development Organization, Vienna.

Verspagen, B. (2004). Innovation and economic growth. In Fagerberg, J., Mowery, D.C. and Nelson, R.R (eds.), *The Oxford Handbook of Innovation*, Oxford University Press, Oxford, UK.

Wagner, C., Brahmakulam, I., Jackson B., Wong, A., and Yoda, T. (2001). *Science and Technology Collaboration: Building Capacity in Developing Countries*. RAND Corporation, Santa Monica, CA.

Building Technological Capabilities through International Market Linkages

Chapter 1

A. Introduction

Technological catch-up for least developed countries requires access to the international knowledge pool and the ability to learn, master and adapt foreign technologies and thereby benefit from international technology diffusion. This process includes transfer of technology, which takes place through several channels. These can be formal (e.g. licensing, foreign direct investment) or informal (e.g. movement of people) and/or market (e.g. interaction with upstream suppliers or downstream customers) or non-market (e.g. technical assistance programmes of official development agencies or NGOs).

The importance of those different channels cannot be established precisely and it varies according to different stages of development, as do developing countries' ability to take advantage of them. Nevertheless, the channels that involve continuous interaction between the acquirer and the supplier of technology are the most likely to be effective channels for knowledge diffusion. The main reason for this is that tacit knowledge is a component of virtually all technologies, but at the same time it is the most difficult to transmit between different agents. Therefore, it is mainly through continuous interaction between agents that tacit knowledge is transmitted. It can thus be assumed that the channels of technology diffusion that involve constant interaction and exchange are more important for LDCs than the others.

The most widespread international market mechanisms that involve continuous interaction between agents leading to knowledge flows are trade and foreign direct investment (FDI). From this, the major channels for international technology diffusion to LDCs can be derived from:

1. Imports of technology embodied in machinery and other capital goods;

2. Interaction with international customers (i.e. exports), particularly through the integration of LDC firms into global value chains;

3. Foreign direct investment;

4. Imports of disembodied technology (i.e. licensing).

The working of those four market mechanisms as channels for diffusion of technology to LDCs is analysed successively in sections to B to E of this chapter.[1]

The critical issue is how effective these channels are in an LDC context. LDCs have over the past 20 years actively integrated into the global economy through trade and investment. Nevertheless, those countries are still at the initial levels of technological development. Their low income levels and the prevalence of poverty entail low levels of physical and human capital. Their national knowledge systems are not well articulated or efficient (UNCTAD, 2006b). Those countries are far away from the world technological frontier. Most domestic firms and farms

Technological catch-up for least developed countries requires access to the international knowledge pool and the ability to learn, master and adapt foreign technologies and thereby benefit from international technology diffusion.

The major channels for international technology diffusion to LDCs are imports of capital goods, integration into global value chains, foreign direct investment and licensing.

operate with rudimentary technologies and carry out little, if any, autonomous research and development (R&D). In these circumstances the working of international market linkages as channels of international technology diffusion may be severely constrained. The evidence presented in this chapter shows the extent of it. Section F summarizes and concludes.

Most LDC firms and farms operate with rudimentary technologies and carry out little, if any, autonomous research and development.

B. Imports of capital goods

By far the most important source of technological innovation in LDCs, as perceived by firms, is new machinery or equipment, according to a large-scale survey of firms in developing countries (chart 3). This is true of domestically owned firms and of foreign affiliates operating in LDCs (Knell, 2006).[2] Machinery and equipment were also found to be the major source of innovation by firms from other developing countries (ODCs).[3]

Chart 3. Three most important sources of technological innovation in LDCs and ODCs, 2000–2005

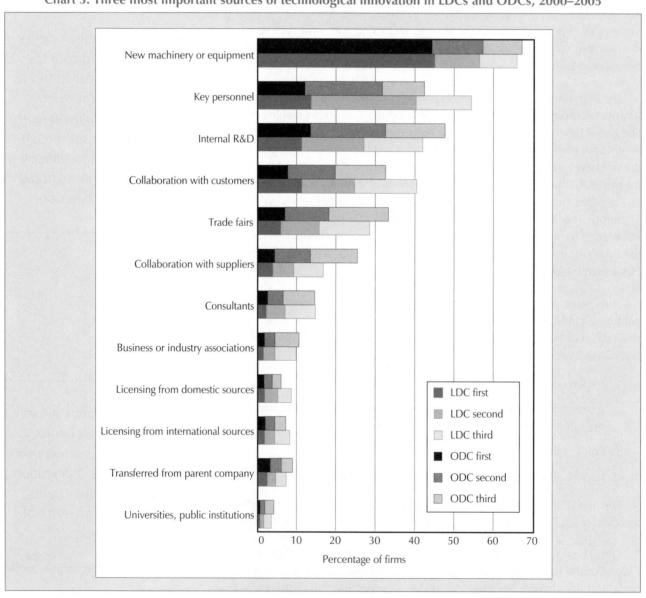

Source: Knell (2006), based on World Bank, Investment Climate Surveys, 2000–2005.

Note: Percentage of replies to the question asking firms to identify the first, second and third most important sources of technological innovation for them. The question was part of a survey questionnaire given to firms located in LDCs and other developing countries, as part of the World Bank's Investment Climate Surveys. In the case of the LDCs, interviews with 2,500 firms were carried out between 2000 and 2005 in Bangladesh, Cambodia, Ethiopia, Madagascar, Mali, Senegal, Uganda, United Republic of Tanzania and Zambia.

It is likely that most of the machinery and equipment operated in LDCs is imported, since those countries have very little capital goods manufacturing capacity. Hence, imports of capital goods are the main source of innovation for firms in LDCs and are a major feature of their technological effort. The presence of a national capital goods industry would reduce the dependence of LDCs on imports. However, the development of domestic capital goods manufacturing capacity typically takes place only at a much later stage of technological catch-up (Justman and Teubal, 1991). Therefore, at the present stage of technological development of LDCs imports remain the main source of capital goods.

Imports of capital goods are the main source of innovation for firms in LDCs and are a major feature of their technological effort.

This section analyses the development in LDCs imports of technology embodied in machinery, equipment and other capital goods between 1980 and 2005. It compares them with those of other developing countries in order to put LDCs in perspective. An analysis is made of different types of capital goods, according to their general characteristics and main end-use (whenever possible), so as to study which types of embodied technologies LDCs have been acquiring internationally over the last 25 years.[4] The trading partners of origin for capital goods are both developed countries and the group of the 20 most technologically advanced developing countries.[5]

Imports of capital goods by LDCs expanded only moderately during the 1980s and 1990s, but since 2003 they increased sharply.

1. TRENDS AND ORIGIN

Imports of capital goods (in nominal terms) by LDCs expanded only moderately during the 1980s and 1990s. Since 2003, however, they increased sharply to reach more than $20 billion in 2005 (chart 4). The strong increase in the more recent years was highly concentrated on oil-exporting countries and Bangladesh, the largest LDC economy.

A significant part of the capital goods imported by LDCs consists of second-hand equipment. Although trade data do not show the extent of this practice,

Chart 4. LDC imports of capital goods, 1980–2005

(Current $, millions)

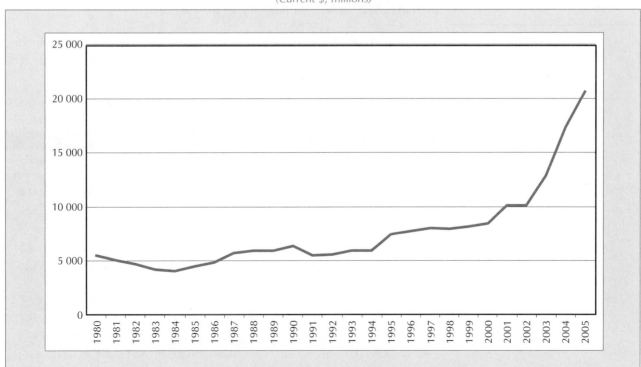

Source: UNCTAD secretariat calculations, based on data from UNDESA Statistics Division.

Note: LDCs exclude Lesotho, Liberia and Timor-Leste. For the definition of capital goods and methodological notes, see the annex.

cursory evidence attests it. In the textile and garment industry, foreign investors often transfer used capital goods from other countries to LDCs when establishing themselves in the new host country (see subsection D.4 of this chapter). It is likely that junior mining companies do the same to some extent.

The sourcing of LDCs' capital goods imports has changed markedly over the last 25 years. While in the 1980s most of them (92 per cent) originated in developed countries, during 2000–2005 this proportion fell to 59 per cent, this reflecting the rise of technologically advanced developing countries as exporters of capital goods. The shift towards this type of South–South trade was driven by the Asian LDCs, which sourced more than half of their capital goods imports from other developing countries in 2000–2005 (table 2). This is mostly explained by the growing regional integration of Asian LDCs not only in terms of international trade, but also in terms of foreign direct investment.

While in the 1980s 92 per cent of LDCs' capital goods imports originated in developed countries, during 2000–2005 this proportion fell to 59 per cent, this reflecting the rise of technologically advanced developing countries as exporters of capital goods.

2. INTENSITY OF CAPITAL GOODS IMPORTS

In order to assess the intensity of capital goods imports in LDCs and its development over time, a series of indicators are presented in table 3. They consist of capital goods imports as a share of GDP, gross fixed capital formation (GFCF), total merchandise imports and total merchandise exports. Lastly, per capita capital goods imports are also shown.

Capital goods imports as a share of GDP and GFCF remained approximately constant during the 1980s and 1990s in the LDCs, but rose marginally in 2000–2005 thanks to higher import values in 2003–2005.[6] Nevertheless, the levels were substantially lower than in other developing countries and the gap widened considerably during the last 25 years (table 3). The share of GDP of capital goods imports was similar in LDCs and ODCs during the 1980s, but it more than doubled to 12 per cent by 2000–2005 in ODCs, while in LDCs it rose to just half that level. On a per capita basis, capital goods imports of LDCs less than doubled to $18 between the 1980s and 2000–2005, while in the ODCs the ratio rose fivefold to $207, a level 11 times higher than in LDCs.

Relative to GDP, capital goods imports in the LDCs were lower than in other developing countries and the gap widened considerably during the last 25 years.

The part of national fixed investment that was dedicated to imported machinery and equipment in the 1980s was higher in the LDCs (27 per cent)

Table 2. Imports of capital goods, by origin, in LDCs and ODCs, 1980–2005
(Percentage ot total capital goods imports)

	1980–1989		1990–1999		2000–2005	
	Developed countries	Developing countries	Developed countries	Developing countries	Developed countries	Developing countries
LDCs	**91.5**	**8.5**	**75.4**	**24.6**	**59.0**	**41.0**
Africa and Haiti	95.0	5.0	88.6	11.4	66.3	33.7
Asia	81.7	18.3	51.2	48.8	43.4	56.6
Islands	92.0	8.0	84.4	15.6	73.8	26.2
Other developing countries (ODCs)	**89.4**	**10.6**	**72.3**	**27.7**	**57.5**	**42.5**
Africa	97.4	2.6	90.8	9.2	83.5	16.5
America	94.4	5.6	85.8	14.2	82.9	17.1
Asia	85.9	14.1	67.2	32.8	51.1	48.9

Source: UNCTAD secretariat calculations, based on data from UNDESA Statistics Division.

Note: LDCs and the regional subgroupings exclude Lesotho, Liberia and Timor-Leste. For the definition of capital goods, capital good groups and country groups, and methodological notes, see the annex.

Table 3. Indicators of the importance of capital goods imports in LDCs and ODCs, 1980–2005
(Percentage, unless otherwise indicated)

	Capital goods imports/ GDP			Capital goods imports/ Gross fixed capital formation			Capital goods imports/ Total merchandise imports			Capital goods imports/ Total merchandise exports			Capital goods imports per capita (Current $)		
	1980–1989	1990–1999	2000–2005	1980–1989	1990–1999	2000–2005	1980–1989	1990–1999	2000–2005	1980–1989	1990–1999	2000–2005	1980–1989	1990–1999	2000–2005
LDCs	**4.5**	**4.5**	**5.9**	**27.0**	**26.0**	**29.5**	**23.6**	**22.1**	**22.4**	**37.4**	**32.9**	**26.5**	**11**	**12**	**18**
Africa and Haiti	5.0	4.7	6.8	32.1	29.0	35.6	25.8	22.6	24.6	34.0	29.7	27.1	14	12	19
Asia	3.3	3.7	4.5	18.0	20.3	21.4	18.7	19.5	18.6	47.8	36.1	23.9	7	10	15
Islands	15.2	19.4	15.2	51.8	70.9	65.2	33.3	41.0	31.7	84.3	134.1	141.9	88	168	159
Other developing countries (ODCs)	**5.3**	**8.5**	**11.9**	**22.5**	**34.4**	**48.6**	**28.1**	**34.6**	**39.2**	**26.3**	**34.6**	**35.9**	**46**	**115**	**207**
Africa	5.5	6.2	7.3	25.6	35.3	43.7	29.1	30.0	30.9	28.7	28.7	27.4	87	74	97
America	3.8	5.4	7.1	17.8	27.3	38.0	33.1	37.6	35.5	28.9	40.2	34.6	81	187	270
Asia	6.2	10.7	14.6	24.9	37.6	52.4	27.3	35.1	41.1	25.8	34.5	37.2	37	110	213

Source: UNCTAD secretariat calculations, based on data from UNDESA Statistics Division.
Notes: As for table 2.

than in ODCs (23 per cent). In 2000–2005, by contrast, this was completely reversed. ODCs devoted almost half of their GFCF to imported capital goods, but LDCs less than one third (table 3). It is likely that this is an indirect indicator of the changing composition of fixed investment, with an increasing share of machinery and equipment in total GFCF of ODCs. This, in turn, possibly points to the increasing technological content of fixed investment in those countries and to their firms' strengthening technological effort. By contrast, comparable technological upgrading of GFCF does not seem to have taken place in LDCs.

Other indicators of the effort to acquire foreign technology embodied in capital goods are provided by their ratios to total merchandise imports and exports. The first ratio points to the priority given to capital goods, as opposed to other imports, such as consumer goods or food. This indicator has been approximately constant at about around 23 per cent in LDCs since 1980, as has the structure of imports of this group of countries. ODCs, by contrast, have strongly redirected their imports towards embodied technology since then, so that the share rose from 28 per cent in the 1980s to almost 40 per cent in 2000–2005 (table 3). Capital goods imports as a share of total exports indicates one possible use of foreign exchange earnings obtained through merchandise trade. It is competing with other uses, such as imports of other goods and payment of foreign debt. Thus, a rising share indicates foreign exchange earned through merchandise exports is increasingly being earmarked for building the productive capacity of the importing country. This indicator has taken opposite (and almost symmetrical) paths in LDCs and ODCs during the last 25 years. In the LDCs capital goods imports declined from 37 per cent of total exports to 27 per cent between the 1980s and 2000–2005. In the other developing countries they rose from 26 per cent to 36 per cent over the same period. Their foreign exchange earnings have been progressively used for building domestic technological capabilities. In LDCs, by contrast, the considerable increase in export earnings in 2000–2005 was not used to finance additional imports of capital goods to a comparable extent (except for oil-exporting economies), because of the only marginal rise in their investment rate.

Country data reveal that the value of capital goods imports is related to the economic weight of national economies and/or to the fact of being a petroleum exporter. Thus, the largest importers are Angola, Bangladesh, Sudan, Myanmar and Yemen (table 4). This reflects a size effect and large capital goods imports associated with the sharp increase in FDI inflows in the oil extractive industry

Data point to the increasing technological content of fixed investment in ODCs and to their firms' strengthening technological effort. By contrast, comparable technological upgrading of fixed investment does not seem to have taken place in LDCs.

In the LDCs capital goods imports declined from 37 per cent of total exports to 27 per cent between the 1980s and 2000–2005. In the other developing countries they rose from 26 per cent to 36 per cent over the same period.

Table 4. Indicators of the importance of capital goods imports for LDCs, by country, 2000–2005

(Period averages)

	Value	Capital goods imports/ GDP	Capital goods imports/GFCF	Capital goods imports per capita
	(Current $ millions)	*(%)*	*(%)*	*($)*
Angola	2101	13.2	112.0	136.8
Bangladesh	1792	3.2	13.5	12.2
Sudan	1026	5.7	30.0	28.7
Myanmar	730	7.9	70.7	15.5
Yemen	720	5.9	31.7	36.3
Ethiopia	617	8.3	39.3	8.2
United Rep. of Tanzania	521	4.8	24.8	14.3
Senegal	451	7.6	34.9	40.6
Zambia	383	8.5	40.4	34.7
Mozambique	369	7.7	33.4	18.9
Cambodia	352	7.9	38.5	26.2
Equatorial Guinea	326	10.9	25.2	702.6
Afghanistan	283	5.8	35.4	12.0
Madagascar	233	5.1	27.9	13.3
Benin	229	7.2	38.3	29.1
Nepal	225	3.8	19.6	8.8
Uganda	213	3.1	14.6	7.9
Mauritania	209	17.4	132.2	74.8
Mali	204	5.4	26.7	18.8
Dem. Rep. of the Congo	188	3.1	27.3	3.4
Guinea	173	5.3	34.7	20.0
Lao PDR	161	7.3	43.6	29.3
Chad	149	6.0	15.0	15.9
Malawi	133	7.1	69.2	10.7
Burkina Faso	133	3.6	14.6	10.2
Haiti	126	3.8	29.4	14.1
Togo	126	7.3	36.1	21.3
Djibouti	122	19.6	154.3	158.5
Sierra Leone	119	11.7	100.1	23.0
Maldives	100	14.2	50.1	348.0
Niger	92	3.9	26.2	7.5
Cape Verde	80	10.8	39.2	165.6
Vanuatu	79	28.8	140.4	387.2
Eritrea	75	9.6	37.8	18.0
Samoa	60	21.6	170.9	331.0
Rwanda	56	3.1	16.2	6.3
Bhutan	52	7.8	12.1	84.6
Gambia	49	11.9	58.0	32.4
Comoros	38	15.3	157.3	51.8
Burundi	33	4.6	37.9	4.5
Central African Republic	27	2.5	40.5	6.8
Solomon Islands	23	7.7	41.0	50.6
Lesotho	20	2.0	4.6	10.3
Sao Tome and Principe	15	27.1	80.5	103.6
Guinea-Bissau	15	6.3	34.5	10.0
Timor-Leste	12	3.6	11.2	12.9
Kiribati	12	21.3	49.4	135.0
Somalia	10	0.5	2.3	1.3
Tuvalu	6	31.7	56.7	587.3

Source: UNCTAD secretariat calculations, based on data from UNDESA Statistics Division.

Note: For the definition of capital goods and methodological notes, see the Annex. Countries are ranked according to import values. Data for Liberia not shown due to due to lack of reliable data.

since the 1990s (see section D of this chapter). Relative indicators reveal that the economies importing incorporated technology most intensively are islands, small economies and, again, oil producers (table 4). This reflects opposite size effects (since the impact of capital goods imports on small economies is greater) and the importance of petroleum extraction. By contrast, the countries with the lowest capital goods import intensity are not only those that have recently experienced armed conflict and therefore have a low investment rate. More surprisingly, some of the major LDC exporters of manufactures (e.g. Bangladesh, Nepal, Haiti and Madagascar) also have very low imports of embodied technology, a fact that indicates their firms' weak technological efforts, which could be expected to be stronger in view of their export structure.

3. Types of capital goods imported

For the purpose of our analysis capital goods have been classified in two different ways.[7] The first classification groups them mainly into two broad categories: machinery and equipment, and transport equipment.[8] The remaining capital goods consist of scientific and measuring instruments, which have always accounted for less than 6 per cent of capital goods imports of both LDCs and ODCs.

The large majority of LDC's capital goods imports over the last 25 years have consisted of machinery and equipment, and their share has increased over time. In 2000–2005 they accounted for over two thirds of LDCs' total capital goods imports, while transport equipment amounted to slightly more than one fourth (table 5). Regionally, the Asian LDCs import machinery and equipment most intensively, as those goods account for more than three fourths of their total capital goods imports. The share is much lower for African and island LDCs.[9] The stronger weight of this type of capital goods in imports of Asian LDCs reflects their higher level of industrialization as compared with other LDCs.

Likewise, in other developing countries capital goods imports are dominated by machinery and equipment and their importance has grown over time. The most important difference between the two groups of developing countries, however, is that the share of imports of transport equipment in ODCs is much lower than in LDCs. This is due, on the one hand, to the higher level of industrialization of the former and, on the other hand, to the presence of domestic industry that produces transport equipment in most of the technologically more advanced developing countries. This means that part of the domestic demand for transport capital goods is met domestically rather than by imports.

The second classification of capital goods focuses on machinery and equipment and scientific and measuring instruments (i.e. excluding transport equipment) and endeavours to identify the type of industry that uses them. This is possible for specialized machinery, but not for general-purpose technologies or for the residual category "other industrial machinery".[10]

Among specialized machinery, the most important category for LDCs is construction, mining and metal crushing, which in 2000–2005 accounted for 13 per cent of their total capital good imports (table 6). This category is relatively more important for African LDCs.[11] Here the share of this type of equipment increased over the last 25 years, while it remained approximately constant in other LDCs and declined in all ODC subregions. At the same time, the share of industrial machinery[12] in African LDCs' capital goods imports declined from 26 per cent in the 1980s to 23 per cent in 2000–2005. The changing composition of African LDCs' capital goods imports reflects the changing patterns of specialization

Some of the major LDC exporters of manufactures have very low imports of embodied technology, a fact that indicates their firms' weak technological efforts.

The large majority of LDC's capital goods imports over the last 25 years have consisted of machinery and equipment, and their share has increased over time.

Asian LDCs import machinery and equipment most intensively, reflecting their higher level of industrialization as compared with other LDCs.

Among specialized machinery, the most important category for LDCs is construction, mining and metal crushing. This category is relatively more important for African LDCs.

Table 5. Imports of capital goods, by broad categories, in LDCs and ODCs, 1980–2005
(Percentage of total capital goods imports)

	1980–1989			1990–1999			2000–2005		
	Machinery & equipment	Transport equipment	Scientific & measuring instruments	Machinery & equipment	Transport equipment	Scientific & measuring instruments	Machinery & equipment	Transport equipment	Scientific & measuring instruments
LDCs	**62.2**	**34.0**	**3.8**	**66.6**	**28.8**	**4.5**	**68.5**	**26.9**	**4.5**
Africa and Haiti	60.9	35.4	3.7	65.6	29.6	4.8	65.0	30.5	4.6
Asia	67.8	27.9	4.3	70.8	24.9	4.3	76.8	18.8	4.4
Islands	45.3	51.8	2.9	50.9	45.6	3.5	56.5	39.7	3.8
Other developing countries (ODCs)	**73.4**	**21.4**	**5.2**	**80.2**	**14.9**	**4.9**	**82.9**	**11.2**	**5.9**
Africa	69.3	25.9	4.8	70.5	23.9	5.6	69.6	24.9	5.5
America	64.2	30.9	4.9	67.9	27.1	5.0	71.0	23.7	5.4
Asia	75.4	19.4	5.2	83.1	12.2	4.7	85.5	8.5	6.0

Source: UNCTAD secretariat calculations, based on data from UNDESA Statistics Division.
Notes: As for table 2.

Table 6. Imports of capital goods, by type of end-use, in LDCs and ODCs, 1980–2005
(Percentage of total capital goods imports)

	Agricultural machinery			Construction, mining, metal-crushing			Power-generating machinery			Textile and leather machinery			Metalworking machinery			Food-processing machinery			Paper, pulp and publishing machinery			Other industrial machinery			ICT capital		
	1980 –89	1990 –99	2000 –05	1980 –89	1990 –99	2000 –05	1980 –89	1990 –99	2000 –05	1980 –89	1990 –99	2000 –05	1980 –89	1990 –99	2000 –05	1980 –89	1990 –99	2000 –05	1980 –89	1990 –99	2000 –05	1980 –89	1990 –99	2000 –05	1980 –89	1990 –99	2000 –05
LDCs	**3.3**	**2.1**	**1.5**	**10.5**	**11.5**	**13.0**	**13.9**	**14.1**	**12.7**	**2.8**	**3.6**	**3.5**	**1.4**	**1.3**	**1.2**	**1.5**	**1.4**	**1.1**	**0.8**	**0.8**	**0.8**	**20.2**	**20.3**	**19.3**	**11.9**	**16.6**	**19.8**
Africa and Haiti	3.7	2.3	1.2	11.3	12.4	15.5	12.1	13.2	11.0	2.5	1.9	0.8	1.3	1.2	0.8	1.5	1.6	1.2	0.6	0.7	0.6	20.0	20.8	19.9	11.7	16.6	18.0
Asia	2.3	1.8	2.0	9.0	10.8	8.9	19.2	15.7	15.7	3.9	7.1	9.2	1.8	1.6	1.9	1.4	1.2	1.0	1.1	1.1	1.0	21.3	20.1	18.5	12.4	16.7	23.1
Islands	1.7	0.9	0.6	5.6	5.8	5.1	10.3	13.9	15.4	0.5	0.5	0.5	0.7	0.6	0.5	0.6	0.5	0.5	0.4	0.4	0.3	15.5	15.8	17.0	13.1	16.0	20.4
Other developing countries (ODCs)	**1.6**	**0.6**	**0.4**	**8.6**	**6.9**	**5.7**	**14.5**	**13.0**	**12.1**	**3.1**	**2.6**	**1.4**	**2.9**	**2.6**	**2.0**	**0.6**	**0.4**	**0.2**	**1.1**	**1.3**	**0.8**	**20.2**	**18.3**	**16.3**	**26.6**	**40.5**	**50.0**
Africa	2.9	1.8	1.3	10.1	9.6	9.0	14.6	13.2	14.0	3.0	2.9	1.7	2.6	2.0	1.5	1.1	1.1	1.0	1.3	1.5	1.3	23.4	22.8	20.6	15.9	21.4	24.8
America	2.0	1.1	0.9	7.7	6.6	5.2	13.9	13.3	14.8	2.6	1.9	1.1	3.2	2.1	1.6	0.7	0.6	0.4	1.3	1.4	0.9	17.4	17.9	17.6	20.9	28.2	33.9
Asia	1.1	0.4	0.2	8.3	6.6	5.5	14.2	12.6	11.3	3.2	2.7	1.5	2.9	2.7	2.0	0.4	0.3	0.2	1.0	1.2	0.7	19.8	17.7	15.6	30.0	44.6	54.3

Source: UNCTAD secretariat calculations, based on data from UNDESA Statistics Division.
Notes: As for table 2.

of those countries over the last 25 years, particularly the de-industrialization that followed trade liberalization and the re-specialization in natural resource extraction (UNCTAD, 2004, 2006b).

The share of ICTs in LDC imports was 30 percentage points lower than in ODCs. This reflects LDCs' slower adoption of the new ICT technologies and, more generally, those countries' lower technology intensity.

Asian LDCs, by contrast, import textile and leather machinery more intensively than any other developing region. This type of equipment accounted for 9 per cent of their total capital goods imports in 2000–2005, while in all other developing regions the corresponding share was below 2 per cent (table 6). In Asian LDCs the proportion of those capital goods has more than doubled over the last 25 years, a fact that reflects the expansion of the garment and textile industry (see subsection D.4 of this chapter).

The most striking difference between the composition of imports of capital goods of ODCs and LDCs is the importance of information and communication technology (ICT) capital. In the former that category accounted for one fourth of total capital goods imports already in the 1980s, and this share doubled to half in 2000–2005. In the LDCs, by contrast, in the early 21st century ICT amounted to just one fifth of total capital goods imports. Although the share of ICT in those imports doubled as compared with the 1980s, it was still 30 percentage points lower than in ODCs. This reflects LDCs' slower pace of adoption of the new ICT technologies and, more generally, those countries' lower technology intensity.

To a certain extent, the fact that ICT capital imports by LDCs are lower than those by ODCs is to be expected, given the lower level of technological development of the former group. Nevertheless, the low uptake of some of those technologies (particularly telecommunications) deprives many of those countries' firms and households of an important tool for economic integration and market efficiency. While the early enthusiasm about the potential contribution of ICTs to development has not been borne out by recent experience, it is widely recognized that those technologies can make a positive contribution to technological upgrading and associated benefits, even in an LDC context (Konde, 2007).

The low uptake of ICTs (particularly telecommunications) deprives many LDC firms and households of an important tool for economic integration and market efficiency.

The share of agricultural machinery in LDCs' total capital goods imports is low (1.5 per cent in 2000–2005) and less than half of its level during the 1980s (table 6). The relative contraction in those imports was driven by African LDCs, where the share declined by 2.5 percentage points, while there was less of a decline in the other LDCs. Those developments are apparently contrary to expectations. First, given the higher share of agriculture in total GDP in LDCs as compared with ODCs, it could have been expected that they would import agricultural machinery more intensively.[13] This is not the case, however, because the agriculture in LDCs is still largely carried on by smallholders on a non-commercial basis and with extremely low levels of automation. Second, it is likely that a Green Revolution (see chapter 2) would lead to greater imports of agricultural machinery in LDCs.

4. IMPLICATIONS

Total capital goods imports by LDCs have lost momentum over the last 25 years. While expanding in nominal terms, they have either been stagnant or risen only marginally when compared with macroeconomic variables or the population. Moreover, they have dramatically fallen behind when compared with imports by other developing countries. The technological effort of ODC firms (in all the subregions) has decisively increased the resources devoted to the acquisition of foreign embodied technology in both absolute and relative terms. While the technological effort to acquire foreign embodied technology was comparable in LDCs and ODCs in the 1980s, the gap has widened considerably since that time. In the LDCs, imports of capital goods have been hampered by structural change, the slow progression of the investment rate and balance-of-payments restrictions.

While the technological effort to acquire foreign embodied technology was comparable in LDCs and ODCs in the 1980s, the gap has widened considerably since that time.

The composition of capital goods imports by LDCs to a large extent mirrors changes in their productive structure and trade specialization and their overall level of technological development. That explains the relatively high and growing share of imports of machinery and equipment destined for the extractive industry in African LDCs (construction, mining and metal-crushing equipment) or for low-value-added manufacturing in Asian LDCs (textile and leather machinery).

Developments in capital goods imports are, moreover, partly associated with the type of FDI that those countries have been attracting in recent years. Therefore, the impact of such imports on the technological capability-building of LDCs depends also on the technology-diffusing effects of the associated FDI projects and on the patterns of TNC insertion in host LDC economies (see section D of this chapter). Imports of capital goods and equipment for mineral resource extraction by African LDCs, for example, have since 2000 been boosted by the surge in investment in this sector (driven mainly by FDI) and by the changes in mining policy. Policy reforms have facilitated access to foreign finance and reduced the cost of importing the equipment and spare parts needed to rehabilitate and expand existing mines and develop new ones (Campbell, 2004).

Capital goods imports are associated with the type of FDI that LDCs have been attracting in recent years.

In summary, imports of capital goods could be expected to play a major role in LDCs' learning of foreign technology and in the domestic accumulation of their firms' technological capabilities. However, this potential is being fulfilled to only a very limited degree for two main reasons. First, the growth in capital goods imports by those countries has been sluggish, in sharp contrast to their dynamic expansion in other developing countries. Second, the types of equipment and machinery imports that have increased most have accentuated the specialization in natural resource extraction and low-value-added manufacturing into which LDCs are locked. By contrast, greater imports of other types of capital goods could have been expected in view of the early stage of technological catch-up of most LDCs (as a Green Revolution would require more agricultural machinery imports) or if a broader diffusion of telecommunication technology were taking place (leading to higher ICT capital goods imports).

> *Importing relatively few capital goods implies that LDC firms are foregoing the possibility of technological learning and adaptive innovation potentially associated with greater imports of technology embodied in those goods.*

Importing relatively few capital goods implies that LDC firms are forgoing the possibility of technological learning and adaptive innovation potentially associated with greater imports of technology embodied in those goods. Moreover, beyond the quantities imported, the crucial issue is whether these firms can make efficient use of these embodied technology imports. However, this is constrained by their low absorptive capacities (see section F of this chapter).

C. Exports and the role of global value chains

> *The global value chain approach emphasizes the importance of international linkages and the increasing varieties of inter-firm arrangements.*

The possibilities available to LDC firms for developing their technological capabilities through exports depend on the linkages they develop with their downstream foreign customers and on the technological effort that they make to learn through those linkages. This is especially true given the changes in international production systems, distribution channels and financial markets, accelerated by the globalization of product markets and the spread of information technologies. The global value chain (GVC) approach emphasizes the importance of international linkages and the increasing varieties of inter-firm arrangements. It helps to explain the strategic role of relationships with key external actors. Thus, it sheds light on how LDC firms can enhance their technological capabilities by exporting (learning-by-exporting) or, alternatively, they can become marginalized from GVCs (Pietrobelli, 2007).

> *Global value chains often represent one of the very few options for local firms and suppliers to secure access to larger (international) markets and to innovative technologies.*

Global value chains are increasingly present in developing countries, also as a result of changes in national and international regulatory frameworks. They often represent one of the very few options — or perhaps the only one — for local firms and suppliers to secure access to larger (international) markets and to innovative technologies. Participation in GVCs may be associated to the upgrading of firms. In this perspective, four types of upgrading have been distinguished for enterprises (Humphrey and Schmitz, 2000):

- *Process upgrading* is transforming inputs into outputs more efficiently by reorganizing the production system or introducing superior technology.

- *Product upgrading* is moving into more sophisticated product lines in terms of increased unit values.

- *Functional upgrading* is acquiring new, superior functions in the chain, such as design or marketing, or abandoning existing lower-value-added functions, so as to focus on higher-value-added activities.

- *Intersectoral upgrading* is applying the competence acquired in a particular function to move into a new sector.

However, whether LDCs' firms and farms will benefit from the relationships with foreign buyers depends on a number of circumstances that may or may not arise. The upgrading process is fraught with difficulties and obstacles, which are particularly great for LDC firms. The following two subsections explain how that process can in principle take place and its applicability to LDCs. An analysis of those exports countries' then highlights how LDC firms have been able to position themselves in GVCs.

1. THE CHANGING NATURE OF GLOBAL VALUE CHAINS

The value chain describes the full range of activities that firms and workers carry out to bring a product from its conception to its end-use and beyond. That includes activities such as design, production, marketing, distribution and support to the final consumer. Chart 5 provides the example of the textile and garments value chain (whose presence in Asian LDCs is analysed in subsection D.4 of this chapter). Rarely do individual companies alone undertake the full range of activities required in order to bring a product from conception to market. The design, production, and marketing of products involve a chain of activities that are often divided among different enterprises, often located in different places and sometimes even in different countries. All activities contribute to total value, but it is crucial to identify those activities providing higher returns (i.e. "premia") along the value chain in order to understand the global distribution of value added. "Rents" often emerge in GVCs, whenever non-competitive structures emerge and the balance of power is unevenly distributed among actors.

At any point in the chain, some degree of governance and coordination is required. This governance may occur through arm's-length market relations or through non-market relationships with different hierarchies: network (implying cooperation among firms of more or less equal power that share their competencies within the chain), quasi-hierarchy and hierarchy (Humphrey and Schmitz, 2000; Pietrobelli and Rabellotti, 2004, 2006a).[14]

The GVC literature also stresses the role played by the GVC leaders, particularly the buyers, in transferring knowledge along the chains. Buyers and retailers

Whether LDCs' firms and farms will benefit from the relationships with foreign buyers depends on a number of circumstances that may or may not arise. The upgrading process is fraught with difficulties and obstacles.

All activities contribute to total value, but it is crucial to identify those activities providing higher returns along the value chain in order to understand the global distribution of value added.

"Rents" often emerge in GVCs, whenever non-competitive structures emerge and the balance of power is unevenly distributed among actors.

Chart 5. The textile and garments value chain

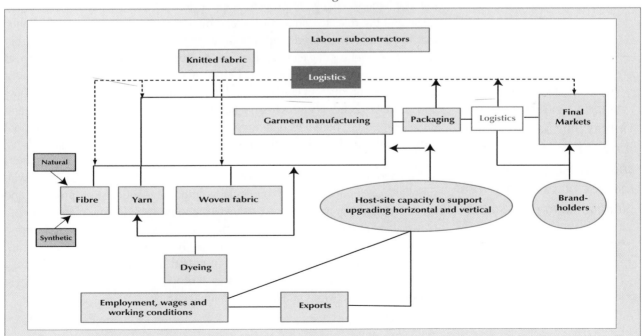

Source: Rasiah (2006a).

increasingly play a role in product development, branding, supplier selection and distribution, and that is especially true for agricultural and fresh produce (Dolan and Humphrey, 2001, 2004; Humphrey, 2005). The increasing "buyer-drivenness" of value chains allows leaders to transfer the so-called low-profit functions to firms in other functional positions along the chain in order to obtain enhanced organizational flexibility (Gibbon and Ponte, 2005). In fact, today the overall process of driving appears to be related to the relations between lead firms and first-tier suppliers, and between first- and second-tier suppliers, and to the allocation of control over the definition of the functions that first-tier suppliers should play. The rise of buyer-driven chains has been facilitated by developments in the national and international regulatory frameworks, trade liberalization, increasingly stringent food (and sanitary) safety regulation, increased currency convertibility, transport market liberalization and improvements, and reduced costs of international communications and transport.

The rise of buyer-driven chains has been facilitated by trade liberalization, increasingly stringent food (and sanitary) safety regulation, increased currency convertibility and reduced costs of international communications and transport.

Those changes open up opportunities for firms in developing country firms (Humphrey, 2005), such as the following:

- Increased processing, much of it close to growing sites.[15] Retailers are often willing to outsource value chain functions to suppliers, providing new opportunities along the chain;

- Increasing product differentiation and investment in innovation;

- Improved systems within supplying countries to respond to the demand for greater emphasis on freshness and agility within the logistics system;

- Emphasis on parts of the supply relationships such as reliable delivery, trust, flexibility in supply and ability to innovate that increase the switching costs for buyers, and may increase the length of contractual relationships for sellers.

Insertion in a quasi-hierarchical chain may offer favourable conditions for process and product upgrading but hinder functional upgrading.

For small firms in less developed countries, participation in value chains is moreover a means of obtaining information about the needs of global markets and gaining access to those markets. Although this information has high value for local small and medium-sized enterprises (SMEs), it is less clear what role the leaders of the GVCs play in fostering and supporting SMEs' upgrading process. Although the lead firm may be the driver for change, it is not necessarily the agent that implements change or provides support to deal with change. It may set the target and the rules to win an order (e.g. by setting a standard or a performance that needs to be achieved) and, insofar as the cost of switching to source from another supplier is not excessive, it may well source elsewhere. Evidence suggests that insertion in a quasi-hierarchical chain may offer favourable conditions for process and product upgrading but hinder functional upgrading (Humphrey and Schmitz, 2000; Pietrobelli and Rabellotti, 2006a; Giuliani, Pietrobelli and Rabellotti, 2005); networks offer ideal conditions for all forms of upgrading, but they are the least likely to occur among producers in developing countries.

In some sectors vertical relations with suppliers of inputs may be particularly important sources of product and process upgrading, as in the case of textiles and most traditional manufacturing.

As innovation studies have shown, in some sectors vertical relations with suppliers of inputs may be particularly important sources of product and process upgrading, as in the case of textiles and most traditional manufacturing. However, in other sectors the major stimuli for technical change may be provided by technology users, organizations such as universities or the firms themselves, as, for example, with software or agro-industrial products (Pavitt, 1984). Table 7 provides relevant information for two types of sectors prevalent in LDCs: resource-based activities and low-tech manufacturing.

2. Participation of LDCs in global value chains

Access to the fastest-growing market segments depends upon satisfying the demands of retailers and competing with other suppliers. Large retailers become gatekeepers to markets, hindering and/or fostering access. These difficult changes represent opportunities but may also threaten exclusion for those suppliers that are unable to respond to the challenge.

Since the mid-1980s lead firms have required more functional capacities (i.e. the range of activities, and the related conditions and skills, that suppliers are required to carry out) from first-tier suppliers in all cases, and sometimes also from second- and third-tier suppliers. At the same time, lead firms require higher performance levels from second-tier suppliers (i.e. compliance with standards for carrying out those activities). These increasing demands by buyers differ by sector and by specific value chain.

Buyers and chain leaders are becoming more and more demanding, but they do not necessarily provide support or transfer knowledge and capabilities. The key agents for knowledge transfer and organization vary from chain to chain. The "lead" firm may not be responsible for ensuring technical competence along the supply chain. In fact, much of the work of value chain organization and management is being outsourced by lead firms, which establish a first tier of suppliers and push responsibility towards them to an increasing extent. First-tier suppliers in turn increasingly rely on a series of second- and third-tier suppliers. Firms from LDCs rarely qualify — that is, they do not have the capacity, skills and volumes — to become first-tier suppliers, and in the best case may become second- or third- tier suppliers.

According to most recent empirical evidence, by far the most demanding entry barrier increases have been for first-tier suppliers (Gibbon and Ponte, 2005). This is perhaps less worrying for LDCs, as no firms from those countries play the role of leader, and very few that of first-tier (or often even second-tier) supplier.

What are the consequences of those increasing demands by buyers for second-tier suppliers in LDCs? The risks involved have been described as the risks of marginalization and exclusion (Gibbon and Ponte, 2005). The former refers to the possibility of downgrading within the same GVC and being relegated to less remunerative and more vulnerable segments of activity, while the latter refers to the eventual inability to enter, and being utterly excluded from global chains.

The processes of exclusion and marginalization differ in different value chains and countries, but the risks have become a standard typical characteristic. However, those risks do not necessarily imply marginalization and exclusion:

Buyers and chain leaders are becoming more and more demanding, but they do not necessarily provide support or transfer knowledge and capabilities.

For the LDCs, the risks involved in increasing demands of buyers in GVCs have been described as the risks of marginalization and exclusion.

Table 7. Patterns of learning and innovation in selected sectoral groups			
Groups	**Industries**	**Learning patterns**	**Description**
Traditional manufacturing	Textiles and apparel, footwear, furniture, tiles	Mainly supplier-driven	• Most new techniques originate from machinery and chemical industries • Opportunities for technological accumulation are focused on improvements and modifications in production methods and associated inputs, and on product design • Most technology is transferred internationally, embodied in capital goods • Low appropriability, low entry barriers
Resource-based activities	Sugar, tobacco, wine, fruit, milk, mining industry	Supplier-driven, science-based	• Importance of basic and applied research led by public research institutes due to low appropriability of knowledge • Innovation is also spurred by suppliers (machinery, seeds, chemicals etc.) • Increasing importance of international sanitary and quality standards, and of patents • Low appropriability of knowledge, but high for input suppliers
Source: Giuliani, Pietrobelli and Robellotti (2005); Pietrobelli and Rabellotti (2006a).			

It is not easy to escape from marginalization, but it is possible, and domestic firms' efforts to build technological capabilities are essential.

In sub-Saharan Africa, there have been relatively few examples of clearly successful upgrading.

the evidence reveals that it is not easy to escape from marginalization, but it is indeed possible, and domestic firms' efforts to build technological capabilities are essential. In some cases, clever strategic alliances with the lead firms may help, as there are specific circumstances where the private sector has direct business motives for investing resources in transferring knowledge and upgrading suppliers. These tend to be time-limited, and are usually directed towards strengthening the ability of suppliers to meet buyers' requirements. However, in some instances public policies explicitly directed to favouring SME inclusion may help (Gomes, 2006).

Analyses on a chain-by-chain basis are necessary in order to identify the consequences for LDC enterprises of the increasing demands made by buyers. To that end, it may be useful to examine the specific opportunities to get a "reward" (i.e. an advantage or a return) and the concrete roles that suppliers may play in getting those rewards (Gibbon and Ponte, 2005). That also helps explore the extent to which LDC producers have attempted to perform those roles, and the opportunities they may have had in that respect. Table 8 presents the structures of rewards in selected GVCs in sub-Saharan Africa, and the roles that local suppliers may play in capturing them.

One of the few cases of detailed studies of specific GVCs in sub-Saharan Africa analyses cotton, clothing, citrus, coffee, cocoa, and fresh vegetables GVCs, concluding that there have been relatively few examples of clearly successful upgrading (Gibbon and Ponte, 2005). Acquiring larger volumes — and economies of scale — appears central in most cases, and this sometimes suggests an interesting scope for regionalization (large regionally integrated markets) and for SMEs growing to medium-sized status.

Several Kenyan exporters consolidated their supply of fresh vegetables to United Kingdom supermarkets in the late 1990s by expanding their scale

Table 8. Structures of rewards in selected global value chains in sub-Saharan Africa

Sector	Reward	Means of obtaining these rewards
Clothing	Security of contracts, ability to compensate for secularly falling prices through larger volumes	• Sales ordered in advance by trading houses and direct sales to retailers • Become a recognized producer of a product type • Meet special delivery conditions (delivery on call-off)
Coffee	Achieve reference prices Medium- and long-term purchasing commitments Considerable premia (direct sales, long-term purchase commitments, multi-season prices)	• Become a non-anonymous seller (typically from large exporter — in Latin America) • Specialize in specialty coffees within the Arabica market • In general, limited opportunities to upgrade in tropical countries (it depends on coffee's physical properties, and most coffee roasters use blends of various origins)
Fresh vegetable citrus	No premium for quality but for producing specific varieties (changing over time) Security of contracts, stability of prices (3–9 months). This in turn allows longer-term planning, planning of larger volumes, economies of scale and cross-subsidization of new product development	• Essentially available to suppliers serving large supermarket chains (mostly in the United Kingdom)
Cocoa	Traditional reward structures for primary producers have disappeared	• Second-tier suppliers (smallholders and cooperatives) can upgrade only by taking on first-tier supplier roles, i.e. engaging in international trading and/or grinding, but this is difficult
Cotton	GVC is less buyer-driven, and rewards reflect global supply/demand balance, including subsidies Premia attached to form of sale (forward, tender) and timing of sale (early market window)	• International cotton trade as a single non-anonymous market bifurcated between coarser and finer cottons — defined in terms of quality and national origins. • Reputational dimensions of national origins matter (difficult to measure and prove quality otherwise) • Upgrading requires improvements in reputation

Source: Gibbon and Ponte (2005), and the cases therein.

(including through investments in the United Republic of Tanzania), improving quality assurance, and diversifying into snow/snap peas and cut flowers. Regarding cotton, the experiences from the United Republic of Tanzania and Zimbabwe are the opposite. While the former experienced downgrading in the 1990s, the Zimbabwean company Cottco consolidated its minor first-tier supplier status by vertically integrating into spinning of cotton knitting yarn, acquired a cotton concession in Mozambique and gained economies of scale in the regional market.

In the coffee value chains the general trend has been one of downgrading of local export companies, now working for foreign-owned exporters (Ponte, 2002a, 2002b). Nevertheless, the few examples of upgrading among second- and third-tier suppliers relate to the following specific instances:

- Participation by mainly private and foreign-owned estates in specialty coffee sales;

- Smallholder cooperatives selling new quality content through fair trade and organic channels;

- In the United Republic of Tanzania, smallholder farm groups selling directly at auction;

- Few local traders establishing wet processing plants, and improving the quality profile of their coffee.

In the clothing sector in Mauritius, many producers upgraded in processes and products (diversification) by increasing their operational scale through investments in Madagascar.[16]

The examples above show how some LDCs have integrated into selected GVCs through FDI from other developing countries, by occupying an upstream position in the chain. In those cases LDCs produce low-value-added goods and occupy the position of third-tier suppliers or further away from final markets.

In some instances, however, foreign buyers have offered interesting potential for upgrading through product differentiation (Lewin, Giovannucci and Varangis, 2004; Linton, 2005), and some lessons may be drawn:

- Finding the right buyer can be an important part of promoting agricultural exports, because of the marketing outlet and support for farmers that buyers may provide.

- Value can be added to products in a variety of ways (e.g. for coffee through organic production, environmental sustainability, origin and characteristics of the produce).

- The buyer may in some cases provide technical assistance (directly or through third parties) to ensure that the quality and consistency of the coffee meet the premium market targeted.

- The link to a specific buyer remained important for achieving certification (e.g. organic and bird-friendly) and identifying the product as a premium product.

The benefits to the producers of a relationship with the buyer are, however, not to be taken for granted, and depend on a host of conditions. Clearly, one of the major risks is suppliers' dependence on a single buyer, which often ends increasing the fragility and vulnerability of suppliers to buyer decisions (IFAD, 2003).

Some LDCs have integrated into selected GVCs through FDI from other developing countries, by occupying an upstream position in the chain. In those cases LDCs produce low-value-added goods and occupy the position of third-tier suppliers or further away from final markets.

One of the major risks is suppliers' dependence on a single buyer, which often ends increasing the fragility and vulnerability of suppliers to buyer decisions.

The uncertain support provided by global buyers and their variable engagement with local suppliers lead some authors to argue that LDCs-based firms should aim at "trading down" (Gibbon and Ponte, 2005). This means consolidating their suppliers' role, focusing on economies of scale, high specialization, and simple and labour-intensive technologies, and aiming at mass markets via large-scale retailers. However, if trading down implies withdrawing from the attempts to develop, strengthen and deepen technological capabilities, it should clearly not be the strategy for LDC suppliers. The search for specific market niches to exploit advanced capabilities always offers potential benefits. However, if technological capability development comes together with "trading down" — that is, a focus on high specialization, economies of scale and firm-size expansion — this may be an option to choose on the basis of a very pragmatic and ongoing assessment. The following subsection examines how LDC firms have fared collectively in terms of trading up/down in international markets.

3. Upgrading and downgrading in LDC exports

Hereafter countries' changing integration into global value chains has been approximated through changes in their world export market shares. An expansion of countries' share in world exports of a product that is associated with the upper end of a value chain (e.g. refined petroleum) means that they have upgraded their specialization within that value chain. Conversely, an expansion of their share in world exports of a product at the lower end of the value chain (e.g. crude petroleum) implies that they have downgraded their specialization in GVCs.

An analysis has been made of LDCs' participation in 24 value chains that cover two thirds of the total merchandise exports of LDCs in 2000–2005. The changing integration into those chains thus has substantial implications for those countries. The value chains analysed are characterized by a relatively high resource intensity, as they refer either to primary products (unprocessed and processed) and/or resource-intensive manufactures. Table 9 shows the integration of LDCs and ODCs into the value chains that were most important for LDC exports during that period.[17]

A focus on all products regardless of processing stage shows whether country groups have increased or decreased their specialization in a particular value chain. Between 1995–1999 and 2000–2005 the specialization of LDCs increased only in petroleum, sugar and a few tropical primary commodities (tobacco and cocoa), given their growing world market shares in those product groups. The specialization of other developing countries, by contrast, grew in 19 of the value chains analysed. With the exception of petroleum, LDCs tend to have a low level of specialization and a relatively small expansion of their specialization in more lucrative value chains (e.g. horticultural products and fish), and at the same time they continue to have a relatively high level of specialization and a rather small expansion in the more traditional value chains (e.g. tobacco, cocoa and sugar).

But it is not just important in which type of value chains countries specialize; it is also important which products within value chains they produce; whether they specialize in products at low processing stages, which are associated with relatively low value added; or whether they specialize in products at higher processing stages, which generally imply higher value added.

LDCs achieved an upgrading of exports between 1995–1999 and 2000–2005 in only seven out of the 24 value chains analysed. In 12 they experienced downgrading, while in three others (plastic, pulp and milk) there was no change. Upgrading in different value chains was achieved by different means:

If trading down implies withdrawing from the attempts to develop, strengthen and deepen technological capabilities, it should clearly not be the strategy for LDC suppliers.

With the exception of petroleum, LDCs tend to have a low level of specialization and a relatively small expansion of their specialization in more lucrative value chains. At the same time they continue to have a relatively high level of specialization and a rather small expansion in the more traditional value chains.

- Aluminium, iron/iron products, artificial fibres and nickel: increased specialization at the upper end of value chain and decreasing specialization at the lower end;

- Fruit: increasing specialization at the upper stages of the value chain and unchanged specialization at the lower end;

- Cotton and wheat: relatively large increase in specialization at the upper end of the value chain and a relatively weak increase in specialization at the lower end.

In the case of two other value chains (livestock/food and cork) the "apparent upgrading" was reached as a result of the decreasing specialization in products at a lower processing stage.

At the same time LDCs experienced downgrading of their exports in 12 value chains:

- Fish, copper and vegetables/fats: increasing specialization at the lower end of the value chain and decreasing specialization at the higher stages;

- Petroleum, vegetables/food, sugar, cocoa, rubber and fur skin: increasing specialization at the lower stages of the value chain and unchanged specialization at the upper end;

- Wood, livestock/leather and tobacco: relatively strong increase in specialization at the lower end of the value chain and a relatively weak increase in specialization at the upper end.

In sum, LDCs rapidly increased their specialization in only a few value chains and they did not manage to significantly upgrade their specialization within value chains. Exports of products in which upgrading occurred amounted to 18 per cent of the total merchandise exports of LDCs in 2000–2005 (including the two cases of "apparent upgrading"). By contrast, the value chains in which downgrading took place accounted for a much higher 52 per cent of those countries' total exports. Hence, those countries' economies have been significantly more affected by downgrading than by upgrading. The increasing consolidation at the lower end of value chains is also reflected by the fact that many LDCs have experienced a collapse of processed primary commodity exports since the 1980s (measured as a share of total merchandise exports) (UNCTAD, 2002), and that many LDCs have experienced a premature de-industrialization since the early 1980s (UNCTAD, 2006b). While the increasing specialization of LDC economies at the lower end of value chains is in line with theories of comparative advantage, it may be considered problematic from the viewpoint of more development-oriented theories, which stress that technological progress and upgrading are preconditions for catching up.

The changing specialization of the group of LDCs sometimes hides considerable differences for geographical subgroups. Between 1995–1999 and 2000–2005 African LDCs upgraded only in cotton, aluminium, wheat and nickel (in the two last products they have only a very weak specialization). Over the same period, Asian LDCs upgraded in cotton, copper, iron/iron products and artificial fibres (in the latter products they have a very limited specialization).

4. IMPLICATIONS

The changing nature of global value chains has led to higher entry barriers for LDC firms that aim at integrating into those chains. The increased power of downstream lead firms and buyers allows them to set the standards (technical,

LDCs rapidly increased their specialization in only a few value chains and they did not manage to significantly upgrade their specialization within value chains.

Exports of products in which upgrading occurred amounted to 18 per cent of the total merchandise exports of LDCs in 2000–2005. By contrast, the value chains in which downgrading took place accounted for a much higher 52 per cent of those countries' total exports.

The changing nature of global value chains has led to higher entry barriers for LDC firms that aim at integrating into those chains.

Table 9. Integration of LDCs and ODCs into selected global value chains, 1995–2005

(Shares in world exports[a], period averages)

Value chains				LDCs			ODCs			World exports
Value chain/ Processing stages	Product	SITC code	1995–1999	2000–2005	Change	1995–1999	2000–2005	Change		($ billion) 2000–2005
			(A)	(B)	(B) – (A)	(C)	(D)	(D) – (C)		
Petroleum (40.13)[b]										
All products			2.1	3.0	0.9	62.6	57.2	-5.4		690.6
Stage I	Petroleum oils, oils from bitumen. materials, crude	333	2.8	4.1	1.3	70.3	62.8	-7.6		478.7
Stage II	All		0.4	0.5	0.0	46.2	44.7	-1.5		211.9
	Petroleum oils or bituminous minerals > 70 % oil	334	0.5	0.5	0.0	47.6	45.6	-2.0		198.1
	Residual petroleum products, n.e.s., related materials	335	0.1	0.2	0.1	27.2	30.6	3.4		13.8
Cotton (14.06)[b]										
All products			2.6	3.7	1.1	54.8	60.2	5.4		195.8
Stage I	Cotton	263	10.8	10.9	0.1	23.9	22.8	-1.1		9.1
Stage II	Textile yarn	651	0.5	0.6	0.1	43.3	50.7	7.4		35.5
Stage III	Cotton fabrics, woven	652	0.2	0.3	0.1	50.0	51.8	1.9		22.1
Stage IV	All		2.8	4.6	1.8	62.6	67.0	4.4		129.1
	Men's clothing of textile fabrics, not knitted	841	4.2	6.0	1.8	61.2	64.0	2.8		43.6
	Women's clothing, of textile fabrics	842	2.0	3.7	1.8	61.4	67.1	5.7		54.8
	Men's or boy's clothing, of textile, knitted or crocheted	843	2.9	5.3	2.4	70.7	72.9	2.1		10.9
	Women's clothing, of textile, knitted or crocheted	844	1.7	3.7	2.0	64.3	70.0	5.7		19.7
Aluminium (2.54)[b]										
All products			0.8	1.4	0.5	17.5	22.0	4.5		94.8
Stage I	Aluminium ores and concentrates (including alumina)	285	8.9	7.5	-1.5	29.5	31.5	2.0		8.3
Stage II	Aluminium	684	0.0	1.2	1.2	17.7	21.1	3.4		58.8
Stage III	Flat-rolled products of alloy steel	675	0.0	0.0	0.0	12.8	21.1	8.3		27.7
Wood (2.30)[b]										
All products			0.9	0.9	0.0	27.6	35.9	8.3		139.0
Stage I	Wood in the rough or roughly squared	247	5.8	7.5	1.7	30.2	23.2	-7.1		10.8
Stage II	All		0.6	0.7	0.1	24.1	27.4	3.3		47.8
	Wood simply worked, and railway sleepers of wood	248	0.8	1.0	0.1	20.3	22.4	2.1		31.4
	Wood manufacture, n.e.s.	635	0.1	0.1	0.0	33.3	36.8	3.5		16.5
Stage III	Furniture & parts; bedding & similar stuffed furniture	821	0.0	0.1	0.0	29.9	42.6	12.7		80.4
Fish (2.19)[b]										
All products			2.5	2.5	0.1	39.7	43.2	3.5		44.5
Stage I	Fish, fresh (live or dead), chilled or frozen	34	2.9	3.1	0.2	34.6	38.1	3.5		30.0
Stage II	All		1.6	1.3	-0.3	49.7	53.9	4.2		14.5
	Fish, dried, salted or in brine; smoked fish	35	2.3	2.2	-0.2	17.3	22.6	5.3		3.0
	Fish, aqua. invertebrates, prepared, preserved, n.e.s.	37	1.4	1.1	-0.3	59.3	62.1	2.8		11.5
Vegetables (1.70)[b]										
Vegetables/ food										
Base product										
Stage I	Vegetables; roots & other edible vegetable products	54	1.5	1.8	0.3	31.0	32.5	1.5		27.2
Food products										
Stage II	All		0.5	0.3	-0.1	45.7	47.9	2.3		37.3
	Margarine and shortening	91	0.1	0.3	0.3	20.9	27.1	6.1		1.7
	Fixed vegetable fats & oils, crude, refined or fractionated	421	0.8	0.6	-0.2	34.9	37.1	2.1		12.6
	Fixed vegetable fats & oils, crude, refined or fractionated	422	0.5	0.3	-0.2	86.1	86.7	0.6		10.7
	Vegetables, roots, tubers, prepared, preserved, n.e.s.	56	0.1	0.1	0.0	28.0	28.4	0.5		12.3

Table 9 (contd.)

Value chains				LDCs			ODCs			World exports
Value chain/ Processing stages	Product	SITC code	1995– 1999	2000– 2005	Change	1995– 1999	2000– 2005	Change	($ billion) 2000–2005
			(A)	(B)	(B) – (A)	(C)	(D)	(D) – (C)	
Vegetables/ textile fibres									
Base product									
Stage I	Vegetables; roots & other edible vegetable products	54	1.5	1.8	0.3	31.0	32.5	1.5	27.2
Textile fibres									
Stage II	Vegetable textile fibres, not spun; waste of them	265	3.1	2.3	-0.8	29.5	22.5	-7.0	0.7
Copper (1.61)[b]									
All products			1.8	1.7	-0.1	40.1	49.1	9.0	48.8
Stage I	Copper ores and concentrates; copper mattes, cement	283	0.2	1.5	1.2	73.8	78.8	5.1	9.2
Stage II	Copper	682	2.1	1.8	-0.4	34.0	42.2	8.3	39.6
Livestock (1.37)[b]									
Livestock/ food									
Base products									
Stage I	Live animals other than animals of division 03	1	2.3	2.1	-0.3	16.4	17.6	1.1	10.1
Food products									
Stage II	All		0.1	0.1	0.0	15.3	16.4	1.1	45.7
	Meat of bovine animals, fresh, chilled or frozen	11	0.1	0.0	-0.1	12.5	18.3	5.9	16.1
	Other meat and edible meat offal	12	0.1	0.1	0.0	17.0	15.4	-1.7	29.7
Stage III	All		0.0	0.0	0.0	19.4	26.2	6.8	9.6
	Meat, edible meat offal, salted, dried; flours, meals	16	0.0	0.0	0.0	4.0	11.6	7.5	2.3
	Meat, edible meat offal, prepared, preserved, n.e.s.	17	0.0	0.0	0.0	24.2	30.8	6.6	7.3
Livestock/ leather									
Base products									
Stage I	Live animals other than animals of division 03	1	2.3	2.1	-0.3	16.4	17.6	1.1	10.1
Leather products									
Stage II	Hides and skins (except furskins), raw	211	1.6	1.9	0.3	8.3	8.5	0.3	5.5
Stage III	Leather	611	1.8	1.9	0.1	43.7	46.5	2.8	17.6
Stage IV	Manufactures of leather, n.e.s.; saddlery & harness	612	0.1	0.1	0.0	40.8	41.4	0.6	1.8

Source: UNCTAD secretariat calculations, based on UNCTAD, GlobStat database.
Notes: The value chains have been identified on the basis of SITC 3-digit level data. The identification of value chains and processing stages involves some judgement. All calculations are based on trade data in current values.
a The numbers in the table have been estimated by calculating the total imports of the world from either LDCs or ODCs as a share of total world imports. b The numbers indicate the value of all products in the value chain as a share of total LDC exports (2000–2005).

quality, environmental) that must be met in order to participate in the chain. Chain leaders, however, rarely help producers to upgrade their technological capabilities so as to become able to fulfil those requirements.

Although LDCs have increased their specialization in some value chains since the mid-1990s, they did not manage to significantly upgrade their specialization within those chains. In quantitative terms, downgrading has been more prevalent than upgrading. In almost all cases LDCs have increased their specialization in relatively basic products at a low stage of processing. This also reflects processes of structural changes and re-specialization that these countries have been undergoing since the 1980s.

These export patterns indicate that little technological upgrading has taken place recently among LDC firms, irrespective of their participation in GVCs. They seem to have responded to growing worldwide demand for raw materials by exporting larger quantities of unprocessed goods whose production entails little value added and limited technological learning. Policies to foster further processing of raw materials have been mainly absent, with some exceptions, as in the case of fisheries exports in Uganda (Kiggundu, 2006).

Export patterns indicate that little technological upgrading has taken place recently among LDC firms, irrespective of their participation in GVCs.

D. Foreign direct investment

The present section examines the contribution of FDI to technological capability-building in the LDCs. It first describes the mechanisms through which the former can in principle contribute to the latter. According to the composition of FDI, it can have different impacts on technological accumulation in host countries. Therefore, the second subsection examines general trends of FDI in LDCs alongside its sectoral composition.[18] Following the same reasoning, the third and fourth subsections analyse the contribution of FDI to LDC knowledge accumulation in two major industries of destination: mining of minerals and garment manufacturing. The final subsection concludes.

1. FDI AND TECHNOLOGY DIFFUSION

It is argued that the arrival of TNCs leads to technological upgrading of domestic firms through technological spillovers via imitation, competition, labour mobility and exports.

It is generally contended that FDI in developing countries contributes to the latter's capital accumulation[19] and to their productivity, as transnational corporations (TNCs) have specific advantages (e.g. production methods, marketing, management) that are generally superior to those of domestic firms. It is moreover argued that the arrival of TNCs leads to technological upgrading of domestic firms through technological spillovers[20] via imitation, competition, labour mobility and exports (which entail exposure to the technology frontier). These spillover effects have the potential to increase the productivity of other firms.

Backward linkages are the most likely channel through which spillovers are transmitted.

Kokko (1994) identifies at least four ways in which technology might be diffused from TNCs to domestic firms in the host economy: (i) demonstration-imitation; (ii) competition; (iii) foreign linkage; and (iv) training. Javorcik (2004) suggests that backward linkages are the most likely channel through which spillovers are transmitted — through (i) direct knowledge transfer from foreign customers to local suppliers; (ii) superior requirements for product quality and on-time delivery introduced by TNCs, which provide incentives to domestic suppliers to upgrade their production management or technology; and (iii) TNC entry into the domestic economy, which increases demand for intermediate inputs, allowing local suppliers to reap the benefits of scale economies.[21] Damijan et al. (2003) argue that the presence of TNCs in the host economy can increase the rate of technical change and technological learning in the economy through knowledge spillovers, which occur as a consequence of introducing new technologies and organizational skills that are typically superior to those in domestic firms. To the extent that domestic firms and TNCs operating in the same sector compete with one another, the latter have an incentive to prevent technology leakage and spillovers from taking place; this can be done using patents, trade secrecy and/or paying higher wages. Görg and Greenaway (2003) argue that TNCs usually do not hand over the sourc of their advantages voluntarily. On the other hand, they may benefit from improved performance from inputs provided by domestic suppliers, and so they can foster the upgrading of the production of local firms.

The materialization of the potential positive impacts of FDI on knowledge accumulation in host countries hinges on a number of conditions, including structural characteristics of host economies and the type of insertion of TNCs in those economies.

However, the materialization of the potential positive impacts of FDI on knowledge accumulation in host countries hinges on a number of conditions, including structural characteristics of host economies, the type of insertion of TNCs in those economies and the job-generating impact of TNCs. First, the structural characteristics of host countries are associated with their absorptive capacity, which in turn depends on the stock of human capital, the dynamism of entrepreneurship, the quality of institutions and the desire for progress (Abramovitz, 1986), as well as infrastructure development. Second, the more TNCs are integrated into host economies, particularly through backward and forward linkages, the more spillover effects are likely to happen. *Mutatis mutandis*, TNCs are not expected to impact positively on microeconomic efficiency and productivity if they operate in enclaves, having minimal contact with domestic firms (Görg and Strobl, 2005; Lall and Narula, 2004; Moss, Ramachandran and Shah, 2005).[22] Third, circulation of knowledge is more likely if the number of jobs generated by TNCs is high, if they are skill-intensive and if there is high labour turnover between foreign affiliates and domestic firms. Fourth, if TNCs simply displace pre-existing domestic firms, the upgrading through competition cannot take place.

Two opposing arguments on technological distance and spillovers have appeared in the literature on FDI and technology transfer. One argument contends that the wider the technology gap between foreign and domestic firms, the more the scope for spillovers (Findlay, 1978). The other argument states that the narrower the technology gap, the easier the technology transfer is (Glass and Saggi, 1998). Görg and Greenaway (2003) and Kokko (1994) suggest that the latter argument is more plausible than the former.

2. Trends and sectoral composition of FDI

FDI inflows into LDCs have increased markedly since the early 1990s (chart 6). Between 2000 and 2005 annual inflows were three times higher than during the preceding 10 years (table 10). On average, 39 of the 50 LDCs received higher annual inflows during the early years of the new century than in 1990–1999. LDCs still account for a marginal part of total FDI flows towards developing countries, but their share rose to 3.5 per cent in 2000–2005, as compared with 2.1 per cent in 1990–1999 and 1.6 per cent in 1980–1989. In the same vein, LDCs accounted for 2.7 per cent of the total FDI stock of developing countries in 2005, up from 1.7 per cent in 1990. On a global scale, FDI inflows in LDCs accounted for 1 per cent of world inflows in 2000–2005 and 0.7 per cent of the world stock in 2005.

In order to put value figures in perspective, indicators of FDI flows and stocks relative to GDP, gross fixed capital formation (GFCF) and population are presented in table 10. They invariably show a continuous deepening of FDI in the LDCs since the 1980s, a trend that has accelerated sharply since 2000. This was more marked than in other developing countries, which also experienced some FDI deepening. FDI inflows as a share of both GDP and GFCF in the LDCs doubled between the 1990s and 2000–2005. While those indicators had been lower than or close to the corresponding ones for other developing countries in the 1980s and 1990s, during the early years of the 21st century LDCs largely surpassed other developing countries on these accounts.

Per capita FDI inflows are lower in LDCs than in other developing countries (table 10). Moreover, the difference between the former and the latter has increased since the 1980s. The reason is that although the rise in FDI flows to LDCs was greater than the rise in flows to other developing countries, this was partly offset by the former's more rapid demographic growth.

The FDI stock as a share of GDP in LDCs rose continuously since 1990 and reached 26 per cent in 2005. This level is similar to that of other developing countries (table 10). These indicators reveal that the surge in FDI into LDCs is a more recent development, as compared with ODCs.

FDI inflows in LDCs are highly concentrated geographically. While African LDCs accounted for 66 per cent of total inflows in the 1990s, this share rose to

TNCs are not expected to impact positively on microeconomic efficiency and productivity if they operate in enclaves, having minimal contact with domestic firms.

FDI inflows into LDCs have increased markedly since the early 1990s, but LDCs accounted for 1 per cent of world inflows in 2000–2005 and 0.7 per cent of the world stock in 2005.

FDI inflows as a share of both GDP and GFCF in the LDCs doubled between the 1990s and 2000–2005 when LDCs largely surpassed other developing countries on these accounts.

Chart 6. FDI inflows in LDCs, 1980–2005

(Current $ millions)

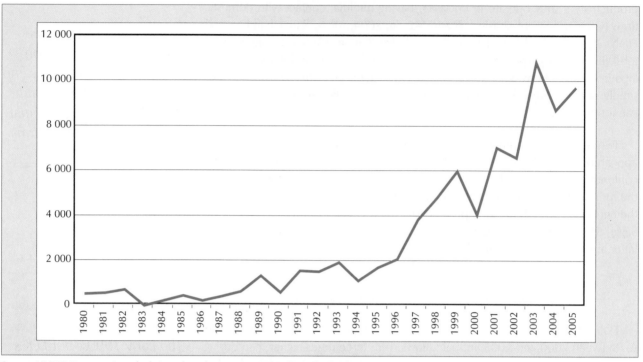

Source: UNCTAD secretariat calculations, based on UNCTAD, FDI/TNC database.

Table 10. Indicators of the importance of FDI in LDCs and ODCs, 1980–2005

	FDI inflows												FDI stock							
	Value ($ millions)			FDI / GDP (%)			FDI / GFCF (%)			FDI per capita ($)			Value ($ millions)				FDI stock / GDP (%)			
	1980-1989	1990-1999	2000-2005	1980-1989	1990-1999	2000-2005	1980-1989	1990-1999	2000-2005	1980-1989	1990-1999	2000-2005	1980	1990	2000	2005	1980	1990	2000	2005
LDCs	**507**	**2 517**	**7 830**	**0.4**	**1.6**	**3.5**	**2.6**	**8.8**	**17.6**	**1**	**4**	**11**	**4 318**	**9 426**	**38 029**	**76 669**	**4.1**	**6.3**	**21.6**	**26.4**
Africa	468	1 669	6 839	0.6	1.8	5.5	3.9	11.0	28.98	2	4	16	3 692	8 329	27 473	62 739	0.0	0.0	0.0	0.0
Asia	25	780	926	0.1	1.2	1.0	0.3	6.6	4.7	0	3	3	557	861	9 600	12 660	1.6	1.7	12.0	11.1
Islands	13	68	65	1.3	3.5	2.4	4.5	13.0	10.4	8	31	25	69	235	956	1 269	8.5	16.4	41.8	37.4
Other developing countries (ODCs)	**19 912**	**111 415**	**210 022**	**0.7**	**2.1**	**2.8**	**3.1**	**8.3**	**11.6**	**6**	**29**	**49**	**134 388**	**377 570**	**1 684 327**	**2 632 623**	**5.4**	**10.4**	**26.1**	**27.3**
Africa	1 739	4 915	11 292	0.5	1.1	1.9	2.3	6.2	11.4	6	13	26	43 389	84 151	209 688	373 263	9.7	20.4	41.3	48.0
America	6 401	38 061	62 531	0.8	2.2	3.1	3.6	11.0	16.7	17	79	119	32 986	101 178	420 740	720 652	4.3	9.1	21.1	29.2
Asia	11 772	68 439	136 199	0.8	2.1	2.8	3.1	7.5	10.1	5	23	41	58 014	192 241	1 053 898	1 538 708	4.5	9.1	26.6	24.1

Source: UNCTAD secretariat calculations, based on data from UNCTAD, FDI/TNC database; and UNDESA Statistics Division.

Note: Indicators of FDI inflows are period averages. All values are in current dollars. LDCs and Islands exclude Timor-Leste.

FDI inflows in LDCs are highly concentrated. Just four petroleum-producing countries received 56 per cent of the LDC total in 2000–2005.

87 per cent in 2000–2005. During this period Asian LDCs received 12 per cent and island LDCs just 1 per cent. The increase in the African share in 2000–2005 was brought about by a small number of recipients of additional FDI flows in that period. Just four petroleum-producing countries — Angola, Sudan, Equatorial Guinea and Chad — received 56 per cent of all FDI inflows during that period. The top 10 FDI recipients accounted for 81 per cent of total inflows, while the other 40 LDCs received the remaining 19 per cent. In other words, the surge in FDI in LDCs in recent years has been led by foreign investment in oil extraction, although most countries have received higher inflows in recent years.

The values and relative indicators of FDI flows and stocks for individual LDCs are presented in table 11. They show that the economies that have attracted FDI most intensively are the four petroleum exporters mentioned above, some island States (Kiribati, Tuvalu and Vanuatu) and Liberia. At the other extreme, with very low FDI intensity, are some other island States (Samoa and Solomon Islands) and some Asian LDCs (Afghanistan, Bhutan and Nepal).

Data on the sectoral destination of FDI in LDCs are fragmentary. Table 12 presents the sectors targeted by foreign investors in selected countries in given years for which data are available. They give the impression that the tertiary sector is the major recipient of FDI inflows in LDCs, as is the case worldwide. Nevertheless, fragmentary evidence indicates that over many years services dominate FDI inflows mainly in island LDCs. In other LDCs FDI is relatively more directed towards the primary sector in the African LDCs and towards industry in the Asian LDCs.

The motivation for FDI in LDCs differs therefore among different regional groupings. The bulk of foreign investment in African LDCs is of the resource-seeking type, while FDI directed towards Asian LDCs is mostly efficiency-seeking and quota-seeking. Market-seeking FDI in LDCs is marginal (given the small size of those countries' markets) as compared with total FDI inflows. It drives mainly FDI in the tertiary sector (e.g. telecom).

Given that mineral extractive industries and garments have accounted for most of FDI inflows into LDCs over the last 15 years, the following subsections analyse the contribution of FDI to domestic technological capability accumulation through TNC activities in those two industries.

The bulk of foreign investment in African LDCs is of the resource-seeking type, while FDI directed towards Asian LDCs is mostly efficiency-seeking and quota-seeking.

3. FDI IN MINERAL EXTRACTIVE INDUSTRIES

The strong increase in FDI in mineral extraction in LDCs (as well as in other developing countries) since the turn of the century was spurred by the sustained and strong rise in the prices of commodities, particularly mineral ones. The upward phase of the price cycle in turn was caused by the imbalance in the commodities market. Starting in the late 1990s, world demand for raw materials rose at a significantly greater pace than previously (mainly owing to the steep rise in consumption in some Asian developing countries, including China), but the supply response was slow. In order to react to the higher pace of demand expansion and take advantage of strong prices, international mining companies actively sought new locations for mineral exploration and extraction. Africa was a major destination for those investments.[23]

Since the late 1990s a few developing countries have emerged as a significant source of outward investment in the mineral industry of LDCs, particularly South Africa and China.

Most foreign companies investing in mining in LDCs have traditionally originated in developed countries (mainly Europe, North America and Australia) and they remain the main host countries of mining TNCs operating in LDCs. Since the late 1990s, however, a few developing countries have emerged as a significant source of outward investment in the mineral industry of LDCs, particularly South Africa and China.

Apart from petroleum extraction, since 2000 international companies have also targeted African LDCs for natural resource exploration and extraction in hard rock mining (mainly metals). They have established operations in many countries, including Burkina Faso, the Democratic Republic of the Congo, Ethiopia, Guinea, Mali, Mauritania, Mozambique, Niger, Sierra Leone, the United Republic of Tanzania and Zambia.

On the recipient side mineral-rich countries, particularly in Africa, have striven to attract higher FDI inflows by radically changing their policies and regulations for the mineral sector since the 1980s.

On the recipient side mineral-rich countries, particularly in Africa, have striven to attract higher FDI inflows by radically changing their policies and regulations for the mineral sector since the 1980s. Frequently adopted in the context of structural adjustment programmes, most of those reforms have resulted in privatizing State-

Table 11. Indicators of the importance of FDI in LDCs, by country, 2000–2005

Country	FDI inflows, 2000–2005 (period averages)				Country	FDI stock, 2005	
	Value ($ millions)	FDI/ GDP (%)	FDI/ GFCF (%)	FDI per capita ($)		Value ($ millions)	FDI stock/ GDP (%)
Angola	1 604	13.6	106.2	109.0	Angola	13 413	46.5
Sudan	1 141	6.4	33.6	32.5	Sudan	7 850	31.8
Equatorial Guinea	1 055	32.4	73.4	2172.2	Equatorial Guinea	7 351	130.1
Chad	566	22.2	52.3	62.3	United Rep. of Tanzania	6 029	46.6
Bangladesh	461	0.8	3.5	3.4	Myanmar	4 862	44.5
United Rep. of Tanzania	442	4.1	21.9	12.0	Liberia	4 031	719.0
Ethiopia	326	4.6	22.6	4.4	Chad	3 857	78.0
Dem. Rep. of the Congo	290	4.3	39.1	5.1	Bangladesh	3 508	5.5
Myanmar	239	2.6	22.9	4.8	Zambia	3 183	43.5
Mozambique	239	5.3	23.3	12.7	Ethiopia	2 752	29.6
Uganda	200	2.9	14.2	7.5	Cambodia	2 471	45.8
Cambodia	173	3.9	19.1	12.8	Mozambique	2 386	35.7
Zambia	158	3.3	15.2	13.9	Dem. Rep. of the Congo	2 333	32.4
Mali	140	3.8	19.0	11.1	Uganda	1 830	20.1
Liberia	134	28.0	295.6	40.2	Senegal	1 126	13.6
Mauritania	97	8.5	64.7	34.0	Yemen	983	6.3
Madagascar	63	1.4	7.9	3.7	Mali	915	17.7
Senegal	59	1.0	4.8	5.4	Togo	686	31.4
Guinea	54	1.6	11.4	5.9	Mauritania	684	40.9
Togo	50	3.1	15.5	8.7	Lao People's Dem. Rep.	669	23.3
Benin	41	1.3	7.2	5.3	Madagascar	651	13.2
Lesotho	38	3.8	8.9	19.6	Guinea	578	18.9
Lao People's Dem. Rep.	24	1.2	7.7	4.4	Lesotho	527	39.5
Gambia	24	5.9	30.7	17.7	Malawi	503	23.5
Yemen	21	0.3	1.4	1.3	Vanuatu	430	130.6
Burkina Faso	18	0.5	2.1	1.5	Eritrea	395	36.7
Cape Verde	18	2.6	9.1	37.5	Benin	290	6.6
Sierra Leone	18	2.1	23.0	3.6	Gambia	289	60.2
Kiribati	17	29.9	69.3	175.4	Rwanda	279	13.2
Timor-Leste	16	4.3	10.9	18.4	Cape Verde	247	23.8
Djibouti	14	2.2	14.0	18.4	Maldives	184	24.0
Eritrea	14	2.1	7.6	3.7	Timor-Leste	167	42.4
Vanuatu	14	4.9	23.8	67.1	Kiribati	151	210.6
Niger	13	0.6	3.9	1.0	Solomon Islands	135	45.3
Maldives	13	1.9	6.9	42.5	Nepal	129	1.7
Malawi	12	0.7	5.7	1.0	Haiti	128	3.3
Haiti	9	0.3	2.0	1.1	Niger	127	3.9
Somalia	7	0.3	1.7	0.9	Central African Republic	112	8.4
Rwanda	6	0.3	1.7	0.7	Djibouti	108	15.3
Nepal	6	0.1	0.5	0.2	Sierra Leone	108	9.3
Tuvalu	6	33.3	59.3	533.0	Burkina Faso	68	1.3
Guinea-Bissau	3	1.3	6.6	2.2	Guinea-Bissau	58	19.4
Sao Tome and Principe	3	5.0	14.4	18.8	Somalia	48	2.2
Burundi	2	0.2	2.3	0.2	Burundi	45	5.3
Central African Republic	1	0.2	0.9	0.4	Samoa	40	9.8
Afghanistan	1	0.0	0.1	0.0	Tuvalu	33	127.2
Comoros	1	0.2	2.2	0.8	Sao Tome and Principe	24	33.4
Bhutan	1	0.1	0.1	0.3	Comoros	24	6.3
Solomon Islands	-2	-0.7	-3.9	-5.2	Afghanistan	22	0.3
Samoa	-3	-0.7	-6.0	-13.7	Bhutan	16	1.7

Source: UNCTAD secretariat calculations, based on data from UNCTAD, FDI/TNC database; and UNDESA Statistics Division.

Note: All values in current dollars. Countries are ranked according to FDI inflows and FDI stock values.

Table 12. Inward FDI inflows in selected LDCs, by sector, 1995–2005								
Country	Year	$ millions				Percentage		
		Primary	Secondary	Tertiary	Total	Primary	Secondary	Tertiary
Bangladesh	2002	17.1	69.5	188.5	275.1	6.2	25.3	68.5
Cape Verde	1995	..	4.6	23.3	27.9	..	16.5	83.5
Cambodia	2002	..	68.9	86.2	155.1	..	44.4	55.6
Ethiopia	2000	40.5	83.7	10.4	134.6	30.1	62.2	7.7
Lao PDR	2001	3.0	13.9	7.0	23.9	12.6	58.2	29.3
Mozambique	2005	45.8	16.5	94.9	157.2	29.1	10.5	60.4
Myanmar	2004	127.9	13.1	4.2	145.2	88.1	9.0	2.9
Nepal	1997/98	5.4	1.7	20.5	27.6	19.6	6.2	74.3
Solomon Islands	1996	130.3	0.6	75.9	206.8	63.0	0.3	36.7
Vanuatu	2002	..	..	6.3	6.3	..	..	100.0

Source: UNCTAD (2006a).

The sweeping changes in African LDCs' mining policy in the 1980s and 1990s were aimed at attracting FDI and increasing exports, in which they have been successful.

owned companies, enhancing geological data, lowering taxes and royalties, granting temporary tax exemptions, eliminating restrictions on the entry of TNCs, introducing import-tax exemptions for equipment, eliminating national content and employment provisions, establishing liberal immigration laws for expatriates, scrapping restrictions on profit and dividend remittances, granting other incentives (e.g. land allocation) and so forth. Examples of this type of policy reform among the LDCs are the mining codes adopted by Guinea (1995), the United Republic of Tanzania (1998), and Mali and Madagascar (1999) (Campbell, 2005).

The sweeping changes in African LDCs' mining policy in the 1980s and 1990s were aimed at attracting FDI and increasing exports, in which they have been successful. Total FDI inflows into African LDCs rose fourfold from an annual average of $1.7 billion in the 1990s to $6.8 billion in 2000–2005 (table 10), the bulk of which was directed to mineral extractive industries (including petroleum). Those countries' mineral exports (including ores, metals, petroleum and related products) increased almost fivefold from $8 billion in 1995 to $38 billion in 2005. The share of those exports in total merchandise exports of African LDCs rose from one quarter in 1995 to almost half 10 years later.[24] This accentuated the re-specialization of those countries in primary extraction.

Typically, TNCs' mineral extraction activities in LDCs are strongly integrated internationally, but weakly embedded into domestic economies.

The dominance of the mineral industry's FDI inflows into LDCs since the 1990s has consequences for the impacts that they can have on domestic technological capability accumulation. Typically, TNCs' mineral extraction activities in those countries are capital-intensive, have little impact on employment, are highly concentrated geographically, have high import content and result in exports of their output as unprocessed raw materials.[25] Most of those operations are totally owned by foreign investors (rather than joint ventures) and a large share of their foreign exchange earnings is retained abroad. Those operations are strongly integrated internationally, but weakly embedded into domestic economies, as they have few forward and backward linkages in host economies (UNCTAD, 2005). In other words, they tend to operate as enclaves.

This type of insertion of FDI projects in domestic economies means that some of the main channels of potential knowledge circulation between TNCs and domestic firms are largely absent: linkages, joint ventures and labour turnover.

This type of insertion of FDI projects in domestic economies means that some of the main channels of potential knowledge circulation between TNCs and domestic firms are largely absent: linkages, joint ventures and labour turnover.[26] The arrival of foreign companies tends to displace small- and medium-scale local miners to marginal areas, rather than establish links with them. This is especially the effect of the entry of medium-sized TNCs, which tend to target older abandoned properties, waste dumps or already known deposits, which are frequently being worked by artisanal miners or by local companies using semi-mechanized methods.

The potential of those FDI inflows to contribute to domestic technological capability-building in host countries is, therefore, very limited. In fact, there is little evidence that the entry of TNCs into mining in those countries is leading to the technological upgrading of domestic firms in the same industry. Where some intermediate technology potentially useful for small- and medium-scale miners has been developed for secondary processing purposes, its distribution and assimilation within the mining community have been limited (Abugre and Akabzaa, 1998).

The changes in mining policy adopted by African LDCs have neglected wider objectives such as articulating the mining sector into broader developmental objectives, for example through backward and forward linkages or domestic value-added processing of minerals. Additionally, they have resulted in weakening State capacity to influence the development process and the developmental impact of mining (Campbell, 2005).

Enhancing the contribution of the mining industry and its TNCs to knowledge accumulation in host countries has not been among the objectives of host countries, owing to the narrow sectoral focus adopted (as opposed to a broader developmental perspective). The goal of generating technology spillovers has generally not been actively pursued, nor has it been an unintended consequence of increased TNC activity. There are few indications that increasing FDI inflows into the oil and hard rock mining industry of African LDCs have been accompanied by greater knowledge flows to those countries beyond the activities of the TNCs themselves.

4. FDI IN GARMENT MANUFACTURING

Foreign direct investment has played an important role in several Asian LDCs in recent years. Bangladesh has since the mid-1990s been the main destination of FDI among those countries. Cambodia and the Lao People's Democratic Republic have been very successful since the 1990s in attracting larger foreign investment inflows. Myanmar received relatively high levels of FDI inflows in 1996–1998, but they fell thereafter, because of political uncertainty and foreign economic sanctions.[27] Poor infrastructure, political instability, being landlocked and/or lack of cross-border synergies have restricted FDI inflows into Afghanistan, Nepal and Bhutan (Rasiah, 2007a).

Garment manufacturing remains the most promising sector for attracting FDI in a wider range of economies — a consequence of both the industry's flexibility in adjusting to unskilled labour,[28] low precision standards and long delivery times, and the preferential access that has emerged from post-MFA developments.[29] The Multifibre Arrangement (MFA) was phased out from 1995 to 2004, but this coincided with the granting of preferential access agreements to LDCs: bilateral trading arrangements between the United States and some Asian LDCs were introduced in 1999 and the Everything But Arms initiative was adopted by the European Union in 2001.[30] This attracted foreign investors seeking export quotas and stimulated local subcontractors to enter garment manufacturing.

FDI has brought scarce capital with superior access to export markets and links with buyers driving value chains. Most Asian LDCs have relied extensively on FDI to drive investment, employment and exports in the garment industry, particularly through foreign firms located in export processing zones (EPZs).

There is little evidence that the entry of TNCs into mining in LDCs is leading to the technological upgrading of domestic firms.

Enhancing the contribution of the mining industry and its TNCs to knowledge accumulation in host countries has not been among the objectives of host countries.

Most Asian LDCs have relied extensively on FDI to drive investment, employment and exports in the garment industry.

Where local firms are important, as in Bangladesh, they participate only in low-value-added subcontracted activities.[31]

The introduction of preferential access to LDCs has influenced FDI inflows of Chinese capital to those countries, as happened in Cambodia. Chinese investment in garment manufacturing in Cambodia amounted to 40 per cent of total FDI in that industry in 2000–2005, with Taiwan Province of China and Hong Kong (China) accounting for 21 per cent. Exports of garments under the Generalized System of Preferences (GSP) accounted for 64 per cent of GSP-related exports from Cambodia in 2004, a sharp rise from 3 per cent in 1995. The impact of garment FDI and exports on Cambodia has been dramatic, with the industry accounting for 72 per cent of manufacturing value added and 15 per cent of GDP in 2004 (Rasiah, 2006b).

Preferential market access conditions offered to LDCs have ensured that their garment exports grew after 2000.

As the MFA was phased out, China's exports grew by an average annual rate of 15.5 per cent in 2000–2005, which led to its attaining a world market share of 27 per cent in 2005 (table 13). China's penetration into global garment markets seems to have accounted for a contraction in production in several economies, with export growth slowing down or exports falling in several Asian economies. Preferential market access conditions offered to LDCs have, however, ensured that their garment exports grew after 2000. Those of Cambodia expanded by 17.8 per cent annually and those of Bangladesh by 10.4 per cent. Exports from the Lao People's Democratic Republic only grew by only 1.8 per cent per annum, while those of Myanmar contracted by 16.2 per cent over the same period (table 13).

The rapid expansion of garment exports from Bangladesh and Cambodia augurs well, suggesting that the industry could act as a good platform to generate jobs, foreign exchange and technological learning to support development. Garments accounted for over 70 per cent of those countries' total exports in 2005. The slow growth in the Lao People's Democratic Republic reflects additional costs involved in carrying out operations in a landlocked country as well as its small labour force. The severe contraction in Myanmar following foreign sanctions is likely to continue unless political circumstances change significantly.

Unless the embedding environment for higher technology activities is strong, firms will participate little in learning and innovation activities, which are pivotal for upgrading and long-term sustainability of garment operations in the LDCs.

However, unless the embedding environment for higher technology activities is strong, firms will participate little in learning and innovation activities, which are pivotal for upgrading and long-term sustainability of garment operations in the LDCs. The analysis below focuses mainly on the impact of FDI inflows on technological learning in garments in Bangladesh, Cambodia, the Lao People's Democratic Republic and Myanmar. A comparison is drawn with other Asian developing economies.[32] The analysis reviews the insertion of those countries' firms in international value chains, upgrading and their technological effort and achievements.

Global value chains and upgrading. When the textile and garment industry in Asian LDCs is analysed from the point of view of global value chains and upgrading, it is seen that none of their firms can be expected to have integrated activities in all processing stages shown in chart 5. In the upstream stages of processing among the Asian LDCs examined only Bangladesh has textile firms, including spinning, weaving, dying, printing and finishing firms. By contrast, firms in Cambodia, the Lao People's Democratic Republic and Myanmar are engaged only in garment manufacturing (Rasiah, 2007b forthcoming; Myint, 2007; Yviengsay and Rasiah, 2007, forthcoming). Their fabric inputs are mainly imported and constitute between 60 and 70 per cent of their production costs. These four economies are net importers of textiles and net exporters of garments, and they reap a trade surplus from the combined textile and garment trade.

No LDC firm can be expected to have integrated activities in all processing stages of the textile/garment value chain.

Table 13. Garment exports of selected LDCs and other countries, 1990–2005

	Value ($ millions)					Share in domestic exports (%)		Average annual growth (%)
	1990	2000	2003	2004	2005	2000	2005[a]	2000–2005
LDCs:								
Bangladesh	643	3 907	4 912	5 686	6 418	77.6	74.2	10.4
Cambodia[b]	0	970	1 600	1 981	2 199	69.8	70.9	17.8
Haiti	63	245	275	303	335	76.9	71.2	6.5
Lao People's Dem. Rep.	0	98	87	99	108			1.8
Lesotho[b]	..	261	290	235	..	77.7	32.4	..
Madagascar[b]	7	309	360	552	530	37.4	69.7	11.4
Myanmar	12	800	692	568	331	48.6	11.3	-16.2
Nepal	50	209	226	..	..	26	34.1	..
Other countries:								
China[c]	9 669	36 071	52 061	61 856	74 163	14.5	9.7	15.5
European Union (25)	-	53 273	68 447	76 887	80 354	2.2	2	8.6
Hong Kong	15 406	24 214	23 158	25 097	27 292	11.9	9.3	2.4
India[b]	2 530	6 178	6 625	6 632	8 290	13.7	8.2	6.1
Indonesia	1 646	4 734	4 105	4 454	5 106	7.6	6	1.5
Mexico[c]	587	8 631	7 343	7 490	7 271	5.2	3.4	-3.4
Pakistan	1 014	2 144	2 710	3 026	3 604	23.8	22.6	10.9
Philippines[c]	1 733	2 536	2 250	2 157	2 276	6.4	5.5	-2.1
Sri Lanka[b]	638	2 812	2 513	2 776	2 877	51.8	45.3	0.5
Thailand	2 817	3 757	3 615	3 985	4 085	5.4	3.7	1.7
Tunisia[b]	1 126	2 227	2 722	3 289	3 332	38.1	31.8	8.4
Turkey	3 331	6 533	9 962	11 193	11 818	23.5	16.1	12.6
United States	2 565	8 629	5 537	5 059	4 998	1.1	0.6	-10.3
Vietnam[b]	..	1 821	3 467	4 441	4 805	12.6	15.2	21.4
World	**108 129**	**197 782**	**232 557**	**259 147**	**275 639**	**3.2**	**2.7**	**6.9**
Memo item: Chinese share in world (%)	8.9	18.2	22.4	23.9	26.9			

Source: UNCTAD secretariat calculations based on WTO (2006: IV. 83).

a Nearest year; b Includes WTO secretariat estimates; c Includes significant exports from export processing zones.

Nazneen (2007, forthcoming) and Myint (2007), suggest that even Bangladesh and Myanmar are not ready to participate in higher-value-added activities. Foreign firms in Myanmar showed positive signs of upgrading, but this was interrupted by the imposition of sanctions in 2001 (Myint, 2007).

In the downstream stages, Bangladesh, Cambodia, the Lao People's Democratic Republic and Myanmar have no domestic brand names sold in major markets.

In the downstream stages, Bangladesh, Cambodia, the Lao People's Democratic Republic and Myanmar have no domestic brand names sold in major markets. Local brands are sold in Bangladesh, but the huge barriers to entry into world garment markets obviously discourage the extension of those brands into larger markets. The country's garment firms could sell own brands in developing economies, but those from Cambodia and the Lao People's Democratic Republic are certainly not ready to invest in building brand recognition.

Lead times — the time taken between the placement of orders by essentially brand-holding buyers and the delivery of orders by contract producers — provide an indicator of competitiveness. It is a combination of throughput time and logistics coordination time, which depends on both the technological capabilities of firms and country infrastructure. Long lead times mean that producer–customer coordination of demand and supply is underdeveloped. Short lead times give producers the flexibility to absorb customization far more than long lead times. That is increasingly important in this industry owing to the quickening pace of fashion changes.

Table 14 indicates the lead times for garments in selected Asian LDCs and ODCs. The former have the longest lead times among the countries shown. Firms from the Lao People's Democratic Republic and Myanmar were the most disadvantaged, taking 90 to 130 days. Cambodia and especially Bangladesh perform better (60–120 days), but lag significantly behind firms from ODCs. Poor logistics coordination and heavy dependence on imports are a major reason why delivery times are high in the four Asian LDCs. The long lead times mean that circular knit garments produced particularly in Cambodia, the Lao People's Democratic Republic and Myanmar are confined to very low margins where fashion changes are not so critical for driving competitiveness. By contrast, firms in China are able to deliver garments faster (40–60 days) than the other economies shown in table 14.

Skills utilization. The skill intensity in Myanmar is the highest among the LDCs examined. It exceeds levels in Indonesia and Thailand and is close to that of China (table 15). Myanmar has invested substantially in education, but now faces demand constraints where labour and human capital supply tends to exceed demand. Hence the skilled labour shares are high, but wages have been lower than those in Cambodia, Indonesia and China. The skill intensity level in Cambodia and the Lao People's Democratic Republic, by contrast, is extremely low. Despite their low skill intensities, those countries' wages are not that much lower than those of China.

Training. Among the sample of garment firms of the Asian countries surveyed, those located in LDCs have the lowest spending on training: around 0.2 per cent of their payroll. That level is considerably lower than that of the other developing countries mentioned in table 15. Garment firms in the Philippines, Indonesia and China reported similar mean training expenditure, amounting to 0.4 per cent of the payroll.

Poor logistics coordination and heavy dependence on imports are a major reason why delivery times are high in the four Asian LDCs.

The skill intensity in Myanmar is the highest among the LDCs examined.

Among the sample of garment firms of the Asian countries surveyed, those located in LDCs have the lowest spending on training.

Table 14. Garment lead times in selected Asian LDCs and ODCs, 2004

(Days)

	Woven	Circular knit
LDCs		
Bangladesh	90–120	60–80
Cambodia	90–120	90–120
Lao People's Dem. Republic	100–130	100–130
Myanmar	90–130	90–130
ODCs		
China	40–60	50–60
India	50–70	60–70
Indonesia	60–90	60–70
Malaysia	60–90	50–60
Sri Lanka	60–90	60–70
Thailand	60–90	50–60
Viet Nam	60–90	60–70

Source: Rasiah (2006a, 2007a).

Note: Lead time is the time taken between the placement of orders (essentially by brand-holding buyers) and the delivery of orders by contract producers.

Chinese firms in Cambodia — which account for the bulk of the garment firms in the country — hardly use any of the training institutions in the country to train employees. That suggests that the engagement of Chinese firms in the country would be seriously affected when the existing preferential access openings in the United States and EU were closed. In Myanmar the contraction in garment exports has discouraged the opening of training centres (Myint, 2007). In the absence of such centres, training in garment firms in the Lao People's Democratic Republic is carried out only in-house in firms. Training centres exist in Bangladesh, but they are focused on reducing injury and downtime rather than on driving upgrading. Other countries have successfully adopted policies to induce training in garment firms, for example Viet Nam, Malaysia and Singapore. But there have been no similar mandatory training policies in Bangladesh, Cambodia, the Lao People's Democratic Republic or Myanmar.

None of the LDCs examined seem to be equipping themselves effectively to sustain expansion in the garment industry when the preferential access instruments are removed.

Foreign machinery suppliers have also participated in training local firms engaged in knitting in Bangladesh and Cambodia. However, the lack of proactive promotion of such avenues of learning has restricted technology absorption in those countries.

The training evidence suggests none of the LDCs examined seem to be equipping themselves effectively to sustain expansion in the garment industry if the preferential access instruments are removed. This has been the case in other countries. In the Philippines and Thailand dwindling employment and exports since the removal of MFA quotas, together with low levels of training expenditure, suggest that garment manufacturing is hollowing out in those countries.[33]

Process technology. Process technology consists of machinery and equipment, layouts, inventory and control techniques, and firm organization, which are important indicators of technological intensity in firms. None of the four Asian LDCs examined is engaged in the manufacturing of machinery and equipment used in the garment industry, hence the role of machinery and equipment imports (section B of this chapter).

Equipment and machinery used in Asian LDCs economies have either been relocated after use in China, Malaysia and Thailand or imported second-hand by domestic producers.

The evidence from Bangladesh, Cambodia, the Lao People's Democratic Republic and Myanmar shows that equipment and machinery used in those economies have either been relocated after use in China, Hong Kong (China), Taiwan Province of China, Malaysia and Thailand or imported second-hand by domestic producers. Only independent knitting machinery and equipment (weft

Table 15. Comparative technological intensity levels of garment firms of selected LDCs and ODCs, 2001–2005

(Percentage, unless otherwise indicated)

	LDCs			ODCs				
	Lao PDR	Cambodia	Myanmar	China	Indonesia	Sri Lanka	Philippines	Thailand
Skill intensity	8.7	12.1	29.7	30.2	25.2	36.3	35.3	29.1
Wage ($)	22.5	21.8	20	25.3	20.2	44.6	41.4	83.3
Training	0.21	0.26	0.2	0.4	0.35	0.29	0.4	0.4
Process technology	0.15	0.19	0.15	0.58	0.32	0.31	0.42	0.48
Adaptive engineering	0.001	0.005	0.001	0.022	0.012	0.017	0.019	0.022

Source: UNCTAD compilation based on UNU-MERIT (2004-2005); NERI (2006); Myint (2007); Rasiah (2007a).

Notes: Data for Cambodia, Myanmar and Lao PDR are for 2005, those for Sri Lanka are for 2002 and those for the other countries are for 2001.

Skills intensity: share of skilled, technical and professional personnel in total workforce (%); wages: mean monthly wage (dollars); training: share of training expenditure in payroll (%); process technology: share of expenditure on changes to organization, layout and processes in total sales (%); adaptive engineering: share of expenditure on product and equipment adaptation in total sales (%).

and warp knitting) from Germany and Taiwan Province of China were imported by some firms Bangladesh and Cambodia. Importing depreciated machinery and equipment was also common earlier in Malaysia, Thailand, the Philippines and Indonesia. Therefore, the much lower process technology intensity in firms from the Lao People's Democratic Republic, Cambodia and Myanmar (table 15 should not be of concern at the moment. What is crucial is whether learning can be driven fast enough for firms in the latter countries to be able to import and use precision equipment and machinery to manufacture higher-value-added garments, as well as support more reliable and quicker logistics coordination with final markets.

Adaptive engineering. Interviews suggest that in Bangladesh and Cambodia firms only invest in automation, machinery and equipment modification and plant layouts to reduce defects and increase yield rates. This type of investment in the LDC garment firms is invariably lower than in the ODCs (table 15), particularly in the Lao People's Democratic Republic and Myanmar. While foreign sanctions have been reported as the prime cause of the decline in investment in upgrading in Myanmar, the structural features of the Lao People's Democratic Republic are seen as the prime deterrent to embedding in the domestic economy.

Anchoring. Evidence suggests that the rapid growth in garment-related FDI inflows, employment and exports has not been accompanied by a corresponding development of the technological capabilities of firms in Bangladesh, Cambodia, the Lao People's Democratic Republic and Myanmar. The Governments of those countries have not devised and implemented an effective policy to develop garment manufacturing and foster its anchoring in the domestic economy, although the industry plays a major role in those economies. Their policy actions have been limited to liberalizing foreign investment regulations, promoting private enterprise, and coordinating investment approvals, customs and basic infrastructure to stimulate the growth of the different segments of activities in the value chains. None of those economies has even imposed training levies on firms to stimulate upgrading.

Governments in Asian LDCs must formulate strategies that will lead to the proactive embedding and diversification of the textile and garment manufacturing activities. Bangladesh has massive labour reserves and hence has the largest garment industry among the LDCs, but unless the infrastructure is improved the size of the industry is unlikely to expand that much more. The political environment in Myanmar has constrained access to the United States market, and thus its higher skills intensities have failed to revive a once promising industry. Cambodia must strengthen governance mechanisms to stimulate learning, which is critical if the garment industry is to follow the direction of Viet Nam. The small labour force and being landlocked have imposed limits on further expansion of the garment industry in the Lao People's Democratic Republic.

5. IMPLICATIONS

There is little evidence of a significant contribution by FDI to technological capability accumulation in LDCs. This is not due to those countries' insufficient "opening" to foreign investors, given the policy changes that they have made since the 1980s and the sharp growth of FDI penetration since the 1990s, which in some respects has become greater than in other developing countries. Rather, its limited contribution is due to the type of integration of TNCs into host countries' economies, the sectoral composition of FDI, the priorities of policies enacted by LDCs and the low absorptive capacity of these countries.

The rapid growth in garment-related FDI inflows, employment and exports has not been accompanied by a corresponding development of the technological capabilities of firms in Bangladesh, Cambodia, the Lao People's Democratic Republic and Myanmar.

Governments in Asian LDCs must formulate strategies that will lead to the proactive embedding and diversification of the textile and garment manufacturing activities.

There is little evidence of a significant contribution by FDI to technological capability accumulation in LDCs.

LDC Governments have liberalized FDI policy regimes and have thus been successful in attracting higher FDI inflows and achieving increases in exports. National Governments have not, however, tried to enhance the impact of higher FDI inflows on domestic technological capability-building or on domestic enterprise development. Consequently, recent inflows into LDCs have led to enclave-type development, with few linkages to the domestic economy. This is true of both natural resource investment — predominant in FDI in African LDCs – – and of light manufacturing, which is more prevalent in Asian LDCs. Although the latter has a higher employment impact, it does not entail technological diffusion through the training and movement of labour, since the type of manufacturing in LDCs is labour-intensive, but involves few skills. Additionally, the establishment of foreign subsidiaries is not accompanied by active training measures that could create knowledge spillovers.

> *LDC Governments have not tried to enhance the impact of higher FDI inflows on domestic technological capability-building or on domestic enterprise development.*

For LDCs to reap some of the technological spillovers usually attributed to the presence of TNCs in host economies, active policy initiatives to that end must be implemented. In addition to attracting FDI, LDCs should introduce policies aimed at maximizing the development and technological learning impacts of foreign investment (see chapter 2 of this Report).

E. Licensing

The use of licensing as a channel for accessing the international knowledge pool (through imports of disembodied technology) is usually considered to be directly related to the income level and technological sophistication of economies. The reason for this is that using this technology diffusion channel effectively requires engineering skills and R&D programmes for adaptation and learning, to a much higher degree than other channels such as capital goods imports (Hoekman, Maskus and Saggi, 2005).

> *The use of licensing as a channel for accessing the international knowledge pool is directly related to the income level and technological sophistication of economies.*

Licensing should therefore be less relevant to LDCs than to other developing countries as a channel for foreign technology diffusion. The data on imports of disembodied technology in table 16 confirm that expectation. Royalty and licence fee payments in these countries are extremely low. Between 2000 and 2005 foreign disbursements amounted to 0.02 per cent of the GDP of the 24 LDCs for which data were available, as compared with 0.36 per cent in other developing countries. On a per capita basis, spending on imports of disembodied technology by LDCs amounted to $0.07 per inhabitant, while in ODCs it was 90 times higher. Imports of disembodied technology by LDCs have grown only moderately since the late 1990s. In 2000–2005 they were on average 14 per cent higher than during the period 1996–1999, but the relative indicators remained stagnant. In other developing countries, by contrast, licence fee payments almost doubled between those two periods, and there was a similar development with regard to the relative indicators (table 16).

> *On a per capita basis, spending on imports of disembodied technology by LDCs amounted to $0.07, while in ODCs it was 90 times higher.*

Licence fee payments are also associated with TNC presence in the country, since most transfer of disembodied technology occurs within multinational corporations (Mendi, 2007). However, it is particularly TNCs in knowledge-intensive sectors that generate that type of intra-firm payments, for example, the information technology and pharmaceutical industries. Since that is not the type of FDI that arrives in LDCs, the strong presence of foreign investment in LDCs (as analysed in section D above) has not entailed a corresponding strengthening of licensing activity in those countries.

Table 16. Indicators of the importance of licensing in LDCs and ODCs, 1996–2005

(Royalty and licence payments, period averages)

	Value ($ thousands)		Licence payments/ GDP (%)		Licence payments per capita ($)	
	1996–1999	*2000–2005*	*1996–1999*	*2000–2005*	*1996–1999*	*2000–2005*
LDCs	**29 044**	**33 250**	**0.02**	**0.02**	**0.07**	**0.07**
Africa	20 231	23 308	0.03	0.03	0.07	0.07
Asia	8 605	9 779	0.02	0.02	0.06	0.07
Islands	207	163	0.03	0.01	0.34	0.24
Other developing countries (ODCs)	**11 771 543**	**22 543 234**	**0.23**	**0.36**	**3.55**	**6.36**
Africa	785 767	1 020 422	0.24	0.27	3.72	4.43
America	2 698 636	3 253 528	0.15	0.17	5.82	6.53
Asia	8 287 140	18 269 284	0.28	0.47	3.14	6.49

Source: UNCTAD secretariat calculations, based on data from World Bank, World Development Indicators online and UNDESA, Statistics Division.

Note: LDCs and regional aggregates are composed of the following countries: Angola, Bangladesh, Benin, Burundi, Cambodia, Cape Verde, Eritrea, Ethiopia, Guinea, Lesotho, Madgascar, Malawi, Mali, Mozambique, Niger, Rwanda, Samoa, Senegal, Sierra Leone, Sudan, Togo, Uganda, United Republic of Tanzania and Zambia.

The diffusion of foreign technology to LDCs through market mechanisms is taking place to a very limited degree, there being very little technological development in those countries, despite the high exposure of LDCs to international trade and capital flows.

F. Conclusions

The diffusion of foreign technology to LDCs through market mechanisms is taking place to a very limited degree, there being very little technological development in those countries, despite the high exposure of LDCs to international trade and capital flows. The main reasons for this lie in the way in which those channels of knowledge diffusion are being accessed by LDCs. The latter are either using market channels too little or they are accessing them intensively, but not in a way that allows their potential for technological learning to develop. The former is true of capital goods imports and licensing, which have virtually stagnated at low levels (in relative terms) in LDCs over the last 25 years. The latter is the case with foreign direct investment and exports: LDCs are quite open to both, but are not capable of using them as effective channels for technology diffusion.

LDCs are either using market channels too little or they are accessing them intensively, but not in a way that allows their potential for technological learning to develop.

The only moderate growth of capital goods imports and licensing in LDCs is in sharp contrast with other developing countries, which have greatly intensified their use of those channels for access to the international knowledge pool. Little licensing activity can be expected in the early stage of technological catch-up, with this channel typically becoming more relevant only in the later stages. Low capital goods imports, by contrast, are a matter of concern, since they are expected to play a major role in diffusion of foreign technologies to LDCs. The sluggishness of those imports means that domestic firms are upgrading their processes and products only marginally. Their technological learning and innovative activity is therefore constrained. The main reasons for the low level of capital goods imports are the de-industrialization of the LDCs since the 1980s, the only moderate rise in the investment rate of those economies and the composition of their fixed capital formation (a relatively small share of which is devoted to machinery and equipment, including ICTs). Nevertheless, even the intensification of capital goods imports and licensing will not on its own guarantee that these international market linkages will work effectively as channels of knowledge diffusion. Policy action is required to make this happen.

The intensification of capital goods imports and licensing will not on its own guarantee that these international market linkages will work effectively as channels of knowledge diffusion. Policy action is required to make this happen.

The positive effects of technology spillovers, upgrading or learning-by-exporting that occur in some ODCs are mostly absent from LDCs.

LDCs' limited and ineffective use of international market linkages to build domestic technological capabilities is worrying since it is precisely those mechanisms that are expected to play a major role in technology diffusion to LDCs in the early stage of catch-up.

Leveraging international market mechanisms to strengthen their role as channels for the diffusion of technology to LDCs requires active policy at the national level as part of broader development strategies geared towards the development of productive capacities.

The levels of FDI inflows and stock of LDCs, as well as their merchandise exports, relative to their economies are comparable to those of other developing countries. Nevertheless, the positive effects of technology spillovers, upgrading or learning-by-exporting that occur in some ODCs (particularly in the late phase of technological catch-up) are mostly absent from LDCs. In the case of FDI, the reasons for this are: (i) the type of foreign investment that those countries have attracted; (ii) the limited linkages of TNCs with domestic economies; and (iii) the lack of policy action aimed at anchoring those activities in the domestic economy or at enabling their potential as technology diffusion channels to unfold. Difficulties in using exports and downstream linkages with international customers as means of technological learning are linked to the changing nature of global value chains, the growing entry barriers and the scarcity of measures taken by chain leaders to help their suppliers to upgrade. Thus, the growing integration of LDCs into international trade and investment flows since the 1980s has not prevented their marginalization from technology flows, as evidenced by the widening knowledge gap and the low-level development of their firms' technological capabilities.

LDCs' limited and ineffective use of international market linkages to build domestic technological capabilities is worrying since it is precisely those mechanisms —particularly international trade and FDI — that are expected to play a major role in technology diffusion to LDCs in the early stage of catch-up. Despite the enhanced contribution that should be made by knowledge aid (see chapter 5 of this Report), market mechanisms will remain the main channels for the diffusion of knowledge to LDCs, provided their presence is accompanied by adequate policy action. Their technology diffusion effects will not occur merely because of the existence of — or even increase in — trade and investment flows, as shown by the experience of LDCs over the last 25 years. Therefore, the recommendations, commonly made, that developing countries (including LDCs) increase their opening to foreign trade and FDI are not pertinent or are at least insufficient. Apart from the questionable effectiveness of such policy lines for technology diffusion, they generally do not apply to most LDCs, since they have already opened up strongly to foreign trade and investment.

For policy-makers in all developing countries, including in LDCs, it is important to realize that the learning associated with these international transactions does not occur automatically. There is, for example, no "fixed quotient" of learning that arrives in developing countries with every "unit" of, say, exports or FDI. Consequently, measures to increase the volume of exports or FDI inflows do not guarantee any increase in learning. Instead, the learning-intensity of such transactions is variable, and the key issue is to raise that learning intensity – to increase the magnitude of knowledge and skill that is acquired "per unit" of exports, imports or inward FDI.[34] In other words, the learning potential of these international transactions is something that can be exploited more or less fully. It is on that variability that policy should focus, and not just on the scale of the transactions (Bell, 2007).

Leveraging international market mechanisms to strengthen their role as channels for the diffusion of technology to LDCs requires active policy at the national level, as well as at the regional and international levels. This is particularly required in the early stage of technological catch-up, when policy action must actively pursue the goal of fostering technological capability-building. Although those interventions comprise S&T policy, they must be part of broader development strategies geared towards the development of productive capacities in all its dimensions, including strengthening domestic absorptive capacity. This issue will be discussed in chapter 2 of this Report.

Notes

1   Diffusion of technology through these four channels derives from interactions between different firms in the context of market transactions. Chapters 4 and 5 of this Report analyse other potentially effective channels for technology transfer to/from LDCs: migration of skilled persons (which usually does not result from market transactions between firms) and knowledge aid (which is a non-market mechanism), respectively.

2   The next major sources of innovation are key personnel, internal R&D and collaboration with customers (see chart 3 and UNCTAD, 2006b: table 35).

3   The crucial importance of capital goods as a source of innovation even in developed countries is confirmed by a survey of European enterprises, which shows that 50 per cent of total innovation expenditure is embodied in plant, machinery and equipment purchased by industrial firms, with own R&D accounting for just 20 per cent (Evangelista et al., 1998, quoted by UNIDO, 2002).

4   The working of trade as a channel for technology diffusion is gauged in different studies through trade openness or total imports (Edwards, 1998; Helliwell, 1992), but these are imprecise proxies for imports of embodied technology. This Report examines capital goods and their main categories in order to gain a better assessment of technology flows through merchandise imports.

5   The Annex provides the list of countries of origin of capital goods.

6   Trends in the intensity of LDCs' capital goods imports are driven by the African and Asian countries. The corresponding indices for island LDCs are substantially higher, due to the small size of these economies (table 3).

7   The precise definition of each category (including its trade classification) is provided in the Annex.

8   Automobiles are dual-use goods and can be either consumer goods or capital goods. Our category of capital goods includes only transport equipment used mostly for production purposes by firms and therefore excludes passenger cars.

9   "African LDCs" refers to most African LDCs plus Haiti. The Annex provides the list of countries included in this grouping, as well as the list of countries that make up the two other groupings: Asian LDCs and island LDCs.

10 The category "scientific and measuring instruments" is reclassified mostly as ICT capital in the second classification of capital goods. Hence the groups presented in table 6 are mainly a further specification of the broad "machinery and equipment" category shown in table 5.

11 Ideally, it would be desirable to separate mining and metal-crushing machinery from construction machinery, so as to highlight the role of natural resource extraction in total capital good imports. These two types of equipment fall, however, into the same category at the 5-digit SITC level (i.e. the most detailed in this trade classification). This is partly due to the fact that in some cases the same types of machinery can be used by both the mining and the construction industries (e.g. earth-moving equipment). Therefore, it was not possible to disentangle them in the trade data set used here.

12 Comprising the following capital good groups: textile and leather machinery; metalworking machinery; food-processing machinery; paper, pulp and publishing machinery; other industrial machinery.

13 In other developing countries, the share of agricultural machinery in total capital goods imports was lower than in LDCs and it has also declined since the 1980s. This, however, mirrors the much lower share of agriculture in GDP and the expansion of domestic supply capacity of agricultural machinery.

14 Gereffi, Humphrey and Sturgeon (2005) identify five different GVC governance patterns.

15 For example, transfer of post-harvest processing of fresh vegetables to producer countries has been observed in Kenya (Humphrey, McCulloch and Ota, 2004).

16 The relocation of activities to Madagascar has led to a strong increase in the country's exports of garments between 2000 and 2005 (table 13).

17 Apart from the value chains shown in table 9, the analysis considered the following: tobacco, iron, fruit, sugar, rubber, plastics, cocoa, pulp, wheat, artificial fibres, milk, fur skin, nickel and cork.

18 The approach is analogous to the one followed in section B of this chapter, which considers the sectoral breakdown of capital goods imports.

19 It is the greenfield part of FDI that brings additional capital to the host economy, but not brownfield investment.

20 Spillovers from FDI occur when the entry or presence of TNCs increases the productivity of domestic firms in a host country and the TNCs do not internalize the value of these benefits.

21 Horizontal spillovers refer to the technology transfer from TNCs to local firms in the same industry. Vertical spillovers take the form of positive externalities via value chains. Backward linkages are contacts between TNCs and their local suppliers. Forward linkages spillovers arise when domestic firms become more productive as a result of gaining access to new, improved or less costly inputs produced by TNCs in upstream sectors.

22 In LDCs natural resource extraction typically develops as enclaves, but this may also be the case of manufacturing and even service projects (e.g. in some cases of industry located in EPZs or tourist facilities) that have little backward or forward linkages with the domestic economy.

23 In this subsection mining refers to the extraction of minerals, including metals and fuels, as well as other minerals.

24 These developments in export values reflect both prices changes (given the cyclical rise in commodity prices just mentioned) and volume increases.

25 The first three features of mining activities are common to most modern mining operations throughout the world, while the two last ones are prevalent in developing countries (including LDCs), but usually not in developed countries (Eggert, 2001).

26 Abugre and Akabzaa (1998) claim that in Africa the "bulk of the investment in the mining sector goes to metallic and precious minerals. There is very limited investment in the non-metallic ores such as lime, phosphate, clay products and salt, all of which require relatively little capital to process but which have the greatest horizontal linkages to, and a higher multiplier effect on, the domestic industry".

27 The United States imposed sanctions on Myanmar in 2001 and by 2004 had terminated all direct imports from the country.

28 The garment industry can operate at both extremes of the skill-wage spectrum (at the low skill-low wage end and at the opposite high skill-high wage end), as well as at intermediate points.

29 Asian LDCs mostly lack the infrastructure and the skills endowments to attract a wide range of industries.

30 The United States and the European Union accounted for about 76 per cent of world garment imports in 2005, while Japan's imports totalled only 8 per cent. Therefore, preferential access to those two markets is very important for LDCs.

31 Although FDI also played a key role in Myanmar, the imposition of sanctions in 2001 led to a contraction in foreign investment and in exports. Domestic capital accounted for 79 per cent of the total number of firms in 2004–2005.

32 The analysis draws on the original findings on technological learning, domestic anchoring of industries and FDI that Rasiah (2007a) prepared for this Report on the basis of data from a series of surveys containing firm-level data on Asian LDCs and ODCs. That paper provides details on the different surveys that have been compiled.

33 The contraction of the garment industry in the Philippines and Thailand might lead to the relocation of firms to the Asian LDCs. Cambodia arguably remains the most appealing of the LDCs examined as regards attracting those firms, but only if further upgrading can be achieved, since the market in the really low-value-added niches is saturated.

34 The same reasoning applies to ODA flows, analysed in chapter 5 of this Report.

References

Abramovitz, M. (1986). Catching-up, forging ahead and falling behind. *Journal of Economic History,* 46 (2): 385–406.

Abugre, C. and Akabzaa, T. (1998). Mining boom: A gain for Africa? *Third World Resurgence,* 93.

Bell, M. (2007). Technological learning and the development of production and innovative capacities in the industry and infrastructure sectors of the least developed countries: What role for ODA? Study prepared as a background paper for *The Least Developed Countries Report 2007*, UNCTAD, Geneva.

Campbell, B. (ed.) (2004). Regulating mining in Africa. For whose benefit? Discussion Paper 26. Nordiska Afrikainstitutet, Uppsala, Sweden.

Campbell, B. (2005). The challenges of development, mining codes in Africa and corporate responsibility. In Bastida, E., Walde, T. and Warden, J. (eds.), *International and Comparative Mineral Law and Policy: Trends and Prospects*. Kluwer Law International, The Hague: 801–822.

Damijan, J., Knell M., Majcen B. and Rojec M. (2003). The role of FDI, R&D accumulation and trade in transferring technology to transition countries: Evidence from firm panel data for eight transition countries. *Economic Systems*, 27 (2): 189–204.

Dolan, C.S. and Humphrey, J. (2001). Governance and trade in fresh vegetables: The impact of UK supermarkets on the African horticulture industry. *Journal of Development Studies*, 37 (2): 147–176.

Dolan, C.S. and Humphrey, J. (2004). Changing governance patterns in the trade in fresh vegetables between Africa and the United Kingdom. *Environment and Planning*, 36 (3): 491–509.

Edwards, S. (1998). Openness, productivity and growth: What do we really know? *Economic Journal*, 108 (447): 383–398.

Eggert, R. G. (2001). Mining and economic sustainability: National economies and local communities. Mining, Minerals and Sustainable Development, No. 19, International Institute for Environment and Development, London.

Evangelista, R., Sandven, T., Sirrilli, G. and Smith, K. (1998). Measuring innovation in European industry. *International Journal of Economics and Business*, 5 (3): 311–333.

Findlay, R. (1978). Relative backwardness, direct foreign investment, and the transfer of technology: A simple dynamic model. *Quarterly Journal of Economics*, 92 (1): 1–16.

Gereffi, G., Humphrey, J. and Sturgeon, T. (2005). The governance of global value chains. *Review of International Political Economy*, 12 (1): 78–104.

Gibbon, P. and Ponte, S. (2005). *Trading Down: Africa, Value Chains and the Global Economy*. Temple University Press, Philadelphia, Penn.

Giuliani, E., Pietrobelli, C. and Rabellotti, R. (2005). Upgrading in global value chains: Lessons from Latin American clusters. *World Development*, 33 (4): 549–73.

Glass, A. and Saggi, K. (1998). International technology transfer and the technology gap. *Journal of Development Economics*, 55 (2): 369–398.

Gomes, R. (2006). Upgrading without exclusion: Lessons from SMEs in fresh fruit clusters in Brazil. In Pietrobelli, C. and Rabellotti, R. (2006b): 71–107.

Görg, H. and Greenaway, D. (2003). Much ado about nothing? Do domestic firms really benefit from foreign direct investment? Discussion Paper Series No. 944, Institute for the Study of Labor (IZA), Bonn.

Görg, H. and Strobl, E. (2005). Foreign direct investment and local economic development: Beyond productivity spillovers. In Moran, T.H., Graham, E. and Blomström, M. (2005): 137–158.

Helliwell, J. (1992). Trade and technical progress. NBER Working Paper No. 4226, National Bureau of Economic Research, Cambridge, Mass.

Hoekman, B., Maskus, K.E. and Saggi, K. (2005). Transfer of technology to developing countries: Unilateral and multilateral policy options. *World Development*, 33 (10): 1587–1602.

Humphrey, J. (2005). Shaping value chains for development: Global value chains in agribusiness. Report for GTZ and Germany's Federal Ministry for Economic Cooperation and Development, Eschborn.

Humphrey, J., McCulloch, N. and Ota, M. (2004). The impact of European market changes on employment in the Kenyan horticulture sector. *Journal of International Development*, 16 (1): 63–80.

Humphrey, J. and Schmitz, H. (2000). Governance and upgrading: Linking industrial cluster and global value chain research. IDS Working Paper No.120, Institute of Development Studies, University of Sussex, Brighton, UK.

IFAD (2003). The adoption of organic agriculture among small farmers in Latin America and the Caribbean: Thematic evaluation. Report No. 1337, International Fund for Agricultural Development, Rome.

Javorcik, B. (2004). Does foreign direct investment increase the productivity of domestic firms? In search of spillovers through backward linkages. *American Economic Review*, 94 (3): 605–627.

Justman, M and Teubal, M. (1991). A structuralist perspective on the role of technology in economic growth and development. *World Development*, 19 (9): 1167–1183.

Kiggundu, R. (2006). Technological change in Uganda's fishery exports. In Chandra, V. (ed.). *Technology, Adaptation and Exports. How some Developing Countries Got it Right*. World Bank, Washington, DC.

Knell, M. (2006). Uneven technological accumulation and growth in the least developed countries. Study prepared for UNCTAD as background paper for *The Least Developed Countries Report 2006*. UNCTAD, Geneva.

Kokko, A. (1994). Technology, market characteristics, and spillovers. *Journal of Development Economics*, 43 (2): 279–293.

Konde, V. (2007). What type of national ICT policies maximize ICT benefits? *ATDF Journal*, 4 (1): 37–48.

Lall, S. and Narula, R. (2004). Foreign direct investment and its role in economic development: Do we need a new agenda? *European Journal of Development Research*, 16 (3): 447–464.

Lewin, B., Giovannucci, D. and Varangis, P. (2004). Coffee markets: New paradigms in global supply and demand. Agriculture and Rural Development Discussion Paper No. 3, World Bank, Washington, DC.

Linton, A. (2005). A niche for sustainability: Fair labour and environmentally sound practices in the specialty coffee industry: Trading morsels, growing hunger, decimating nature: Linking food and trade to development and the environment. Princeton University, NJ.

Mendi, P. (2007). Trade in disembodied technology and total factor productivity in OECD countries. Research Policy, 36: 121–133.

Moran, T.H., Graham, E., and Blomström, M. (2005). *Does Foreign Direct Investment Promote Development?* Institute for International Economics Center for Global Development, Washington, DC.

Moss, T.J., Ramachandran, V. and Shah, M.K. (2005). Is Africa's skepticism of foreign capital justified? Evidence from East African firm survey data. In Moran, T.H., Graham, E. and Blomström, M. (2005): 337–366.

Myint, M.M. (2007). Staggered garment production in Myanmar, mimeo.

Nazneen, A. (2007, forthcoming). The garment industry in Bangladesh. *Journal of Contemporary Asia*.

NERI (2006). Survey of manufacturing firms. Funded by the Sasakawa Foundation, National Economic Research Institute, Vientienne.

Pavitt, K. (1984). Sectoral patterns of technical change: Towards a taxonomy and a theory. Research Policy, 13 (6): 343–373.

Pietrobelli, C. (2007). Upgrading, technological capabilities and competitiveness in LDCs: Global value chains, clusters and SMEs. Study prepared for UNCTAD as a background paper for *The Least Developed Countries Report 2007*, UNCTAD, Geneva.

Pietrobelli, C. and Rabellotti, R. (2004). Upgrading in clusters and value chains in Latin America: The role of policies. Sustainable Development Department Best Practices Series No. MSM-124, Inter-American Development Bank, Washington, DC.

Pietrobelli, C. and Rabellotti, R. (2006a). Clusters and value chains in Latin America: In search of an integrated approach. In Pietrobelli, C. and Rabellotti, R. (2006b): 1–40.

Pietrobelli, C. and Rabellotti, R. (eds.) (2006b). *Upgrading to Compete: Global Value Chains, Clusters and SMEs in Latin America*. Harvard University David Rockefeller Center for Latin American Studies and the Inter-American Development Bank, Cambridge, Mass and Washington, DC.

Ponte, S. (2002a). Brewing a bitter cup? Deregulation, quality and the re-organization of coffee marketing in East Africa. *Journal of Agrarian Change*, 2 (2): 248–72.

Ponte, S. (2002b). The "Latte Revolution"? Regulation, markets and consumption in the global coffee chain. *World Development* 30 (7): 1099–1122.

Rasiah, R. (2006a). Post-MFA implications for garment manufacturing in least developed economies. Paper presented at the conference Future of Garment Manufacturing in Developing Economies, organized by CICP and FES. 2–4 June, Phnom Penh.

Rasiah, R. (2006b). Sustaining development through garment exports in Cambodia. Study prepared for UNCTAD as a background paper to *The Least Developed Countries Report 2006*, UNCTAD, Geneva.

Rasiah, R. (2007a). Garment exports from South, East and Southeast Asian LDEs. Study prepared for UNCTAD as a background paper for *The Least Developed Countries Report 2007*, UNCTAD, Geneva.

Rasiah, R. (2007b, forthcoming). The garment industry in Cambodia. *Journal of Contemporary Asia*.

UNCTAD (2002). *The Least Developed Countries Report 2002: Escaping the Poverty Trap.* United Nations publication, sales no. E.02.II.D.8, Geneva and New York.

UNCTAD (2004), *The Least Developed Countries Report 2004: Linking International Trade with Poverty reduction*. United Nations publication, sales no. E.04.II.D.27, New York and Geneva.

UNCTAD (2005). *Economic Development in Africa: Rethinking the Role of Foreign Direct Investment*. United Nations publication, sales no. E.05.II.D.12, Geneva and New York.

UNCTAD (2006a). *FDI in Least Developed Countries at a Glance 2005/2006*. United Nations publication, UNCTAD/ITE/IIA/2005/7, Geneva and New York.

UNCTAD (2006b). *The Least Developed Countries Report 2006: Developing Productive Capacities*. United Nations publication, sales no. E.06.II.D.9, Geneva and New York.

UNIDO (2002). *Innovative Technology Transfer Framework Linked to Trade for UNIDO Action*. UNIDO, Vienna.

UNIDO (2005). *Industrial Development Report 2005: Capability Building for Catching-up*. UNIDO, Vienna.

UNU-MERIT (2004-2005). Survey data on Cambodian, Indian, Malaysian and Sri Lankan industrial firms. Funded by UNU-MERIT, DFID and the World Bank, Maastricht and DC.

WTO (2006). International Trade Statstitics 2006. Geneva.

Yviengsay, I. and Rasiah, R. (2007, forthcoming). Garment exports from Lao: Reaching the Natural Limits. *Journal of Contemporary Asia*.

Annex

Definition of capital goods and groups. The definition of capital goods is mostly based on the BEC (Broad Economic Categories) Rev.3 classification of the United Nations. It comprises the following categories (with the respective BEC Rev.3 codes):

41   Capital goods (except transport equipment)

42   Parts and accessories *(of Capital goods under heading 41)*

521   Industrial *(Transport equipment)*

53   Parts and accessories *(of Industrial transport equipment under heading 521)*

Capital goods have been loosely classified in two ways. The first is a general classification that divides them into the following groups (with the respective SITC Rev.3 codes):

1. Machinery and equipment (612.1, 629.2, 657.7, 657.9, 692, 695, 711, 712, 713, 714, 716, 718, 721, 722, 723, 724, 725, 726, 727, 728, 731, 733, 735, 737, 741, 742, 743, 744, 745, 746, 747, 748, 749, 751, 752, 759, 761.2, 762.8, 763.8, 764, 771, 772, 773.2, 776, 778, 812.1, 821.3, 881.2, 881.3, 894.6, 895.1)

2. Scientific and measuring instruments (774, 871, 872, 873, 874, 897.4)

3. Transport equipment (625.2, 625.3, 782, 783, 784, 786, 791, 792, 793)

The second classification singles out (whenever possible) capital goods by their main end-users or by type of general-purpose technology. It divides them into the following groups (with the respective SITC Rev.3 codes):

1. Agricultural machinery (721, 722)

2. Construction, mining, metal crushing (723, 728)

3. Power-generating machinery (711, 712, 713, 714, 716, 718, 771, 772, 773.2, 812.1)

4. Textile and leather machinery (724)

5. Metalworking machinery (731, 733, 735, 737)

6. Food-processing machinery (727)

7. Paper, pulp and publishing machinery (725, 726)

8. Other industrial machinery (612.1, 629.2, 657.7, 657.9, 692, 695, 741, 742, 743, 744, 745, 746, 747, 748, 749, 778, 821.3, 871, 881.2, 894.6, 895.1, 897.4)

9. ICT capital (751, 752, 759, 761.2, 762.8, 763.8, 764, 774, 776, 872, 873, 874, 881.3)

10. Transport equipment (as above)

Definition of country/territories groups. The following country groups have been used:

1. *Developed countries/territories:* Andorra, Australia, Austria, Belgium, Canada, Channel Islands, Cyprus, Czech Republic, Denmark, Estonia, Faeroe Islands, Finland, France, Germany, Gibraltar, Greece, Holy See, Hungary, Iceland, Ireland, Isle of Man, Israel, Italy, Japan, Latvia, Liechtenstein, Lithuania, Luxembourg, Malta, Monaco, Netherlands, New Zealand, Norway, Poland, Portugal, San Marino, Slovakia, Slovenia, Spain, Sweden, Switzerland, United Kingdom, United States.

2. *Technologically advanced developing countries/economies:* the 20 developing countries/economies with the highest ranking in UNIDO's ITA (index of industrial and technological advancement): China, Hong Kong (China), India, Indonesia, Jordan, Republic of Korea, Malaysia, Pakistan, Philippines, Singapore, Taiwan Province of China, Thailand, Turkey, Argentina, Brazil, Costa Rica, El Salvador, Mexico, South Africa, Tunisia (source: UNIDO, 2005).

3. LDC subregional groupings:

3.1. Africa and Haiti: Angola, Benin, Burkina Faso, Burundi, Central African Republic, Chad, Democratic Republic of the Congo, Djibouti, Equatorial Guinea, Eritrea, Ethiopia, Gambia, Guinea, Guinea-Bissau, Haiti, Lesotho, Liberia, Madagascar, Malawi, Mali, Mauritania, Mozambique, Niger, Rwanda, Senegal, Sierra Leone, Somalia, Sudan, Togo, Uganda, United Republic of Tanzania, Zambia.

3.2. Asia: Afghanistan, Bangladesh, Bhutan, Cambodia, Lao People's Democratic Republic, Myanmar, Nepal, Yemen.

3.3. Islands: Cape Verde, Comoros, Kiribati, Maldives, Samoa, Sao Tome and Principe, Solomon Islands, Timor-Leste, Tuvalu, Vanuatu.

Methodological notes. Mirror trade data have been used to estimate capital goods imports, with developed countries and technologically advanced developing countries (as defined above) as reporters and developing countries as partners. Raw data were downloaded from UNDESA Statistics Division, Comtrade database, in January 2007.

National Policies to Promote Technological Learning and Innovation

Chapter

2

A. Introduction

This chapter examines the role of national policy in promoting technological learning and innovation in the least developed countries (LDCs). Section B considers briefly what the Governments of the LDCs are currently doing to promote science, technology and innovation. It does so by examining how science and technology issues are treated in poverty reduction strategy papers (PRSPs) and analyzing the findings in the context of current development policy thinking. The evidence shows that, although the LDCs are concerned with promoting sustained economic growth as the basis for poverty reduction, the treatment of technological change as a source of economic growth is generally weak. The rest of the chapter proposes how LDC Governments might rectify this deficiency.

The analysis is based on the commonly accepted insight that processes of technological change in rich countries, where firms are innovating by pushing the knowledge frontier further, are fundamentally different from such processes in developing countries, where innovation primarily takes place through enterprises learning to master, adapt and improve technologies that already exist in more technologically advanced countries. Science, technology and innovation (STI) policies to promote technological development should be different in technologically leading countries from in follower countries, including LDCs. In short, STI policy in LDCs, as in all developing countries, should be geared to technological catch-up with more technologically advanced countries through technological learning and innovation. Innovation in this context occurs when firms commercially apply knowledge which is new to them, even if it is not new to the world or to the country.

Science, technology and innovation (STI) policies to promote technological development should be different in technologically leading countries from in follower countries, including LDCs.

The rest of the chapter seeks to clarify what this implies for the design and implementation of STI policy in LDCs. Section C sets out some general considerations on the nature and scope of STI policy. Sections D and E suggest how the catch-up concept can be applied in an LDC context by firstly outlining typical learning and innovation trajectories during catch-up, and secondly considering the implications of those trajectories for LDCs, which are at the early stages of the catch-up process. Section F raises some issues regarding the capacity of LDC Governments to design and implement policies of the types proposed in the chapter. The conclusion summarizes the major messages of the chapter.

B. How science and technology issues are treated in PRSPs: Recent country experience in comparative perspective

1. RECENT COUNTRY EXPERIENCE

It is difficult to construct a systematic picture of policies to promote science, technology and innovation in the LDCs. However, many LDC Governments prepare PRSPs and these documents give a good indication of the priority which is given to science and technology issues in national policy. Analysis of the PRSPs prepared during the period 2004–2006 in 11 LDCs — including six African LDCs, four Asian LDCs and Haiti — indicates that the incorporation of science and technology issues in PRSPs is generally weak (Warren-Rodriguez, 2007). Nevertheless, some attention has been paid to a number of specific issues, notably applied agricultural research and extension, technical and vocational training, investment in electricity and telecommunications networks, and increased use of information and communication technologies (ICTs), particularly for use of ICTs for better governance.

Only four of the 11 countries include science and/or technology in their PRSPs as a priority policy for poverty reduction.

In particular, the analysis (table 17) shows that:

- Only four of the 11 countries include science and/or technology as priority policy for poverty reduction, with the United Republic of Tanzania and Uganda focusing on the importance of science, and Mozambique and Bangladesh focusing on the importance of technological development.

- Only three of the 11 countries (Bangladesh, Mozambique and the United Republic of Tanzania) include a specific section or paragraph on science and technology issues.

- Only three of the 11 countries (Bangladesh, Lesotho and Sierra Leone) include explicit and specific science and technology initiatives to enhance technology transfer and acquisition through either international trade or foreign direct investment (FDI).

- Only three of the 11 countries (Bangladesh, the United Republic of Tanzania and Uganda) include specific initiatives to support basic research.

- Only four of the 11 countries (Bangladesh, Sierra Leone, Uganda and the United Republic of Tanzania) include specific initiatives for applied research outside agriculture.

- Only four of the 11 countries (Bangladesh, Cambodia, Lesotho and the United Republic of Tanzania) make explicit reference to the need to expand business development services that support technological upgrading efforts by local firms.

Nine of the 11 countries include some reference to initiatives aimed at agricultural research, and all 11 countries include initiatives to promote agricultural extension.

- Only three of the 11 countries (Bangladesh, Lesotho and Uganda) include specific science and technology initiatives in all three levels of education – primary, secondary and higher.

- Only six of the 11 countries include policies to promote best practices and quality standards by local firms, typically though the creation and capacitation of local standards and metrology institutions.

There are nevertheless some science and technology-related areas which the PRSPs do address, most notably:

- Seven of the 11 countries include some reference to initiatives aimed at agricultural research, including some, such as Burkina Faso, which include a detailed breakdown of intended activities by crop.

- Nine of the 11 countries include initiatives to promote agricultural extension.

- All 11 countries include specific initiatives to expand technical and vocational education, and all mention its importance.

- All 11 countries identify the need to extend and upgrade electricity networks, and 10 of them also stress the importance of rural electrification.

- Six of the 11 countries acknowledge the importance of improving general telecommunications networks, but only five mention the importance of extending this infrastructure to rural areas.

Table 17. How S&T is treated in the PRSPs of selected LDCs

	Bangladesh	Bhutan	Burkina Faso	Cambodia	Haiti	Lao PDR	Lesotho	Mozambique	Sierra Leone	Uganda	United Rep. of Tanzania
Was S&T considered a priority area in the PRSP document?	Y	N	N	N	N	W	N	Y	N	Y	Y
Is there a specific section/paragraph covering S&T issues?	Y	N	N	N	N	N	N	Y	N	N	Y
Are specific S&T initiatives included at the level of:											
• trade policies	Y	N	N	N	N	N	N	W	Y	W	N
• FDIs	Y	N	N	N	N	W	Y	W	N	N	W
Does the PRSP include specific S&T initiatives in											
• primary education	Y	N	N	N	N	W	Y	N	N	Y	N
• secondary education	Y	N	Y	N	N	W	Y	Y	Y	Y	N
• higher education	Y	N	N	N	N	W	Y	Y	Y	Y	Y
Are infrastructural technology concerns treated in the PRSP?											
• electricity networks											
- general	Y	Y	Y	Y	Y	Y	Y	Y	Y	Y	Y
- rural	Y	Y	Y	Y	N	Y	Y	Y	Y	Y	Y
• telecommunication networks											
- general	Y	W	Y	Y	Y	W	Y	W	W	Y	W
- rural	Y	N	Y	Y	N	W	Y	N	W	Y	N
• ICT extension											
- general	Y	N	N	W	W	W	Y	Y	Y	W	Y
- rural	Y	N.A.	N.A.	N	N	W	N	N	Y	N	N
Are there projects aiming at increasing technological awareness through:											
• basic R&D activities	Y	N	N	N	N	N	N	N	N	Y	Y
• applied R&D activities in agricultural research	Y	W	Y	W	N	Y	N	Y	Y	Y	Y
• applied R&D in industrial/engineering research	Y	N	N	N	N	N	N	N	Y	Y	Y
• technical and vocational education training	Y	Y	Y	Y	Y	Y	Y	Y	Y	Y	Y
Are there sector-specific technology extension programmes:											
• in agriculture	Y	Y	Y	W	W	Y	Y	Y	Y	Y	Y
• in business development services	Y	W	W	Y	N	N	Y	N	N	W	Y
• in product standards and best practices	Y	N	N	Y	N	Y	N	Y	Y	Y	N

Source: UNCTAD secretariat based on Warren-Rodriguez (2007).

Note: Y = yes, N = no, W = weak, N.A. = not available.

- However, nine of the 11 countries include specific initiatives to apply ICT to improve public administration and public service delivery.

- Seven of the 11 countries intend to promote renewable energy resources (e.g. solar and wind power).

These results are important, as the sample of PRSPs is representative of the latest generation of PRSPs in LDCs. As shown in the *Least Developed Countries Report 2004*, the PRSP approach has evolved considerably since it was first introduced at the end of 1999. In particular, there has been a shift away from an exclusive emphasis on increasing social sector expenditures in the context of debt relief, towards poverty reduction strategies whose first pillar is to ensure strong and sustainable growth (see UNCTAD, 2004: 272–273). With this renewed focus on economic growth as the basis for poverty reduction, there is greater concern with sources of economic growth. One would expect that this would logically lead to consideration of the role of technological progress. As we shall discuss in more detail below, most major growth theories identify technological change as being at the heart of growth processes. But as the evidence above shows, this has not occurred. In short, *the new focus on economic growth as the basis of poverty reduction in the latest generation of PRSPs has not generally been associated with a focus on technological progress as a key source of economic growth.*[1]

The new focus on economic growth as the basis of poverty reduction in the latest generation of PRSPs has not generally been associated with a focus on technological progress as a key source of economic growth.

2. A COMPARATIVE PERSPECTIVE

The weak treatment of technological change reflects the marginalization of technology policies within structural adjustment programmes of the 1980s and 1990s, and the omission of technology issues from the PRSP approach which replaced such programmes in 2000.

Technological development was an integral, though very imperfect, aspect of efforts to promote development in LDCs prior to structural adjustment.

Most LDCs began their structural adjustment a little later than other developing countries. However, since 1988, two thirds of the LDCs have been intensively engaged in reform processes (UNCTAD, 2000: part II, chapter 4). Although there were some problems of implementation, the process of economic liberalization was pushed by policy conditionality associated with aid and debt relief programmes, and pulled by the belief of many policymakers in the 1990s that liberalization was the best way to ensure the benefits of globalization reached LDCs. Whatever the balance of impulses, many LDCs have undertaken rapid and comprehensive reforms, which have continued during the PRSP era. This has created a totally different policy environment from that at the end of the 1980s. A telling indicator of the depth of reforms is the fact that two thirds of the LDCs had an open trade regime according to the International Monetary Fund's index of trade restrictiveness in 2002, and the LDCs had actually undertaken more trade liberalization than other developing countries (UNCTAD, 2004: part II, chapter 5).

Technology policy was not considered as part of structural adjustment programmes. Key institutions and incentives for agricultural and industrial development which were created prior to the1980s as part of development plans were dismantled as economic policy moved decisively in the direction of economic liberalization and privatization.

Technological development was an integral, though very imperfect, aspect of efforts to promote development in LDCs prior to structural adjustment. Thus, for example, many LDCs had agricultural marketing boards which were intended to serve a variety of functions, including research and the provision of services which supported technological upgrading of export crops. But technology policy was not considered as part of structural adjustment programmes. Key institutions and incentives for agricultural and industrial development which were created prior to the1980s as part of development plans were dismantled as economic policy moved decisively in the direction of economic liberalization and privatization.

The decline and fragmentation of science and technology infrastructure (research institutes, universities and technology policy coordination bodies) were particularly severe in African LDCs in the 1990s (see UNESCO, 2005). In Bangladesh, a broad set of publicly funded research and development (R&D) institutes has been maintained, and Nepal, which established a Ministry of Science and Technology in 1996, has continued to support technological development in its five-year planning process. But in both cases, low levels of public funding for research institutes are a problem (UNESCO, 2005: 257–259), and in Bangladesh, as the case study in chapter 3 of this Report shows, the disarticulation between public research and development institutes and productive sectors remains a key constraint on learning at the enterprise level.[2]

The introduction of the PRSP approach in late 1999 has reinforced the marginalization of science and technology issues in LDC policy processes.

The introduction of the PRSP approach in late 1999 has reinforced the marginalization of science and technology issues in LDC policy processes. The approach is based on the important principle of domestic ownership and there has been a genuine effort to encourage the emergence of home-grown policies which can provide the basis for a more effective partnership with donors. However, given weak state capacity and also the tension between policy conditionality and domestic ownership, most PRSPs tend to be concerned with strengthening and deepening the earlier economic reform processes. They embody so-called second generation reforms, which pay particular attention to social allocation of public resources and seek improved governance, including reducing corruption and promoting an overall improved investment climate. Promoting technological change is not part of the vision, and it is conspicuously absent from the PRSP

Source Book of the World Bank, which is intended as a guide to policymakers (Klugman, 2002).

It is important that LDC Governments give much more attention to technological progress as a source of economic growth. This requires a more radical rupture from past structural adjustment policies. As the World Bank (2005) recognizes, the key lesson from economic reforms of the 1990s was not that they failed to integrate social considerations and poverty reduction issues. Rather, it was that they failed to promote economic growth. In particular:

- Economic reforms "enabled better use of existing capacity but did not provide sufficient incentives for expanding that capacity" (ibid., 10).

- They "often mistook efficiency gains for growth" (ibid., 11).

- They "exaggerated the gains from improved resource allocation and their dynamic repercussions, and proved to be both theoretically incomplete and contradicted by the evidence" (ibid., 11).

- "Expectations that gains in growth would be won entirely through policy improvements were unrealistic" (ibid., 11).

- "Means were often mistaken for goals – that is, improvements in policies were mistaken for growth strategies, as if improvements in policies were an end in themselves" (ibid., 11).

From this diagnosis, it is argued that:

- "Going forward, the pursuit of policy reforms for reform's sake should be replaced by a more comprehensive understanding of the forces underlying growth" (ibid., 11).

- "Removing the obstacles that make growth impossible may not be enough: growth-oriented action, for example, on technological catch-up, or encouragement of risk-taking for faster accumulation, may be needed" (ibid., 11).

From the perspective of this Report, it is important that LDC Governments elaborate development strategies which are designed to promote sustained economic growth and poverty reduction through the development of their productive capacities. PRSPs, which often now function as medium-term public expenditure frameworks, can be embedded within such long-term development strategies. Technological development issues, as well as trade development issues, should be integral aspects of the broader development strategy and can be integrated within poverty reduction strategies through the development strategies.

If LDCs ignore the need for adopting policies to promote technological progress as a basic source of economic growth, they are likely to be increasingly marginalized within the global economy. The problem of marginalization is not simply a question of the very low level of technological development in LDCs indicated in the introduction of this Report. It also reflects the fact that promoting technological change is at the heart of Organisation for Economic Co-operation and Development (OECD) efforts to promote economic growth in LDCs (Weiss, 2005). It also has been a central component of development strategies in the most successful developing countries and is becoming important in more and more developing countries.

Policies to promote technological catch-up were an integral component of developmental success in East Asian developing countries (UNCTAD, 1994; Akyuz, 1998; Nelson and Pack, 1999), and successful models are being adapted in

It is important that LDC Governments give much more attention to technological progress as a source of economic growth.

If LDCs ignore the need for adopting policies to promote technological progress as a basic source of economic growth, they are likely to be increasingly marginalized within the global economy.

follower countries such as Malaysia and Viet Nam. In Latin America, science and technology policies were marginalized in the early period of structural reforms. But the Economic Commission for Latin America and the Caribbean (ECLAC) has, since 1990, been advocating the adoption of mesolevel and microlevel productive development policies alongside macroeconomic reforms (see for example, ECLAC, 1990, 1995, 2004). These ideas are now taking concrete shape as more and more countries are adopting productive development policies, including policies to promote STI (Peres, 2006). Some argue that what is emerging is a new "open-economy industrial policy", in which proactive measures are used to promote infant export industries rather than infant import-substitution industries (see Melo, 2001; Schrank and Kurtz, 2005). A recent review of these new industrial policies has concluded that although these policies are very widespread in Latin America, they are as yet "timid and inconsistent" (Melo and Rodriguez-Clare, 2006: 54), partly owing to negative associations with old-style import-substitution industrial policy and partly owing to budgetary constraints and institutional weaknesses. Moreover, the effectiveness of the new open-economy science and technology policies has also been questioned (Cimoli, Ferraz and Primi, 2005). However, Schrank and Kurtz (2005, 2006) provide empirical evidence which suggests that the new open-economy industrial policy is actually accelerating export growth rates in countries where they are being most intensively applied. Moreover, Melo and Rodriguez-Clare (2006: 57) argue that the current phase is best understood as a policy learning phase through which "productive development policies can develop their potential to effectively contribute to the goals of growth and modernization".

Similarly, in Africa there has recently been an important surge of interest at the regional level in science and technology issues, with the New Partnership for Africa's Development (NEPAD) and the African Union both promoting new regional initiatives to revive science and promote centres of excellence (NEPAD, 2005). Technological development was actually at the heart of the African solution to the economic crisis of the 1970s — as set out in the Lagos Plan of Action — before it was overtaken by the structural adjustment programmes, which focused on getting price incentives right. These initiatives are thus returning to a promising road already identified but not yet travelled.

In retrospect, it is clear that, although structural adjustment programmes addressed some real policy failures, they threw out the baby with the bathwater. The broad revival of interest in policies to promote technological change, partly inspired by the East Asian success, is indicative of wide restlessness to find a new, post-Washington-Consensus policy model as well as of the intuition that it is in this area — promoting technological change — that it is possible to find more effective policies to promote growth and poverty reduction. If LDCs do not participate in this policy trend, they will be increasingly marginalized in the global economy, where competition increasingly depends on knowledge rather than the simple possession of natural resources.

The broad revival of interest in policies to promote technological change, partly inspired by the East Asian success, is indicative of wide restlessness to find a new, post-Washington-Consensus policy model as well as of the intuition that it is in this area — promoting technological change — that it is possible to find more effective policies to promote growth and poverty reduction.

C. The nature and scope of STI policies

Although the weak focus on technological change within national policies to promote economic growth and poverty reduction is striking, some might argue that STI policies are a luxury which LDCs cannot afford at their stage of development. This view may partly be based on a misunderstanding of the role of technological change in development. But it also could be founded on a narrow conception of a science, technology and innovation policy. In the past, a science policy was often associated with the funding of scientific research and the training of scientists. Similarly, technology policy has been closely associated with the development of specific technologies, particularly to support new high-tech industries. However, these notions of science and technology policies have now been superseded by a broader notion of what STI policy is and how it can be implemented. This section sets out features of this broader notion.

1. LINEAR VERSUS SYSTEMS MODELS OF INNOVATION

In the past, the scope of STI policy has been highly influenced by a linear model of innovation which suggests that basic science leads to applied science, which in turn causes innovation. The policy implication of this science push model of innovation is simple. According to Arnold and Bell (2001: 5), "If you want more innovation (and therefore economic development), you should fund more science".

This science-push model of innovation was very influential in the design of technology policies in OECD countries in the 1950s and 1960s, and it has also influenced the approach to science and technology in developing countries and LDCs. For example, in the 1960s many African LDCs established research and development (R&D) institutes as a means of acquiring technology. At the same time, they set up policy institutions such as national research councils or ministries for science and technology, and money budgeted for science and technology was spent on these R&D institutes and policy institutions. In this approach, "S&T policy was interpreted to mean R&D policy" (Oyelaran-Oyeyinka, 2006: 45).

There are various problems with the science-push model of innovation. One glaring weakness has been the lack of relevance of public research institutions to the needs of the productive sectors and the irrelevance of scientific research efforts to commercial market needs. This weakness is quite apparent in the LDCs, where "sparse, often disconnected R&D activities have little if any links with the needs of domestic enterprises or farmers organizations" and where the dearth of linkages between formal public research institutes and domestic production dissipate the considerable inputs already invested over the years" (UNCTAD, 2006a: 251). Evidence from investment climate surveys indicates that in recent years only 0.4 per cent of the companies considered universities or public institutes the most important channel for technology acquisition, and only 3.4 per cent of the firms reported that universities and public institutes were their first-most, second-most or third-most important source of technology acquisition (ibid., table 35).

The weakness of the supply-push model has led to an alternative approach — a demand-pull model of innovation. In essence, this retains a linear model of innovation but the initial impulse for innovation does not come from science-push but rather from demand-pull. Instead of the public sector being the main science and technology provider, the expressed demands of the private sector are meant to provide the motor for technological change. Recent technology policies in Latin America reflect this approach (Cimoli, Ferraz and Primi, 2005) and illustrate an attempt to achieve greater articulation between public sector technological agencies and the private sector. This has involved a shift in the science and technology priorities of the public agencies from basic research to the provision and commercialization of technological services, mainly oriented to support production process management and quality control. Moreover, technology funds have been established to subsidize technological development projects of private firms and training. They have also been used to promote the development of private-sector technological services providers, thus facilitating the emergence of a technological services market.

There are various problems with the science-push model of innovation. One glaring weakness has been the lack of relevance of public research institutions to the needs of the productive sectors and the irrelevance of scientific research efforts to commercial market needs.

Evidence from investment climate surveys in LDCs indicates that in recent years only 0.4 per cent of the companies considered universities or public institutes the most important channel for technology acquisition.

Both the supply-push and demand-pull models of innovation are now viewed as oversimplified views of how innovation occurs (Arnold and Bell, 2001). As a result, a different model of innovation has emerged which suggests that innovation depends on the existence of a variety of agents and institutions (much greater in scope than technology providers and technology users) and that the effectiveness of innovation depends on the interactions between these agencies and institutions.

In this systems model of innovation, the ability and propensity of an enterprise to innovate not only depends on its access to knowledge from research institutes or technology services centres (pushed or pulled), but also on many other factors including: access to finance; access to human resources; adequate basic physical infrastructure; firm-level capabilities; inter-firm linkages and collaboration; general business services; demand conditions; and the framework conditions including the investment climate, general cultural propensity towards entrepreneurship and levels of literacy. There is no longer a single source of innovation (scientific research) but multiple sources, including interactions among enterprises and sectors.

The systems approach to innovation has become widely accepted within OECD countries (OECD, 1997). The focus for STI policies is upon improving "national innovation systems". Such systems are defined as "that set of distinct institutions which jointly and individually contributes to the development of diffusion of new technologies and which provides a framework within which Governments form and implement policies to influence the innovation process. As such it is a system of interconnected institutions to create, store and transfer the knowledge, skills and artifacts which define new technologies" (Metcalfe, 1995). The main elements of such a system are illustrated schematically in chart 7.

> *In this systems model of innovation, the ability and propensity of an enterprise to innovate not only depends on its access to knowledge from research institutes or technology services centres (pushed or pulled), but also on many other factors including...*

> *... access to finance; access to human resources; adequate basic physical infrastructure; firm-level capabilities; inter-firm linkages and collaboration; general business services; demand conditions; and the framework conditions including the investment climate, general cultural propensity towards entrepreneurship and levels of literacy.*

Chart 7. Major components of a national innovation system

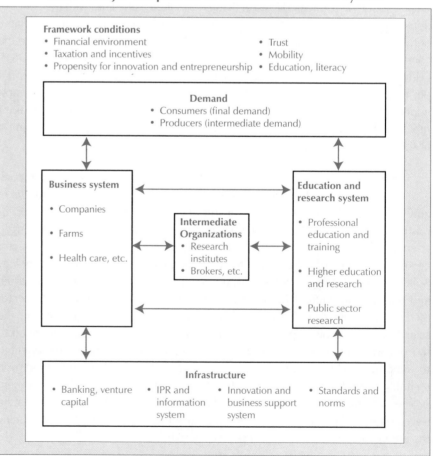

Source: Arnold and Bell (2001)

It is important that, in their approach to the design and implementation of STI policy, LDC Governments also adopt a systems approach. But in this Report, it is suggested that it may be premature to seek to establish national innovation systems. Rather, the aim should be to develop local and sectoral innovation systems, as illustrated in box 1, and to increase the absorptive capability of domestic knowledge systems. The latter idea will be discussed in more detail below.

Box 1. Chilli production in Bangladesh: how the innovation system works in practice

The fertile Jamalpur chars — temporary islands formed by siltation in river deltas — in Bangladesh are well known for their high-quality chilli production. Although the chars are very fertile, there is a lack of basic infrastructure and the chilli-growers often lack market information and have weak linkages with external actors.

To strengthen the sustainable innovation systems linked to local chilli production, the United Kingdom Department for International Development is funding the Crop Post-Harvest Research Programme, which aims to identify and strengthen linkages among all actors involved in the chilli supply chain.

Box chart 1 shows that all the actors involved in enhancing the local innovation systems are closely related. The arrows in the chart refer to the flows of goods and knowledge among these actors. The strongest links between the char-dwellers and the mainland actors are to be found in the private sector. Information from the private sector and the public extension services is passed on to the local char-dwellers by so-called input dealers. Local middlemen provide market access for local products, although national chilli processors and retailers are also starting to develop direct links with the char-dwellers (highlighted by the dashed line). Non-governmental organizations act as promoters, while the research team builds linkages between the public and private sectors and locals. The research team bridges the gap between the private-sector research institute, which is currently introducing new chilli seed varieties, and the other actors. It is also providing training to private- and public-sector agents to make this system viable and sustainable on its own.

The actors need to be: (a) flexible, in order to adapt to the evolving needs of the partners; (b) accountable to other actors; and (c) interactive, as the evolution of activities over time and among the actors is considered to be key to the success of intervention in technology markets.

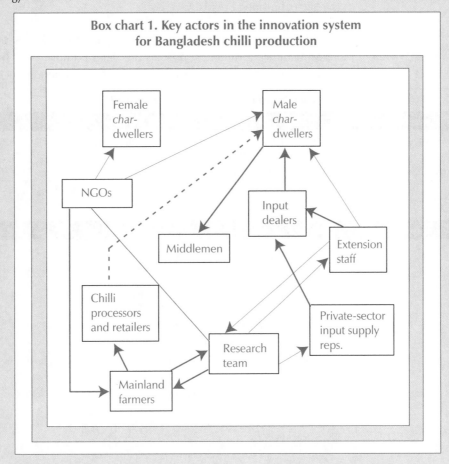

Box chart 1. Key actors in the innovation system for Bangladesh chilli production

Source: Biggs, S. and Hatsaert, H., 2004.

2. EXPLICIT AND IMPLICIT INSTRUMENTS OF STI POLICY

The systems model of innovation has important implications for the scope of public action. The supply-push model of innovation leads to a narrowly-defined STI policy which focuses on scientific research. The systems approach to innovation rather suggests that innovation depends upon a large number of policies and institutions. It implies that the instruments of STI policy should not only include measures to stimulate the supply side of technology development, but also measures to stimulate the demand for technology development, measures to strengthen the links between supply and demand, and measures which address framework conditions.

Table 18, which builds on Dodgson and Bessant (1996), summarizes some of the relevant STI policy tools. At the top of the table are explicit measures which are concerned with human resources development for science and technology, public science and technology infrastructure, and policies to affect technology imports. Public science and technology infrastructure includes such institutions as public research centres, technology advisory centres, agriculture and industrial extension agencies, and business support services, which are all concerned with the supply of knowledge within domestic knowledge systems. At the bottom of the table are implicit measures which affect the willingness and ability to undertake the investments, in both physical capital and human skills, necessary for innovation.

The implicit measures are fairly standard and include public physical infrastructure investment; financial and fiscal policies which increase the incentive for investment and innovation; trade policy and competition policy; public enterprises and public procurement; and regulation, notably in relation to intellectual property rights.

What is particularly critical in this regard for LDCs is that both physical infrastructure and financial policies are central implicit STI policy instruments. With regard to physical infrastructure, public investment is necessary to crowd in

It is important that, in their approach to the design and implementation of STI policy, LDC Governments also adopt a systems approach.

The systems approach to innovation suggests that innovation depends upon a large number of policies and institutions.

Table 18. Explicit and implicit instruments of STI policy	
Explicit policy instruments	**Examples**
Human resource development	General education systems, universities and polytechnics, technical and vocation, education and training, apprenticeship schemes
Science and technology infrastructure	Public research laboratories, research associations, research grants, technology centres
Information	Networks, advisor centres, consultancy services, specialist libraries, databases
Technology import policy	FDI policy, licences
Implicit policy instruments	**Examples**
Physical infrastructure	Power, roads, communication
Direct financial support	Grants, subsidies, loans, provisions of equipment or services, loan guarantees
Indirect financial support	Schemes encouraging investment in innovation, venture capital
Trade	Trade agreements, tariffs, currency regulation
Public procurement	Central or local government purchasing and contracts, R&D contracts
Taxation	Company, personal, indirect and payroll taxation, tax allowances
Regulation	Patents, regulations (e.g., in environmental control), inspectorates, monopoly and anti-trust legislation
Public enterprise	Innovation by publicly-owned industries, use of these as pioneering facilities, establishment of new industries
Political	Planning, regional policies, honours and awards for innovation, encouragement of mergers or joint ventures
Public services	Procurement, maintenance, supervision, and innovation in public services such as telecommunications, transport and health care

Source: Based on Dodgson and Bessant (1996).

private sector investment and innovation. But innovation is a risky process which often involves capital investment and resource mobilization. Access to finance and adequate financial incentives are conditions without which innovation will not take place. In this regard, development banks are particularly important at early stages of a catch-up process and venture capital funds become important later. A variety of fiscal policies are used to stimulate pioneer investments, including tax holidays, accelerated depreciation allowances, investment tax credits, duty-free imports of capital goods and reduced capital goods. Moreover, beyond measures to ensure that entrepreneurs have access to finance — which might involve, for example, special agencies for SMEs or even the establishment of technology banks for bigger projects — pioneer investors can benefit from credit subsidies or loan guarantees, which partially socialize risks.

Access to finance and adequate financial incentives are conditions without which innovation will not take place.

Trade policy is also important for the innovation process. In the classic case of technology acquisition in the Republic of Korea, protectionist measures using temporary tariff barriers were combined with export promotion measures to support initial acquisition of technology and implementation of production and then to encourage upgrading (Kim, 1980). More recently, there are important lessons for LDCs from the cases of Viet Nam and Mauritius and a number of other successful developing countries which have adopted a gradual approach to trade liberalization. Competition policy also matters, and policy may be designed to achieve a balance between the beneficial effects of competitive pressures together with those arising from coordination. Thus, the creation of dynamic and innovative clusters of economic activity is now regarded as a critical feature of innovation policies in many countries. Regulation policy, in particular in relation to intellectual property rights (IPRs), is also important, and will be discussed in chapter 3. Public procurement can be a powerful source of demand for innovation and public sector enterprises can play a role in stimulating innovation. This can occur, for example, in the example which public service organizations set in their innovative practices. Sometimes, too, Governments may have to set up demonstration enterprises, which can show the viability and profitability of new activities. The activity of the Chilean Economic Development Agency (CORFO) and Fundación Chile all exemplify this.

Trade policy is also important for the innovation process.

3. Old industrial policy versus new innovation policy

Articulating this array of instruments of STI policy in a way which stimulates firms and farms to undertake innovation, in the sense of introducing products and production processes which are new to them, is a complex task. In the past, explicit technology policies were often implemented as part of an industrial policy which sought to develop strategic sectors through a combination of tariff protection, direct subsidies and prohibitions on certain kinds of technology transfer. These policies worked well in some successful East Asia countries, where firms were subject to performance criteria or effective monitoring in line with specified development targets (see Amsden, 2001). But in many other cases, industrial policy – and the associated technology policy – became hostage to special interest groups and resulted in wasted scarce resources. Nevertheless, as noted earlier in this chapter, there has been a revival of interest in industrial policy in recent years. The new industrial policy is very different from the old industrial policy, in that it focuses on promoting entrepreneurship and innovation through a mixed, market-based model with the Government and private sector working closely together. This new approach to industrial policy can offer significant insights for Governments in the design and implementation of STI policies, which are relevant not only within manufacturing, but more generally in agriculture, industry and services.

The new industrial policy which focuses on promoting entrepreneurship and innovation through a mixed, market-based model with the Government and private sector working closely together can offer significant insights for Governments in the design and implementation of STI policies.

In the new industrial policy — which is sometimes renamed an entrepreneurial policy or an innovation policy — the State acts as a facilitator of learning. The private sector is perceived as the main agent of change. But the Government facilitates the process of entrepreneurial search and discovery for viable new economic activities (see Rodrik, 2004; Kuznetsov and Sabel, 2005). There are significant risks involved, which implies the need for a partnership and synergies with the public sector to socialize risks. Coordinated action is also often necessary, as returns from the investment of one entrepreneur depend on investments in other sectors. The state catalyzes and coordinates private investment and innovation through market-based incentives aimed at reducing risks and sharing benefits.

This approach to STI policy has a number of features. First, it is based on a strategic vision of national priorities for economic and technological development, which must be elaborated within the broader context of social and economic objectives.

Second, Government policy is directed towards addressing systemic failures which occur in knowledge accumulation and technology development. Important sources of market failure – incomplete appropriability, uncertainty and indivisibilities — have long been recognized in processes of scientific research (Arrow, 1962). But the systems approach to innovation draws attention to wider systems failures in both market and non-market institutions. The most basic one is the low level of firm capabilities. But low levels of non-market interactions between actors in the system may also contribute to poor innovative performance. Against this background, public action should seek to enhance the performance of the market system and to create the conditions needed to ensure that the economic system achieves socially desirable goals which would be unobtainable through market forces alone. Such socially desirable goals might include the endogenization of certain technological activities (such as R&D or training in design and engineering) within private firms, or the promotion of economic diversification so that the economy is not locked into unstable economic structures which do not generate sufficient job opportunities. For countries at the earliest stages of the catch-up process, the case for public action is particularly strong. There are various system failures:

- Investment and innovation are discouraged by fundamental uncertainty. The costs of investment and innovation are high but benefits are uncertain and come later.

- Investment and innovation are also discouraged when all costs are borne by the firm itself but externalities mean that others gain part of the benefits.

- There are also major coordination risks when the profitability of investment and innovation by one economic agent depends on other agents also undertaking investment.

Third, government policy should play a catalytic role in the sense that policies should over time increasingly stimulate market forces to promote innovation and learning. Such policies have been called "market-stimulating" technology policies (Lall and Teubal, 1998: 1382). They encompass measures to stimulate the development of markets for technology support services.

Fourth, technology policies should encompass a mixture of functional, horizontal and vertical policies (ibid., 1370). Functional policies are intended to improve the working of markets economy-wide, in particular in factor markets, without favouring particular sectors or activities. Vertical policies are sectoral-specific, and seek to promote technological learning and innovation within particular sectors. Horizontal policies are concerned with promoting generic

---

In the new industrial policy — which is sometimes renamed an entrepreneurial policy or an innovation policy — the State acts as a facilitator of learning.

Government policy is directed towards addressing systemic failures which occur in knowledge accumulation and technology development.

Government policy should play a catalytic role in the sense that policies should over time increasingly stimulate market forces to promote innovation and learning.

technological learning and innovation activities within firms that are socially desirable and cross-sectoral (Teubal 1996).

Finally, incentives and public institutions which promote learning and innovation should be carefully designed to ensure their effectiveness. Rodrik (2004) summarizes a number of good practices as follows:

- Incentives should be provided only to activities which are new to the national economy (that is, pioneer activities) and which thus fosters diversification.

- There should be clear benchmarks/criteria of success and failure, and winners should be rewarded and losers abandoned.

- There must be a built-in sunset clause; thus, public support will be withdrawn after an appropriate amount of time has elapsed.

- Public support should target activities (such as learning design and engineering skills), not sectors, and although these activities may be sector-specific, they should be cross-cutting as far as possible.

- Any activities that are subsidized must have a clear potential of providing spillovers and demonstration effects.

- Support measures should be designed, implemented and monitored by agencies with demonstrated competence.

- Such agencies should be politically accountable and closely monitored.

- The agencies must maintain clear lines of communication with the private sector.

- Mistakes will be made, so transparency is important.

- Support measures must be adaptable to take account of the evolution of the industries concerned.·

STI policies in LDCs need to be founded on a strategic vision for national economic development and integrated within their national development strategies.

D. Applying the catch-up concept in an LDC context: Typical learning and innovation trajectories

The underlying strategic objective of policymakers should be to promote technological catch-up with more technologically advanced countries.

STI policies in LDCs need to be founded on a strategic vision for national economic development and integrated within their national development strategies. In general terms, such strategies will involve concerted efforts to increase domestic value-added, productivity and international competitiveness by increasing the knowledge content of economic activity and to promote diversification through learning and innovation. But this Report argues that the underlying strategic objective of policymakers should be to promote technological catch-up with more technologically advanced countries.

The focus on technological catch-up as a basic objective can help policymakers because "the "gap" with the state of technology in leader countries helps define the capabilities that are needed and the direction in which resources should be allocated" (Arnold and Bell, 2001:19). But policy analyses of the catch-up process have gone further and identified typical trajectories of learning and innovation which occur during the catch-up process. This is particularly important for LDCs, as catch-up is a process which takes time and involves cumulative learning in which earlier, simpler capabilities and activities provide the basis for developing more advanced capabilities and activities. An important lesson from successful experience is that development strategies should adopt this step-by-step process, and STI policies which are an integral part of such strategies should evolve during the process of technological catch-up as business capabilities and domestic knowledge systems develop and as the structure of the national economy changes. The typical learning and innovation trajectories during catch-up provide the basis for identifying how strategic priorities, incentives and institutions of STI policy can change over time as technological catch-up occurs.

In broad terms, analysts have identified two different stages of the catch-up process: (a) an early catch-up stage in which simple technologies are adopted in mature low-tech, and medium-tech industries; and (b) a late catch-up stage in which more complex technologies are adopted in medium and high tech industries which are in a consolidation phase where process technology is still changing rapidly (see Kim and Dahlman, 1992; Pack, 2000; Amsden and Chu, 2003). The late catch-up stage is relevant for countries which have already established simple industries but do not operate at the world technological frontier and no longer can compete on the basis of low wages and unskilled labour.

The typical learning and innovation trajectories during catch-up provide the basis for identifying how strategic priorities, incentives and institutions of STI policy can change over time as technological catch-up occurs.

The two stages of the catch-up process are distinguished by the complexity of the types of industries which are developing. However, by focusing on individual industries within each stage, analysts have gone further and identified three broad phases of learning and innovation through which a new sector develops within a country. These are: firstly, the initiation of production by importing foreign technology and implementing production; secondly, local diffusion of new products and processes as more firms adopt the technology; and thirdly, industrial upgrading through incremental technological improvements to process and product design, and also associated marketing improvements. For some industries, such industrial upgrading is associated with a shift from producing for local markets to producing for export markets. This three-phase sequence was initially observed by Kim (1980) and has been found to apply in a range of industries in East Asia, such as garments, machine tools and motorcycles (Otsuka, 2006) (see chart 8). It should be noted that the phases can overlap somewhat and that they "are not necessarily sequential" (Kim and Dahlman, 1992). However, successful assimilation of foreign technologies within a country involves all three phases — initial implementation by pioneer investors, local diffusion and upgrading.

Chart 8. Phases of development of an industry during catch-up

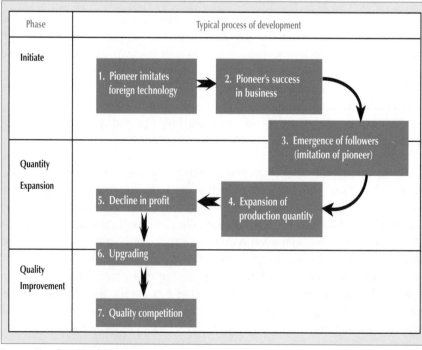

Source: Based on Otsuka (2006).

From a policy perspective, what is important is that appropriate policies to promote technological learning and innovation are different during the early stage of the catch-up process from the late stage, and different policy measures are required to promote initial acquisition of foreign technology, local diffusion and upgrading. How policy does and should change over time during the catch-up process has been most fully elaborated by Linsu Kim on the basis of the case of the Republic of Korea (Kim 1980; Westphal, Kim and Dahlman, 1985; Kim and Dahlman, 1992), and by Morris Teubal, who has sought to generalize on the basis of Israel's experience (Avnimelech and Teubal, 2006, 2008 forthcoming; Sercovitch and Teubal, 2007). Box 2 summarizes how policy changed from the early to the late part of the catch-up process in the Republic of Korea.

The assimilation and absorption of existing technologies involve costs and risks, and their success depends on technological efforts of various kinds and the development of various technological capabilities at the level of the firm and the farm. For agriculture, learning involves inventive adaptation of material inputs to local ecological conditions, often blending knowledge and techniques from elsewhere with traditional knowledge. For industry and services, learning is required to develop tacit technological know-how. Tacit knowledge develops through training, experience and watching. Such tacit knowledge is important because various adaptations are required in establishing and operating new facilities. The development of firm-level capabilities and support systems is thus vital for successful assimilation of foreign technology.[3]

Analysis within East Asia has indicated that, in the early stages of catch-up, the development of production and investment capabilities at the firm level is vital.

Analysis within East Asia has indicated that, in the early stages of catch-up, the development of production and investment capabilities at the firm level is vital (see table 19). As Dahlman, Ross-Larson and Westphal (1987: 774) succinctly put it: "The central issue of technologically developing countries is not acquiring the capability to invent products and processes. It is acquiring the capability to use existing technology — to produce more efficiently, to establish better production facilities, and to use the experience gained in production and investment to adapt and improve the technology in use. This requires technical and operating

Table 19. Elements of production and investment capability
Production capability
Production management - to oversee the operation of established facilities
Production engineering - to provide the information required to optimize the operation of established facilities, including:
• Raw material control - to sort and grade inputs, seek improved inputs • Production scheduling - to coordinate production processes across products and facilities • Quality control - to monitor conformance with product standards and upgrade • Troubleshooting - to overcome problems encountered in the course of operation • Adaptations of processes and products - to respond to changing circumstances and to increase productivity
Repair and maintenance of physical capital - according to regular schedule or when needed
Marketing - to find and develop uses for possible outputs and to channel outputs to markets
Investment capability
Manpower training - to impart skills and abilities of all kinds
Pre-investment feasibility studies - to identify possible projects and to ascertain prospects for viability under alternative design concepts

Project execution - to establish or expand facilities, including:
• Project management - to organize and oversee the activities involved in project execution
• Project engineering - to provide the information needed to make technology operational in a particular setting, including:
  - Detailed studies - to make tentative choices among design alternatives
  - Basic engineering - to supply the core technology in terms of process flows, material and energy balances, specifications of principal equipment, plant layout
  - Detailed engineering - to supply the peripheral technology in terms of complete specifications for all physical capital, architectural and engineering plans, construction and equipment installation specifications
• Procurement - to choose, coordinate and supervise hardware suppliers and construction contractors
• Embodiment in physical capital - to accomplish site preparation, construction, plant erection, manufacture of machinery and equipment
• Start-up of operations - to attain predetermined norms

Source: Westphal, Kim and Dahlman (1985).

Box 2. The evolution of technology policy during catch-up: the case of the Republic of Korea

The Republic of Korea has achieved a phenomenal rate of economic growth and poverty reduction through rapid capital accumulation and technological change associated with employment expansion and rising labour productivity. Technology policies were adopted to accelerate the acquisition of technological capabilities. These policies sought to influence the supply of technology and the demand for technology and to lubricate the linkages between supply and demand. The policies, and their effectiveness, evolved over time in the course of continuous technological change.

During the early stage of catch-up, when domestic firms started developing technological capabilities in relatively simple industries with mature technologies, the most important policies for technology acquisition were implicit policies: both trade policy and financial policy stimulated demand for technology. Trade policy involved a combination of tariff protection to stimulate domestic business start-ups and export promotion to push firms to become internationally competitive, as well as some protection for the domestic machinery industry to enable capital goods to be imported at international prices. The financing of purchases by supplier's credits which carried lower rates of interest than those on the domestic market also increased the attractiveness of capital goods imports. Another factor that was basic to the whole process of technology acquisition, diffusion and upgrading was heavy early investment in human resource development, in addition to encouraging the emergence of large firms (chaebols) which could take advantage of economies of scale as well as take the lead in developing technological capabilities in successively more complex industries.

Public research institutes were set up but played a minimal role in technology development: rather, they helped local firms strengthen their bargaining power in relation to foreign technology suppliers. The Government also encouraged the development of local consulting engineering firms by stipulating that the major contractors for all engineering projects should, if possible, be local firms, with foreign partners as minor participants. In the early stages of catch-up, these engineering service firms did not play a major role in the local diffusion of technology, although inter-firm mobility of personnel was important. The scientific and technological information centre set up by the Government was not very well utilized either, as mature technologies were easily imitated through reverse engineering. The Government also took initiatives to strengthen public-sector research and development by means of tax incentives and preferential financing. However, these measures were broadly ineffective during the early stage of catch-up, as the major technological task was to reverse-engineer mature foreign products. The Ministry of Science and Technology was created, but "its activities were largely ignored by action-oriented ministries that shaped industrial policies in promoting production and exports in labour-intensive mature industries" (Kim and Dahlman, 1992: 441).

In short, in the early stages, "in the absence of demand for technological change, the direct instruments to strengthen the supply of technological capability and to provide linkages [between supply and demand] were ineffective" (Kim and Dahlman, 1992: 445): indirect technology promotion measures, which stimulated demand, were more important.

During the later stages of catch-up, from the 1980s onwards, when firms from the Republic of Korea were importing more complex technologies in medium- and high-tech industries that were in a consolidation phase in the sense that process technologies were still changing rapidly, this situation changed. Policies affecting the domestic supply of technology, and in particular the Republic of Korea's own research and development programme, assumed more importance, and policies to stimulate demand, increase supply and link the two all worked effectively together.

The demand side of technology acquisition and upgrading was stimulated through government procurement. The Government liberalized foreign direct investment and foreign licensing, put more pressure on domestic firms to increase competitiveness through gradual trade liberalization and revised intellectual property laws to pre-empt imitative product development. The Government also established an effective technology transfer centre and technical information centres, which became increasingly popular with users. Measures to promote the development of capital goods producers were also taken (quantitative restrictions, import licensing and domestic content requirements) and this induced local producers to develop technological capabilities to meet the increasing demand for capital goods. Technology extension services were also important for the diffusion of best practices, particularly to small and medium-sized enterprises.

The Government of the Republic of Korea also actively promoted R&D activities at this stage of catch-up, and achieved a major increase in private-sector R&D efforts. The instruments used by the Government included: (a) tax incentives (reduced tariffs on imports of R&D equipment; the deduction of annual non-capital R&D expenditure and the cost of human resource development from taxable income; accelerated depreciation on industrial R&D facilities; and a tax credit for investment in R&D facilities); (b) preferential financing for R&D activities (from a technology fund within the National Investment Fund, the Industrial Development Fund, the Korea Development Bank's Technology Development Fund, industrial technology funds earmarked specifically for automation and the development of new material, and the Small and Medium Industry Promotion Fund); (c) direct R&D grants; and (d) venture capital creation. In 1987, preferential financing accounted for 64 per cent of total expenditure on research and development in the manufacturing sector.

Box table 1 summarizes the different roles of the private sector, universities and government research institutes in R&D activities through the early to late stages of catch-up.

Source: Kim and Dahlman (1992); Kim and Yi (1997).

Box 2 (contd.)

Box table 1. Evolution of R&D activities in the Republic of Korea			
	Initial stage	**Intermediate stage**	**Knowledge-intensive stage**
Business R&D	• Little R&D investment • Imitative reverse-engineering • Limited engineering	• Formative stage • Advanced reverse engineering • Development and engineering	• Dominant role in the nation's R&D • Globalization of R&D • Research, development and engineering
University R&D	• Minimal role • Undergraduate teaching oriented	• Formative stage • Informal links with industry	• Basic research being strengthened • Stronger formal links with industry
Government research institute R&D	• Strengthening industry's bargaining power in technology transfer • Training experienced researchers • Reverse engineering of advanced technologies • Leading role in the nation's R&D	• Expansion of government-supported research institutes network • Incubating experienced researchers • Leading role in national R&D policies	• Leading role in national R&D projects • Technical support for SMEs

Source: Kim and Yi (1997).

capabilities and also, in particular, design and engineering skills (see Bell, 2007). Successful latecomer firms successively develop more complex technological capabilities and associated organizational and marketing skills.[4] This begins with simple assembly operation and graduates towards more complex tasks such as process adaptation and R&D as the firm moves closer towards the technology frontier of leading firms (Hobday, 1995). Relationships with foreign buyers can be an important source of technological learning. In such cases, successful firms graduate over time from original equipment manufacture, to given production specification, to own-design manufacture and finally own-brand manufacture (table 20)[5].

Over time, technological development through catch-up depends not simply on the deepening of these capabilities at the enterprise level, but also on the widening of these capabilities through their development and application in an increasing variety of economic activities. Typically, as a poor economy gets richer, its economy is likely to become more diversified through the introduction of new sectors of economic activity. Recent research has shown that there is a strong association between the level of sectoral diversification within an economy and its level of per capita income (Imbs and Waczairg, 2003).

Over time, technological development through catch-up depends not simply on the deepening of these capabilities at the enterprise level, but also on the widening of these capabilities through their development and application in an increasing variety of economic activities.

In this process, the relative importance of agriculture generally declines as economies develop. There are multiple patterns of economic change. However,

Table 20. Learning trajectories of latecomer firms in East Asia (1950s–1990s): process technology, product technology and marketing					
1950s–1990s – Simple activites → → → → → → → → **Complex activites**					
Marketing	Simple OEM/sub-contracting → → → → → ODM → → → OBM				
Process technology	Simple assembly	Process adaptation	Incremental improvements	Process development	Applied research	Process R&D
Product technology	Assessment selection	Reverse engineering	Prototype development	Design for manufacturing	New design	Product R&D

Source: Hobday, 1995.

Note: OEM is original equipment manufacture; ODM is own-design manufacture; OBM is own-brand manufacture.

accumulated capabilities and experience enable the emergence of more technologically complex and knowledge-intensive activities. Moreover, there is also a strong directionality to the widening of technological capabilities which arises because of dynamic inter-sectoral linkages. These may reflect technological interdependencies among sectors of economic activity in which technological capabilities in one sector can be used in another sector. More important than this, however, is the stimulus for innovation which comes through backward and forward linkages, in which technological change which lowers prices or improves quality in one sector opens new profitable investment and innovation opportunities in the linked activities.

One such development trajectory has been identified in relation to the development of clusters of productive activity associated with the development of natural resources. This sequence of structural change may develop from agricultural farming activities, forestry or mining. The typical pattern of development of a mature production cluster has been described as having four stages:

- *Phase 1:* The natural resource is extracted and exported with minimum essential processing. Inputs, machinery and engineering services are all imported.

- *Phase 2:* Processing export activities are initiated. Import substitution with local production of some inputs and equipment is begun (typically under license for the domestic market). Domestic production engineering capabilities develop.

- *Phase 3:* Exporting of goods and services originally produced for import substitution purposes (for example, basic machinery for undemanding markets) is begun. More sophisticated processed goods are exported. Engineering services are of domestic origin.

- *Phase 4:* Processed goods of great variety and complexity, inputs and machinery for demanding markets, design engineering services and specialized consultancy services are all exported.

Another typical pattern of structural change which has been identified involves a transition from primary and light industry to large-scale processing industries (such as steel, cement and petrochemicals), the emergence of a capital-goods sector and its transformation into a key sector, and the emergence of high-technology industry (Justman and Teubal, 1991). These three types of structural change are not necessarily sequential or all relevant for small countries. A capital-goods sector can emerge from primary production, and not necessarily stem from the demands of large-scale processing industries. However, the development of the latter provides a strong stimulus to the former. The transformation of the capital goods into a key sector occurs when capital goods industries become the locus of accumulated knowledge and experience in a particular group of technologies, accelerating their diffusion across industries. The emergence of high-tech industries requires more complex technological capabilities than the other two phases, and it is thus likely to emerge after strong engineering capabilities have been established and these skills built upon.

The emergence of high-tech industries requires more complex technological capabilities than the other two phases, and it is thus likely to emerge after strong engineering capabilities have been established and these skills built upon.

E. Applying the catch-up concept in an LDC context: Some strategic priorities

Policies to promote technological learning and innovation need to be adapted to the specific context of LDCs. They are in the early stage of a process of technological catch-up and are generally at the start of the learning and innovation trajectories which typically occur during catch-up. This has particular implications for both strategic priorities and instruments of STI policy.

Technological catch-up will require a pro-growth macroeconomic framework which can ensure adequate financial resources for sustained technological learning and innovation, as well as a pro-investment climate which stimulates demand for investment. Technological catch-up in LDCs will also require the co-evolution of improvement in physical infrastructure, human capital and financial systems, along with improved technological capabilities within enterprises and more effective knowledge systems supporting the supply of knowledge and linkages between creators and users of knowledge. Improving physical infrastructure, human capital and financial systems is absolutely vital because many LDCs are at the very beginning of the catch-up process and have major deficiencies in each of these areas.

The following statistics stand out from the *Least Developed Countries Report 2006*:

- Basic human capital is very weak in the LDCs. The average length of schooling for the adult population in 2000 was three years. This is less than half the 2000 average level for other developing countries (7.1 years) and is less than the level of schooling was in other developing countries in 1960. Although the level of formal education in LDCs is almost double the 1980 level, the education gap between LDCs and other developing countries is larger than it was in 1960. In 2002, 34 per cent of the total population aged 15–24 and 41 per cent of the female population aged 15–24 was illiterate.

- Physical infrastructure necessary for modern and mass production is also very weak in the LDCs. In 2003, the level of telephone mainlines and fixed and mobile phones per capita was 11 per cent of the level in other developing countries and 3 per cent of the level in OECD countries. In 2002, electricity consumption per capita in the LDCs was 7 per cent of the level in other developing countries and 1.6 per cent of the level in OECD countries. Only 16 per cent of the LDC population is estimated to have had access to electricity that year, compared with 53 per cent in other developing countries and 99 per cent in OECD countries.

- The domestic financial systems are also very weak and characterized by dualistic and segmented structures. The formal financial system is not working to support long-term productive investment in most LDCs. Between 1980 and 2003, a period in which most LDCs undertook financial liberalization, domestic credit to the private sector stagnated at around 14 to 15 per cent of GDP. In contrast to other developing countries, domestic credit as a share of GDP almost doubled, from 30 per cent to 60 per cent, over the same period.

Without improvement in these foundations for development, it is difficult to see how technological change will take place. But it is important that LDC Governments and their development partners go beyond this. In this regard, it

Policies to promote technological learning and innovation need to be adapted to the specific context of LDCs. They are in the early stage of a process of technological catch-up and are generally at the start of the learning and innovation trajectories which typically occur during catch-up.

Improving physical infrastructure, human capital and financial systems is absolutely vital because many LDCs are at the very beginning of the catch-up process and have major deficiencies in each of these areas.

But it is important that LDC Governments and their development partners go beyond this.

is possible to identify six major strategic priorities for LDCs at the start and early stages of catch-up:

1. Increase agricultural productivity, in particular by promoting a Green Revolution in basic staples.

2. Promote the formation and growth of domestic business firms.

3. Increase the absorptive capacity of the domestic knowledge system.

4. Leverage more learning from international trade and FDI.

5. Foster agricultural growth linkages and natural resource-based production clusters.

6. Upgrade export activities.

In order to ensure poverty reduction, strategic priorities of STI policy should be articulated with a view to promoting economy-wide expansion of productive employment opportunities.

In order to ensure poverty reduction, these strategic priorities should be articulated with a view to promoting economy-wide expansion of productive employment opportunities. This means that there is need for technological change in both agricultural and non-agricultural activities. Attention should also be given to innovation in non-tradable activities as well as tradables. As Sachs (2004a, 2004b) has pointed out, the choice of more labour-intensive techniques is much easier for non-tradables than for tradables, as the latter have to be internationally competitive.

1. PROMOTING AGRICULTURAL PRODUCTIVITY GROWTH IN BASIC STAPLES

Technological advances in small-scale agricultural production and trade are often critical in initiating a catch-up process.

Agricultural activities are the major source of livelihood in most LDCs and also constitute a significant portion of GDP. Sustainable agricultural intensification is becoming a necessity in more and more LDCs, as rural population density rises and the opportunities for agricultural growth through expansion of the agricultural land area are becoming exhausted. The productivity gaps with other countries also indicate that there are major potentials for income generation through agricultural productivity growth. Technological advances in small-scale agricultural production and trade are often critical in initiating a catch-up process. In this regard, promoting a Green Revolution in basic staples should be a top priority of STI policy in many LDCs.

Promoting a Green Revolution in basic staples should be a top priority of STI policy in many LDCs.

As has been seen from past experience, the first stage in promoting a Green Revolution should be to establish the basics for agricultural productivity growth (see chart 9). These include: investing in rural physical infrastructure, particularly roads and (where appropriate) irrigation systems; establishing adaptive and experimental research stations; investing in extension; and, where necessary, pursuing land reforms (Dorward et al., 2004). After establishing the basics for a Green Revolution, policies should widen the uptake of the new technology. In order to do so, it is necessary to kick-start markets through government interventions to enable farmers access to seasonal finance and seasonal inputs and output markets at low risk and low cost. This often involves subsidies and also special agencies which provide a bundle of services. The importance of government interventions to kick-start markets is evident in the historical experience of the Green Revolution. However, once farmers become used to the new technologies, when volumes of credit and input demand build up, then the private sector can take over. Such state withdrawal should take place in late catch-up stage, though the Government may start to prepare for this in the later phases of early catch-up.

Getting the agricultural knowledge and information system right is a key ingredient of establishing the basics. It is important that LDCs in very early catch-

Chart 9. Policy phases to support agricultural transformation in favoured areas

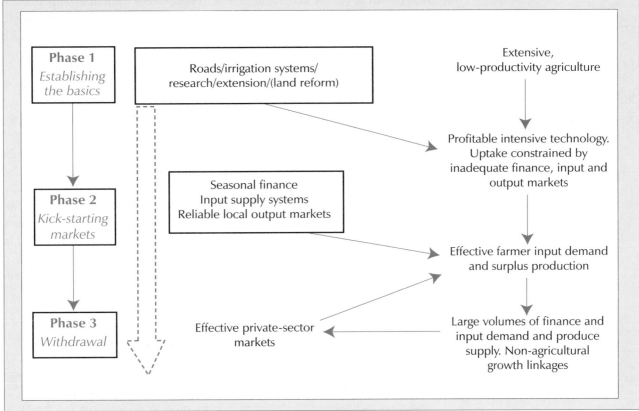

Source: Dorward et al. (2004).

up phase not only develop their adaptive research capabilities for agriculture, but also seek to capitalize on the potentials of the traditional knowledge of farmers. Public research efforts within national agricultural research systems should thus seek to be more closely integrated with farmers' needs and experience. Adaptive research should include development of modern varieties which are suitable for diverse ecosystems and can be integrated into local farming systems. This has in the past proved difficult in Africa. But Otsuka (2004) suggests that it may be possible to promote an organic Green Revolution in East Africa based on organic fertilizer (manure and compost) through keeping cross-bred dairy cows and goats and by using trees with nitrogen-fixing capacity for nutritious fodder. He also suggests that the New Rice for Africa (NERICA), a primarily upland rice, could be developed if rice research programmes were strengthened in West Africa and East and Southern Africa. These programmes could develop second-generation upland NERICA, which would be resistant to pests and diseases, as well as lowland NERICA. Byerlee and Eicher (1997) also indicate the importance of revitalizing maize research capacity for re-energizing Africa's emerging maize revolution. In many countries, agricultural extension systems were expanded through donor support but, as this support has declined, it has been impossible to sustain these systems. This has led to experimentation with different public-private sector mixes in the delivery of extension services. The effectiveness of these experiments is a critical issue which needs close attention (Chapman and Tripp, 2003).

It is important that LDCs in very early catch-up phase not only develop their adaptive research capabilities for agriculture, but also seek to capitalize on the potentials of the traditional knowledge of farmers.

Addressing coordination failures which arise in adoption of new commercial practices requires institutional innovations. In the past, commodity marketing boards were the key institutional innovation which provided multiple functions. They obviously had numerous deficiencies. However, current agricultural market liberalization policies have been premature in most LDCs. They have sought to dynamize rural economies before domestic markets for credit, inputs and technology are adequately established, and even, in some cases before the basic physical infrastructure, research and extension efforts have taken place. The challenge which many LDCs now face is to devise new institutional innovations which can enable the spread of the Green Revolution and which do not fall into the traps of the old marketing boards, but also fill the institutional vacuum which many poor farmers and low-density and remoter regions face.

Addressing coordination failures which arise in adoption of new commercial practices requires institutional innovations.

Broad-based agricultural productivity growth in basic staples — a Green Revolution — is the surest base for substantial poverty reduction. But an important condition for success for such a Green Revolution is that there is a market for increased output. Given the rising rates of urbanization in many LDCs, there is a potential domestic market. However, there is also an increasing tendency for food consumption in LDCs to be met by food imports, including subsidized food imports from rich countries. It may be necessary therefore for LDCs to consider temporary protection in agricultural sectors against subsidized food imports. This should only be temporary and designed to enable the build-up of competitiveness by domestic farmers and the wide uptake of Green Revolution technologies. In successful cases, for example with the introduction of modern varieties of rice in Viet Nam, countries have moved from being a net food importer, to being self-sufficient, to being able to meet domestic demand and also export.

2. FORMATION AND GROWTH OF DOMESTIC BUSINESS FIRMS

Whereas LDC Governments recognize the importance of promoting technical change in agriculture, there is a general failure to recognize the importance of promoting technological learning and innovation in non-agricultural activities.

Whereas LDC Governments recognize the importance of promoting technical change in agriculture, there is a general failure to recognize the importance of promoting technological learning and innovation in non-agricultural activities. But this is an important aspect of sustained development trajectories. Moreover, it is becoming critical in the LDCs because of the growing non-agricultural labour force and the concomitant need to generate productive employment outside agriculture.

At the start of the catch-up process, business firm formation is critical for initiating technological learning and innovation.

At the start of the catch-up process, business firm formation is critical for initiating technological learning and innovation. Business firms are the basic locus of non-agricultural technological learning and innovation, and a major problem facing many LDCs is the lack of such firms. The business sector is characterized by a missing middle. At one end of the spectrum, there are a multitude of informal microenterprises, most of which are characterized by the use of basic and traditional technologies, and cater to the basic consumption needs of restricted and relatively small local markets. At the other end of the spectrum are a few large firms, which are mainly capital intensive, resource based, import dependent or export assembly oriented. These firms are often wholly or minority-owned foreign affiliates or state-owned enterprises. They are not large by international standards but they dominate the business landscape in most LDCs. Between these extremes, there are very few formal-sector SMEs and those small firms which exist do not tend to grow into medium and large firms (UNCTAD, 2006a).

Many informal microenterprises only enable people to subsist. But there are some more dynamic petty activities and their transformation into organized small-scale enterprises can be achieved through "upgrading skills and managerial capacities and improving their managerial capacities and improving their systemic competitiveness through a set of converging affirmative actions such as preferential access to credit, technology and markets" (Sachs, 2004b: 14). Essentially, the key capabilities which are required are building core competences, in particular operating, craft and technician capabilities, as well as business management capabilities. In this regard, technical and vocational education and training can play a key role.

Collective entrepreneurship can also be a powerful mechanism for both diffusing and upgrading best practices. This can build on existing collective entrepreneurship practices, such as saving and credit rotation associations, or sectoral and territorial groupings of producers and traders who seek economies of scale, e.g. by sharing capital equipment. How collaborative action in the fields of technology, design and marketing can be promoted is a key issue. The encouragement of clusters of activity, e.g. through public infrastructure provision, is likely to be an important field for public policy.

Collective entrepreneurship can also be a powerful mechanism for both diffusing and upgrading best practices.

It is important to recognize that whilst informal microenterprises provide an important safety net against destitution for many households, investment and innovation are carried out by formal firms. Moreover, large firms are often more innovative than small firms. Thus, beyond encouraging the transformation of microenterprises into small firms, efforts should be made to ensure that those firms can grow. Fostering linkages between large firms and SMEs can be very important for this process.

3. INCREASING THE ABSORPTIVE CAPABILITY OF THE DOMESTIC KNOWLEDGE SYSTEM

The domestic knowledge systems which constitute the technological infrastructure supporting technological learning and innovation are dualistic and segmented. The production activities which create most employment and livelihoods in the LDCs are based on traditional or indigenous knowledge and traditional knowledge systems. These have great potential as a reservoir of creativity, but are largely de-linked from the modern knowledge systems. The latter, like the formal financial institutions, also have major weaknesses, notably: (a) there are weak linkages within the system between different specialized suppliers of knowledge (national laboratories, research institutes, universities, technology transfer agencies, etc.); (b) knowledge creators are de-linked from the local productive apparatus and creating knowledge on the basis of a R&D-centered linear model of innovation rather than responding to demand, which in any case is very weak; (c) the modern knowledge system has often been donor-driven; and (d) modern knowledge systems in LDCs are not well connected with international knowledge systems (UNCTAD, 2006a).

The domestic knowledge systems which constitute the technological infrastructure supporting technological learning and innovation in the LDCs are dualistic and segmented.

Increasing the absorptive capability of domestic knowledge systems requires three major types of policy measure. Firstly, there is a need for education and training which increases the pool of relevant human skills. Secondly, there is a need for incentives to promote the development of technological learning and innovation routines within domestic firms. Thirdly, there is a need for the creation of a set of institutions which increase knowledge linkages among domestic firms, between foreign firms who have invested in LDCs and domestic firms, and between domestic firms and the rest of the world. In the early stage of catch-up, this is likely to involve the creation of specialized, publicly-funded agencies which act as intermediary organizations in various ways, as well as the development of dynamic local clusters of economic activity. However, a long-term goal should be to foster the development of engineering firms, intermediate goods producers and capital goods suppliers. The development of these specialized agents is possible when there is demand for technology services (for example, local technology consultancy firms or engineering contractors).

Increasing the absorptive capacity of domestic knowledge systems is a basic strategic priority.

(a) Human capital and skills

With regard to education and training, it is important that basic skills related to technology use, operation and maintenance, and business management are strengthened. This requires attention to technical and vocational education and training. But advanced human capital is also very weak in the LDCs. In recent years, tertiary enrolment has been only 6 per cent of the population aged 20 to 24, compared with 23 per cent in other developing countries. Within tertiary enrolment, the share of enrolments in science and agriculture is approximately the same as in other developing countries, but the share of engineering enrolments is just over half the level in other developing countries (UNCTAD, 2006a). LDCs need to develop their pool of design and engineering skills. This will require enterprise-based learning as well as formal education.

Outmigration of high-skill workers is also a problem in many LDCs. This issue will be taken up in chapter 4.

It is important that basic skills related to technology use, operation and maintenance, and business management are strengthened.

(b) Financial incentives for learning and innovative investment

The second major area of policy to increase the absorptive capability of the domestic knowledge system is the provision of incentives for technological learning and innovation by domestic firms. This goes beyond basic firm formation. Undertaking innovation is a risky and costly activity, and the technological effort entailed in search, acquisition, introduction and upgrading of technology may entail significant sunk costs. As a result the promotion of technological learning and innovation by domestic firms requires financial resources and incentives. As will be discussed in chapter 3, there are major limits to the relevance of IPRs as an incentive mechanism for innovation in the context of catch-up. Indeed, they may have a damaging effect in discouraging informal mechanisms of technology acquisition. Against this background, other incentive mechanisms are important.

Financial incentives are often necessary to endogenize learning routines and dynamic technological capabilities within firms. These are provided in rich countries for R&D. Moreover, they have been an important instrument in all countries which have successfully pursued a catch-up strategy (see, in particular, Amsden, 2001). They should not be ignored by countries in the early catch-up stage. Such incentives have taken various forms, including credit subsidies, various types of fiscal allowances and matching grants for innovation projects. But it is important that their provision is based on competitions and that they are also linked to achievement of certain technological goals. Moreover, the aim of these incentives should be to endogenize learning routines and innovation capabilities in domestic firms so that the financial support is no longer necessary. Box 3 summarizes some key features of innovation funds operating in Nicaragua.

Financial incentives are often necessary to endogenize learning routines and dynamic technological capabilities within firms.

An important issue is what kinds of projects should be supported this way. This should be related to the capabilities one seeks to develop at the firm level. Whereas R&D in the form of adaptive invention is absolutely vital for agriculture, enterprise-level design and engineering capabilities are much more important during this stage in non-agricultural activities. What matters are capabilities learned through the act of investment. In this regard, financial incentives for pioneer investments may be justified because of their spillover effects.

(c) Increasing linkages in the domestic knowledge system

Whilst the development of the technological capabilities of domestic firms must be the foundation of efforts to increase the absorptive capability of the domestic knowledge system, it is also important to increase linkages among domestic firms, between domestic firms and foreign firms who have undertaken FDI in LDCs, and also between domestic firms and the rest of the world. At the start of catch-up, increasing the linkages in the domestic knowledge system is likely to involve the creation of specialized, publicly-funded agencies, which act as intermediary organizations in various ways, and the promotion of innovative clusters. Later, the

---

Box 3. An Innovation Fund for small and medium-sized enterprises: the Nicaraguan example

Aiming at upgrading domestic innovative capacity and relaxing the constraints faced by small and medium-sized enterprises — notably, high interest rates, short repayment terms and a lack of alternative financing methods — the Nicaraguan Government introduced the Innovation Fund. The Innovation Fund covers three agents: (a) enterprises; (b) technology service providers, such as research and educational institutions and laboratories; and (c) Government policymakers. The relation among these three agents is key to the process of technology diffusion and to the successful working of the fund.

The Innovation Fund is a financing mechanism that provides incentives to SMEs to invest in technological innovations. The incentives, in the form of subsidies, are given to: (a) SMEs (defined as firms with less than 100 employees), where they cover 60 per cent of the cost of the innovation project, up to a maximum of $30,000; (b) associations of up to five SMEs, where they cover 80 per cent of the innovation project, up to a maximum of $100,000; and (c) technological service providers, where they also cover 80 per cent of the innovation project, up to a maximum of $100,000.

The innovation projects financed with the help of these subsidies mainly cover four technology-related areas: (a) technological innovation; (b) innovation in information and communications technologies; (c) organizational innovation; and (d) commercial and market development activities. While the first two areas contain "traditional" innovative activities such as technology upgrading, R&D design, product development, software development and the management of information systems, the remaining two areas cover new technology-related activities that range from new management models and engineering and associated managerial capabilities to technology acquisition, metrology, the implementation of standards, market research, technological monitoring and participation in international technological fairs.

The role of technological service providers is particularly important as they help small and medium-sized enterprises to identify needs and formulate their technology-upgrading proposals, which are then sent to the Government for approval. After the projects have been submitted to the Government for funding, the SMEs contract the necessary services and purchase the necessary technology and submit a request for reimbursement of the costs incurred. The entire process, from planning to reimbursement, takes an average of 9–12 months.

An ex post analysis of the validity and applicability of the Innovation Fund shows that all the SMEs that received financial support developed new products, new markets and quality control measures. They also introduced new information and communications technology equipment and trained their employees, and expected to see their sales increase.

The Nicaraguan experience shows that Governments have the capacity not only to promote technological innovation but also to stimulate the supply of technological services and specialized technical assistance to SMEs. The SMEs themselves displayed two key qualities: dynamism and flexibility.

In view of the role played by technological service providers, there is a need to facilitate the establishment of technological service centres that provide needs-based services to SMEs — including training, quality controls, designing and engineering capabilities and market studies during the preparatory and maturity phases of the domestic technological upgrading process.

Source: Oyanguren, 2007.

---

development of domestic specialized technological agents — engineering firms, machinery producers, business consultancy firms — is important.

Public technology centres can play an important role in both stimulating demand and providing technological services before a commercial market for the provision of such services exists. Such centres should stimulate demand from the private sector for developing technological capabilities and assist search and acquisition of technology. As Justman and Teubal (1995: 266) put it in describing the key role of basic technology infrastructure:

> "At initial stages of the development of a traditional (low-tech or mid-tech) industry there may be neither supply nor demand for essential skills, and a cooperative effort may be necessary to articulate the needs of local industry and to elicit a mutual commitment to a path of progressive development. The role of basic TI [technology infrastructure] is to mediate between the technological needs of the industry and potential sources of supply...[It does so] by providing information and advising local industry regarding the availability of foreign technology...stimulating local demand for foreign technology by helping local industry redefine its needs in terms of possibilities that the new technology offers i.e. 'user-need determination';

It is also important to increase linkages among domestic firms, between domestic firms and foreign firms who have undertaken FDI in LDCs, and also between domestic firms and the rest of the world.

and increasing the effective supply of technology inputs by stimulating investment in adapting them to local needs and promoting local sources of supply (including technical consultants)."

The UNCTAD Centres for Innovation and Enterprise Development provide one example of such agencies (box 4).

One focus of policy action should be to foster the establishment and development of dynamic clusters of firms. Such clusters help to remedy the problem of the "missing middle".

One focus of policy action should be to foster the establishment and development of dynamic clusters of firms. Such clusters help to remedy the problem of the "missing middle". Clustering can be considered a major facilitating factor for a number of subsequent developments, including division of labour and specialization, the emergence of a wide network of suppliers, the appearance of agents who sell to distant national and international markets, the emergence of specialized producer services, the emergence of a pool of specialized and skilled workers, and the formation of business associations. These are the so-called external economies deriving from clustering.

These positive developments in cluster do not necessarily take place automatically. Oyelaran-Oyeyinka and McCormick (2007) study several African clusters, and suggest that, although they are all geographically and sectorally bounded groups of producers, some are continuously learning and innovating, while others appear to be trapped in a pattern of poor markets, low-quality products, and lack of imagination. It is therefore the role of policy to foster the establishment of institutions that favour collective action among the firms and institutions of the cluster. This may include supporting the creation of backward ties with suppliers and subcontractors and forward ties with traders and buyers, or within bilateral horizontal linkages between two or more local producers, through joint marketing of products, joint purchase of inputs, order sharing, common use of specialized equipment, joint product development, and exchange of expertise and market information (Nadvi and Schmitz, 1999).

Marketization of basic technological services and the development of specialized technological agents — engineering firms, intermediate goods producers, machinery producers, business consultancy firms — should be a long-term goal.

Over time, policy should also seek to build domestic markets for the services associated with technology centres as well as spin off commercially viable innovations to a country. This may not be achieved in the early catch-up phase. But marketization of basic technological services and the development of specialized technological agents should be a long-term goal. These agents — engineering firms, intermediate goods producers, machinery producers, business consultancy firms — are very important for facilitating rapid diffusion of knowledge among producers and their local proximity facilitates adaptation and innovation in ongoing operation and in new investments. Dahlman, Ross-Larson and Westphal (1987) identify the emergence of these agents as a key part of the success of newly industrializing economies, and draw the conclusion that, "It is thus necessary to foster an environment that promotes the formation and growth of local technological agents and their interaction with local users of their services so that technological possibilities are matched to local conditions and requirements in an efficient way" (p.773).

4. LEVERAGING MORE LEARNING FROM INTERNATIONAL TRADE AND FDI

As discussed in the previous chapter, international market linkages are not presently functioning well as channels of technological acquisition by domestic firms in the LDCs. Policy action is required to leverage more learning from international trade and FDI. To this end, the following goals should be pursued:

- Strengthening the embeddedness of transnational corporation activity in the domestic economy by stimulating the creation of backward and forward linkages.

Box 4. Centres for Innovation and Enterprise Development

Centres for Innovation and Enterprise Development (CIEDs) represent a novel institutional response to the challenge of promoting innovation in manufacturing firms in developing countries. CIEDs constitute an emerging network of change-generating agencies designed to promote technological innovation in manufacturing SMEs and to stimulate the development of networks for innovation among firms and between firms and local knowledge-producing institutions (universities, R&D institutes, engineering consultancy firms, etc.) In Africa, CIEDs are now operational in Côte d'Ivoire, Ghana, the United Republic of Tanzania, and Zimbabwe.

CIEDs focus mainly on: (a) building and sustaining awareness of the need for innovation; (b) strengthening the ability of firms to identify weaknesses in strategy and operations, as well as bottlenecks in production; and (c) serving as the link between firms and a network of support structures and suppliers who can help firms overcome their problems.

Indigenous small and medium-sized enterprises form the primary clientele of CIEDs. In some cases the latter work with larger firms, especially where such work could promote innovation at the level of small and medium-sized enterprises. CIEDs help their clients to locate appropriate sources of expertise and provide assistance in negotiations and project preparation. Typical projects include: industrial and management audits; work studies and process re-engineering; maintenance management; materials management and sourcing of raw materials, equipment and spare parts; technical training; market analysis for existing or new products; and upgrading product quality to meet local and external market requirements.

The nature of the innovation process — even at the level of the firm — requires very close cooperation between CIEDs and existing business support structures, as well as technology development organizations in each country. At the local level, strategic partnerships will be formed with organizations like Empretec, which have already established strong links with manufacturing enterprises and their associations. Linkages will also be forged with other organizations which have experience in promoting enterprise innovation.

Technology is the main point of departure for engaging with manufacturing firms, and CIEDs work primarily with enterprise-level personnel to generate and implement innovative solutions to problems encountered within firms. Any external inputs from consultants or experts drawn from the science and technology, R&D or other institutions in the country are complementary to efforts within the firms. This is a cardinal principle that distinguishes CIEDs from most other business-development service providers and helps to ensure the sustainability of CIED initiatives.

CIEDs' focus on firms helps to stimulate demand for business development services. As firms begin to define their problems and enhance their ability to identify and implement technological innovation projects, they also begin to recognize those resources which must be sourced externally. This helps to strengthen the market for technical and other business development services and also to ensure that such services respond to the real needs of the firms.

In order to improve the learning experience at firm level, participatory approaches to project identification and implementation are used to the fullest extent possible, to ensure that knowledge acquisition and deployment are maximized within the firm. High-impact and lower-cost projects are tackled first so as to minimize financial burdens on firms. Higher-cost projects are phased in gradually as firms build up their internal knowledge and confidence and hence their capacity to handle more capital-intensive activities.

CIEDs seek to generate a continuous process of analysis and action within their client firms. To this end, they use three diagnostic tools at various stages of their interaction with manufacturing firms. The first of these diagnostic tools, known as a change assessment and screening tool (CAST), is designed to help in the selection of potentially innovative firms. The second and third diagnostic tools, known as a general information-seeking tool (GIST) and an in-depth enterprise assessment system (IDEAS), are used to assist firms in analysing their problems and identifying possible solutions.

Source: UNCTAD, 2002.

- Fostering development of SMEs so as to enable them to supply both transnational corporations active in the domestic market and export markets, and to integrate into global value chains.

- Using investment projects in natural resource-based activities (particularly mining) as growth poles by diversifying economic activity vertically and horizontally around one given project.·

These goals can be achieved through a series of policy mechanisms, including:

- Negotiating with transnational corporations for commitments on minimum levels of local sourcing. This should be decided on a case-by-case basis, taking into account the supply capacity of domestic firms. In some cases, such

Policy action is required to leverage more learning from international trade and FDI.

efforts to establish local sourcing are pursued by transnational corporations themselves or by pressure from international financial institutions that co-finance projects.

- Negotiating with transnational corporation objectives of local further processing of primary products, particularly in the case of natural resource extraction.

- Favouring the establishment of joint ventures with domestic firms when transnational corporations establish themselves in the countries.

- Negotiating with transnational corporations on minimum levels of employment of nationals, so as to foster domestic skills accumulation.

- Imposing training levies and establishing training centres, particularly those related to clusters centering on a given type of activity.

- Providing technical assistance to small firms and farms, in order to raise their awareness on standards (technical, environmental, hygienic, etc.) so as to enable producers to meet higher requirements from domestic and international downstream buyers. This can be done at the cluster level and through collective institutions and joint actions, involving small producers together with buyers, chain leaders and transnational corporations.

- Using public procurement as a means of fostering SME development.

- Supporting the development of national standards infrastructures, especially for certification and testing.

- Establishing stakeholder coordination councils to facilitate strong and horizontal interfaces between all critical economic agents (SMEs, other domestic firms, transnational corporations, and training and research institutions) in the development of industries to connect and coordinate all critical economic agents relevant to upgrading and improving the competitiveness of their activities.

Access to capital goods should be facilitated by reducing their total cost to domestic firms.

Access to capital goods should be facilitated by reducing their total cost to domestic firms. This can be achieved through trade and fiscal policy mechanisms (e.g. tax rebates, accelerated depreciation, etc.). These types of measures have been part of the mining code reforms adopted in several African countries (see chapter 1, section B of this Report) and should be extended to other sectors, including industry and agriculture.

The increasing share of developing country partners in flows of both trade and FDI of LDCs points to another area of intervention for the purpose of increasing technological capabilities of LDCs. Given the smaller technological distance of LDCs from other developing countries (as compared with developed countries), the impact of technological imports from the latter on LDCs may be higher, as they require less developed domestic absorptive capability. Equally, inflows of FDI from ODCs are likely more conducive to technological learning in host economies. The reasons for this are not only the already-mentioned shorter technological distance, but also the fact that these inflows tend to take more the form of joint ventures with local partners and create more linkages (UNCTAD, 2006b).

South–South links should be actively pursued by LDCs as a means of contributing to national technological catch-up.

South–South links should be actively pursued by LDCs as a means of contributing to national technological catch-up. This may take place in the context of regional integration schemes or through the joint undertaking of supra-national development projects that try to exploit the complementarities of different economies in the same region.

5. Promoting diversification through
dynamic inter-sectoral linkage effects

Besides deepening technological capabilities, a strategic priority of early catch-up should be to promote economic diversification through the development of new activities. This should be an essential element of STI policy in LDCs. Diversification can emerge in unexpected ways if policy facilitates entrepreneurial search and discovery in general. But inter-sectoral linkage effects also mean that there are certain economic activities for which supply and demand conditions are likely to be more propitious. In this regard, there are two areas which are particularly appropriate for LDCs. These are: (a) the development of agricultural growth linkages, and (b) the development of natural resource-based production clusters.

(a) Agricultural growth linkages

In association with promoting agricultural productivity growth, policy should encourage industries and services spurred by agricultural growth linkages. Past experience shows that agricultural growth linkages are a powerful mechanism through which more dynamic informal-sector microenterprises have been transformed into organized small firms. The development of local food processing industries through forward linkages from agriculture is a major mechanism for developing manufacturing experience and skills. Moreover, increasing demand for local consumer goods and simple capital goods, which stems from the rising incomes associated with agricultural productivity growth, provides a major stimulus for microenterprises to transform into small firms. The focalization of physical infrastructure development as well as organizational delivery of public services on market towns can encourage the development of clusters of rural non-farm activities linked to growing agricultural activities.

Past experience shows that agricultural growth linkages are a powerful mechanism through which more dynamic informal-sector microenterprises have been transformed into organized small firms.

(b) Natural resource-based production clusters

Efforts should also be made to develop natural resource-based production clusters through adding value to natural resources and exploring the possibilities for import substitution with local production of some inputs and equipment and the development of domestic production engineering capabilities.

The following measures have been suggested to develop natural resource-based production clusters:

- Identify, in conjunction with the private sector, the development potential of the activities linked to simple natural resource extraction, including the supply of inputs and equipment, processing activities of growing complexity, and related services, including in particular engineering and consultancy services;

- Identify the activities of the production cluster which require more foreign investment, because of the advanced nature of their technology and their access to international markets, to guide national efforts to attract the most suitable transnational corporations to the country;

- Identify key technologies for developing the production cluster, promote the local mastery and updating of those technologies through selective design and engineering policies and, if necessary, research and development, both in domestic enterprises and in research institutes, and promote the updating and adaptation of technology through missions abroad, licenses, joint ventures and programmes for co-financing consultancy activities in respect of key technologies; and

Efforts should also be made to develop natural resource-based production clusters through adding value to natural resources and exploring the possibilities for import substitution with local production of some inputs and equipment and the development of domestic production engineering capabilities.

Identify short-, medium- and long-term infrastructural needs of the cluster, including physical infrastructure, science and technology infrastructure and human resources (Ramos, 1998: 124–125).

Promoting diversification through dynamic inter-sectoral linkage effects is likely to require targeted policies which include financial incentives. As the example of the development of the leather industry in Ethiopia shows, it may also involve a complex institutional arrangement involving multiple actors (see box 5).

Promoting diversification through dynamic inter-sectoral linkage effects is likely to require targeted policies which include financial incentives.

6. Upgrading exports

An important feature of most LDCs is the non-dynamic nature of their exports. Thus, a final strategic priority should be upgrading their exports. Technological support for export development requires targeted policies. From past experience, successful cases may be initiated either by Governments who identify potential new opportunities where sustainable comparative advantage can be created, or by entrepreneurs who initiate activities which are new to the country without any initial support from the Government (Chandra and Kolavalli, 2006). However they start, their consequent development is supported by public action to promote both the diffusion and upgrading of technology. These activities may be directed to support traditional agricultural exports, such as cotton or coffee; new niche agricultural products, such as pineapples or cut flowers; labour-intensive industries, such as garments or leather products; or the tourism industry.

Technological support for export development requires targeted policies.

There is intense global competition in all these activities, so upgrading is particularly important. One of the most important developing sectors has been garments, and in that sector the trigger for initiating the process has come through trade preferences. This has supported the acquisition of technology and also some diffusion. However, a critical weakness is the lack of upgrading. This threatens the sustainability of these activities.

Box 5. The value chain of the leather goods industry in Ethiopia

Ethiopia has a comparative advantage in semi-processed leather, finished leather and leather products. The goal of the Ethiopian Government is to make use of this comparative advantage to transform the raw material into finished products.

Box chart 2 summarizes the three main stages of the value chain in the production of finished leather goods, namely, (a) the supply of livestock, (b) tanning and (c) the manufacture of leather products. Growth and competitiveness in the leather sector can only be achieved if the bottlenecks and constraints found at each stage of the value chain are tackled efficiently.

Having the largest livestock population in Africa, Ethiopia has a plentiful supply of raw material: hides and skins have been its second-largest export, preceded only by coffee. The marketing chain for trade in hides and skins stretches from the rural farmer and rural markets to small dealers, town traders and tanneries. The hides and skins produced in slaughterhouses are auctioned to big traders and tanneries. Potential improvements at this stage of the value chain include better preservation and handling of the hides and skins, the prevention of livestock disease, better quality and the introduction of incentive schemes and a pricing structure.

The 1975 ban on the export of raw hides and skins led to an increase in the number of hides and skins processed in Ethiopia. Several new tanneries are currently being built with a view to increasing the production of finished leather. Small and medium-sized tanneries exist alongside large ones. Improvements in quality did not match progress in speeding up the processing of hides and skins during the import-substitution period. Poor manufacturing capabilities, little innovation, heavy indebtedness and poor production capacity are some of the constraints on expansion of manufacturing in this sector.

To improve the learning and technological capabilities of local firms, national actors should intervene to provide services to enterprises and should continuously interact with them. The Ministry of Agriculture initially coordinated all the efforts to make improvements in this sector and checked that Ethiopian standards for hides and skins were met. In 1999, these functions were transferred to the Ethiopian Livestock Marketing Authority, an independent organization. The other agency involved in stand-ard-setting in this area is the Quality and Standards Authority of Ethiopia. Horizontal linkages between these organizations are essential if the value added of the exports of hides and skins is to be increased. Other agencies are responsible for providing incentives: the Ministry of Trade and Industry, for example, is responsible for setting up training institutes to raise the level of

Box 5 (contd.)

qualifications of workers in the leather sector, and a "productivity improvement centre" is engaged in training activities and in work to improve quality and upgrade leather-processing techniques. Unfortunately, the centre is not subsidized by the Government and, as a result, is poorly equipped and has only a limited impact.

The leather sector has enormous potential for development. Some key institutions and support structures already exist, but the services provided are not always of very high standard. All improvements in quality and productivity must take place across all stages of the industry's value chain. It is not enough to focus only on upgrading the processing and manufacture of leather for export purposes: the quality of the raw material also needs to be improved.

Box chart 2. Ethiopian leather sector: value chain and existing linkages to support institutions

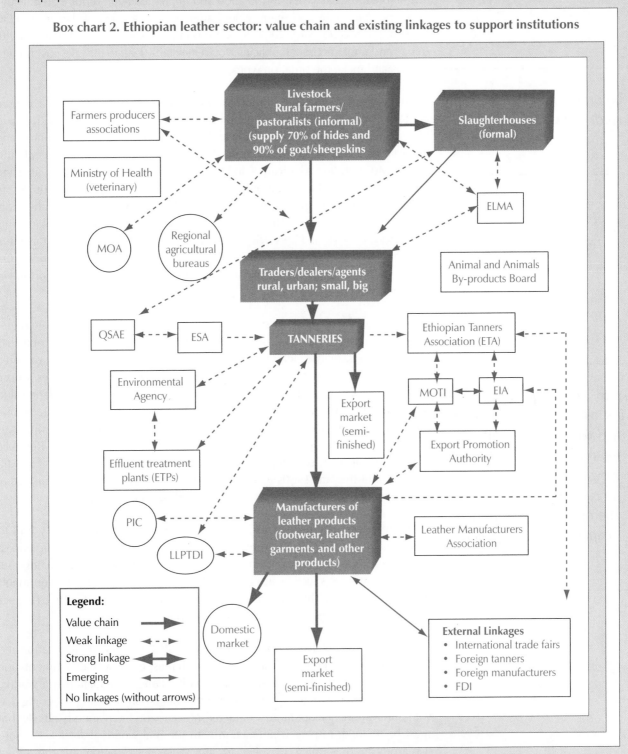

Source: UNCTAD, 2002.

Notes: MOA - Ministry of Agriculture; QSAE - Quality & Standards Authority of Ethiopia; ESA - Ethiopian Standards Authority; MOTI - Ministry of Trade & Industry; LLPTDI - Leather and Leather Products Training Development Institute; PIC - Productivity Improvement Centre; ELMA - Ethiopian Leather Manufacturers' Association; EIA - Ethiopian Investment Authority.

F. The question of state capacity

1. THE IMPORTANCE OF POLICY LEARNING

The sceptics would argue that the types of STI policies described above can hypothetically work, but they are inappropriate for LDCs because state capacities are simply too weak. Their formulation and implementation require an effective developmental state and many would argue that this is impossible in an LDC context (see Mkandawire, 2001, for various impossibility theses). Any attempt to design and implement such policies would inevitably lead to massive government failures and make the situation worse.

The problem of state capacity needs to be seen in dynamic rather than static terms.

This argument has some substantive basis in that it is true that at present there are major deficiencies in governmental capacity in LDCs, particularly with regard to long-neglected STI issues. Many institutions simply lack the technical and financial means to undertake the tasks that they are mandated to achieve. In this regard, Mozambique is indicative. In 2004, that country's National Standards and Quality Institute had a staff of only 13 people, of which only five had university degrees, and were earning about $200 a month. The agency had no laboratory or calibrating facilities. Of the 100 people working at the National Engineering Laboratory, only 10 had university degrees, and most of these held management positions, whilst 15 others had technical secondary education qualifications. On top of the lack of qualified technicians, these institutions are heavily underfunded (Warren-Rodriguez, 2007: 41).

However, the problem of state capacity needs to be seen in dynamic rather than static terms. The static perception that LDCs have weak state capacities ignores the possibility of learning through policy practice. The Republic of Korea and Taiwan Province of China are now regarded as exceptional cases whose exceptionally competent bureaucracies enabled the successful formulation and implementation of catch-up policies. But the Koumintang bureaucracy that initiated and sustained rapid catch-up growth in Taiwan Province of China was notorious for its corruption and incompetence until the 1950s and the Republic of Korea was actually sending its bureaucrats to Pakistan and Philippines for extra training until the late 1960s (Chang and Cheema, 2001). Thus, very successful development experiences did not begin with ideal state capacities.

From a dynamic perspective, just as firms learn over time by doing, Governments also learn by doing. The key to developing state capacity in relation to STI issues is therefore to develop such capacity through policy practice.

There is certainly a need to build a highly competent bureaucracy and to build governmental capacity in relation to STI issues, which should encompass human resource development, institution building and adequate financing. But from a dynamic perspective, just as firms learn over time by doing, Governments also learn by doing. The key to developing state capacity in relation to STI issues is therefore to develop such capacity through policy practice.

From this perspective, Teubal (1996) suggests that in relation to innovation and technology policy, there is a policy cycle which must begin with experimentation and search for what works best. As he puts it, "Policy formulation is a gradual process requiring actual experience in implementation (learning by doing). As with innovation, its optimum characteristics cannot be planned initially but must be learned, in part in interaction with the real world" (p.1180). Because it is a process of learning, mistakes are inevitable. But Governments should not be seeking some unique economy-wide optimum but making a smaller set of incremental choices and establishing mechanisms to evaluate outcomes and react to what has been learned. Teubal argues that in the initial infant stage of technology policy, horizontal policies should predominate and that, over time, as policy experience is gained, it becomes more possible to successfully implement vertical policies.

The incremental learning approach to policy formulation and implementation should apply to all government policies (Moreau, 2004). But it is notable that with regard to technological catch-up, there are a significant number of models of what works, mainly derived from Japan and East Asian development experience. These models provide a fund of experience which can be drawn on in the learning process. They cannot, of course, be transferred without adaptation to other contexts. But what is significant is that there is a diverse range of experience, including pioneer late industrializers such as the Republic of Korea and Taiwan Province of China, and also followers such as Malaysia, China and Viet Nam. The availability of these policy models for successful catch-up experience contrasts markedly with the lack of models for successful poverty reduction strategies. Governments that are expected to be competent to formulate and implement these poverty reduction strategies, which are policy experiments totally new to the world and without any prior working examples of sustained success, should be expected to be competent enough to formulate and implement policies for technological catch-up.

2. GOVERNMENT–BUSINESS RELATIONS

Government bureaucracy should be competent and independent. But beyond this, an important lesson from successful catch-up experiences is that the Government does not act as an omniscient central planner, but rather formulates and implements policy through a network of institutions which link Government to business. The establishment of intermediary government-business institutions should be a priority in good governance of technological learning and innovation. A good model for this is the deliberation council system established in Japan in the 1950s for the implementation of its industrial policy (see UNCTAD, 1994: part II, chapter 1). This system consisted of a set of industry-specific councils (or boards of enquiry) which consisted of business leaders, former government officials, academics, journalists and representatives from consumer groups, as well as the worlds of labour and finance. Their role was information-gathering, interest coordination and persuasion, and through their operation, policies were not unilaterally decided and enforced by the Government. Such institutions were widely adopted in East Asia in countries seeking technological catch-up, including the Republic of Korea, Malaysia and Thailand (World Bank, 1993: 181–187).

The establishment of government-business links can ensure that the Government has access to information. But it is important that despite this, Government retains its independence. Financial incentives and other forms of support to the private sector must be given on the basis of merit, through competitive selection processes and monitored in relation to specified results-oriented performance standards. In this framework, governmental support is not a giveaway but rather provided in return for the achievement of results by the private sector which support the achievement of the societal goals embodied in the strategic vision. Amsden (2001) identifies this "reciprocal control mechanism" as the key institutional innovation in successful catch-up. Similarly, Chandra and Kolavalli (2006) show that in all cases of successful establishment of new export industries, Governments played an important role in supporting technological learning and innovation. However, "the practice of providing support to favourite firms within an industry was not followed" (ibid. 16).

Corruption will simply sabotage an effective STI policy of the type discussed here. A basic condition for success is that policies to promote technological

The incremental learning approach to policy formulation and implementation should apply to all government policies. But it is notable that with regard to technological catch-up, there are a significant number of models of what works.

An important lesson from successful catch-up experiences is that the Government does not act as an omniscient central planner, but rather formulates and implements policy through a network of institutions which link Government to business.

learning and innovation do not favour or protect special interest groups ("cronyism"). In this regard, it is worth noting that, as well as performance standards and structured competition for government support, the strategic vision plays an important function. It is not simply a coordination framework but also "a conceptual framework for resisting partisan efforts to bend industrial policy in their favour" (Justman and Teubal, 1988: 246). Making the strategic vision explicit is thus very important.

3. THE ADMINISTRATIVE ORGANIZATION OF STI POLICY

Good governance of technological learning and innovation is likely to require organizational restructuring within the state apparatus itself owing to the cross-sectoral nature of technological learning and innovation.

Good governance of technological learning and innovation is likely to require organizational restructuring within the state apparatus itself owing to the cross-sectoral nature of technological learning and innovation. As a result of this feature, many agencies are required to be involved in promoting innovation (see box 5). Many countries have started to establish ministries of science and technology to take a lead on science and technology issues. But the mere establishment of a ministry of science and technology can be counter-productive, as it can lead to an overemphasis on science and an underemphasis on innovation at the sectoral level (Juma, 2007). Warren-Rodriguez (2007) illustrates well how the cross-sectional nature of technological development coupled with inter-ministerial fragmentation of decision-making lead to the marginalization of the science and technology issues in the PRSP action matrix, despite a strong general commitment to technological learning and innovation.

The appropriate organizational structure for integrating technological development issues into policy processes needs careful consideration. One model, suggested by Forsyth (1990: 173) is to have a technology policy unit within the Ministry of Planning (or senior policy coordination unit), together with technology experts in relevant sectoral ministries, including trade, industry, agriculture and education. The technology policy unit should also be in close contact with the ministry of finance with regard to fiscal measures and financial provision of technological activities. Another model is provided by the Nordic countries' approach to innovation policy, such as the establishment of national technology agency and Science and Technology Policy Council in Finland (Nordic Industrial Fund, 2003). Whatever the precise format, this institutional issue must be addressed, once again through a learning approach, as a condition for successful design and implementation of policies to promote technological learning and innovation.

4. THE IMPORTANCE OF NATIONAL POLICY SPACE

A final condition for successful design and implementation of policies to promote technological learning and innovation is the existence of national policy space in the sense that Governments have sufficient room to manoeuver to adopt independent economic policies in line with their development objectives.

A final condition for successful design and implementation of policies to promote technological learning and innovation is the existence of national policy space in the sense that Governments have sufficient room to manoeuver to adopt independent economic policies in line with their development objectives. In this regard, there are two critical issues.

Firstly, as they are more aid-dependent, LDCs are much more subject to conditionality or the pressure of expectations on what is regarded as reasonable policy. The PRSP approach aims to enhance domestic ownership, but in practice the tension between conditionality and ownership has not been resolved, and only a few LDCs have started to elaborate home-grown policies. LDC development partners should facilitate experimentation required by the types of STI policies proposed here and facilitate policy learning. This should include improved policy coherence between macroeconomic and microeconomic development objectives, as too stringent macroeconomic stabilization may undermine the evolution of the conditions necessary for innovation and learning.

Secondly, whereas the international trade regime may not be highly binding, the international IPR regime is potentially a major problem for technological development in all developing countries seeking to catch-up, including LDCs. This issue is taken up in more detail in the next chapter.

G. Conclusions

The basic message of this chapter can be summarized in seven basic points.

Firstly, LDC Governments are concerned with promoting sustained economic growth as a basis for poverty reduction, but the treatment of technological change as a source of economic growth is generally weak in their PRSPs.

Secondly, the weak treatment of technological change reflects the marginalization of technology policies within structural adjustment programmes, which have been particularly intensely implemented within the LDCs, the omission of technology issues from the PRSP approach, and the failure to embed PRSPs — which are essentially three-year public expenditure plans — within broader development strategies that include actions to promote technological change. It is vital that LDCs now devise such development strategies. There is widespread restlessness in many developing countries, including LDCs, to find a new, post-Washington consensus policy model. A focus on promoting technological change as a sequential, cumulative process can be at the heart of a new approach. Priority actions in three-year poverty reduction strategies can be derived from the broader development strategy. Thus, LDC Governments should integrate an STI policy into their development and poverty reduction strategies.

Thirdly, the STI policy should focus on promoting technological learning and innovation within enterprises, both firms and farms. This is best achieved with a systems model of innovation rather than a linear model which focuses on scientific research and expects that to generate technological development and innovation. It is also best achieved with a mixed market-based approach in which the Government and the private sector work closely together. Public action should facilitate entrepreneurial search and discovery, catalyse private investment and innovation through market-based incentives, and address coordination failures where the profitability of investment depends on interrelated action in different sectors.

Fourthly, the basic strategic objective of STI policy should be to promote technological catch-up with more advanced countries. Successful developing countries have adopted policies to promote technological learning and innovation which are geared towards achieving technological catch-up with more advanced countries. There is no reason why LDC Governments should not do likewise. Indeed, unless the LDCs adopt policies to stimulate technological catch-up with the rest of the world, they will continue to fall behind other countries technologically and face deepening marginalization in the global economy.

Fifthly, policies to promote technological catch-up need to be appropriate to the level of technological development, economic structure and capabilities of the Governments and business sector of the LDCs. Most LDCs are in the early stage of a process of catch-up and are generally at the start of the learning and innovation trajectories which typically occur during catch-up. Technological catch-up in LDCs

LDC Governments should integrate an STI policy into their development and poverty reduction strategies.

The STI policy should focus on promoting technological learning and innovation within enterprises, both firms and farms.

will require the co-evolution of improvement in physical infrastructure, human capital and financial systems together with improved technological capabilities within enterprises and more effective knowledge systems supporting the supply of knowledge and linkages between creators and users of knowledge. Catch-up involves both the deepening of technological capabilities at the enterprise level and the widening of those capabilities through their development and application in an increasing variety of economic sectors. In that regard, it is possible to identify six major strategic priorities which will be relevant for many LDCs:

- Increase agricultural productivity in basic staples, in particular through promoting a Green Revolution;

- Promote the formation and growth of domestic business firms;

- Increase the absorptive capacity of domestic knowledge systems;

- Leverage more learning from international trade and FDI;

- Foster diversification through agricultural growth linkages and natural-resource-based production clusters;

- Upgrade export activities.

Sixthly, those priorities should be articulated with a view to economy-wide expansion of employment opportunities in order to ensure poverty reduction. That will require technological change in agricultural and non-agricultural activities, and in tradables and non-tradables.

Seventhly, LDC Governments currently have weak capacities to formulate and implement STI policies within development strategies. But this does not mean that such capacities cannot be developed. Governments should adopt an incremental learning approach to policy formulation and implementation. They should also ensure that there is a network of intermediary government–business institutions to ensure good governance of technological learning and innovation. Finally, attention should be given to the administrative organization of STI policy as it is a cross-cutting issue which cannot be left to a ministry of science and technology alone.

Technological catch-up in LDCs will require the co-evolution of improvement in physical infrastructure, human capital and financial systems together with improved technological capabilities within enterprises and more effective knowledge systems supporting the supply of knowledge and linkages between creators and users of knowledge.

Notes

1   Box, Ulmanen and Steinhauer (2004) reach a similar conclusion in relation to science and technology plans in African, Caribbean and Pacific (ACP) countries. Although the Cotnou Partnership Framework encourages the development of scientific, technological and research infrastructure, science and technology issues are rarely referred to in the Country Support Strategy papers of ACP countries.

2   For further discussion of the state of science and technology in Nepal, see Nepal and Karki (2002). Waast (2002) provides a very revealing discussion on the state of science in Africa, whilst the status of science and technology infrastructure is discussed in Akin Adubifa (2004), Khalil-Timany (2002) and Lall and Pietrobelli (2003).

3   Within LDCs, there are many examples of failures of assimilating and operating transferred industrial technology because of weak firm-level capabilities. The typical symptoms are repeated breakdowns of machinery, a high incidence of down time, low product quality standards, failure to reach rated capacity of equipment, carrying large margins of unplanned excess capacity and excessive unit costs. The causes of these failures include: "(i) the inability to hire labour with the required manual skills; (ii) unforeseen complexity of the process stemming from the failure to make an adequate prior technical appraisal of equipment; (iii) lack of local repair and maintenance facilities; (iv) unsuitability of the process for the assigned task; (v) failure of machinery manufacturer to provide adequate after-sales service and to supply spare parts when needed; (vi) inherent faults in the equipment; (vii) inexperience of management in organizing and running an industrial operation; and (viii) poor financial appraisal" (Forsyth, 1990: 127).

4. For further discussion of these technological capabilities, see Lall (1992, 2004), UNIDO (2002).

5. Under original equipment manufacture (OEM), the latecomer firm produces a finished product to the precise specification of a foreign buyer. The foreign firm then markets the product under its own brand name, through its own distribution channel and often involves the foreign partner in the selection of capital equipment and the training of managers, engineers and technicians as well as providing advice on production, financing and management.

References

Akin Adubifa, O. (2004). An assessment of science and technology: Capacity-building in sub-Saharan Africa. ATPS Special Paper Series No. 19, African Technology Policy Studies Network, Nairobi, Kenya.

Akyuz, Y. (1998). East Asian development: New perspectives. Special issue of *Journal of Development Studies*, 34 (6): 1–137.

Amsden, A.H. (2001). *The Rise of "the Rest": Challenges to the West from Late-Industrializing Economies*. Oxford University Press, New York.

Amsden, A. and Chu W.W. (2003). *Beyond Late Development: Taiwan's Upgrading Policies*. MIT Press, Cambridge, Mass.

Arnold, E. and Bell, M. (2001). Some new ideas about research and development. In *Partnerships at the Leading Edge: A Danish Vision for Knowledge, Research and Development*. Report of the Commission on Development-Related Research, funded by DANIDA, Ministry of Foreign Affairs, Copenhagen.

Arrow, K.J. (1962). Economic welfare and the allocation of resources for innovation. In Nelson, R.R., *The Rate and Direction of Inventive Activity*. Princeton University Press, NJ.

Avnimelech, G. and Teubal, M. (2006). Innovation and technology policy (ITP) for catching-up: A three phase life cycle framework for industrializing economies. Studies and Perspectives Series No. 69, United Nations Economic Commission for Latin America and the Caribbean, Buenos Aires.

Avnimelech, G. and Teubal, M. (2008, Forthcoming). From direct support of business sector R&D/innovation to targeting venture capital/private equity: A catching-up innovation and technology policy life cycle perspective. In *Economics of Innovation and New Technology*, forthcoming, special issue on the governance of technological knowledge, 17 (1).

Biggs, S. and Hatsaert, H. (2004). Strengthening poverty reduction programmes using and actor-oriented approach: Examples from natural resources innovation systems. Agricultural Research and Extension Network Paper No. 134, Overseas Development Institute, London.

Box, L., Ulmanen, J.H. and Steinhauer, N. (2004). Review of science and technology plans in ACP countries. Paper prepared for Technical Centre for Agricultural and Rural Cooperation, Maastricht.

Bell, M. (2007). Technological learning and the development of production and innovative capacities in the industry and infrastructure sectors of the least developed countries: What roles for ODA? Study prepared for UNCTAD as a background paper for *The Least Developed Countries Report 2007*, UNCTAD, Geneva.

Byerlee, D. and Eicher, C.K. (1997). *Africa's Emerging Maize Revolution.* Lynne Reinner Publishers, Boulder, CO and London.

Chandra, V. and Kolavalli, S. (2006). *Technology, Adaptation and Exports: How Some Developing Countries Got It Right*. World Bank, Washington, DC.

Chandra, V. and Kolavalli, S. (2006). Technology, adaptation and exports: How some countries got it right. Chapter 1 in Chandra, V. (ed.), *Technology Adaptation and Exports: How Some Developing Countries Got It Right*, World Bank, Washington, DC.

Chang, H.J. and Cheema, A. (2001). Conditions for successful technology policy in developing countries — learning rents, state structures, and institutions. Discussion Paper Series No. 2001-8, UNU-INTECH, Maastricht.

Chapman, R. and Tripp, R. (2003). Changing incentives for agricultural extension: A review of privatized extension in practice. AGRN Network Paper No. 132, Agricultural Research and Extension Network, London.

Cimoli, M., Ferraz, J.C. and Primi, A. (2005). Science and technology policies in open economies: The case of Latin America and the Caribbean. Productive Development Series No. 165, UN-CEPAL, Santiago, Chile.

Dahlman, C.J., Ross-Larson, B. and Westphal, L.E. (1987). Managing technological development: Lessons from the newly industrializing countries. *World Development*, 15 (6): 759–775.

Dodgson, M. and Bessant, J. R. (1996). *Effective Innovation Policy: A New Approach*. International Thomson Business Press, New York.

Dorward, A., Fan, S., Kydd, J., Lofgren, H., Morrison, J., Poulton, C., Rao, N., Smith, L., Tchale, H., Thorat, S., Urey, I. and Wobst, P. (2004). Institutions and policies for pro-poor agricultural growth. *Development Policy Review*, 22 (6): 611–622.

ECLAC (1990). *Changing Production Patterns with Social Equity*. United Nations publication, sales no. E.90.IIG.6, Santiago, Chile.

ECLAC (1995). *Latin America and the Caribbean: Policies to Improve Linkages with the Global Economy*. United Nations publication, sales no. E.95.II.G.6, Santiago, Chile.

ECLAC (2004). *Productive Development in Open Economies*. Thirtieth Session of the Economic Commission for Latin America and the Caribbean, 28 June – 2 July, San Juan, Puerto Rico.

Forsyth, D.J.C. (1990). *Technology Policy for Small Developing Countries*. Macmillan, Houndmills, Basingstoke and London.

Hayami, Y. and Ruttan, V. (1985). *Agricultural Development: An International Perspective*. John Hopkins University Press, Baltimore, MD and London.

Hobday, M. (1995). *Innovation in East Asia*. Edward Elgar, Aldershot, England and Brookfield, Vermont.

Imbs, J and Wacziarg, R. (2003). Stages of diversification. *American Economic Review*, 93 (1): 63–86.

Juma, C. (2007). Speech at the global forum on Building Science, Technology and Innovation Capacity for Sustainable Growth and Poverty Reduction. World Bank, 13–15 February, Washington, DC.

Justman, M. and Teubal, M. (1986). Innovation policy in an open economy: A normative framework for strategic and tactical issues. *Research Policy*, 15 (3): 121–138.

Justman, M. and Teubal, M. (1991). A structuralist perspective on the role of technology in economic growth and development. *World Development*, 19 (9): 1167–1183.

Justman, M. and Teubal, M. (1995). Technological infrastructure policy (TIP): Creating capabilities and building markets. *Research Policy*, 24 (2): 259–281.

Khalili-Timamy, M.H. (2002). State of science and technological capacity in sub-Saharan Africa. ATPS Special Paper Series No. 12, African Technology Policy Studies Network (ATPS), Nairobi.

Kim, L (1980). Stages of development of industrial technology in a developing country: A model. Research Policy No. 9: 254–277. Reproduced in Kim, L. (2000), *Learning and Innovation in Economic Development*. Edward Elgar, Cheltenham, UK and Northampton, Mass.

Kim, L. and Dahlman, C.J. (1992). Technology policy for industrialization: An integrative framework and Korea's experience. *Research Policy*, 21 (5): 437–452.

Kim, L. and Yi, G. (1997). The dynamics of R&D in industrial development: Lesson from the Korean Experience. *Industry and Innovation*, 4 (2): 2–8.

Klugman, J. (ed.) (2002). *A Sourcebook for Poverty Reduction Strategies*, 2 volumes, World Bank, Washington, DC.

Kuznetsov, Y. and Sabel, C. (2005). New industrial policy: Solving economic development problems without picking winners. Presentation for the World Bank Institute, 13 June, World Bank, Washington, DC.

Lall, S. (1992). Technological capabilities and industrialization. *World Development*, 20 (2): 165–186.

Lall, S. (2004). Reinventing industrial strategy: The role of government policy in building industrial competitiveness. G-24 Discussion Paper Series No. 28, UNCTAD, Geneva.

Lall, S. and Pietrobelli, C. (2003). *Failing to Compete: Technology Development and Technology Systems in Africa*. Edward Elgar Publishing, Cheltenham UK and Northampton, Mass.

Lall, S. and Teubal, M. (1998). "Market-stimulating" technology policies in developing countries: A framework with examples from East Asia. *World Development*, 26 (8): 1369–1385.

Lele, U. and Ekboir, J. (2004). Technology generation, adaptation, adoption and impact: Towards a framework for understanding and increasing research impact. Working Paper No. 31964, World Bank, Washington, DC.

Melo, A. (2001). Industrial policy in Latin America and the Caribbean at the turn of the century. Research Department Working Paper No. 459, Inter-American Development Bank, Washington, DC.

Melo, A. and Rodriguez-Clare, A. (2006). Productive development policies and supporting institutions in Latin America and the Caribbean. Competitiveness Studies Series, Working Paper No. C-106, Inter-American Development Bank, Washington, DC.

Metcalfe, J. (1995). The economic foundations of technology policy: equilibrium and evolutionary perspectives. In Stoneman, P. (ed.), *Handbook of Economics of Innovation and Technology Change*. Blackwell, Oxford.

Mkandawire, T. (2001). Thinking about developmental states in Africa. *Cambridge Journal of Economics*, 25 (3): 289–314.

Moreau, F. (2004). The role of the state in evolutionary economics. *Cambridge Journal of Economics*, 28 (6): 847–874.

Nadvi, K. and Schmitz, H. (1999). Industrial clusters in developing countries. Special issue of *World Development*, 27 (9).

Nelson, R. and Pack, H. (1999). The Asian miracle and modern growth theory. *Economic Journal*, 109 (457): 416–436.

NEPAD (2005). Africa's science and technology consolidated plan of action. The New Partnership for Africa's Development, South Africa.

Nepal, C. and Karki, B.R. (2002). Promoting business and technology incubation for improved competitiveness of small and medium-sized industries through application of modern and efficient technologies in Nepal. In United Nations Economic and Social Commission for Asia and the Pacific (ESCAP), *Promoting Business and Technology Incubation for Improved Competitiveness of Small and Medium-Sized Industries Through Application of Modern and Efficient Technologies*, Thailand.

Nordic Industrial Fund (2003). Good practices in Nordic innovation policies. Report produced by STEP Centre for Innovation Research, Oslo.

OECD (1997). *National Innovation Systems*. Organization for Economic Co-operation and Development, Paris.

OECD (2007). Working party on statistics: Disaggregating technical co-operation. Document DCD/DAC/STAT(2007)3, Organisation for Economic Co-operation and Development, Paris.

Otsuka, K. (2004). Possibility of Green Revolution in Sub-Saharan Africa, in FASID Open Forum XI. The Possibility of a Green Revolution in East Africa, FASID, Tokyo, Japan.

Otsuka, K. (2006). Lecture 1: The economics of industrial cluster. Presentation prepared for Seminar on Cluster-Based Industrial Development, 24 May, Hanoi, Viet Nam.

Oyanguren, R. L. (2007). Nicaraguan Innovation Fund for SMEs: Government instrument to promote exports and national competitiveness by helping businesses to find, adopt and adapt useful technologies. Presentation to the Global Forum on Building Science, Technology and Innovation Capacity for Sustainable Growth and Poverty Reduction, 13–15 February, World Bank, Washington, DC.

Oyelaran-Oyeyinka, B. (2006). *Learning to Compete in African Industry: Institutions and Technology in Development*. Ashgate Publishing, Aldershot, England and Burlington VT.

Oyelaran-Oyeyinka, B. and McCormick, D. (2007). *Industrial Clusters and Innovation Systems in Africa: Institutions, Markets and Policy*. United Nations University Press, Tokyo, New York and Paris.

Pack, H. (2000) Research and development in the industrial development process. In Kim, L. and Nelson, R. R. (Eds.), *Technology, Learning and Innovation: Experiences of Newly Industrializing Countries*. Cambridge University Press, Cambridge, UK.

Peres, W. (2006). The slow comeback of industrial policies in Latin America and the Caribbean, *CEPAL Review* No. 88, Economic Commission for Latin America and the Caribbean, Santiago.

Ramos, J. (1998). A development strategy founded on natural resource-based production clusters, CEPAL Review No. 66, Economic Commission for Latin America and the Caribbean, Santiago.

Rodriguez-Clare, A. (2005). Microeconomic interventions after the Washington Consensus. Research Department Working Paper No. 524, Inter-American Development Bank, Washington, DC.

Rodrik, D. (2004). Industrial policy for the twenty-first century. Paper prepared for United Nations Industrial Development Organization (UNIDO), Vienna.

Sachs, I. (2004a). From poverty trap to inclusive development in LDCs. *Economic and Political Weekly*, 39 (18): 1802–1811.

Sachs, I. (2004b). Inclusive development strategy in an era of globalization. Working Paper No. 35, Policy Integration Department – World Commission on the Social Dimension of Globalisation, International Labour Office, Geneva.

Schrank, A. and Kurtz, M. (2005). Credit where credit is due: Open economy industrial policy and export diversification in Latin America and the Caribbean. *Politics and Society*, 33 (4): 671–702.

Schrank, A. and Kurtz, M. (2006). Open economy industrial policy in Latin America and the Caribbean. Paper prepared for Responding to Globalization in the Americas: the Political Economy of Hemispheric Integration, LSE/ISA, London.

Sercovich, F. and Teubal, M. (2007). Innovation, technological capability and competitiveness: the policy issues in evolutionary perspective. Paper presented at the UNCTAD Meeting of Experts on FDI, Technology and Competitiveness: A Conference in Honour of Sanjaya Lall, 8–9 March, Geneva.

Singh, R.M. (2001). Development of science and technology in Nepal. *Science Technology & Society,* 6 (1): 159–178.

Teubal, M. (1996). A catalytic and evolutionary approach to horizontal technology policies (HTPs). *Research Policy*, 25 (8): 1161–1188.

Teubal, M. (1997). R&D technology policy in NICs as learning process. *World Development,* 24 (3): 449–460.

UN Millennium Project Task Force on Science, Technology and Innovation (2005). *Innovation: Applying Knowledge in Development*. Earthscan, London and Sterling VA.

UNCTAD (1994). *Trade and Development Report 1994*. United Nations publication, sales no. E.94.II.D.26, Geneva.

UNCTAD (1995). Strengthening of linkages between the national research and development systems and industrial sectors; Contribution of technologies, including new and emerging technologies, to industrialization in developing countries, E/CN. 16/1995/8, Geneva.

UNCTAD (2000). *The Least Developed Countries Report 2000*. United Nations publication, sales no. E.00.II.D.21, Geneva.

UNCTAD (2002). Investment and Innovation Policy Review of Ethiopia. UNCTAD/ITE/IPC/Misc.4, Geneva.

UNCTAD (2004) *The Least Developed Countries Report 2004*. United Nations publication, sales no. E.04.II.D.27, Geneva and New York.

UNCTAD (2006a). *The Least Developed Countries Report 2006: Developing Productive Capacities*. United Nations publication, sales no. E.06.II.D.9, Geneva and New York.

UNCTAD (2006b) *World Investment Report 2006: FDI from Developing and Transition Economies: Implications for Development*. United Nations publication, sales no. E.06.II.D.11, Geneva.

UNESCO (2005). *UNESCO Science Report 2005*. Paris.

UNIDO (2002). Industrial Development Report 2002/2003. *Competing Through Innovation and Learning*. Vienna.

Waast, R. (2002). The state of science in Africa: An overview. A survey conducted by the Institut de Recherche pour le Développement, Paris.

Warren-Rodriguez, A. (2007). Science and technology and the PRSP Process: A survey of recent country experiences. Study prepared for UNCTAD as a background paper for *The Least Developed Countries Report 2007*, UNCTAD, Geneva.

Weiss, L. (2005). Global governance, national strategies: How industrialized states make room to move under the WTO. *Review of International Political Economy,* 12 (5): 723–749.

Westphal, L.E., Kim, L. and Dahlman, C.J. (1985). Reflections on the Republic of Korea's acquistion of technological capability. Reproduced in Kim, L., *Learning and Innovation in Economic Development*. Edward Elgar, Cheltenham, UK and Northampton, MA.

Westphal, L.E. (2001). Technology strategies for economic development in a fast changing global economy. *Economics of Innovation and New Technology*, 11: 4–5.

World Bank (1993). *The East Asian Miracle: Economic Growth and Public Policy*. World Bank, Washington, DC.

World Bank (2005). *Economic Growth in the 1990s: Lessons from a Decade of Reform*. World Bank, Washington, DC.

Intellectual Property Rights and Other Incentive Mechanisms for Learning and Innovation

Chapter

3

A. Introduction

Building strong domestic productive capacities is central to faster economic growth and diversification in LDCs. The objective of this chapter is to explore the current controversies about how a strong intellectual property rights (IPR) regime, as encouraged by the Agreement on Trade-Related Aspects of Intellectual Property Rights (TRIPS), affects the economic development processes of LDCs and the range of policy issues related to facilitating technological development, through the lens of development economics rather than a narrow legalistic perspective. It will begin with an overview of some of the general global IPR trends, seen through the prism of LDCs (section B), and discuss the "knowledge trade-off" underlying the rationale for IPRs and its applicability to LDCs (section C). It will then examine some of the available secondary evidence regarding the impact of IPRs on learning and innovation and present the findings of an original case study on the impact of IPRs on innovation in the domestic processing sector in Bangladesh (section D). The chapter will also assess the impact of TRIPS and TRIPS-plus obligations on the learning trajectories of LDCs and whether prescribed flexibilities for LDCs are working as promised. Section E, on policy implications, will revisit some widely used incentive and policy mechanisms and section F will consider several new proposals for improving knowledge governance. Conclusions and main policy recommendations are set out in section G.

The term "intellectual property rights" (IPRs) refers to those legal rules, norms and regulations that prevent the unauthorized use of intellectual products.

B. Trends in intellectual property protection

1. INTELLECTUAL PROPERTY PROTECTION AND THE GOVERNANCE OF KNOWLEDGE

The term "intellectual property rights" (IPRs) refers to those legal rules, norms and regulations that prevent the unauthorized use of intellectual products. IPRs cover a broad range of subjects, inter alia, patents, copyrights, trademarks, geographical indications, industrial designs and trade secrets. The chapter will focus, however, on patents and copyright. Intellectual Property (IP) essentially consists of two domains: one deals with industrial products (which includes patents, trademarks, industrial designs and geographical indications of source) and the other with artistic products (which are covered by copyright and related rights). Once IPRs are established, its owner enjoys certain specified rights in terms of its duration (20 years for patents and life plus 50 years for copyrights). IPRs can be issued on products and processes: patents are usually issued for a technical device, or engineering principle after an investigation into its anteriority,

IPRs cover a broad range of subjects, inter alia, patents, copyrights, trademarks, geographical indications, industrial designs and trade secrets.

and in exchange for the public divulging of the technical details. Patents can also be granted, inter alia, for crops, genes, and drugs. A patent confers negative rights, i.e., the right to exclude others from certain activities (TRIPS Article 28).

The copyright is granted for the expression of an idea, not the idea itself. It essentially provides the "right to copy" an original creation, such as poems, theses, plays, literary works, choreographic works, musical compositions, audio recordings, paintings, drawings, sculptures, photos, software, radio and television broadcasts, and sometimes industrial designs.

The growing economic importance of intellectual property has been accompanied by more qualitative changes in intellectual protection, all of which point to a considerable tightening of the rules governing access to knowledge.

The boundary between those domains has, in some respects, been eroding in recent years, owing to the fast rates of diffusion of scientific innovations that blur the boundaries between patentable and copyrightable subject matters and its more widespread use as a source of corporate profits, as well as to the convergent use of new technologies across sectors in what is increasingly being referred to as the "knowledge economy" (OECD, 1999).[1] Measuring the knowledge economy is subject to methodological and statistical shortfalls of various kinds, not least the limits of existing economic categories and classifications (Foray, 2000: chapter 1). The "copyright industries" have not only grown significantly in recent years, but have also expanded beyond their traditional core to encompass a wider set of activities in which knowledge is an important input in the production process. According to recent estimates for the United States, copyright industries contribute between 7 and 11 per cent of output and between 4 million and 8.5 million jobs. At the same time the number of patent applications has been growing rapidly, and licensing and cross-licensing (section B of this chapter) are being used more frequently.

These trends, which attest to the growing economic importance of intellectual property, have been accompanied by more qualitative changes in intellectual protection, all of which point to a considerable tightening of the rules governing access to knowledge. The 1990s witnessed a series of major changes in the patent system that reduced patentability thresholds for patents and expanded the scope of legitimate subject matter to include genetically modified organisms (GMOs), software and business methods. The reform of the United States copyright law in the late 1990s, which extended the duration (term) of copyright to a life plus 70 years model,[2] culminating in the Digital Millennium Copyright Act (1998), was followed by the European Union Copyright Directive (EUCD) in 2001. There have also been other legislative changes in the advanced economies to strengthen enforcement, such as the EC Database Directive, which provides exclusive rights on non-creative databases. Moreover, concerns are intensifying as regards increased use of "defensive patents" or strategic use of patents (Hall, 2005), as well as over increasing restrictions on statutory private use exceptions or "fair use"(Burk and Cohen, 2001; UNCTAD and ICTSD, 2003a; Musungu, 2005). The process of tightening intellectual property protection has been reflected in the increased control over knowledge, information and culture by a small number of very large corporations often operating in highly concentrated markets (Teece, 1995; Macmillan, 2005; David and Foray, 2003). Indeed, the protection of intellectual property has in recent years moved from a defensive to an offensive corporate strategy, including deterring entry of potential rivals (Robledo, 2005), as patents and copyrights are increasingly seen as a unique means of generating value from intangible assets.

Over the last two decades, together with policy advice from donors and multilateral organizations, developing countries, including LDCs, have been strongly encouraged to broaden the scope of IP protection, irrespective of their own needs and conditions.

However, efforts to tighten protection have not been confined to domestic legislation. Over the last two decades, as a result of strong corporate lobbying in some key sectors, together with policy advice from donors and multilateral organizations, developing countries, including LDCs, have been strongly encouraged to broaden the scope of IP protection, irrespective of their own needs and conditions. This pressure has been channelled through multilateral, regional and bilateral obligations: the TRIPS Agreement, the WIPO Internet treaties (1996), regional free trade agreements, bilateral investment treaties and a number of other international trade agreements.

Advocates of stringent IPRs have insisted that they will encourage technology transfer, stimulate innovation and bring collateral benefits by strengthening the investment climate and attracting more foreign direct investment (FDI), which in turn will improve welfare (Pires de Carvalho, 2002; Sykes, 2002; Fisch and Speyer, 1995). Consequently, intellectual property has been labeled a "power tool for economic development and wealth creation" (Idris, 2003). But there are strong opposing arguments.

2. Some trends in IP protection, worldwide and in LDCs

Although patent systems diverge significantly across countries, patent statistics can be regarded as one measure of a country's inventive activity and related technology flows (WIPO, 2006). Recent patenting trends indicate that patent filings worldwide have grown on average by 4.8 per cent per annum over the past 10 years (reaching 1.6 million in 2004); and patents granted have also increased at a similar rate. However, while some emerging economies (India, Brazil and Mexico) are making increasing use of the patent system, it remains highly concentrated with the United States, Japan, the Republic of Korea, China and the European Patent Office accounting for 74 per cent of all patents granted (WIPO, 2006).

The available data on patenting trends in LDCs from WIPO and the World Bank (World Development Indicators online) are not totally consistent (tables 21 and 22). However, they both show similar patterns, namely:

- LDCs share of global patents is insignificant; and

- Overall in LDCs patent applications by non-residents exceeded those by residents.

The World Bank data also show that there was a downward trend in domestic patenting activity by LDC residents (chart 10 and table 21).

According to available data, between 1998 and 2004, trademarks and industrial designs played a far greater role than patents for LDC residents. Data on industrial design applications suggest that in Bangladesh, residents made 680 applications, compared with 251 in Yemen and 123 in Madagascar (table 22).

Advocates of stringent IPRs have insisted that they will encourage technology transfer, stimulate innovation and bring collateral benefits by strengthening the investment climate and attracting more FDI, which in turn will improve welfare. But there are strong opposing arguments.

Recent patenting trends indicate that patent filings worldwide have grown on average by 4.8 per cent per annum over the past 10 years... But LDCs' share of global patents remained insignificant.

Chart 10. Patent applications in LDCs by residents and non-residents, 1990–2004

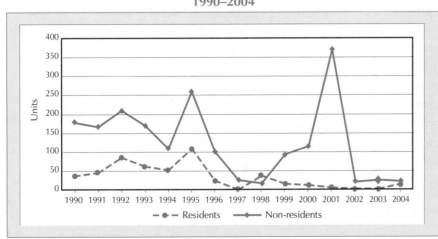

Source: World Bank, *World Development Indicators*, online, 2007.

Table 21. Patent applications by LDC residents and non-residents, 1990–2004

Year	Patent applications, non-residents	Patent applications, residents
1990	179	39
1991	168	47
1992	210	86
1993	171	63
1994	109	53
1995	260	110
1996	102	25
1997	26	2
1998	18	39
1999	95	16
2000	117	13
2001	372	7
2002	22	4
2003	26	3
2004	24	16

Source: World Bank, *World Development Indicators,* online, 2007.

Table 22. Industrial property applications in LDCs, by residents and non-residents, latest years

Country	Year	Patent applications Residents	Non-residents	Trademark applications Residents	Non-residents	Industrial design applications Residents	Non-residents
Bangladesh	2003	58	260	4 085	1 310	680	10
Benin	1998	..	..	20 908	3 008	..	..
Bhutan	1997–2002	..	..	7	2 020	..	..
Burundi	2002	..	..	20	132	..	..
Cambodia	2003	..	..	297	1 559	..	..
Djibouti	2000	..	..	408ª	..	..	..
Gambia	2001	..	55	..	..	..	9
Haiti	1999	1	5	150	1306	..	..
Lao People's Democratic Republic	2002	..	..	19	672	..	..
Lesotho	2001	1	54	..	19	..	1
Madagascar	2002	4	..	162	293	123	..
Malawi	2002	..	1	138	440	10	12
Mauritania	2002	6	..	9	..	0	..
Mozambique	2001	1	52	..	..	..	12
Nepal	2001	3	11	1 148	418	3	18
Rwanda	1999	..	4	5	124	..	..
Samoa	2000	..	15	16	357	0	0
Sierra Leone	2001	1	51	..	..	..	9
Sudan	2001	1	54	..	..	..	9
Uganda	2001	2	58	..	14	..	9
United Republic of Tanzania	2001	2	54	..	16	..	11
Yemen	2004	63	788	6 865	24 169	251	50
Zambia	2001	6	25	213	582	7	9

Source: UNCTAD secretariat compilation based on WIPO, Guide To Intellectual Property Worldwide, Country Profiles, last updated September 2006.

Note: Data are available only for the above-reported LDCs.

a Denotes figure for non-residents and residents combined. Data on the composition of patents are not available.

Non-resident applications were not as significant, with the exception of Yemen (50 applications made). As regards trademark applications by residents, 20,908 applications were made in Benin, compared with 6,865 in Yemen and 1,148 in Nepal, while non-resident applications were sizeable in several LDCs (table 22). The low level of patenting activity by LDC residents mirrors low levels of R&D expenditure. According to the most recent data, gross domestic expenditure on R&D (GERD) in Burkina Faso amounted to 0.17 per cent of GDP, while the percentage was 0.0064 per cent for Lesotho, 0.12 per cent for Madagascar, 0.67 per cent for Nepal, 0.34 per cent for Sudan, 0.81 per cent for Uganda, 0.0081 per cent for Zambia and 0.6 per cent for Bangladesh (chapter Introduction to this Report, table 1). This compares with, for example, 1.3 per cent in China and 0.98 per cent in Brazil.

As regards licensing activities in LDCs, available data indicate that licensing has not increased on a per capita basis since the conclusion of the TRIPS Agreement: licence payments on a per capita basis were the lowest in the world ($0.07) between 2000 and 2005, and have remained unchanged since the period 1996–1999. The comparable figure in other developing countries was $6.36 per capita (in 2000–2005), which was almost double the figure for the previous period (1996–1999): $3.55 (chapter 1, table 16).

Between 1998 and 2004, trademarks and industrial designs played a far greater role than patents for LDC residents.

3. LDCs in the TRIPS-based policy regime

It is generally accepted that the issue of intellectual property entered multilateral trade negotiations in the Uruguay Round largely as a result of the concerted pressure of the United States, European and Japanese pharmaceutical and international entertainment companies (Shukla, 2000; Drahos and Braithwaite, 2004).

In line with their WTO obligations under the TRIPS agreement, WTO members must also comply with most provisions of the Paris Convention on Industrial Property and the Berne Convention on Literary and Artistic Works, and particularly provisions of the Treaty on Intellectual Property in Respect of Integrated Circuits. Currently, 35 LDCs are parties to the Paris Convention and 29 are parties to the Berne Convention (table 23). As a result, LDCs are obliged to apply the same "minimum" IP standards as soon as the transitional periods expire or upon graduation. In many cases, TRIPS-plus regulations impose on LDCs even higher standards and obligations than on other WTO members.

As regards licensing activities in LDCs, available data indicate that licensing has not increased on a per capita basis since the conclusion of the TRIPS Agreement: licence payments on a per capita basis are the lowest in the world ($0.07) (between 2000 and 2005), and have remained unchanged since the period 1996–1999.

The 1994 TRIPS Agreement obliges all signatory countries to grant patents for any inventions, whether products or processes, in all fields of technology, provided that they are new, involve an inventive step and are capable of industrial application, without discrimination as to the place of invention, the field of technology and whether products are imported or locally produced (Article 27). Since the conclusion of the TRIPS Agreement, IP protection has been extended to include items that were previously unprotected in most developing countries, such as computer programmes, integrated circuits, plant varieties and pharmaceuticals. The original transition period granted to all LDC members of the WTO (until 2006) was extended until 1 July 2013, and until 2016 for pharmaceutical products and related processes.

The TRIPS Agreement[5] recognized that the implementation of high standards of IP protection would be difficult for LDCs to implement immediately, granting a 10-year transition period and providing for technical assistance for "the preparation of laws and regulations on the protection of intellectual property rights as well as for the prevention of their abuse".

Table 23. LDC membership in selected intellectual property conventions, as at February 2007

	Paris Convention (Industrial Property)	Berne Convention (Literary and Artistic Works)	WIPO Copyright Treaty
WTO LDCs			
Angola			
Bangladesh	X	X	
Benin	X	X	
Burkina Faso	X	X	X
Burundi	X		
Cambodia	X		
Central African Republic	X	X	
Chad	X	X	
Dem. Rep. of the Congo	X	X	
Djibouti	X	X	
Gambia	X	X	
Guinea	X	X	
Guinea-Bissau	X	X	
Haiti	X	X	
Lesotho	X	X	
Madagascar	X	X	
Malawi	X	X	
Maldives			
Mali	X	X	X
Mauritania	X	X	
Mozambique	X		
Myanmar			
Nepal	X	X	
Niger	X	X	
Senegal	X	X	X
Sierra Leone	X		
Solomon Islands			
Togo	X	X	X
Uganda	X		
United Rep. of Tanzania	X	X	
Zambia	X	X	
Non-WTO LDCs			
Afghanistan			
Bhutan	X	X	
Cape Verde		X	
Comoros	X	X	
Equatorial Guinea	X	X	
Eritrea			
Ethiopia			
Kiribati			
Lao PDR	X		
Liberia	X	X	
Rwanda	X	X	
Sao Tome and Principe	X		
Samoa			
Somalia			
Sudan	X	X	
Timor-Leste			
Tuvalu			
Vanuatu			
Yemen			
Total	**35**	**29**	**4**

Source: UNCTAD secretariat compilation based on http://www.wipo.org.

The TRIPS Agreement incorporates a number of flexibilities — such as compulsory licensing[6], parallel imports[7] and fair use/fair dealing (or statutory private use, as employed in European continental copyright law, e.g. France, Germany, Italy, etc.)[8] — that the LDCs can utilize in order to make possible the use of TRIPS-compatible norms in a manner that enables them to pursue their own regulatory policies. However, this does not imply that flexibilities are necessarily utilized. Firstly, TRIPS flexibilities are not utilizable in the LDCs unless legislation is drafted to incorporate them into national laws. Secondly, under regional arrangements for IP protection, many of those flexibilities cannot be utilized owing to membership of regional IP organizations, such as Organisation Africaine de la Propriété Intellectuelle (OAPI) (12 out of whose 16 members are LDCs; table 24) and the African Regional Intellectual Property Office (ARIPO). Thirdly, those flexibilities cannot be used because of commitments undertaken at the bilateral level[9] (table 25).

Other flexibilities include exceptions to patent rights such as the Bolar exception, government use and experimental use exceptions. Developing countries are advised to interpret the flexibilities in the widest way possible, and to incorporate explicit provisions into their national patent laws (CIPR, 2002). With respect to exceptions to patent rights,[10] under TRIPS, LDCs have considerable flexibility as regards promotion of transfer of technology, prevention of abuse of intellectual property rights and protection of public health. However, TRIPS-plus regulations limiting flexibilities, already operative in many LDCs, are likely to have an adverse impact on their access to the global pool of knowledge, which may further constrain national policy. When the Agreement on Trade-Related Investment Measures (TRIMs) (which discourages local content requirements) is also taken into account, it is clear that LDC prospects for effective industrial policy and learning are greatly diminished (UNCTAD, 2006c).

The TRIPS Agreement incorporates a number of flexibilities, but this does not imply that flexibilities are necessarily utilized...

... Firstly, TRIPS flexibilities are not utilizable in the LDCs unless legislation is drafted to incorporate them into national laws. Secondly, under regional arrangements for IP protection, many of those flexibilities cannot be utilized owing to membership of regional IP organizations. Thirdly, those flexibilities cannot be used because of commitments undertaken at the bilateral level.

Table 24. LDC membership in regional intellectual property organizations, 2007		
LDC	**ARIPO**	**OAPI**
Benin		X
Burkina Faso		X
Central African Republic		X
Chad		X
Equatorial Guinea		X
Gambia	X	
Guinea		X
Guinea Bissau		X
Lesotho	X	
Malawi	X	
Mali		X
Mauritania		X
Mozambique	X	
Niger		X
Senegal		X
Sierra Leone	X	
Somalia	X	
Sudan	X	
Togo		X
Uganda	X	
United Republic of Tanzania	X	
Zambia	X	
Total	**10**	**12**

Source: UNCTAD secretariat compilation based on African Regional Intellectual Property Organization (ARIPO), http://www.aripo.org; and Organisation Africaine de la Propriété Intellectuelle (OAPI), http://www.oapi.wipo.net.

Table 25. Intellectual property requirements in bilateral agreements between the United States and selected LDCs

	TRIPS-plus area	Definition of Investment includes Intellectual property
Bilateral United States–LDC BIT Agreements		
United States–Bangladesh Bilateral Investment Treaty (1986)	Requirement to accede to the Budapest Convention (micro-organisms)	Article 1c) "Investment" means every kind of investment owned or controlled directly or indirectly, including equity, debt; and service and investment contracts; and includes…. (iv) Intellectual property, including rights with respect copyrights and related patents, trade marks and trade names, industrial designs, trade secrets and know-how, and goodwill;
United States–Democratic Republic of the Congo Bilateral Investment Treaty (1984)		Article I c) "Investment" means every kind of investment, owned or controlled directly or indirectly, including equity, debt, and service and investment contracts; and includes: (iv) intellectual and industrial property rights, including rights with respect to copyrights, patents, trademarks, trade names, industrial designs, trade secrets and know how, and goodwill;
United States–Mozambique Bilateral Investment Treaty (1998)		Article 1 d) "investment" of a national or company means every kind of investment owned or controlled directly or indirectly by that national or company, and includes investment consisting or taking the form of: (v) intellectual property, including:copyrights and related rights, patents, and confidential business information, trade and services markes, and trade names; rights in plant varieties, industrial designs, rights in semiconductor layout designs, trade secrets, including know how (vi) rights conferred pursuant to law, such as licences and permits; (e) "covered investment under this treaty" means an investment of a national or company of a Party in the territory of the other Party;
United States–Senegal Bilateral Investment Treaty (1990)		Article I (c) "Investment" means every kind of investment, owned or controlled directly or indirectly, including equity, debt, and service and investment contracts; and includes: (iv) intellectual and industrial property rights, including rights with respect to copyrights, patents, trademarks, trade names, industrial designs, trade secrets and know-how, and goodwill;
Bilateral United States–LDC Trade Agreements		
United States–Cambodia Trade Relations and Intellectual Property Rights Agreement	Article 11(1)d : Requirement to join UPOV Convention Article 13(5) Extension of TRIPS copyright terms of duration from 50 to 75 years.[a] Article XVIII (1) a. Requirement for patenting in all fields of technology. TRIPS-plus because no exclusion for animals or plants, as possible under TRIPS Article 27 (3) b. Each Party shall make patents available for any inventions, whether products or processes, in all fields of technology, provided that such inventions are new, result from an inventive step and are capable of industrial application. For the purposes of this Article, a Party may deem the terms inventive step and capable of industrial applications" to be synonymous with the terms non-obvious and "useful," respectively.	
United States–Laos Bilateral Trade Relations Agreement	Includes Intellectual Property Chapter Article 13 (2)d: Requirement to join UPOV Convention Article 18 (5) : Patenting in all fields of technology . TRIPS-plus because no exclusion for animals or plants, as possible under TRIPS Article 27 (3) b. "Patents shall be available and patent rights enjoyable without discrimination as to the field of technology or whether products are imported or locally produced". Article 15 (4): Extension of TRIPS copyright terms of duration from 50 to 75 years[b]	The Agreement includes a specific chapter on Intellectual Property Rights. Definition of Intellectual property rights: Article 28 1 (d): "'intellectual property rights´ refers to copyrights and related rights, trademarks, patents, protection of integrated circuit layout designs and encrypted satellite signals, trade secrets, and protection of plant breeders' rights"

Sources: UNCTAD secretariat compilation based on Agreement between the United States and the Kingdom of Cambodia on Trade Relations and Intellectual Property Rights Protection done at Washington, in duplicate, October 4, 1996. Agreement between the United States and the Lao People's Democratic Republic on Trade Relations, 1997 (http://tcc.export.gov/Trade_Agreements/All_Trade_Agreements/indexasp).

Notes: a Article 13(5): "Whenever the term of protection of a work, other than a photographic work or work of applied art, is calculated on a basis other than the life of a natural person, such term shall be no less than 75 years from the end of the calendar year of first authorized publication…"

b Article 15 (4): "Each Party shall provide that, where the term of protection of a work is to be calculated on a basis other than the life of a natural person, the term shall be no less than 75 years from the end of the calendar year of the first authorized publication of the work or, failing such authorized publication within 25 years from the creation of the work, not less than 100 years from the end of the calendar year of the creation of the work".

The inclusion of TRIPS-plus clauses in regional arrangements, in addition to BITs, FTAs and other preferential agreements, can limit the use of flexibilities.[11] The stringent TRIPS-plus standards required, either at the time or immediately following accession to the WTO, are yet another example of the asymmetric treatment accorded in multilateral forums to the most vulnerable and weakest members of the international community.

Even with its inbuilt flexibilities, the TRIPS Agreement is highly problematic for LDCs owing to the high transaction costs involved in complex and burdensome procedural requirements for implementing and enforcing appropriate national legal provisions. LDCs generally lack the relevant expertise and the administrative capacity to implement them. Furthermore, although the Doha Declaration of 2001 was an improvement over TRIPS, especially in the area of health and access to medicines, it does not address the building of technological capacity. Since most LDCs lack sufficient awareness about the full use of flexibilities, WIPO, in cooperation with UNCTAD, should play a more active role in informing those countries about the full range of their possible use.

LDCs generally lack the relevant expertise and the administrative capacity to implement the legal provisions of the TRIPS Agreement.

The majority of non-African LDCs seem to confer patent protection for pharmaceutical products by applying the legislation of the countries whose colonies they once were (Correa, 2007). Despite the extension period, practically all African LDCs have followed suit, and this includes the granting of patents for pharmaceuticals. In the spirit of Article 66.1 of the TRIPS Agreement and paragraph 7 of the Doha Declaration (2001), which exempt LDCs from both making available and enforcing patents, and test data protection, they have the option of not enforcing granted patents and allowing competition in the relevant product market.

Various flexibilities allow LDCs to use TRIPS-compatible norms in a manner that enables them to pursue their own public policies, and to establish economic conditions supportive of their economic development objectives. While these flexibilities are mainly defined in terms of more generous implementation times, they also include exemptions in areas such as public health, where rules on compulsory licensing, parallel imports and experimental use are more relaxed. Table 25 provides a non-exhaustive list of selected examples regarding the nature of TRIPS-plus requirements in both bilateral investment agreements and bilateral trade agreements between a number of LDCs and their partners. For example, Article 11 D of the trade relations and intellectual property agreement between the United States and Cambodia (1996) limits Cambodia's scope for flexibility with respect to adopting a particular type of sui generis system for plant protection, which requires Cambodia to join the International Convention for the Protection of New Varieties of Plants (the UPOV Convention).[12]

Various flexibilities allow LDCs to use TRIPS-compatible norms in a manner that enables them to pursue their own public policies, and to establish economic conditions supportive of their economic development objectives.

Similarly, the Lao People's Democratic Republic and Bangladesh have entered into bilateral agreements with the United States that contain TRIPS-plus requirements (table 25). Moreover, the European Union and Bangladesh Cooperation Agreement on Partnership and Development (1999) encourages Bangladesh's adoption of the UPOV Convention by 1 January 2006. The EU Cotonou Agreement (2000) with ACP countries includes patenting for biotechnological inventions and plant varieties, as well as legal protection of databases, as part of its list of intellectual property rights falling within the scope of the Agreement.[13] All African LDCs belong to the ACP group.

(a) Free trade agreements and TRIPS-plus obligations

Owing to the TRIPS Agreement's inbuilt flexibilities, more stringent IP requirements have been negotiated in regional and bilateral agreements. The inclusion of these so-called TRIPS-plus clauses further limits the use of the flexibilities negotiated at the multilateral level, as witnessed in the mushrooming of Free Trade Agreements (FTAs), whose number has increased sixfold in just two decades (Roffe and Vivas, 2007). For example, some FTAs require that countries not make use of parallel imports, extend the duration of the copyright, while others restrict the grounds for compulsory licences. Some FTAs also impose data exclusivity clauses which restrict the use of the patent holder's test data as the basis for granting safety approval of the generic versions of the same drug.[14] For example, compliance with TRIPS and "going beyond TRIPS"[15] are one of the eligibility requirements for benefits under the preferential scheme of the United States' African Growth and Opportunity Act (AGOA).[16]

(b) Regional cooperation and regional intellectual property systems in the LDCs

Regional cooperation may offer some advantages as regards lower transaction costs and regional harmonization, but also disadvantages if regional commitments are of a TRIPS-plus nature, implying a higher level of commitments than stipulated under the TRIPS Agreement (table 24). LDC members of OAPI cannot take advantage of an extended transition period or a longer extension on pharmaceutical product protection (granted at Doha) unless the Bangui Agreement is amended specifically for that purpose (CIPR, 2002). The Bangui Agreement includes TRIPS-plus commitments that require TRIPS compliance prior to the agreed LDC extension deadline. The Bangui Agreement furthermore contains no exclusions from patentability. Unless amended, the Bangui Agreement will continue to restrict the issuance of compulsory licences to a greater extent than required by TRIPS.[17] The LDCs concerned should seriously consider the implications of that restriction.

4. CALLS FOR REFORM

After two decades of steadily increasing IP protection there are growing concerns about how far that process has gone. Increasingly, developing countries, including the LDCs, are concerned that the development dimension is not sufficiently integrated into global IP policymaking. In 2004, WIPO launched discussions on a Development Agenda, prompted by the recognition of global knowledge asymmetries and the need for greater integration of a development dimension into global IP policymaking. (CIPR, 2002; WIPO, 2007b). [18]

Recently, the Committee on Proposals Related to a WIPO Development Agenda (WIPO, 2007b) called for reform of the current IPR regime that would promote a better-balanced international system adapted to the requirements of developing countries. That reform would emphasize "the transfer of technology and access to knowledge and information, crucial to developing countries in stimulating innovation and creativity" (WIPO, 2007b: 15). During recent WIPO meetings on the Development Agenda (February 2007), various developing countries, including several LDCs, expressed their concerns about the possible adverse impact of stringent IPRs on the condition of the poor and strongly emphasized the need for impact assessment before the implementation of new IP instruments. The philosophy underlying the Development Agenda at WIPO is that IP protection should be enacted in accordance with the level of development of different countries and that protection of private interests should be balanced with that of the larger public interest (section E of this chapter). In a similar vein, the Secretary-General of the United Nations, Mr. Ban Ki-moon, has stated that "[t]he rules of intellectual property rights need to be reformed, so as to strengthen technological progress and to ensure that the poor have better access to new technologies and products" (www.un.org/ecosoc).

More stringent IP requirements have been negotiated in regional and bilateral agreements. The inclusion of these so-called TRIPS-plus clauses may limit the use of the flexibilities negotiated at the multilateral level, especially so in the mushrooming of Free Trade Agreements.

After two decades of steadily increasing IP protection there are growing concerns about how far that process has gone. Increasingly, developing countries, including the LDCs, are concerned that the development dimension is not sufficiently integrated into global IP policymaking.

Similar concerns reflect the fact that in a world where most developing countries, and just about all LDCs, are net importers of technology and depend on externally generated knowledge, the current IPR regime may hinder or prevent catch-up strategies. This locks poorer countries even more firmly into a low-technology, low-valued added growth path and further widens the knowledge divide between those countries and developed countries, where 97 per cent of the world's patents are currently held (UNESCO, 2005). Accordingly, assessing the impact of growing Intellectual Property Protection (IPP) on the learning process in LDCs cannot be divorced from its overall impact on development.

Moving beyond current arrangements means seeing IPRs not as an end in themselves, but as a means for development, growth and poverty reduction. Three options are currently under consideration. The first of these recognizes that current agreements still leave some room to achieve objectives with respect to the promotion of the transfer of technology, and seeks to design strategies that can make full use of that space (UNCTAD, 2006c). The second option suggests that given the technological constraints facing developing countries, some degree of roll-back (or opting out) is needed in the TRIPS agreement to better accommodate development needs (Rodrik, 2001; South Centre, 2002). The third option seeks to create new modalities for IPP that will better accommodate developing country needs. Those options, which need not be mutually exclusive, will be taken up in greater detail in section E.

The current IPR regime may hinder or prevent catch-up strategies, thus locking poorer countries even more firmly into a low-technology, low-value-added growth path and further widening the knowledge divide between those countries and developed countries.

C. Economics of IPRs and its applicability to LDCs

1. IPRs AND THE KNOWLEDGE TRADE-OFF

Ideas are among the most complex creations of human endeavour. Understanding what exactly they are and the creative processes behind them has alternately fascinated and frustrated philosophers and social thinkers for millennia. Economists tend to take a more prosaic perspective. Ideas matter to the extent that they fuel innovations and enhance economic growth and welfare. The positive impact of innovation on economic growth has been widely accepted in the economic literature, as far back as Adam Smith's pin factory. Indeed, in many accounts innovation is the primary engine of long-term development; to borrow the title of an article by two leading historians of technological development, innovation is "how the west grew rich" (Rosenberg and Birdzell, 1986). Certainly, the greater the number of individuals, firms or countries that have access to superior products and processes, and the sooner they have such access, the more widespread and substantial will be the economic benefits (Baumol, 2002). For poorer countries, seeking to initiate and sustain catch-up growth, access to the knowledge possessed by those higher up the development ladder is generally considered to offer a key ingredient in a virtuous circle of strong capital formation and technological progress.

Moving beyond current arrangements means seeing IPRs not as an end in themselves, but as a means for development, growth and poverty reduction.

That said, conventional economics has struggled to integrate innovation into its models, leaving it as at best a "sideshow...excluded from the central ring of the main performance" (Baumol, 2002). In part that is because of the determination of conventional economists to reduce innovation to the workings of the price mechanism. At its worst this leaves innovation as a *deus ex machina* set of freely available and clearly codified instructions that shifts the production possibility frontier, and whose contribution to economic welfare can be easily traced through changes in relative prices. More constructively, innovation is seen as a profit-seeking activity linked, in particular, to R&D. Accordingly, leaving the market to produce and disseminate new ideas may not be desirable because information problems lead to too many or too few resources being devoted to innovative activity. In particular, because producing new ideas involves the commitment of time and money (often in the form of specialized assets) with an uncertain outcome, it tends to be a high-fixed-cost activity vulnerable to copying by competitors. However, unlike in the case of a public good, it is possible for the creator of an idea to exclude others from using it, although this may damage social welfare by stopping the flow of ideas from reaching those who could use it most effectively. By implication, managing this knowledge trade-off needs non-market (social) mechanisms, of which (intellectual) property rights are seen as the most compatible with the working of market forces.

That perspective still tends to define innovation as pioneering activity to develop a new product or processes and is rooted in the rational behaviour of the firm. It also tends to assume that knowledge spills over rather easily from its original source. It thus underestimates the peculiar properties of knowledge as an economic good that makes innovation a much more complex process than is allowed in equilibrium models (Foray, 2000). In particular, it fails to acknowledge the tacit and local nature of much knowledge, which renders imitation arduous, since it underestimates the interactive and cumulative nature of the learning process that accompanies the production of knowledge.

Strengthening incentives to innovate depends on a broad range of economic, social and political factors, including the knowledge ecology, or the set of institutions that enable access to, and production and use, of knowledge for learning and innovation.

Strengthening incentives to innovate depends on a broad range of economic, social and political factors, including the knowledge ecology, or the set of institutions that enable access to, and production and use, of knowledge for learning and innovation (Dasgupta, 2007). The knowledge ecology represents the institutional framework devised to optimize access to, and production and use of, knowledge. The existence of property rights and the rule of law are certainly amongst the inducement incentives, but they do not act alone. A degree of political stability as well as clear-sighted leadership will also have a role in encouraging a climate where citizens are willing to invest in change, as will basic social factors such as health and safety standards and life expectancy. However, a range of government policies with respect to taxation, competition, human capital and the investment climate will be important in establishing the incentives to encourage the development of absorptive capacity at both firm and national levels. At the same time, the banking and financial system will have a pivotal role in releasing resources for capability building (Rogers, 2004).

Thus, the effectiveness of inducement mechanisms for innovation will largely depend on a country's knowledge ecology, or the institutional framework devised to encourage the risk-taking involved in any innovative endeavour, and not merely R&D, and the level of its technological absorptive capacity, or the ability of a firm to recognize the value of new, external information, assimilate it and apply it to commercial ends (Cohen and Levinthal, 1990).

As discussed in chapter 2 of this Report, the market mechanism needs to be supported in order to generate the climate for Schumpeterian entrepreneurship and innovation. The role of IPRs as inducement mechanisms for innovation can be evaluated adequately only in that context. Thus, unlike in conventional economics, the institutions associated with innovation are constantly evolving and adapting to unpredictable circumstances. In particular, the destructive consequences of innovation mean that it generates adjustments which can be disruptive and costly for (a not necessarily small) subset of citizens, while its intangible, cumulative and interactive dimensions mean that an array of "social capabilities" (Abramowitz, 1986) are implicated in the innovation process and in such a way that initial conditions have a very strong bearing on subsequent success. This also implies that innovation is a more coordinated process than suggested by conventional models and one which rests on a socio-economic contract between the Government, firms and consumers based on the notion of balance between the rights of the inventors and those of the wider public, and which is, moreover, also committed to making considerable resources available to learning at the micro, meso and macroeconomic levels of innovative activity.

2. IPRs, LEARNING AND IMITATION

Catch-up growth is partly determined by the size of the technology gap which separates the developing from the more advanced economies, and partly by the capability of developing countries to discover new technologies and to absorb more advanced technology already available from abroad (Rogers, 2004). That makes learning a central factor in any successful productive system, but also one that must be calibrated to different levels of economic and industrial development. In the case of LDCs, learning will principally revolve around absorbing already existing techniques and adapting them to specific local conditions, namely by imitation. Such imitation ranges from illegal duplication of standard products to deriving inspiration from the latest cutting-edge gadgets. But in most cases of imitation some kind of "reverse engineering" will be essential, based on a variety of skills and activities which would support a purposive search for relevant information and its development through effective interactions within and among firms and other institutions familiar with knowledge acquired from abroad. In that respect, strong IPR protection is likely to hinder rather than to facilitate technology transfer and indigenous learning activities in the early stages of industrialization (Kim, 2000; CIPR, 2002; Teece, 2005).

In the LDCs, learning will principally revolve around absorbing already existing techniques and adapting them to specific local conditions, namely by imitation. But in most cases of imitation some kind of "reverse engineering" will be essential.

The leading channels for accessing technology from abroad include imported goods, FDI and foreign licensing (see chapter 1 of this Report). The kind of knowledge needed in each case is likely to be different and tailored, policies and institutions will have to be devised to handle the technology transfer challenge. Empirical studies seem to support the hypothesis that stronger IPRs favour licensing through easing the enforcement of contracts and raising imitation costs, and possibly increased FDI inflows (Yang and Maskus, 1998). This contention, however, remains to be tested in the LDCs and is the subject of further research. Moreover, given the broader determinants of FDI and licensing arrangements and recent trends in LDCs (section B of this chapter), it is likely that imitation, based on imported capital goods and informal channels of technology transfer will be crucial for technological progress in most LDCs. However, even here, various social capabilities or absorptive capabilities will be needed if local firms are to benefit from the potential spillovers from imported technology, as has been corroborated by the case study in Bangladesh (subsection D.3 of this chapter).

Firms' capacity to tap into knowledge systems and build technological capabilities is determined by several factors, for example informal interactions with other actors in the knowledge system within which firms operate, such as universities (for human capital provision), financial institutions (for venture capital and financing of research), industrial infrastructure (for manufacturing products or acquiring information related to production) and entrepreneurial associations (for marketing and assessment of market-based conditions). Other actors in the knowledge system provide incentives (or disincentives) for interaction, thereby facilitating (or limiting) a firm's ability to build its technological capabilities (Chesbrough and Teece, 1996). As a consequence, the learning efficiency of firms depends on numerous country-specific institutional, infrastructural and cultural elements that predetermine interactive capabilities, organizational efficiencies and mobility of skills, including a country's knowledge ecology (OECD, 1999).

IPRs can be deemed as beneficial when they foster the development of firm-based innovative capabilities through diffusion of knowledge, technology transfer, foreign direct investments and licensing, among others. However, it is just as possible that patents can block technology transfer under certain circumstances.

Intellectual property rights can play an important role in stimulating R&D investments only where absorptive capabilities already exist, provided the compliance costs do not exceed the benefits. But in countries that lack absorptive capabilities, innovation is likely to remain, at best, underdeveloped in the face of greater protection.

Intellectual property rights can play an important role in stimulating R&D investments only where absorptive capabilities already exist, provided the compliance costs do not exceed the benefits. But in countries that lack absorptive capabilities, innovation is likely to remain, at best, underdeveloped in the face of greater protection. IPRs can be deemed as beneficial when they foster the development of firm-based innovative capabilities through diffusion of knowledge, technology transfer, foreign direct investments and licensing, among others. However, it is just as possible that patents can block technology transfer under certain circumstances. Firms may withhold technological information from particular countries for competitive reasons, a strategy that is facilitated by globalized IPRs (Gehl Sampath, 2006). The spectrum of anti-competitive deployment of patents that can hinder learning by firms through imitation and reverse engineering looms large in the context of weak competition enforcement in most developing economies (Maskus, 2005). Even where there is no such blockage, the higher costs (for inputs, seeds and intermediate products) may act as a deterrent, particularly in some industries (Sampat et al. 2003). These findings are broadly corroborated by the case study in the domestic processing sector in in Bangladesh (Gehl Sampath, 2007a; subsection D.3 of this chapter).

Making claims about the unequivocal impact of intellectual property on innovation is also rendered difficult by the fact that knowledge generation, accumulation and diffusion processes are different across sectors and technologies. Mansfield's study on the comparative importance of patents in different industries showed that patents were most important for the development and introduction of products in two industries — the pharmaceutical and chemical industries — where they accounted for over 30 per cent of development activities (Mansfield, 1998). In other sectors, firms tend to rely on a variety of other appropriability mechanisms to protect their innovations, such as secrecy and first-mover advantages, often far more than on patents (Cohen et al., 2001; Arundel, 2001).

Even within sectors where intellectual property is important, a variety of strategic motives prompt firms to use patents as an appropriability mechanism. Such motives include the use of patents as negotiating levers or as tools for prevention of infringement suits, blocking innovations from competitors or capturing extra value for innovative efforts. Excessive market power accumulated through patents can be used by firms to control diffusion of inventions and research results (Gallini and Trebilcock, 1998), and/or to cover entire areas of research or preserve market shares by accumulating "sleeping patents" that help capture extra value for innovative efforts (Barton, 1998; Kanwar and Evenson, 2001; Dumont and Holmes, 2002). Not surprisingly, in a comparative survey of the manufacturing sectors in the United States and Japan, Cohen et al., (2001) found strategic uses of patents to be common in the manufacturing sectors in both countries, with a higher prevalence of strategic patenting in Japan. The electronics industry is also a good example of strategic patenting. Thumm (2004) notes from the results of a survey of the Swiss biotechnology industry that, apart from protecting one's own technology from imitation, the second most prominent reason for patenting was to prevent competitors' patenting and application activities.

Recent attention concentrated on strengthening property rights as the way to establish the right innovation climate is likely to have been damaging for LDCs where the premium is on imitation. That produces an environment that chokes off the kind of reverse engineering options that were successfully used in a previous generation of late industrializing economies. As illustrated by the case study in Bangladesh, without imitation, learning will be made extremely difficult for countries with low technological capacities that rely on licensing for technology transfer only to a very limited degree,[19] (subsection D.3 of this chapter). The result, as recognized in a recent UNIDO report, may be a widening knowledge gap (UNIDO, 2006).

Property rights can be an obstacle to development insofar as their application directly imposes limits on access to ideas; restricts the policy space needed to build social capabilities; places a heavy burden on development budgets; increases the potential for anti-competitive activity; and reduces technology flows to the poorest countries. Although, these problems may not be immediately felt in low-income economies as IPRs are tightened (Maskus, 2004), because innovation is a cumulative process linked to continuous learning at various levels of society, it would be misleading to conclude that they are absent.

Although a number of econometric studies on the relationship between IPRs and technology transfer indicate a positive association of both variables,[20] there is little conclusive evidence about the positive impact of IPRs on technology inflows (Correa, 2007). In particular, there is no evidence to suggest that increased protection of IPRs in developing countries will lead to more opportunities for accessing the latest technologies,[21] or that the local rate of innovation will increase. While the availability of IPRs reduces the risk for potential transferors and may encourage formal modes of transfer (such as licensing), the increased power that IPRs give leaves it within title-holders' discretion whether or not to transfer the technologies they possess, and to determine the price and other conditions thereof.[22]

Empirical research on the East Asian economies (Japan, Republic of Korea, Taiwan Province of China) the most successful catch-up economies of the recent (and perhaps any) era, suggests that relatively weak IPR protection encouraged technological learning during the early industrialization phase (Kumar, 2002). The experience of the Republic of Korea's technological development shows that during the implementation of its catch-up strategy, "foreign technology transfer played a vital role in building the existing knowledge base of Korean firms. Simple, mature technologies could be easily obtained free of charge, through informal mechanisms, because they were readily available in various forms. Even if such technology were patented, foreign patent holders were lenient in controlling such duplicative imitation, as it was no longer useful for sustaining their international competitiveness" (Kim, 2003).

If adequate protection and enforcement of IPRs are genuinely intended to enhance development, policymakers should seriously consider differentiation of IPP in line with countries' level of economic and technological development. Otherwise the "one-size-fits-all" approach can be a recipe for disaster for developing countries, particularly for least developed countries. Developing countries should strengthen their own absorptive capacity for long-term solutions that would enable them to identify relevant technology available elsewhere, strengthen their bargaining power in transferring technology on more favourable terms, assimilate that technology quickly once transferred, imitate and produce creatively and eventually generate their own IPRs (Kim, 2000).

Empirical research on the East Asian economies suggests that relatively weak IPR protection encouraged technological learning during the early industrialization phase.

The "one-size-fits-all" approach can be a recipe for disaster for developing countries, particularly for least developed countries.

3. PATENT EXCESS IN THE KNOWLEDGE ECONOMY

The traditional consensus on the benefits of stronger IPRs is breaking down. The current IPR regime has been associated with excessive extension of copyright and increasing "strategic use" of patents, both of which are welfare-reducing (Davis, 2002; Bennet, 2002; Robledo, 2005). In many industries, the increasing number of patent applications can be explained not by the need to promote more innovations but by purely rent-seeking purposes — for example, defensive use of

IP portfolios to deter litigation by other firms. This can be used against possible new entrants who might affect the oligopoly rents available to the incumbents, and, therefore, as a tool to deter or even block innovation (Robledo, 2005).

As a result, many industries and technological fields are now characterized by the formation of "patent thickets" — an expression that describes the proliferation of overlapping and not clearly delineated patents. Efforts and costs devoted to sorting out conflicting and overlapping IPR claims are increasing, as is uncertainty about the nature and extent of legal liability in the use of knowledge inputs. Moreover, because the current copyright system grants exclusive rights only to producers of knowledge, and not to users of ideas and knowledge, persistent and divisive disputes contribute to a growing hostility towards traditional IP systems (Steinmueller, 2003).

At the same time, there is growing recognition that patents may not even be necessary since other mechanisms may be more efficient in stimulating innovation, particularly for countries in the "initiation phase" of technological learning. The characteristics of knowledge as a semi-public good do not prevent the first inventor from generating sufficient competitive advantages if the supply of copies of the invention is not immediate — hence the fact that being first is an asset that can be converted into positive prices, even in a private competitive market (Boldrin and Levine, 2004).

Certainly, historical experience confirms that copyright is not needed in order to stimulate creative activity (Gana, 1995). And those who have suggested that innovation is a much more collaborative process argue that the common heritage of information and knowledge ("the Republic of Science") is being threatened and eroded through extended IP protection for works created many years ago.[23]

In the knowledge-intensive global economy, copyright's capacity to limit access to knowledge will necessarily have an adverse impact on LDCs that need access in order to contribute to and benefit from the global research, information and communication system. Knowledge is cumulative and excessive copyright protection is likely to have an adverse impact on LDCs, since they are primarily users of imported knowledge, rather than creators. Developing countries are of the view that they are entitled to less restrictive access to all categories of works, without imposition of excessive technological protection measures (TPM) control mechanisms, especially as regards personal use, research and education (Knopf, 2005; Smiers, 2005).

Moreover, where overprotection distorts the efficient operation of the market for knowledge and ideas, poorer countries are likely to be the biggest losers. The elasticity of supply of creativity should be considered important criteria for determining the appropriate level of protection in the market for ideas, as well as consumer response to the price of creative works (Johnson, 2005).

D. Evidence of the impact of IPRs on learning

1. GENERAL EVIDENCE

A broad overview of the empirical literature strongly suggests that the effects of IPRs on technology transfers to developing countries depend on a country's level of development, the specific technological fields involved, the level of individual

In many industries, the increasing number of patent applications can be explained not by the need to promote more innovations but by purely rent-seeking purposes.

Efforts and costs devoted to sorting out conflicting and overlapping IPR claims are increasing, as is uncertainty about the nature and extent of legal liability in the use of knowledge inputs.

firms' absorptive capacity, the lifecycle of technologies, the sector in which IPRs are applied, the type of technology used and general market conditions (UNCTAD and ICTSD, 2003a and 2006; UNIDO, 2006; Todo, 2002; Primo Braga and Fink, 1998).[24] That view is corroborated by the case study in Bangladesh (Gehl Sampath, 2007a; subsection D.3 of this chapter). As countries' capacity to innovate depends on a whole range of economic, social and political factors, including intellectual property rights, fiscal policies, competition and finance, macroeconomic and monetary factors (especially the banking and credit system), it is almost impossible to isolate the strength of certain inter-related variables in the innovative process.

Indeed, the absence of IPP may be necessary in order to allow learning through imitation at the initial levels of technological development. IPRs may pre-empt duplicative imitation of foreign technologies which was crucial in the process of technological catching-up of the Republic of Korea and Japan (Kim, 1997). Another telling example is the successful development of the Indian pharmaceutical industry. On the basis of a strong technological capacity in chemistry and pharmaceutical formulation, the Indian generics pharmaceutical industry became a global provider of low-cost medicines and active ingredients in the absence of product patent protection (Chaudhuri, 2005).

There seems to be broad consensus (as implied by Article 66.1 of the TRIPS Agreement) that "in the early stages of their industrial growth, countries are primarily interested 'in being able to imitate imported technologies freely, calling for limited protection" (Maskus, 2005: 60). In addition, internalized forms of technology transfer, (i.e. those taking place intra-firm) are likely to be preferred by technology holders or constitute the only viable option when the absorptive capacity in the recipient country is low and imitation by domestic firms is unlikely. Logically, IPRs will play a neutral role since the transferred technology remains under the foreign firm's control and knowledge spillovers are not common in local firms, even in TNC subsidiaries (Correa, 2007). This was also found to be the case in the manufacturing sector in Bangladesh (Gehl Sampath, 2007a; subsection D.3 of this chapter). Moreover, studies by Glass and Saggi (2002) and Helpman (1993) suggest that the rate of global innovation declines with a reduction in the rate of imitation due to stronger IPRs.

The stated fundamental objective of the TRIPS Agreement is to encourage domestic innovation and international technology diffusion: however, since its adoption, the North South technological gap has continued to grow (Correa, 2007), and the knowledge divide has increased between countries (UNESCO, 2005). Empirical evidence of a causal relationship between stronger IPRs and an increasing level of technology transfer post-TRIPS is non-existent. Moreover, the evidence about whether stronger IPRs stimulate formal technology transfer via trade, FDI, and licensing is also mixed and inconclusive (UNCTAD and ICTSD, 2003a). Benefits, to the extent that they exist, are more likely to come from acceleration in the domestic deployment of advanced technology by the affiliates of foreign firms (Branstetter, 2005). There is more evidence that stronger IPRs will hinder informal channels of inward technology transfer, for example reverse engineering and copying, because of their increased costs for developing countries (CIPR, 2002; UNCTAD and ICTSD, 2003a). Moreover, literature demonstrates a growing concern that stronger IPRs will increase monopoly positions in respect of knowledge, thereby restricting opportunities for learning and technology transfer (David, 2005; Gehl Sampath, 2006; Hoekman, Maskus and Saggi, 2005; Maskus and Reichman, 2005).

The effects of IPRs on technology transfers to developing countries depend on a country's level of development, the specific technological fields involved, the level of individual firms' absorptive capacity, the lifecycle of technologies, the sector in which IPRs are applied, the type of technology used and general market conditions.

The stated fundamental objective of the TRIPS Agreement is to encourage domestic innovation and international technology diffusion: however, since its adoption the North–South technological gap has continued to grow.

Weak patents can help local firms in the early stages of industrialization to build their technological capabilities by permitting imitation and reverse engineering.

An UNCTAD study of 87 countries found wide differences between developing countries with respect to the impact of strengthened TRIPS; the importance of patents fluctuates considerably according to the technological nature of the activity they are engaged in and the technological maturity of the economy (Lall, 2003). The econometric cross-section evidence suggests a U-shaped relationship between the strength of patents and income levels; the intensity of patenting initially falls with increasing income as countries build local capabilities by copying, and then rises as they engage in more domestic innovative efforts. The turning point is $7,750 per capita (in 1985 prices), a figure well above that found in LDCs. The study suggests that weak patents can help local firms in the early stages to build their technological capabilities by permitting imitation and reverse engineering, as borne out by the experience of the newly industrializing South-East Asian economies (Republic of Korea and Taiwan Province of China). Similarly, research by Kim, based on the Korean experience, suggest that "stronger IPR protection will hinder rather than facilitate technology transfer and indigenous learning activities in the early stages of industrialization when learning takes place through reverse engineering and duplicative imitation of mature foreign product" and he argues that "only after countries have accumulated sufficient indigenous capabilities with extensive science and technology infrastructure to undertake creative imitation in the later stage does IPR protection become an important element in technology transfer of industrial activities" (Kim, 2003).

The strengthening and the expansion of patent protection do not seem to have stimulated innovation in developing countries so far. In Mexico, a study found no increase in domestic patenting after the substantial changes made to the patent law (1991), while a significant increase in foreign patenting was observed (Aboites, 2003). In the case of Brazil, in the period 1990–2001 only 27 patent applications were filed by domestic enterprises in the pharmaceutical sector — one of the most active in patenting worldwide — compared with 2,934 applications made by foreign companies (Elias, 2004).

The strengthening and the expansion of patent protection do not seem to have stimulated innovation in developing countries so far.

Another important consideration for the analysis of the role of IPRs in LDCs concerns the relationship between innovation and firm size: literature points to important asymmetries in the potential benefits of IPRs for small and large firms, even in developed countries — that is, patenting and enforcement of IPRs increase with firm size and the level of innovative activity (Curran and Blackburn, 2000). Studies on the relationship between patenting and firm size indicate that patenting is rare among SMEs, which prefer to protect their innovations through informal means such as trade secrets, trust and contracts (Curran and Blackburn, 2000; Correa, 2003). The findings from the case study in Bangladesh also corroborate the hypothesis that innovation varies with firm size (subsection D.3 of this chapter). Poor managerial capacity and skill level of workers, poor financing or lack of access to financial capital, poor support services, weak industrial and social infrastructure, a poor marketing and distribution network and a poor technological knowledge base make the use of innovation-related IPRs illusory for most SMEs in LDCs (Correa, 2003). In addition, obtaining patents and maintaining them in force is a very costly process. The acquisition of a patent is generally subject to a fee and requires costly legal advice on how to draft the specifications and claims appropriately. In many LDCs there are few, if any, patent attorneys. Even when a patent is obtained, the maintenance fees (that prevent the patent from lapsing) are largely unaffordable for most SMEs (Kitching and Blackburn, 1998).[25] Even more significant costs may be incurred in monitoring possible infringements and enforcing IPRs. Patent litigation may be extremely risky and expensive, especially if foreign grants have been obtained, and beyond the reach of most small and medium enterprises (SMEs).[26]

Historical experiences from a number of East Asian economies (Japan, Republic of Korea and Taiwan Province of China) demonstrate that systems with weak IP protection are better able to promote and facilitate incremental innovation, absorption and diffusion of technology, particularly in SMEs. Evidence from countries such as Brazil, the Philippines, Japan and Switzerland suggests similar findings. The Republic of Korea, for example, had almost no IP protection during the early stages of its industrialization (Amsden, 1989). The experience of late industrializers in Europe points to much the same conclusion (Chang, 2002).[27] Similarly, in the United States international copyright was not respected until the 1890s (Yu, 2007).

Historical experiences demonstrate that systems with weak IP protection are better able to promote and facilitate incremental innovation, absorption and diffusion of technology, particularly in SMEs.

2. FIRM-LEVEL EVIDENCE

Mounting empirical evidence about the impact of IPR regimes on innovation, from studies that evaluated the reliance of the United States and European firms on IPRs as a method for acquiring better protection for their technical know-how, shows that firms prefer to rely on methods other than IPRs, such as trade secrecy and lead times, in protecting their intellectual assets.[28] The most important surveys of United States firms indicate that patents are not a very important tool for capturing the benefits of innovation (except in the pharmaceutical industry), although their impact varies between sectors. The pharmaceutical industry is one of the few sectors where patents are an important part of the inducement mechanisms. More recent empirical studies tend to confirm those earlier findings (Cohen, Nelson and Walsh, 2000; Scherer, 2005).

This type of evidence implies that an exclusive focus on patents as the solution to knowledge generation may be misplaced and that patents are only a small part of the "tool box" used to capture rents from innovation (Cowan and Harrison, 2001), except with regard to the pharmaceutical industry and some high-tech industries.

Exclusive focus on patents as the solution to knowledge generation may be misplaced and that patents are only a small part of the "tool box" used to capture rents from innovation.

Empirical evidence about the impact of IPRs in developing countries in general is scant and ambiguous (CIPR, 2002; UNCTAD and ICTSD, 2003a). A recent study on the impact of IPRs in Mexico found that they play no role in stimulating innovation in the maize-growing industry (Léger, 2005). Other studies from countries with lagging scientific and technological infrastructure suggest that IP protection has not been a significant determinant of growth (Maskus, 2005). The case study of 155 firms in Bangladesh finds that IPR protection, an inducement to innovation, is better suited to TNCs operating in Bangladesh (conducive to rent-seeking), than to technological learning and innovation in local LDC firms (Gehl Sampath, 2007a; subsection D.3 of this chapter).

Competition, rather than IPR-based monopoly, can be a powerful incentive for innovation, as is illustrated by the Indian semiconductors industry (Jensen and Webster, 2006). Other studies suggest that IPP is not usually the driving force behind R&D (Hart, 1994). In the area of software in particular, non-proprietary models such as "open source" schemes have been very effective in supporting a vibrant process of innovation.

In the area of software in particular, non-proprietary models such as "open source" schemes have been very effective in supporting a vibrant process of innovation.

3. EVIDENCE FROM AN LDC: THE CASE OF BANGLADESH

Bangladesh, the country chosen for this study, is in many ways exceptional in the LDC category owing to its thriving domestic processing sector, which is actively engaged in exporting textiles and ready-made garments (RMGs), processed food products and generic drugs. For example, Bangladesh now exports a wide range of pharmaceutical products (therapeutic class and dosage forms) to 67 countries. In order to evaluate the impact of IPRs on innovation in an LDC, an original in-depth study on the impact of intellectual property rights as an incentive to innovate in the domestic processing sector in Bangladesh was commissioned by UNCTAD and conducted by Padmashree Gehl Sampath between October 2006 and May 2007, for this Report (Gehl Sampath, 2007a). The study used both quantitative and qualitative techniques in order to explore the impact of intellectual property rights on three domestic processing sectors in Bangladesh: agro-processing, textiles and garments, and the pharmaceutical sector. The choice of sectors was prompted by their relative economic importance to the economy, the relative importance of IPRs and varying degrees of sectoral technological intensity. Both the agro-processing and textiles and garments sectors are low-technology, whereas the pharmaceutical sector is a patent-intensive, high- technology sector.

The study had three main stages. In the first stage, a background report and a pilot survey on the state of innovation and the main incentives that play a role in driving innovation in the domestic processing sector were prepared jointly with a local research team in Bangladesh. The second stage consisted of 155 firm-level surveys using the data generated through the background report and pilot survey. A semi-structured questionnaire covering all three sectors was given to each firm. Of the firms surveyed, 50 were in the agro-processing sector, 60 were in the textiles and garments sector, and 45 were in the pharmaceutical sector. The third stage consisted of face-to-face interviews conducted with a cross-section of firms, as well as a variety of other actors, including leading professional associations, agencies and relevant government departments. Those interviews were used as case studies to interpret the results of the survey. More than 105 persons (including CEOs and top-level management) were interviewed for the study.

As a least developed country, Bangladesh is exempt from implementing the general provisions of the TRIPS Agreement until 2013, and has a further extension until 2016 for implementing its provisions on patents and clinical test data in the area of pharmaceutical products and related processes (in accordance with the Doha Declaration). However, the country is currently working towards gradual compliance with the TRIPS Agreement, and has a bilateral agreement with the EU to comply with its provisions before 2013. The EU–Bangladesh Commission is negotiating several aspects of the latter agreement, a part of which also provides that Bangladesh will make its intellectual property institutions TRIPS-compliant. The Bangladeshi Parliament is expected to amend the country's trademark, patent and copyright legislation, after a lengthy inter-agency approval and clearance process, in order to make it TRIPS-compliant.

Bangladesh's knowledge infrastructure is very weak when judged by conventional indicators such as R&D investments as percentage of GDP, centres of excellence for basic and applied research in both the public and private sectors of the economy or scientists and researchers per million inhabitants (UNCTAD, 2006b; chapter Introduction of this Report, table 1). Therefore, the study defined innovation not in the strict sense of that term, but as the application of new practices and production of all products and process technologies that are new to the firms in question (Nelson and Rosenberg, 1993). Those incremental innovations ranged from small changes in process technologies that lead to significant improvements in production methods, to new organizational techniques that lead to improved delivery efficiency for existing products or to the production of new technologically improved products. Innovation was measured by the number of new product and process developments applied by the firms in the past five years.

As a least developed country, Bangladesh is exempt from implementing the general provisions of the TRIPS Agreement until 2013, and has a further extension until 2016 for implementing its provisions on patents and clinical test data in the area of pharmaceutical products and related processes (in accordance with the Doha Declaration)...

... However, the country is currently working towards gradual compliance with the TRIPS Agreement, and has a bilateral agreement with the EU to comply with its provisions before 2013.

The study analysed the process of learning and innovation in the three domestic processing sectors and the various factors that influence innovation in Bangladesh.[29] It considered a large range of firm-level factors and their impact on new product or process innovation in the three sectors, such as the contribution of scientific/skilled manpower, the quality of local infrastructure services for new product and/or process development, financial constraints and availability of venture capital, collaboration with local universities, local R&D institutes, intellectual property protection, participation in local SME development schemes, participation in government–firm technology transfer coordination councils, and the transfer of personnel between local firms or R&D institutions. It sought to measure both the direct impact of intellectual property rights on promoting R&D and enhancing the innovative performance of firms, and the indirect impact on innovative activities, in terms of technology transfer, licensing and technology sourcing through foreign subsidiaries.

The survey covered large, medium-sized and small firms equally across all three sectors. A medium-sized firm employs between 300 and 500 workers in the textiles and garments sector and about 500 employees in the pharmaceutical sector. The agro-processing sector has a large number of very small home-based units (with fewer than 10 employees). In the textiles and garments sector, the survey covered specialized textile mills, ready-made garment firms and the traditional handloom sector (one of the oldest creative industries in the region). In the agro-processing sector, the focus was on the general food-processing industry, which uses, for example, spices, grains, cereal and flour to produce and market processed food products, as opposed to any specialized niche, such as shrimp farming or rice products. The pharmaceutical sector survey covered both indigenous pharmaceutical firms and subsidiaries of TNCs operating within Bangladesh.

The survey found no observable positive IPR impact on licensing, technology transfer or technology sourcing through foreign subsidiaries.

(a) Innovation incentives and the role of intellectual property rights

Innovative capacity within local firms is very low across all three sectors. The study finds that the presence of intellectual property rights in the local context does not play a role either as a direct incentive for innovation or as an indirect incentive enabling knowledge spillovers (through various technology transfer mechanisms such as licensing, imports of equipment and government–firm technology transfer). Currently, intellectual property rights within the country are benefiting mostly TNCs operating in the local market, as the local firms are not sufficiently specialized to protect their innovations. IPRs in any case may not be appropriate for the types of incremental innovations in which most firms engage.

Table 26 contains a summary table of the survey, based on descriptive statistics on innovation, contribution of technology transfer to new product/process innovations and other potential indirect impacts of intellectual property rights on knowledge spillovers to local firms. It shows that a large number of local firms considered themselves to be involved in new product/process innovations. There was no observable positive IPR impact on licensing, technology transfer or technology sourcing through foreign subsidiaries. Half of the agro-processing firms, 96 per cent of pharmaceutical firms and 55 per cent of textiles and ready-made garments (RMG) firms surveyed considered various sources of technology transfer, both public and private, to be of very little importance for new product/process innovations at the firm level. Other benefits of IPR protection in the local context that are usually referred to in the general literature on the topic, such as licensing and technology sourcing through foreign subsidiaries, hardly play any role. Only 4 per cent of agro-processing firm, 2 per cent of pharmaceutical firms and 7 per cent of firms in the textiles and RMG sector considered IPR protection

Half of the agro-processing firms, 96 per cent of pharmaceutical firms and 55 per cent of textiles and RMG firms surveyed considered technology transfer from external sources, both public and private, to be of very little importance for new product/ process innovations at the firm level.

Table 26. Innovation, sources of knowledge and indirect effects of IPRs at the firm level in Bangladesh

	Agro-processing		Pharmaceuticals		Textiles	
	Number	% of firms	Number	% of firms	Number	% of firms
New product development						
No	9	18.0	2	4.4	11	18.3
Yes	41	82.0	43	95.6	49	81.7
New process development						
No	10	20.0	31	68.9	6	10.0
Yes	40	80.0	14	31.1	54	90.0
Impact of various sources of knowledge on new product/process innovation						
Technology licensing[a]	1	2.0	1	2.2	2	3.3
Tech sourcing from foreign subsidiaries	1	2.0	0	0.0	2	3.3
Firm's own innovation efforts	18	36.0	7	15.6	25	41.7
Other sources[b]	30	60.0	37	82.2	31	51.7
Number of firms	50		45		60	

Source: Gehl Sampath (2007a) based on field survey, 2006–2007.

a Including through IP protection.

b "Other sources" was defined by the firms as mainly imitation and copying.

The only important sources of innovation at the firm level are attributable to firms' own indigenous innovation efforts and imitation and copying from others.

to be of any use. The only important sources of innovation at the firm level are attributable to firms' own indigenous innovation efforts, and imitation and copying from others (the "other sources" category in the table).

(b) Sector-specific results

Sector-specific inquiry aimed at identifying the main drivers for innovation at the firm level and whether IPRs play a direct or indirect role for innovation, substantiated the results of the analysis in the previous sections of the study. Table 27 contains descriptive statistics on several variables, such as government incentives and skilled manpower for new product/process development at the firm level across the three sectors. The values contained are the mean between 1 (very weak) and 5 (very strong); thus, any rating above 2.5 indicates that the variable is important for new product/process development at the firm level. The table shows that skilled manpower and good local infrastructure play a very important role as regards new product/process innovations. This validates the analysis in the previous sections of the study. Government incentives play an important role in respect of the textiles and RMG sector and the agro-processing sector, since both receive cash incentives for export performance. The table also shows that intellectual property protection does not play an important role as far as new product/process development is concerned.

Skilled manpower and good local infrastructure play a very important role as regards new product/process innovations. Government incentives play an important role in respect of the textiles and RMG sector and the agro-processing sector, since both receive cash incentives for export performance. Intellectual property protection does not play an important role as far as new product/process development is concerned.

Those explanatory variables were considered together with several other quantitative variables, such as employment and R&D investments, in order to estimate a bivariate probit model for a firm's incentives to engage in new product/process innovations. The dependent variable is a dummy variable which distinguishes innovative from non-innovative firms, on the basis of new product and process development efforts carried out over the last five years. For an independent variable to be included in the set of regressors, it has to be present in the three data sets, so that its effect across the three sectors can be compared and its effect in the pooled model assessed.[30]

In addition to separate models for each sector, a pooled model was estimated. The poolability of the slope coefficients, that is those associated with the exogenous explanatory variables, was tested using a Chow-type likelihood ratio test, and the null hypothesis was not rejected. The results are set out in table 28, and the pooled model with different sector intercepts is thus the more preferred model. The first

Table 27. Factors contributing to new product/process development in Bangladesh			
Contribution to product development	Pharma biotech	Textiles & RMG	Agro-processing
Government incentives	1.066	2.754	2.980
Skilled manpower	2.493	3.100	3.540
Collaboration with univs.	1.177	2.435	2.520
Collaboration with DRIs	1.087	2.364	2.400
Intellectual property protection	1.219	2.000	2.280
Good local infrastructure	1.980	2.799	2.860
Venture capital	1.581	2.017	2.240
Local SMIs	1.131	2.029	2.200
Mobility of staff between public and private sector	1.444	2.137	2.420
Loom & dye tech. contrib.	-	2.398	-
Number of firms	**45**	**60**	**50**

Source: As for table 26.

Note: Figures in table represent the mean of rankings between 1 (very weak) and 5 (very strong).

three pairs of columns form the general model with different slope parameters, and the last pair of columns shows the more preferred restricted model (pooled data). The general model reported in the first three pairs of columns was first tested against an even broader general model where all the potential incentives for new product/process innovations at the firm level were considered, and the set of regressors included IPRs, intensity of collaboration, areas of government/ other institution support, education of staff and level of training, and financial support constraint variables. It was found that those variables do not play any role with regard to the likelihood of their being involved in new product/process development in the three sectors in Bangladesh, and they were thus excluded from the model.

The results of the model can be interpreted as described below.

Firstly, the results of the study indicate that R&D expenditures, expressed as a percentage of total sales, play a negative role in both new product and new process development, as all three sectors mainly engage in very low-value-added activities, which are labour-intensive rather than R&D-intensive. The limited R&D that is being carried out is relatively removed from the needs of local production in all three sectors (see also UNCTAD, 2006b: chapter 6). The Government's current policies may even exacerbate this situation, as they are too narrowly focused on limited areas (promotion of exports and macroeconomic stabilization) and mainly favour urban, large and middle-sized private entrepreneurs. Consequently, public policies should be expanded to promote learning at the firm level, which would assist firms in their efforts to engage more in knowledge-intensive, value-added production and processing activities.

Secondly, larger firms (in terms of full-time employment) are less frequently involved in new product and new process development. That result can be explained by the fact that the data set is composed of a large number of small and medium-sized firms, (owing to the composition of the sectors, agro-processing and handloom production generally being small-scale). The smaller the firm is, the larger its relative R&D expenditure, and hence the result just mentioned.

Thirdly, intellectual property rights do not contribute to new product or process development in any of the three sectors (see also table 27). Most firms in the agro-processing sector did not believe that those rights played a major role either positively or negatively. They had major concerns about their impact on seed

The results of the study indicate that the limited R&D that is being carried out in public research institutions is relatively removed from the needs of local production.

Public policies should be expanded to promote learning at the firm level, which would assist firms in their efforts to engage more in knowledge-intensive, value-added production and processing activities.

Table 28. New product/process development in Bangladesh: Bivariate probit ML estimation results

Variable	Co-efficient	(Std. error)	Co-efficient	(Std. error)	Co-efficient	(Std. error)	Co-efficient	(Std. error)
	Agro-processing		Pharma biotech		Textiles		Pooled data	
New product development								
R&D intensity 2001–2005 (in log)	-0.169	(0.114)	0.072	(0.195)	-0.152**	(0.064)	-0.174***	(0.052)
Employment (FTEs in log) 2001–2005	-0.570**	(0.252)	0.000	(0.412)	-0.191	(0.121)	-0.294***	(0.099)
Collaboration with industry association	0.934	(0.793)	0.000 (assumed)		0.417	(0.446)	0.874***	(0.337)
Agro-processing	-	-	-	-	-	-	-2.414***	(0.548)
Textiles	-	-	-	-	-	-	-1.643***	(0.456)
Intercept	2.180	(1.588)	2.150	(3.005)	1.141	(0.974)	3.600***	(0.894)
New process development								
R&D intensity 2001–2005 (in log)	-0.219**	(0.089)	0.072	(0.195)	0.019	(0.108)	-0.115**	(0.053)
Employment (FTEs in log) 2001–2005	-0.336*	(0.180)	0.000	(0.412)	-0.703	(0.459)	-0.353***	(0.114)
Agro-processing	-	-	-	-	-	-	-2.317***	(0.521)
Textiles	-	-	-	-	-	-	-0.895**	(0.454)
Intercept	0.247	(1.191)	2.150	(3.005)	6.025	(3.944)	3.443***	(0.944)
Number of firms	50		45		60		155	
Log-likelihood	-17.095		-9.221		-26.947		-58.519	

Source: As for table 26.

Significance levels: * 10%; ** 5%; *** 1%.

availability and seed price. Larger firms tended to regard IPRs as more beneficial than did smaller firms, seeing them as a tool them which they could protect their products and secure economic benefits. Other firms, which considered IPRs to be detrimental to innovation, based their assessment on the indirect impact of IPRs on increasing prices of seeds and other inputs. However, at this stage it is difficult to assess with any conclusiveness the impact of rising seed prices on agricultural produce in Bangladesh resulting from application of IPRs. Most agro-processing firms do not produce agricultural inputs in-house, and the inefficiencies in post-harvest techniques and lack of organized sale of agricultural produce within the country do not permit a rigorous assessment of the impact of increased seed prices on agricultural produce.

In the textiles and RMG sector, most of the firms interviewed did not believe that IPRs played any role as an inducement to innovation, since they simply assembled the final output according to precisely given, buyer-determined specifications. Firms noted that that since they did not possess any indigenous design-related capabilities, IPRs could not be an inducement to innovation. Regarding whether they benefited from IPR protection in terms of increased collaboration with external firms, the general view was that the buyer firms did not help them in their efforts to upgrade technology or to enhance innovative capabilities since this would help them to create better backward linkages, especially in knitwear, and enhance the bargaining power of the local firms. Most local firms considered that such knowledge-sharing would be inimical to the interests of the buyer firms, which benefited from the low prices in the market due to the local firms' lack of bargaining power.

The firms in the pharmaceutical sector are mainly engaged in the formulation of active pharmaceutical ingredients (APIs), (requiring manufacturing skills only), and are striving to build capacity in order to engineer APIs (requiring knowledge-intensive chemical synthesis skills). Since foreign firms can obtain patents on their products in the country, the local firms were concerned that this might adversely affect their efforts to venture into reverse engineering of APIs. The patents on pharmaceutical products (approximately 50 per cent of the 182 granted in 2006) are not on local innovations. This points to the existence of other reasons for patenting, such as strategic use, monopoly profits, and prevention of parallel imports (Gehl Sampath, 2007a). This issue, however, needs to be explored further. As regards the indirect impact of IPRs on firms' activities, most firms in the survey have been unsuccessfully engaged in negotiating technology transfer in order to increase their that API capacity, reverse engineering skills and other such know-how. However, even those firms that have been successful in negotiating agreements with foreign firms considered that IPRs were not a helpful factor in promoting foreign collaboration for access to technology.

Firms that collaborate closely with industry associations are more likely to engage in new product development.

Fourthly, firms that collaborate closely with industry associations are more likely to engage in new product development; however, the variable "collaboration with industry association" plays no role in new process development. That finding is consistent with the study's analysis, which indicates that firms mainly seek support and lobby for policy change through professional associations, so as to make up for the absence of an institutional and policy framework that could stimulate and support innovation. Finally, ceteris paribus, firms in the agro-processing and textiles sectors are less frequently involved in new product and new process development than those in the pharmaceutical sector. Maximum-value-addition activities are currently taking place in the pharmaceutical sector. The textiles and RMG sector, although a high foreign exchange earner, has relatively lower value-addition capacity.

As already mentioned, the broader general model where all the potential incentives for new product/process innovations at the firm level were considered, including IPRs, intensity of collaboration, areas of government/other institution support, education of staff and level of training, and financial support constraint variables, showed that such variables do not play any role with regard to the likelihood of their being involved in new product/process development in the three sectors in Bangladesh. That points to one of the most critical issues facing all three sectors equally: the underdeveloped state of the domestic knowledge system as a whole and firms' low absorptive capacity. As noted above, the lack of engineering and scientific skills and public support for technological upgrading constitutes a significant barrier to learning. Strategic policy support that strengthens the absorptive capacity of firms, and enables them to move from labour-intensive to knowledge-intensive activities, is urgently needed to remedy that constraint on enhanced sectoral competitiveness.

Lack of engineering and scientific skills and public support for technological upgrading constitutes a significant barrier to learning. Strategic policy support that strengthens the absorptive capacity of firms, and enables them to move from labour-intensive to knowledge-intensive activities, is urgently needed.

In the agricultural sector, more research that meets the needs of the agro-processing sector needs to be conducted, including adaptive research on enhancing variety and ensuring the availability of fruit and vegetables all year round, as well as livestock research, according to field interviews. The scope of the New Agriculture Extension Policy, which focuses mainly on extension services for cereal crops, needs to be broadened in order to benefit the agro-processing sector. Most importantly, there is a need for inclusive policy action that also caters to the needs of the majority of the rural agro-processing firms. Similarly, the survey indicates that more concerted policy effort is required to promote the build-up of API capacity in Bangladesh. Such policy responses extend beyond property rights. Strategic policy action is needed in order to improve the impact and conduct of public sector research in universities and public research institutes in particular, so as to upgrade technologically, as required in the globally competitive pharmaceutical sector. Similarly, low value-addition capacity in the textiles and RMG sector emphasizes the need for policy support institutions. For

More concerted policy effort is required to promote the build-up of processing capacity in the pharmaceutical sector in Bangladesh.

all three sectors, the lack of government support to subsidize learning is a problem that should be addressed in the near future. Creation of human resources at the secondary and tertiary levels should be targeted. Policy incentives are required in order to translate individual capabilities into organizational capabilities so that human resources currently available in the three sectors can be harnessed appropriately.

Table 29 contains the survey firms' rankings in critical areas of support for engaging in more knowledge-intensive activities. The figures present the mean of rankings between 1 (least important) and 5 (most important). As the table shows, firms across all three sectors consider policy support to be critical in several areas, including science and technology support institutions, testing and quality evaluation facilities, and financial support.

(c) Summary of key findings

This study has conducted an in-depth investigation of innovation and competitiveness in three sectors of domestic processing in Bangladesh: the agro-processing, the textile and RMG and the pharmaceutical sectors. The objective was to evaluate the relative importance of IPRs as a firm-level incentive. The findings seek to contribute to the growing literature on intellectual property rights and development, and also make the case for broadening the discourse on the nature of knowledge and learning activities in LDCs beyond IPRs.

Innovative capacity within local firms remains very low across all three sectors. The survey finds that the presence of intellectual property rights in the local context does not play a role either as a direct incentive for innovation or as an indirect incentive enabling knowledge spillovers (through various technology transfer mechanisms such as licensing, imports of equipment or government–firm technology transfer). At the present time, intellectual property rights are benefiting mostly the TNCs operating in the local market, as local firms are not sufficiently specialized to protect their innovations under the current IPR regime. This regime in any case may not be appropriate for the types of incremental innovations in which most firms engage. The majority of local firms considered themselves to be involved in new product/process innovations; however, there was no observable positive IPR impact on licensing, technology transfer or technology sourcing through foreign subsidiaries. Over half of the agro-processing firms, and of the textiles and RMG firms (55 per cent in both cases) and the great majority of pharmaceutical firms surveyed (96 per cent) considered technology transfer from

Policy incentives are required in order to translate individual capabilities into organizational capabilities so that human resources currently available in the three sectors can be harnessed appropriately.

The survey finds that the presence of intellectual property rights in the local context does not play a role either as a direct incentive for innovation or as an indirect incentive enabling knowledge spillovers (through various technology transfer mechanisms such as licensing, imports of equipment or government–firm technology transfer).

Table 29. Areas of policy support for enhancing the innovative performance of firms			
Areas of policy support for innovative performance	Pharma Biotech	Textiles & RMG	Agro-Processing
Science and technology support institutions	3.734	3.651	3.940
Testing and quality evaluation facilities	4.179	3.785	3.620
Professional associations	-	4.584	3.500
Market research and intelligence	4.023	4.232	3.400
Overseas market promotion	4.178	3.685	3.280
Export credit program	2.890	3.284	3.420
Financial incentives	4.176	3.850	3.320
SME support	1.419	2.931	2.960
Number of firms	45	60	50

Source: As for table 26.

Note: Figures in table represent the mean of rankings between 1 (very weak) to 5 (very strong).

external sources, whether public or private, to be of very little importance for new product/process innovations. Only a small number (4 per cent) of agro-processing firms, 2 per cent of pharmaceuticals firms and 7 per cent of firms in the textiles and RMG sector considered IPR protection to be of any use. The only important sources of innovation at the firm level are the firms' own indigenous innovation efforts and innovation through imitation and or copying.

The firms in the pharmaceutical sector were very concerned that since foreign firms could obtain patents on their products in the country, this might adversely affect their efforts to venture into reverse engineering of APIs. As regards the indirect impact of IPRs on firms, most firms surveyed have been unsuccessfully engaged in the process of negotiating technology transfer in order to increase API production capacity, reverse engineering skills and other such know-how. Even those that have been successful in negotiating agreements with foreign firms considered that IPRs were not a helpful factor in promoting foreign collaboration for access to technology.

The domestic knowledge system is very weak in Bangladesh, characterized by weak industrial and scientific infrastructure, poor collaboration and sectoral interlinkages, and lack of skills and institutional support for technological upgrading. In that context, the study finds that the relative importance of IPRs for domestic processing sectors of varying technological intensity, as expected (on the basis of the experience in developed economies, and as indicated by economic literature), may not hold for LDCs. The overall finding is that IPRs are equally unimportant across the three sectors, largely owing to domestic firms' inability to engage in knowledge-intensive activities.

In conclusion, the findings indicate that policy matters in reducing the collateral damage that occurs when nascent sectors in LDCs are exposed to global competition. Coherent national policies that focus strategically on enabling innovation in the three sectors will play a key role in transforming those sectors into more competitive modes and enable local firms to deal with any harmful effects of IP protection. Furthermore, the findings indicate that without proactive and strategic public policy, in support of learning and innovation, the granting of IPRs does not generate higher levels of technological learning in domestic processing firms in Bangladesh (Gehl Sampath, 2007a).

The overall finding is that IPRs are equally unimportant across the three sectors, largely owing to domestic firms' inability to engage in knowledge-intensive activities.

The findings indicate that without proactive and strategic public policy in support of learning and innovation, the granting of IPRs does not generate higher levels of technological learning in domestic processing firms in Bangladesh.

E. IPR regimes and LDCs: Policy implications

As knowledge becomes an increasingly important productive asset in today's globalizing world, IP will play a more and more prominent role in the organizing of economic activity. But that role is not necessarily "development-neutral". Indeed, expanded IPP is associated with the proliferation of legal monopolies and related barriers to entry, which makes it harder for developing countries to compete in innovation-based markets. In today's knowledge-intensive global economy, those trends are accentuating the asymmetrical economic processes stacked against weaker participants.[31]

As knowledge becomes an increasingly important productive asset in today's globalizing world, IP will play a more and more prominent role in the organizing of economic activity.

The expected beneficial impacts of change in policy regimes are predicated on the notion that knowledge is the same as information and is a transferable commodity. However, contrary to conventional wisdom, technical change, learning, innovation and knowledge accumulation are endogenous processes — that is, knowledge is not a downloadable commodity. Previously, there had been some hope that the combined effect of globalization and ICTs would be a powerful driver and facilitate the process of development strategies based on catching up. Indeed, as the relevant data suggest, knowledge-based research and innovation activities (e.g. R&D, patents, licences and publications) are more unevenly distributed between the developed and developing countries than before; indeed, despite ICTs and stronger IPRs, there are clear signs of an increasing knowledge and technology divide (Johnson and Segura-Bonila, 2001; UNIDO, 2006).

Technical change, learning, innovation and knowledge accumulation are endogenous processes — that is, knowledge is not a downloadable commodity.

Equating "information" with "knowledge" may be the reason for exaggerated expectations regarding IPRs. But tacit knowledge cannot be transferred: it can occur only through the time-consuming process of interactive learning, learning by doing and learning by using. Furthermore, both tacitness and codification of knowledge is an obstacle to easy knowledge absorption, because of global knowledge asymmetries and "context specificities" that characterize knowledge. Knowledge is context-specific; it is socially and culturally embedded and dependent on the level of research and absorptive capacity in the recipient countries. Successful knowledge transfer presupposes the existence of domestic knowledge systems (i.e. a pro-innovation policy framework, infrastructure and appropriate institutional development, producer competence and learning, imitative capabilities and innovation capabilities at the firm level). The findings of the case study in Bangladesh corroborate the view that the local policy framework and a strategic vision have a critical role to play in the learning process (Gehl Sampath, 2007a).

The current pattern of IPP has undermined many countries' short- and medium-term technological learning prospects.

Most LDCs do not yet have the above discussed prerequisites in place (UNCTAD, 2006b: chapter 6). Without an adequate knowledge infrastructure and institutional framework to capture the potential benefits of new ideas and information, the benefits claimed for IPR-induced technology transfer are not likely to be forthcoming. Effective absorption of imported technologies crucially depends on the learning capacity of the recipient firms. A growing body of research suggests that the promised benefits of harmonized IPR regimes — leading to increased (external) knowledge flows and enhanced innovation, leading in turn to income convergence and poverty reduction — have largely bypassed most LDCs. Indeed, the current pattern of IPP has undermined many countries' short- and medium-term technological learning prospects. While TRIPS-based knowledge governance has provided a degree of confidence for foreign investors, in many LDCs this has been accompanied by sluggish domestic investment performance and a decline in their domestic technological performance. The expectation that property rights alone, without improvements in the wider knowledge ecology, would enhance their catch-up growth strategies has generally not been fulfilled. What is still missing is a credible relationship between incentives and outcome.

Throughout history, a stronger IP system has tended to be the result of technological development rather than its precondition.

Throughout history, a stronger IP system has tended to be the result of technological development rather than its precondition. Available evidence suggests that stronger patent rights are likely to increase payments from developing to developed countries without having a favourable impact on domestic technological capacity. And while FDI may strengthen patent rights in middle-income and large developing countries, this is not the case in the poorest ones. This is confirmed by the case study of 155 firms in the domestic processing sector in Bangladesh (with the exception of the pharmaceutical sector as a whole, which is dominated by TNCs). The findings of the Bangladesh case study indicate that IPR policies are not considered to be of particular importance to local firms in LDCs, which are not yet capable of innovation in the strict sense of that term (subsection D.3). Rather, low-income countries should focus on strengthening their absorptive and learning capacities, enhance the efficacy of their domestic knowledge systems and improve their knowledge ecology.

The TRIPS-based regulatory framework has transformed the conditions for learning in LDCs (most of which did not even have IP legislation prior to the adoption of the TRIPS Agreement, and many still do not) and unduly focused the attention of policymakers on the harmonization of IPP with what already exists in the advanced countries, but "the appropriate intellectual property regime for a developing country is different from that for an advanced industrial country"(Stiglitz, 2005: 2).

IPRs provide an incentive to innovate, but like any other incentive, it works only in certain contexts (Scotchmer, 2004). IPRs are not a magic tool that can boost innovation without other essentials, such as a critical level of skills, information, capital and markets.[32] Generally, it seems clear that patents stimulate innovation only marginally, if at all, in countries with weak scientific and technological infrastructure (at the initiation stage of technological learning). As the findings of the Bangladesh case study indicate, IPRs play no role in stimulating innovation in the textiles and garments and food processing sectors.

IPRs are unlikely to play a significant role in promoting local learning and innovation in countries with low absorptive capabilities in the "initiation" phase, which is marked by an absence of the basic conditions for patents to operate as incentives for innovations, namely high R&D investments and capacity for reverse engineering and low-cost production (Foray, 2004). In the second, "internalization", stage, local firms can learn through imitation under a flexible IPR regime, while technology owners face a growing risk of imitation, and tensions between domestic and foreign firms increase. It is only in the third stage — the "generation" stage — that local innovative firms in the most dynamic sectors can fully benefit from intellectual property protection (Kim, 2003).[33]

Even if, under certain conditions, IPRs were to positively encourage technology transfer through licensing, LDCs are unlikely to become significant recipients of licensed technology. The low technical capacity of local enterprises constrains their ability to license in technology, while the low GDP per capita in LDCs is not likely to stimulate potential transferors to engage in such arrangements (Yang and Maskus, 2005; section E of chapter of this Report).

In that context, any policies directed at increasing the transfer and dissemination of technologies should be actively supplemented by complementary measures aimed at strengthening firms' capacity to effectively absorb new knowledge through adaptation and knowledge expansion throughout society.

Licensing, as a channel for technology transfer, is also likely to be of little importance to firms in LDCs, as IPRs, particularly patents, promote innovation in profitable markets only where firms have the required capital, human resources and managerial capabilities. Similarly, licensing is out of reach for firms without a critical level of absorptive capacity. However, only in the "generation" stage of technological development can the benefits of IPRs offset the costs and constraints imposed on domestic research and production capacities.

For LDCs, improving their knowledge ecology, namely the institutional framework that creates the capacity to access, produce and use knowledge throughout the economy, will require far more than IP protection. The process of knowledge transfer is complex, costly and time-consuming. Advocates of strong IP protection tend to underestimate the difficulties involved in learning and in the knowledge-transfer process. The standard assertion that thanks to strong IPRs, knowledge can now travel freely and cheaply between countries is simply not realistic, as it disregards the complex dynamics of knowledge governance. Available evidence indicates that the expectation that more stringent levels of IP

Low-income countries should focus on strengthening their absorptive and learning capacities, enhance the efficacy of their domestic knowledge systems and improve their knowledge ecology.

The TRIPS-based regulatory framework has transformed the conditions for learning in LDCs and unduly focused the attention of policymakers on the harmonization of IPP with what already exists in the advanced countries.

The appropriate intellectual property regime for a developing country is different from that for an advanced industrial country.

protection will necessarily stimulate learning has not been met, as illustrated by the case study in Bangladesh (subsection D.3).

The current transformation of the international IPR system exhibits inherent market failures which are not Pareto optimal, insofar as (i) it increases the "excludability" of R&D results and reduces knowledge diffusion and informational spillovers; and (ii) by focusing on licensing and patenting as the salient mechanism of technology transfer, the IPR regime imposes incentives that threaten to crowd out other (superior) mechanisms. Another cause for concern is that the diversity of institutional arrangements is threatened. The post-TRIPS perspective that IPRs are the only means of valorizing intangible capital, and should therefore be the commonly used yardstick for the pricing of knowledge and ideas, is questionable.

The space for public research and knowledge-sharing is shrinking: functions that were previously assumed to be in the public domain can no longer be so assumed, owing to a growing trend toward commoditization of publicly-funded research outputs, including of data and information resources (David, 2006d; Okediji, 2004, 2006; Nelson, 2004). No longer is it safe to assume that publicly funded research will be distributed freely. Privatized or restricted information flows will inevitably slow down developing countries' learning capacities and pace of innovation; this will make it more difficult to improve on existing technologies and products, and thus slow down the process of technological upgrading (Sampat, 2003). Since technologies in the public domain can play an important role in the development of productive capacities in LDCs, restricting access to the existing pool of knowledge in the public domain, via strong IPRs, may hinder those countries' learning potential. The shrinking of the public domain can only exert an adverse impact on the LDCs' learning trajectories.

Developing country firms largely rely on informal learning mechanisms, such as imports of capital goods and equipment, imitation and reverse engineering, as important mechanisms for knowledge access and learning. That fact is confirmed by the findings from the case study in Bangladesh (subsection D.3). This implies that if an LDC is seeking to attract more FDI or promote entrepreneurial activities at home, it should address constraints related to efficient knowledge governance, growth and technology infrastructure before dealing with IPR issues. The relevant policy question is to ask at what stage of development, economic and market-based incentives (such as patents) start to "kick in". Furthermore, a stronger patent system may create new problems for LDCs as it tends to increase the adverse effect of excessive IPRs elsewhere. In a globalised economy, the strengthening of IP protection in economies that are rapidly catching up may even create negative externalities for LDCs, thereby slowing down their catch-up growth processes.[34]

In addition, owing to increased copyright protection (life plus 50 years), information flows are constricted more generally. Access to copyrighted materials has become more limited, as has the right to make reproductions for educational purposes. That may have an adverse impact on access to copyrighted works for education, research and knowledge diffusion in general. Although the TRIPS Agreement allows some degree of unauthorized copying via the "fair dealing" exception, these exceptions are increasingly being eroded via technological protection measures (TPMs) or digital rights management systems used to control access to or use of their marks by authorized users. That implies that the application of stringent IP standards may impede access to textbooks, journals and other educational material in poor countries by requiring the consent of, and likely payment to, the IPR holders prior to copying (CIPR, 2002). Experts are even more concerned about its impact on the Internet, which, despite its enormous potential for broadening access to education and knowledge dissemination in

The space for public research and knowledge-sharing is shrinking: functions that were previously assumed to be in the public domain can no longer be so assumed, owing to a growing trend toward commoditization of publicly-funded research outputs, including of data and information resources.

Restricting access to the existing pool of knowledge in the public domain, via strong IPRs, may hinder those countries' learning potential. The shrinking of the public domain can only exert an adverse impact on the LDCs' learning trajectories.

poor countries, can be constrained via application of encryption technologies that can override the principle of fair use or fair dealing by making every exception or limitation subject to the "three step test" (TRIPS Article 13). The principle of fair use needs to be preserved in cyberspace through both national and international regulation (Okediji, 2001, 2006).

1. One size does not fit all and the need for flexibility in IPR systems

The fact that the costs and benefits of a stronger IPR system are unequally distributed between the users and producers of knowledge, and that the low-income countries are likely to bear high costs without receiving much benefit in return (at least in the short and mid-term), creates a strong case for adapting the system to the particular country context. Given the countries' heterogeneities and the differences in their knowledge ecologies, the one-size-fits-all principle is suboptimal (CIPR, 2002). Avoiding general solutions to IPR management is recommended. The poorest nations clearly need flexibility as well as ad hoc mechanisms to build a sound and viable technological base.

The costs and benefits of a stronger IPR system are unequally distributed between the users and producers of knowledge, and low-income countries are likely to bear high costs without receiving much benefit in return.

2. What kind of technical assistance is needed?

Serious concerns have been expressed that the type of technical assistance provided to LDCs so far has not met the requirement contained in Article 66.2.,[35] namely that "[d]eveloped country Members shall provide incentives to enterprises and institutions in their territories for the purpose of promoting and encouraging technology transfer to least developed country Members in order to enable them to create a sound and viable technological base". To date, the technical assistance provided to LDCs has focused on designing and implementing IPR legislation consistent with the TRIPS Agreement, and not on their needs with regard to building "a sound and viable technological base". As such, it responds far more to the interests of IP rights holders than to the fundamental development concerns of LDCs (Correa, 2007; Kostecki, 2006).

F. Alternative knowledge governance models

Given the social inefficiencies inherent in the post-TRIPS IP regime, related to excessive privatization and commoditization of knowledge, the challenge in the policy design of alternative mechanisms is how best to address the dilemma of the knowledge trade-off — that is, how to simultaneously support and encourage increased knowledge access, production and use? What is the design of "superior" solutions to the knowledge trade-off dilemma associated with proprietary models? How to preserve access to essential technological knowledge that can contribute to incremental improvements, local innovations and capacity-building, and how to best create conditions for effective knowledge governance? What kind of catching-up mechanisms could substitute for imitation? Which new policy mechanisms can better meet the objectives of simultaneously encouraging and supporting the production of new knowledge while facilitating broad and rapid access to new knowledge? Logically, solutions will depend on the nature of knowledge and the cost structure of the markets for ideas (Johnson, 2005).

To date, the technical assistance provided to LDCs has focused on designing and implementing IPR legislation consistent with the TRIPS Agreement, and not on their needs with regard to building "a sound and viable technological base".

Providing broad and immediate access to information is important for two kinds of knowledge: essential knowledge for passive consumption (such as new molecules and compounds that enable the production of new drugs or vaccines); and cumulative knowledge or knowledge as productive capital (for active use), such as new information technologies that would enable incremental innovation and new applications in traditional sectors (Machlup, 1983; Foray, 2000, 2007).

Five sets of "solutions" for alternative policy designs are proposed: they relate both to improving the efficiency of the global IPR system (proprietary solutions) and to the use of non-IP mechanisms (non-proprietary solutions).

1. The first set of solutions deals with the improvement of the patent system itself at a global level, which may be a necessary (but not sufficient) condition for LDCs to benefit from a fully harmonized IPR system (i.e. calibration of standards and norms for countries at varying levels of development).

2. The second set involves using fully the internal flexibility offered by TRIPS to extend exclusion rights. The key issue is providing countries with the capacity to fine-tune their system in line with their needs and conditions, including via: (i) limitation on exclusion rights (exceptions and compulsory licensing); (ii) limitation on exclusion rights in terms of subject matter; and (iii) inclusion of new subject matters (e.g. traditional knowledge) in the international policy agenda.

3. The third set is related to the use TRIPS' external flexibilities, which consist of using the power of legal and regulatory institutions to reconstruct the research and information commons and support open source initiatives as a way of mitigating the adverse effects of the highly protectionist IPR environment by promoting the low-cost research and innovation model in LDCs.

4. The fourth set does not involve the direct manipulation of legal tools but is aimed at avoiding monopoly price distortions associated with IPRs (patent buy-outs and creation of incentives for price discrimination).

5. The fifth set of solutions is related to increasing R&D incentives in the area of neglected needs (public–private partnerships, advance purchase commitments).

Perhaps the most promising model for LDCs is offered by the open source mechanism, associated with the new knowledge economy paradigm. A shift in the nature of the innovation process is currently taking place in the most developed innovation systems (Von Hippel, 2005). The open source option involves a fast collaborative and incremental process, operating without patents but in a legally structured environment. The mechanism is mainly based on voluntary contributions of innovators to solve a problem collectively and then share it openly. While such models are not new, the Internet has greatly increased their productivity. As a result, this model has been widely diffused in many fields, such as software, biomedical technologies and consumer products, as illustrated by unprecedented incremental rates of innovation in software development, where high rates of innovation are correlated with rich information spillovers. The open nature of these projects emphasizes collaboration, lack of price-based competition and collective efficiency. Unrestricted access to innovation and release of data, codes, information and knowledge, all in the public domain, support incremental and cumulative innovation. This method of innovation has proved to be particularly efficient in supporting incremental and cumulative innovation. The essence of the model is the accumulation of small inventive steps, which are shared within a community and form a collective invention. Open Source software also operates in a legal environment, using, inter alia, GPL (General Public License) or "copyleft" license; other models use Community Source License Agreements (used by Sun Microsystems), etc.

Perhaps the most promising model for LDCs is offered by the open source mechanism.

The open source option involves a fast collaborative and incremental process, operating without patents but in a legally structured environment.

The objective of open source models is to create information and knowledge commons with important welfare implications in terms of: (i) no deadweight loss from above-marginal-cost pricing (directly associated with IPRs); and (ii) a built-in mechanism for price reduction, thereby increasing social welfare. In open source models, competition is based largely on the quality of post-product service rather than in the product development stage. Market entry costs are lower as entry is immediate; since innovation is shared; fixed costs of product development are significantly lower than in proprietary (IP) models. For innovators to be motivated to produce knowledge, there is no need for strong "rights to exclude", for exclusivity is not required in order to capture economic returns. Moreover, the model benefits from scale and network effects, as researchers and developers share new knowledge with their counterparts outside their own laboratories and firms. Access, production and use of new knowledge are achieved without the high social costs and inefficiencies associated with traditional proprietary models. This model is particularly applicable to LDCs because of its cost advantages and greater possibilities for learning thanks to the willingness of the innovators to share knowledge and ideas (David, 2005; Ghosh and Schmidt, 2006).

Fully exploiting the scope of TRIPS flexibilities is a crucial issue linked to the issue of the technical capabilities to use the opportunities offered by the system.

Other non-IP-based incentive mechanisms include: (i) subsidizing research (provision of funding for R&D through grants, tax credits, and work in government laboratories); (ii) developing prizes; and (iii) trade secrets. Additionally, other mechanisms that should be considered include: (i) legal provisions to stimulate firms to implement multipart pricing (Lanjouw, 2002); (ii) compulsory licensing; (iii) patent buy-outs (Kremer, 1998); (iv) advanced purchase commitments (Kremer); (v) public–private partnerships (Moran, 2005); (vi) information commons and open source initiatives (Maurer, 2003; Lessig, 2004; Nelson, 2005; David, 2005);[36] and (vii) compensatory liability regime ("use and pay system") (Reichman and Lewis, 2005).

1. LEARNING TO USE FLEXIBILITIES: THE ROLE OF NATIONAL AND REGIONAL IP OFFICES

Fully exploiting the scope of TRIPS flexibilities (limitations, exceptions or extensions, such as compulsory licensing, fair use or fair dealing and parallel imports) is a crucial issue linked to the issue of the technical capabilities to use the opportunities offered by the system. The institutional capacity of national IP offices is critical, since those mechanisms are difficult to implement; sophisticated knowledge and competences in law and international agreements may therefore be required.

It is essential that national patent offices build their legal competences for using those mechanisms more effectively; the considerable flexibility offered by TRIPS would then be better exploited by LDCs.

That is why a TRIPS provision involves the obligation for the developed countries to provide technical assistance to the LDCs (Article 67). It is also essential that the national patent offices build their legal competences for using those mechanisms more effectively; the considerable flexibility offered by TRIPS would then be better exploited by LDCs.

In contrast to patent protection, the costs incurred and the time spent by competitors in IP protection under trade secrets has no acquisition costs, while overcoming the secrecy barrier through legitimate reverse engineering may in some cases be substantial. Trade secret protection, however, may not be a valid option when the technology can be easily traced from a product put on the market. Additionally, enforcement of trade secrets may impose significant procedural burdens.

2. Utility models

Utility models have been implemented in a large number of developed and developing countries.[37] Box 6 summarizes the differences between utility models and patents.

Utility models are essentially suited to protecting "minor" or incremental innovations and can be acquired more easily and at lower cost than patents. In all countries where utility models are recognized, the great majority of applications and grants are in respect of domestic applicants, in contrast with patents, where foreign applicants largely dominate, particularly in developing countries.

The extent to which a system of utility models may be useful in LDCs is debatable. Given the low level of development of manufacturing activities in LDCs, it is unclear whether there is a sufficient flow of (minor) innovations that can be captured by the system. Also, it is unclear whether the availability of utility models protection will necessarily encourage such innovations. However, as most LDC firms rely on mature technologies and imported machinery and equipment, it is unlikely that at this stage utility models could be of great value to them, but this could change as their technological capacity is upgraded. Utility models protection seems, in any case, a better starting point than patents.

In addition to the traditional channels of technology transfer and dissemination, alternative means and mechanisms, such as joint research, country-level technology-sharing consortia, patent pools and technology-sharing consortia at the regional level, could be explored.

In addition to the traditional channels of technology transfer and dissemination, alternative means and mechanisms, such as joint research, country-level technology-sharing consortia, patent pools and technology-sharing consortia at the regional level, could be explored.

Joint research initiatives involving various firms and research institutions may enable LDCs to put together the human and financial resources needed to undertake well-defined projects. Significant efforts should be made, however, to overcome the lack of an innovation culture and to build up the required inter-firm and inter-institutional trust and operational methods. The role of "bridging institutions", such as financial entities, specialized NGOs, business and farmers' associations, and public extension and technology support services, would be crucial for linking possible partners and helping them to define common objectives and procedures (UNCTAD, 2006b).

Transfer and dissemination of technology could also be boosted through country-level technology-sharing consortia. Members of the consortia that receive technology from one or more suppliers may mutually support absorptive efforts and reduce the costs of incorporation of new technologies.[38] As in the case of joint research initiatives, a great deal of collaboration by bridging institutions

---

Box 6. Utility models and patents

- The requirements for acquiring a utility model are less stringent than for patents. While the requirement of "novelty" has always to be met, that of "inventive step" or "non-obviousness" may be much lower or absent altogether. In practice, protection for utility models is often sought for innovations of a rather incremental character which may not meet the patentability criteria.
- The term of protection for utility models is shorter than for patents and varies from country to country (usually between 7 and 10 years without the possibility of extension or renewal).
- In most countries where utility model protection is available, patent offices do not examine applications as to substance prior to registration. This means that the registration process is often significantly simpler and faster, taking, on average, six months.
- Utility models are much cheaper to obtain and to maintain.
- In some countries, utility model protection can be obtained only for certain fields of technology, and for products but not processes.

Source: WIPO at www.wipo.org/sme/en/ip_business/utility_models/.

would be necessary for setting up consortia among firms with low technological development.

Patent pools organized by technology suppliers in particular fields may also help to provide access to required technologies, where the latter are protected under patents. A patent pool is an agreement between two or more patent owners to license (one or more) of their patents to (one or more) third parties. The benefit accruing to LDCs from patent pools would require the agreement of patent owners to license their technologies free or at a pre-determined royalty rate. Patent pools can reduce transaction costs, as individual negotiations are avoided. Given that LDCs' markets represent a tiny portion of global markets, licensing conditions under patent pools could encourage exporting in order to enable potential licensees to exploit economies of scale from external markets.

The generally accepted view is that joint ventures offer greater opportunities for the transfer of technology than do other modalities of firm governance, since domestic partners share in the ownership and management of the enterprise that receive new technologies. There may be inter-firm cooperation, via joint research, technology-sharing consortia or other modalities, at the national and regional levels, although firms tend to prefer linkages with companies in more advanced countries that can offer up-to-date technologies, access to markets and other learning advantages, rather than to link up with firms at the same level of knowledge. Monitoring technologies in the public domain is an important source of learning for LDCs; therefore, restrictions on this option will curtail their options and learning possibilities.

While our discussion is by no means exhaustive, it suggests that in addition to IPP, a panoply of tools and mechanisms exists, many of which are already being used successfully in other developing countries to enhance knowledge governance. Policymakers in LDCs, in collaboration with their international development partners, would be well advised to explore those alternatives.

G. Conclusions and recommendations for improving knowledge governance

The 1994 TRIPS Agreement initiated a move towards minimum global standards on patentable subject matters with far-reaching implications for the catch-up growth strategy of LDCs. In the context of the single undertaking of the Uruguay Round, developing countries, including the LDCs, undertook to align large parts of their IP legislation with the legislation of the major industrial economies in the hope that greater intellectual property protection would lead to more innovation and increased technology transfer. However, the expectation that this would yield higher rates of technology transfer, FDI and innovation has not been met. The relationship between strong IP protection and development is not straightforward; the impact of strong IP protection depends on a country's knowledge ecology (the institutional framework that enables access to, and production and use of, knowledge for learning and innovation) and the level of its technological absorptive capacity, or the ability of a firm to recognize the value of new, external information, assimilate that information and apply it to commercial ends. Strong IP protection may induce FDI and innovation in countries with developed knowledge systems; however, in economies with weak domestic knowledge systems, as is the case in all LDCs, strong IP protection limits policy options and may even be negative, if associated with increased prices for inputs and restricted opportunities for imitation. Despite a differential sectoral

Inter-firm cooperation, via joint research, technology-sharing consortia or other modalities, at the national and regional levels can offer up-to-date technologies, access to markets and other learning advantages.

In addition to IPP, a panoply of tools and mechanisms exists, many of which are already being used successfully in other developing countries to enhance knowledge governance, which policymakers in LDCs, in collaboration with their international development partners, would be well advised to explore.

impact, those findings are corroborated by the case study of the impact of IPRs on innovation in the domestic processing sector in Bangladesh (subsection D.3).

The knowledge systems in the LDCs are very weak. Initiating a sustainable process of knowledge governance that could accelerate the development of productive capacities in those countries is a daunting task, but not an impossible one. Several initiatives proposed in this Report may alleviate the constraints faced by LDCs so that they can better integrate into the global knowledge economy. Such initiatives crucially depend on the learning capacity to upgrade the capabilities of different domestic actors, with a large input of development-oriented technical assistance and foreign cooperation.

The enterprise is the locus where technology learning and innovation take place. Any process of technological upgrading is inconceivable without the strengthening of entrepreneurial capacity, but this cannot be achieved via technology policies alone. Even in the absence of restrictions on accessing knowledge, no policy initiative, no matter how well designed, will catalyse learning until local firms begin to acquire the financial, managerial and technological capabilities necessary for incorporating new technologies and innovating accordingly. This process also requires institutions to provide technical support and establish linkages between local participants and external knowledge sources, e.g. technology providers, research partners, FDI partners, public and private R&D institutions, Internet content providers, other firms, educational and research institutions, NGOs, academic institutions, business associations and specialized technology institutions. Therefore, complementary institutional and organizational innovations need to dovetail with the learning process in order to enhance the technological absorptive capacities of the countries concerned.

A number of thorny issues arise with respect to the role of IPRs in the LDCs. Economists have found it extremely hard to measure the costs and benefits of IPRs, particularly at different stages of development. It seems clear, however, that IPRs do not automatically lead to learning and innovation, and may even jeopardize them. This is confirmed by the case study of the textiles and garments, agro-processing and pharmaceutical sectors in Bangladesh (Gehl Sampath, 2007a; subsection D.3). As argued by most experts, in the area of IPRs "one size does not fit all", and this implies that in the design and implementation of IPR policies it is necessary to consider the impact of varying levels of development and countries' initial conditions (CIPR, 2002; UNCTAD and ICTSD, 2005; Correa, 2000; UNIDO, 2006; UNCTAD, 2006a, 2006b and 2006c; World Bank, 2001). IPR protection has historically followed rather than anticipated economic and technological development.

Developing countries were subject under the TRIPS Agreement to the same standards of protection as those applicable to developed countries, subject only to transitional periods that have already expired. The same treatment was accorded to the LDCs; only longer transitional periods, renewable upon request, were permitted. As a result, LDCs are obliged to apply the same "minimum" IP standards as soon as the transitional periods expire or upon graduation. In many cases, TRIPS-plus regulations impose on LDCs even higher standards and obligations than on other WTO members.

However, TRIPS Article 66.1 recognizes that LDCs need a more flexible approach to IPRs, including the total lack of protection, in order to develop "a sound and viable technological base". LDCs still have the opportunity — until 2013 (and until 2016, in the case of pharmaceuticals) — to undertake an imitative path of technological development, as developed countries did in the past. However, that window of opportunity may close in a period shorter than

In economies with weak domestic knowledge systems, as is the case in all LDCs, strong IP protection limits policy options and may even be negative, if associated with increased prices for inputs and restricted opportunities for imitation.

Any process of technological upgrading is inconceivable without the strengthening of entrepreneurial capacity, but this cannot be achieved via technology policies alone.

that enjoyed by the majority of developed countries, and although LDCs may have the freedom to imitate, foreign markets will be closed to their products, as higher standards of IP protection have almost become universalized. Since interactive learning is a time-consuming, cumulative process involving many agents, our recommendation is as follows:

- It is recommended that the transitional period for LDCs should not be subject to an arbitrarily predetermined deadline, but become enforceable only once those countries have reached, "a sound and viable technological base" (as stated in the TRIPS preamble).

Moreover, TRIPS Article 66.2 requires the granting of incentives to promote transfer of technology to the LDCs. The Decision of 19 February 2003 and the Doha Declaration are steps forward in the implementation of that provision, but concrete measures to facilitate access to technologies by LDCs are either non-existent or insufficient. It remains unclear which measures that could effectively contribute to mobilizing technology transfer by developed countries' enterprises to LDCs need to be adopted by developed countries. As required by Article 66.2, incentives should be given directly to enterprises and institutions, in developed countries, since that is where most of the technologies are located. That obligation cannot be met merely through cooperation provided by public agencies.

- It is recommended that the concept of "transfer of technology", for the purposes of compliance with Article 66.2, be elucidated by the WTO, so as to make it clear that developed countries' Governments should provide firm-based incentives for the transfer of IPR and non-IPR-protected technology, and that "technology" should be understood as manufacturing methods, formulae, designs, and basic and detailed engineering — that is, knowledge that may be effectively applied to upgrade the technological capacity of LDCs' recipients, as opposed to a simple transfer of general training and technical assistance or scientific cooperation. ·

Furthermore,

- It is recommended that developed countries effectively implement their obligations under Article 66.2 of the TRIPS Agreement by adopting special incentives, specifically aimed at facilitating the transfer of technology to LDC enterprises (such as tax breaks and subsidies), including machinery and equipment. With a view to avoiding any inconsistencies with other WTO rules and reducing uncertainty for prospective technology suppliers, the wording specifically allowing such incentives may be incorporated into the GATT Agreement on Subsidies and Countervailing Measures.·

An approach consistent with the concept underlying Article 66.2 should not be limited to the granting of incentives whose impact with regard to securing successful outcomes is doubtful. Although LDCs can delay the granting of patents in all areas, this only permits LDC firms to exploit inventions patented abroad in their own markets. This exemption is likely to have only a limited impact in terms of setting up competitive production facilities in LDCs (in which internal economies of scale are not likely to be achieved). Despite the fact that IPRs are "private rights", WTO member countries have no limitation on adopting, in the context of the WTO's special and differential treatment, measures exempting exports originating from LDCs from patent infringement actions in their jurisdictions.[39] In practice, such exemptions may benefit only a narrow range of products manufactured in LDCs, but may provide a strong incentive for investment and technological learning in particular areas with spillover effects in other sectors of LDCs' economies.

It is recommended that the transitional period for the LDCs should not be subject to an arbitrarily predetermined deadline, but become enforceable only once those countries have reached, "a sound and viable technological base".

It is recommended that the concept of "transfer of technology", for the purposes of compliance with Article 66.2, be elucidated by the WTO and that "technology" should be understood as manufacturing methods, formulae, designs, and basic and detailed engineering.

IPR-related technical assistance to LDCs should be premised on the understanding that the introduction of IPRs may entail significant costs with little, if any, benefits to LDCs.

It is recommended that developed countries effectively implement their obligations under Article 66.2 of the TRIPS Agreement by adopting special incentives, specifically aimed at facilitating the transfer of technology to LDC enterprises.

- It is recommended that the technical assistance provided by WIPO and other organizations be unbiased and, development-focused, and inform LDCs about all the flexibilities allowed by the TRIPS Agreement. The content and forms of delivery of IPRs-related technical assistance should be defined by the recipient Government, in accordance with its own priorities and development objectives and in full consultation with other stakeholders, including public-interest-oriented NGOs.

- It is recommended that studies assessing the economic impact of IPR regimes on the development of productive capacities in LDCs be carried out, with the assistance and cooperation of all relevant partners, inter alia those from the wider international community, including UNCTAD and civil society.

Moreover, certain LDCs acceding to the WTO have been required to forgo the transitional periods enjoyed by the original LDC members and to provide TRIPS-plus protection in several areas. There is no legal or economic justification for such requirements. This burden should not be imposed on new WTO members, in view of the recognition — in Article 66.1 of the TRIPS Agreement — that IPRs may constrain rather than accelerate the development of a viable technological base.

It is recommended that the LDCs currently in the process of accession to the WTO not be required to provide accelerated and TRIPS-plus protection.

- It is recommended that the LDCs currently in the process of accession to the WTO not be required to provide accelerated and TRIPS-plus protection, and be granted the same transitional periods as those granted to other LDC members.

- It is recommended that LDCs use to the fullest extent possible the flexibilities allowed by the TRIPS Agreement (parallel imports, compulsory licences, permissible exceptions to exclusive rights, fair use, etc.) and seek to avoid the erosion of such flexibilities through FTAs, BITs or trade agreements, or in the context of accession to the WTO.

- It is recommended that the inclusion of IPRs as "covered investments" be reviewed in any further bilateral or regional agreement.

1. RECOMMENDATIONS AS PER TRIPS FLEXIBILITIES

It is recommended that LDCs use to the fullest extent possible the flexibilities allowed by the TRIPS Agreement (parallel imports, compulsory licences, permissible exceptions to exclusive rights, fair use, etc.) and seek to avoid the erosion of such flexibilities through FTAs, BITs or trade agreements.

- It is recommended that the international community reconsider the development dimension of the TRIPS Agreement, with a view to meeting the need for a balanced approach and pro-development IPR regime, especially with regard to LDCs.

- It is recommended that greater flexibility be built into the current patent system, with a view to obtaining more and longer special and differential treatment for LDCs.

- With a view to accommodating technological and knowledge asymmetries between economies, it is recommended that LDCs be granted LDC-specific IP standards with regard to novelty, nature of inventions, terms of protection and calibrated disclosure.

- It is recommended that with respect to TRIPS-plus provisions on patents, the scope of limitations and exceptions be increased in order to allow greater flexibility for IPR users. The full use of exceptions and limitations should be granted to LDCs, especially with regard to research and fair use.

- It is recommended that there be more flexibility in determining the terms of protection and the conditions for issue of compulsory licenses.

2. Recommendations aimed at improving learning capacities

The LDCs should consider the following measures aimed at improving their learning capacities:

- LDCs should be afforded special arrangements to provide them with access to information and knowledge in the public domain, which is increasingly being eroded owing to the widespread application of stringent IPRs.

- It is recommended that IPR provisions be excluded in FTAs with LDCs.

- It is recommended that as regards the terms of licensing, licensing conditions be reviewed with a view to accommodating LDC-specific market conditions, including factor prices.

- It is recommended that the current TRIPS-plus policy regime trends (through FTAs and BITs) be reversed.

- It is recommended that LDC-based resources and knowledge be pooled in the search for economies of scale and collective efficiency solutions in all IPR-related institutional arrangements, including in multilateral forums.

- It is recommended that guidelines be developed in Patent Offices with respect to patentability criteria — that is, to examine applications carefully rather than simply copy international standards (in drafting national legislation).

- It is recommended that national legislation be drafted with a view to providing clear criteria definitions in line with countries' own conditions and needs, without discrimination aimed at preventing the "ever greening" of patents phenomenon (i.e. extension of patents that do not add value).

- It is recommended that third parties be introduced to challenge the granting of patents (as done, for example, in Israel, Pakistan India and Viet Nam).

All of the above should be reviewed with a view to making the IP system a positive force rather than a barrier to development.

As regards alternative non-proprietary mechanisms for knowledge governance, the LDCs, in collaboration with the international community, should explore a panoply of existing mechanisms, which are being successfully used in many other countries, in order to stimulate learning and knowledge governance — patent buy-outs, price discrimination mechanisms, public–private partnerships, subsidizing research (directly and indirectly) via grants, tax credits, fiscal measures to support R&D and other types of innovative activities, developing prizes, government-based advance market commitments, open source collective mechanisms, information and knowledge commons, compensatory liability regime ("use and pay system"), joint research initiatives of various kinds, local as well as regional technology-sharing consortia, joint research ventures and licensing agreements with technology transfer clauses. Moreover, improving linkages between S&T institutions and the enterprise sector is highly recommended.

- It is recommended that in order to encourage institutional diversity for enhanced knowledge ecology, a plurality of options be explored with a view to accelerating technological learning and innovation.

The underlying assumption of this Report is that the main challenge which policymakers in LDCs need to address is how to improve the knowledge ecology,

It is recommended that the international community reconsider the development dimension of the TRIPS Agreement, with a view to meeting the need for a balanced approach and pro-development IPR regime, especially with regard to LDCs.

It is recommended that IPR provisions be excluded in FTAs with LDCs.

It is recommended that LDC-based resources and knowledge be pooled in the search for economies of scale and collective efficiency solutions in all IPR-related institutional arrangements, including in multilateral forums.

devise supportive policy frameworks and consider the plurality of options available with a view to better managing and benefiting from their own as well as already available knowledge resources. Establishing proprietary IP systems and creating property rights are but one response, among a number of responses, to a more generic and fundamental problem, which is how to create and improve their knowledge ecology. That challenge goes beyond fine-tuning the existing IPR regime.

Notes

1 This rapprochement has been intensifying since the introduction of software patents in the United States (an area subject to copyright in the TRIPS Agreement). Not all WTO Members have followed the United States approach.

2 This trend is identified with the "copyright maximalist" agenda that is currently being seriously challenged (David, 2005; Macmillan, 2003, 2005; South Centre, 2002, 2007; Musungu, 2005; Smiers, 2005; CIPR, 2002; Kozul-Wright and Jenner, 2007 forthcoming; Maskus and Reichman, 2005).

3 With respect to patent applications, data are available for only 17 LDCs; for varying years between 1999 and 2004.

4 See World Bank, World Development Indicators online.

5 Article 66.1 provides as follows: "In view of the special needs and requirements of least-developed country Members, their economic, financial and administrative constraints, and their need for flexibility to create a viable technological base, such Members shall not be required to apply the provisions of this Agreement, other than Articles 3, 4 and 5, for a period of 10 years from the date of application as defined under paragraph 1 of Article 65."

6 Compulsory licensing occurs when a Government allows someone else to produce the patented product or process without the consent of the patent owner. WTO rules on compulsory licences are outlined in Article 31 of the TRIPS Agreement and were reaffirmed in the Doha Declaration, adopted in 2001 (http://www.wto.org).

7 Parallel importation refers to "the importation of a good or service as to which exhaustion of an IPR has occurred abroad" (Resource Book on TRIPS and Development, UNCTAD and ICTSD, 2005: 93).

8 "Fair dealing" refers to the right granted by copyright laws to reproduce limited portions of copyrighted works without infringing the legitimate interest of the authors or copyright owners. This right exists in the United Kingdom and other regions whose copyright ordinances are derived from the United Kingdom, such as Australia, Canada, New Zealand and Hong Kong (China). In the United States, the term "fair use" is adopted.

9 See the WTO General Council Decision of 30 August 2003 for a system to address this issue.

10 Apart from a provision that exceptions should not unreasonably conflict with normal exploitation by the patent, taking into account the legitimate interests of third parties, Article 30 of the TRIPS Agreement does not define the scope or nature of permissible exceptions.

11 The issue of TRIPS-plus standards has been a sensitive one during stalled United States–Southern African Customs Union (SACU) free trade agreement negotiations with Lesotho being included.

12 Either the UPOV 1978 or the UPOV 1991 Convention.

13 See Article 46 (5) of the Agreement.

14 Some FTAs also restrict the use of test data for off-patent products.

15 "The extent to which the country provides protection of intellectual property rights consistent with or greater than the protection afforded under the Agreement on Trade-Related Aspects of Intellectual Property Rights described in section 101(d)(15) of the Uruguay Round Agreements Act".

16 AGOA has been in force between the United States and 48 sub-Saharan African countries since 2000, including 26 LDCs (source: http://www.agoa.gov/eligibility/country_eligibility.html).

17 This restriction does not apply to LDC members of ARIPO, which have more flexibility to mould their own patent legislation and practice.

18 See WIPO (2007b), Correa (2007), UNCTAD and ICTSD (2005) and UNIDO (2006).

19 Only 7 per cent of firms in LDCs engage in licensing (UNCTAD, 2006b).

20 See, for example, Maskus (2005: paragraphs 41–74).

21 In Brazil, for example, only one out of 176 "transfer of technology" contracts in the pharmaceutical sector registered with the National Institute of Intellectual Property included the exploitation of a patent. In 138 cases the use of trademarks was licensed (Elias, 2004).

22 The exception to this pattern occurs when there is a credible threat of compulsory licence or government use in accordance with Article 31 of the TRIPS Agreement. One example is the case brought before the South African Competition Commission by COSATU and others against GlaxoSmithKline, South Africa (Pty) Ltd and Boehringer Ingelheim, which eventually led to the negotiation of voluntary licences.

23 See the extensive literature, e.g., David and Foray (2003); Foray (2000, 2007); Von Hippel (2005); Jaffe and Lerner (2004); Suthersanen, Dutfield and Chow (2007); Nelson (2004).

24 For an exhaustive study of theory and evidence about the role of IPRs in technology transfer, see UNIDO (2006).

25 In contrast to patent protection, the protection under trade secrets has no acquisition costs, while competitors' cost and time involved in overcoming the secrecy barrier by legitimate reverse engineering may in some cases be substantial.

26 This is equally valid for SMEs in developed economies.

27 See Von Hippel (1981); Levin, et al. (1987); Cohen, Nelson and Walsh (2000); Scherer (2005); Arundel (2001).

28 See the empirical study by Levin, et al. (1987), which found that firms in 130 lines of business reported that patents were the least important means of securing competitive advantage for new products. See study by Cohen, Nelson and Walsh (2000), which concluded that in many different industries, being first to manufacture a product far outweighs the benefits of monopoly rents associated with patents.

29 Its results are corroborated by another broader study on the pharmaceutical sector in Bangladesh, which looks at all other components in the domestic knowledge system (such as universities, public research institutes, hospitals and clinics), in addition to the firms (Gehl Sampath, 2007b).

30 The main technology source variables were included when estimating the model for agro-processing only and pharmaceutical biotechnology only. None of them is significant, and they are jointly insignificant in each sector.

31 UNCTAD (2006c); CIPR (2002); Foray (2000, 2004); Correa (2000); Sampat (2003); Maskus and Reichman (2005).

32 There is strong evidence, for instance, suggesting that patents do not encourage R&D in pharmaceuticals for diseases prevalent in developing countries, as large pharmaceutical companies concentrate on projects leading to profitable drugs and tend to ignore those for which the effective demand is low (CIPR, 2002) .

33 For an analysis of patenting strategies, see Granstrand (1999) and OECD (2005).

34 According to the New York Times, TRIPS has become a mechanism for transferring rents from the South to the North. According to World Bank figures, the net obligation resulting from TRIPS amounts to more than $40 billion annually, which developing countries owe to American and European corporations (*New York Times*, 17 April 2007).

35 The Decision of the TRIPS Council of November 2005 also stipulates that in order to help LDCs draw up the information to be presented, and "with a view to making technical assistance and capacity building as effective and operational as possible, the WTO shall seek to enhance its cooperation with WIPO and with other relevant international organizations". The WTO has set up a working group on trade and transfer of technology to address this issue.

36 For a more extensive discussion of these mechanisms, see Foray (2007).

37 Utility patents are used in many countries, including Argentina, Armenia, Austria, Belarus, Belgium, Brazil, Bulgaria, China, Colombia, Costa Rica, Czech Republic, Denmark, Estonia, Ethiopia, Finland, France, Georgia, Germany, Greece, Guatemala, Hungary, Ireland, Italy, Japan, Kazakhstan, Kenya, Kyrgyzstan, Malaysia, Mexico, Netherlands, members of the African Organization of Intellectual Property, members of the Andean Community, Philippines, Poland, Portugal, Republic of Korea, Moldova, Russian Federation, Slovakia, Spain, Tajikistan, Trinidad and Tobago, Turkey, Ukraine, Uruguay and Uzbekistan.

38 As amply demonstrated in the literature on the economics of innovation, and contrary to Arrow's concept of a passive, automatic and costless process, the adoption of technologies requires deliberate efforts and investment (Radosevic, 1999).

39 The details of such an exemption should be carefully worked out in order to avoid fraud in its implementation as well as legal challenges based on eventual limitations imposed on the exercise of pre-existing rights.

References

Aboites, J. (2003). Innovación, patentes y globalización. In Aboites, J. and Dutrénit, G. (eds.), *Innovación, Aprendizaje y Creación de Capacidades Tecnológicas*. Universidad Autónoma Metropolitana, Mexico City.

Abramovitz, M. (1986). Catching-up, forging ahead and falling behind. *Journal of Economic History,* 46 (2): 385–406.

Amsden, A.H. (1989). *Asia's Next Giant: South Korea and Late Industrialization*. Oxford University Press, New York.

Arundel, A. (2001). The relative effectiveness of patents and secrecy for appropriation. *Research Policy*, 30 (4): 611–624.

Barton, J.H. (1998). The impact of contemporary patent law on plant biotechnology research. In Eberhart, S.A., et al. (eds.), *Intellectual Property Rights III: Global Genetic Resources: Access and Property Rights*. Crop Science Society of America (CSSA), Madison.

Baumol, W. (2002). *The Free Market Innovation Machine: Analyzing the Growth Miracle of Capitalism*. Princeton University Press, Princeton, NJ.

Bennett, D. (2002). The power of patents and their strategic use (The 2002 Law Journal), *Business North Carolina*, Oct. 64.

Boldrin, M. and Levine, D.K. (2004). The case against intellectual monopoly – 2003 Lawrence R. Klein Lecture. *International Economic Review*, 45 (2): 327–350.

Boyle, J. (2004). A manifesto on WIPO and the future of intellectual property. *Duke Law & Technology Review,* No. 9.

Branstetter, L.G. (2005). Do stronger patents induce more local innovation? In Maskus, K. and Reichman, J.H. (eds.), *International Public Goods and Transfer and Technology: Under a Globalized Intellectual Property Regime*. Cambridge University Press, Cambridge.

Burk, D.L. and Cohen, J.E. (2001). Fair use infrastructure for rights management systems. *Harvard Journal of Law & Technology*, 15 (1): 41–83.

Chang, H.J. (2002). *Kicking Away the Ladder: Development Strategy in Historical Perspective*. Anthem Press, London.

Chaudhuri, S. (2005). *The WTO and India's Pharmaceuticals Industry: Patent Protection, TRIPS and Developing Countries*. Oxford University Press India, New Delhi.

Chesbrough, H.W. and Teece, D.J. (1996). When is virtual virtuous? Organizing for innovation. *Harvard Business Review*, 74 (1): 65–73.

CIPR (2002). Integrating intellectual property rights and development policy. Report of the Commission on Intellectual Property Rights, London.

Cohen, W. and Levinthal, D. (1990). Absorptive capacity: A new perspective on learning and Innovation. *Administrative Science Quarterly*, 35 (1): 128–152.

Cohen, W.M, Nelson, R.R., and Walsh, J. (2000). Protecting their intellectual assets: Appropriability conditions and why US manufacturing firms patent (or not). NBER Working Paper No. 7552, National Bureau of Economic Research, Cambridge, Mass.

Cohen, W., Goto, A., Nagata, A., Nelson, R. and Walsh, J. (2001). R&D spillovers, patents and the incentives to innovate in Japan and the United States. *Research Policy,* 31 (8-9): 1349–1367.

Correa, C. (2000). Emerging trends: New patterns of technology transfer. In Patel, S., Roffe, P. and Yusf, A. (eds.), *International Technology Transfer: The Origins and Aftermath of the United Nations Negotiations on a Draft Code of Conduct*. Kluwer Law International, The Hague.

Correa, C. (2003). Do small and medium enterprises benefit from patent protection? In Pietrobelli, C. and Sverrisson, A. (eds.), *Linking Local and Global Economies: Organisation, Technology and Export Opportunities for SMEs*. Routledge, London and New York.

Correa, C. (2007). Technology transfer and IPRs. Study prepared as a background paper for *The Least Developed Countries Report 2007*, UNCTAD, Geneva.

Cowan, R. and Harrison, E. (2001). Intellectual property rights in a knowledge-based economy. Research Memoranda No. 26, UNU-MERIT, Maastricht.

Curran, J. and Blackburn, R. (2000). *Researching the Small Firm*. Sage, London.

Dasgupta, P. (2007). *Economics: A Very Short Introduction*. Oxford University Press, Oxford.

David, P.A. (2005). Economic development, growth and the ICT connection. Presentation prepared for the WSIS Thematic Meeting — Economic and Social Implications, 17–19 January, Antigua.

David, P.A. (2006a). Property and the pursuit of knowledge: IPR issues affecting scientific research. *Research Policy*, 35 (6): 767–771.

David, P.A. (2006b). Reflections on the patent system and IPR protection in the past, present and future. Stanford Institute for Economic Policy Research (SIEPR) Discussion Paper No. 05–15, Stanford University, Stanford, CA.

David, P.A. (2006c). Towards a cyber infrastructure for enhanced scientific collaboration: Providing its "soft" foundations may be the hardest part. In Kahin, B. and Foray, D. (eds.), *Advancing Knowledge and the Knowledge Economy*. MIT Press, Cambridge, Mass.

David, P.A. (2006d). Using IPR to expand the research common for science: New moves in "legal" jujitsu. A presentation to the Intellectual Property Rights for Business and Society Conference, DIME-EU Network of Excellence, 14–15 September, London.

David, P.A. and Foray, D. (2003). Economic fundamentals of the knowledge society. *Policy Futures in Education*, 1 (1): 20–49.

David, P.A. and Hall, B.H. (2006). Property and the pursuit of knowledge: IPR issues affecting scientific research. *Research Policy*, 35 (6): 767–771.

Davis, L. (2002). The strategic use of patents in international business department of industrial economics and strategy. Copenhagen Business School, Proposal for a workshop paper delivered to the 28th Annual EIBA Conference, Athens, Greece.

Drahos, P. and Braithwaite, J. (2004). *Who Owns the Knowledge Economy? Political Organising Behind TRIPS*. Earthscan, London.

Dumont, B. and Holmes, P. (2002). The scope of intellectual property rights and their interface with competition law and policy: Divergent paths to the same goal? *Economics of Innovation and New Technology*, 11 (2): 149–162.

Elias, L.A. (2004). Transferência de tecnologia: indicadores recentes sobre a indústria farmacêutica. Paper submitted to the conference 10 anos do TRIPS: Democratização do Acesso à Saúde, São Paulo, mimeo.

Fisch, G. and Speyer, B. (1995). TRIPS as an adjustment mechanism in North–South trade. *Economics*. 55/56: 85–93.

Foray, D. (2000). *The Economics of Knowledge*. MIT Press, Cambridge, Mass.

Foray, D. (2004). The patent system and the dynamics of innovation in Europe. *Science and Public Policy*, 31 (6): 449–456.

Foray, D. (2007). Knowledge, intellectual property and development in LDCs: Toward innovative policy initiatives. Study prepared for UNCTAD as a background paper for *The Least Developed Countries Report 2007*, UNCTAD, Geneva.

Gallini, N.T. and Trebilcock, M. (1998). Intellectual property rights and competition policy: A framework for analysis of economic and legal issues. In Anderson, R. and Gallini, N. (eds.), *Competition Policy and Intellectual Property Rights in the Knowledge-Based Economy*. University of Calgary Press, Calgary.

Gana, R.L. (1995). Has creativity died in the third world? Some implications of the internationalization of intellectual property. *Denver Journal of International Law*, 24 (1): 109–144.

Gehl Sampath, P. (2006). Breaking the fence: Patent right and biomedical innovation in "technology followers". UNU-MERIT, Maastricht.

Gehl Sampath, P. (2007a), Intellectual property in least developed countries: pharmaceutical, agro-processing and textiles and RMG in Bangladesh. Study prepared for UNCTAD as a background paper for *The Least Developed Countries Report 2007*, UNCTAD, Geneva.

Gehl Sampath, P. (2007b). Innovation and health in developing countries: Can Bangladesh's pharmaceutical sector help? UNU-Merit, Maastricht.

Ghosh, R. and Schmidt, P. (2006). Open source and open standards: A new frontier for economic development, UNU-MERIT, Maastricht.

Glass, A. and Saggi, K. (2002). Intellectual property rights and foreign direct Investment. *Journal of International Economics*, 56 (2): 387–410.

Granstrand, O. (1999). *The Economics and Management of Intellectual Property: Towards Intellectual Capitalism*. Edward Elgar, Cheltenham and Northampton, United Kingdom and Mass.

Hall, B.H. (2005). Government policy for innovation in Latin America. Presentation at the Barcelona Conference on R&D and Innovation in the Development Process, a Report to the World Bank, Barcelona.

Hart, M. (1994). Getting back to basics: Reinventing patent law for economic efficiency. *Intellectual Property Journal*, 8 (2).

Helpman, E. (1993). Innovation, imitation and intellectual property rights. *Econometrics*, 61 (6): 1247–1280.

Hoekman, B.M., Maskus, K.E. and Saggi, K. (2005). Transfer of technology to developing countries: Unilateral and multilateral policy options. *World Development*, 33 (10): 1587–1602.

Idris, K. (2003). *Intellectual Property: A Power Tool for Economic Growth*. World Intellectual Property Organization (WIPO), Geneva.

Jaffe, A. B. and Lerner, J. (2004). *Innovation and Its Discontents: How Our Broken Patent System is Endangering Innovation and Progress, and What to Do About It*. Princeton University Press, Princeton, NJ.

Jensen, P.H. and Webster, E. (2006). Firm size and the use of intellectual property rights. *The Ecomomic Society of Australia in the Economic Record*, 82 (256): 44–55.

Johnson, B. and Segura-Bonilla, O. (2001). Innovation systems and developing countries: Experiences from the SUDESCA project. DRUID Working Paper No. 01–12, Danish Research Unit for Industrial Dynamics, Aalborg.

Johnson, W.R. (2005). The economics of ideas and the ideas of economists. *Southern Economic Journal*, 73 (1): 2–12.

Kaddar, M. and Gaulé, P. (2004). Le marché mondial des vaccins: Évolution et dynamisme. *Réseau Médicaments et Développement*, 29: 1–4.

Kanwar, S. and Evenson, R.E. (2001). Does intellectual property protection spur technological change? Economic Growth Center Discussion Paper No. 831, Yale University, New Haven, CT.

Kim, L. (1997). *Imitation to Innovation: The Dynamics of Korea's Technological Learning*. Harvard Business School Press, Boston.

Kim, L. (2000). The dynamics of technological learning in industrialization. Discussion Paper Series No. 2000–7, UNU-INTECH, Maastricht.

Kim, L. (2003). Technology transfer and intellectual property rights: Lessons from Korea's experience. Issue Paper No. 2, UNCTAD-ICTSD project on IPRs and Sustainable Development, Geneva.

Kitching, J. and Blackburn, R. (1998). Intellectual property management in the small and medium enterprise (SME). *Journal of Small Business and Enterprise Development*, 5 (4): 327–335.

Knopf, H. (2005). Towards a positive agenda for international copyright reform from a developed country's perspective. Paper presented at the UNCTAD-ICTSD Dialogues: Intellectual Property and Sustainable Development: Revising the Agenda in a New Context, 24-28 October, Bellagio.

Kostecki, M. (2006). Intellectual property and economic development: What technical assistance to redress the balance in favour of developing nations? Issue Paper No. 14, UNCTAD-ICTSD Programme on IPRs and Sustainable Development, Geneva.

Kozul-Wright, Z. and Jenner, P. (2007, forthcoming). Creative destruction of the music industry and the copyright in the knowledge-driven economy. DIME Working Paper Series, University of Birkbeck, UCL, London.

Kremer, M. (1998). Patent buyouts: A mechanism for encouraging innovation. *Quarterly Journal of Economics*, 113 (4): 1137–1167.

Kumar, N. (2002). Intellectual property rights, technology and economic development: Experiences of Asian countries. Background paper prepared for the Commission on Intellectual Property Rights, Study Paper No. 1B, New Delhi.

Lall, S. (2003). Indicators of the relative importance of IPRs in developing countries. Issue Paper No. 3, UNCTAD-ICTSD Project on IPRs and Sustainable Development, Geneva.

Lanjouw, J. (2002). A new global patent regime for diseases: U.S. and international legal issues. *Harvard Journal of Law & Technology*, 16 (1): 85–124.

Léger, A. (2005). Intellectual property rights and their impacts in developing countries: An empirical analysis of maize breeding in Mexico. Institutional Change in Agriculture and Natural Resources (ICAR) Discussion Paper No. 0505, Humboldt University, Berlin.

Lessig, L. (2004). *Free Culture: How Big Media Uses Technology and the Law to Lock Down Culture and Control Creativity*. Penguin Books, New York.

Levin, R.C., Klevorick, A.K., Nelson, R.R. and Winter, S.G. (1987). Appropriating the returns from industrial research and development. *Brookings Papers on Economic Activity*, 1987 (3): 783–831.

Machlup, F. (1983). What do we mean by the optimum utilization of knowledge? In Boulding, K.E. and Senesh, L. (eds.), *The Optimum Utilization of Knowledge: Making Knowledge Serve Better Betterment*. Westview Press, Boulder, CO.

Macmillan, F. (2003). Copyrights commodification of creativity. University of London, London (http://www.oiprc.ox.ac.uk/EJWP0203.pdf).

Macmillan, F. (2005). *New Directions in Copyright Law volume 1*. Edward Elgar, Cheltenham and Northampton, United Kingdom and Mass.

Mansfield, E. (1998). Academic research underlying industrial innovations: Sources, characteristics and financing. *Review of Economics and Statistics*, 77 (1): 55–65.

Maskus, K. (2004). Comments for TRIPS Plus Ten: Economic implications. Presentation prepared for SIDA/ICTSD Conference, 24 September, Stockholm.

Maskus, K. (2005). The role of intellectual property rights in encouraging foreign direct investment and technology transfer. In Fink, C. and Maskus, K. (eds.), *Intellectual Property and Development: Lessons from Recent Economic Research*. World Bank and Oxford University Press, Washington, DC.

Maskus, K. and Reichman, J.H. (2005) (eds.). *International Public Goods and Transfer and Technology: Under a Globalized Intellectual Property Regime*. Cambridge University Press, Cambridge.

Maurer, S.M. (2003). New institutions for doing science: From databases to open biology. Paper presented to the European Policy for Intellectual Property Conference on Copyright and Database Protection, Patents and Research Tools and Other Challenges to the Intellectual Property System, 24–25 November, The Netherlands.

Moran, M. (2005). A breakthrough in R&D for neglected diseases: New ways to get the drugs we need, *PLoS Medicine*, 2(9): 828–832.

Musungu, S. (2005). Rethinking innovation, development and intellectual property in the UN: WIPO and beyond. Issues Paper No. 5, Quaker International Affairs Programme, QIAP, Ottawa.

Nelson, R.R. (2004). The market economy and the scientific commons. *Research Policy*, 33 (3): 455–471.

Nelson, R.R. (2005). Linkages between the market economy and the scientific commons. In Maskus, K. and Reichman, J.H., *International Public Goods and Transfer and Technology - Under a Globalized Intellectual Property Regime*. Cambridge University Press, Cambridge.

Nelson, R.R. and Rosenberg, N. (1993). Technical innovation and national systems. In Nelson, R. (ed.), *National Innovation Systems: A Comparative Analysis*. Oxford University Press, Oxford.

OECD (1999). The knowledge-based economy: A set of facts and figures. Organisation for Economic Co-operation and Development, Paris.

OECD (2005). Intellectual property rights. Directorate for Financial and Enterprise Affairs, Competition Committee, Organisation for Economic Co-operation and Development, DAF/COMP(2004)24, Paris.

Okediji, R.L. (2001). Givers, takers, and other kinds of users: A fair use doctrine for cyberspace. *Florida Law Review*, 53 (107).

Okediji, R.L. (2004). Fostering access to education, research and dissemination of knowledge through copyright. UNCTAD-ICTSD dialogue on moving the pro-development IP agenda forward: Preserving public goods in health, education and learning, 29 November–3 December, Bellagio.

Okediji, R.L. (2006). The international copyright system: Limitations, exceptions and public interest considerations for developing countries. Issue Paper No. 15, UNCTAD-ICTSD Project on IPRs and Sustainable Development, Geneva.

Pires de Carvalho, N. (2002). *The TRIPS Regime of Patent Rights*. Kluwer Law International, The Hague.

Primo Braga, C.A. and Fink, C. (1998). Reforming intellectual property rights regimes: Challenges for developing countries. *Journal of International Economic Law*, 1 (4): 537–554.

Radosevic, S. (1999). *International Technology Transfer and Catch-up in Economic Development*. Edward Elgar, Cheltenham and Northampton, UK.

Reichman, J., and Lewis, T. (2005). Using liability rules to stimulate local innovation in developing countries: application to traditional knowledge. In Maskus and Reichman (2005): 337–365.

Robledo, A.R. (2005). Strategic patents and asymmetric litigation costs as entry deterrence mechanisms. *Economic Bulletin*, 15 (2): 1–9.

Rodrik, D. (2001). The global governance of trade as if development really mattered. United Nations Development Programme, New York.

Roffe, D. and Vivas, D. (2007). Maintaining Policy Space for Development: A Case Study on IP Technical Assistance in FTAs, International Centre for Trade and Sustainable Development (ICTSD), Issue Paper No. 19. Intellectual Property and Sustainable Development Series, Geneva.

Rogers, M. (2004). Absorptive capability and economic growth: how do countries catch-up? *Cambridge Journal of Economics*, 28: 577–596.

Rosenberg, N. and Birdzell, L. (1986). How the West grew rich: The economic transformation of the industrial world. *Journal of Economic History*, 47 (2): 595–596.

Saggi, K. (2000). Trade, foreign direct investment, and international technology transfer: A survey. World Bank Policy Research Working Paper No. 2349, World Bank, Washington, DC.

Sampat, B. (2003). Recent changes in patent policy and the "privatization" of knowledge: Causes, consequences, and implications for developing countries. In Sarewitz, D., et al., *Knowledge Flows and Knowledge Collectives: Understanding the Role of Science and Technology Policies in Development*. Project for the Global Inclusion Program of the Rockefeller Foundation, New York.

Scherer, F.M. (2005). *Patents: Economics, Policy and Measurement*. Edward Elgar, Cheltenham and Northampton, United Kingdom and Mass.

Scotchmer, S. (2004). *Innovation and Incentives*. MIT Press, Cambridge, Mass.

Shukla, S.P. (2000). From GATT to WTO and beyond. WIDER Working Paper No. 195, UNU-WIDER, Helsinki.

Smiers, J. (2005). Abandoning copyright: a blessing for artists, art and society http://www.hku.nl/hku/show/id=95113.

South Centre (2002). Weak IPRs have helped development. South Center, Geneva.

South Centre (2007). Development and intellectual property under the EPA negotiations. Policy Brief No. 6, South Centre, Geneva.

Steinmueller, E. (2003). Information society consequences of expanding the intellectual property domain. Issue Report No. 38, Socio-economic Trends Assessment for the Digital Revolution (STAR). Science and Technology Policy Research (SPRU), Sussex.

Stiglitz, J. (2005). Intellectual-property rights and wrongs. *The Daily Times (Pakistan)*, 16 August: 1–3.

Suthersanen, U. (2005). Paper prepared for the UNCTAD/ICTSD/BA Regional Arab Dialogue on IPRs, Innovation and Sustainable Development, 26–28 June, Alexandria.

Suthersanen, U. (2006). Utility models and innovation in developing countries. Paper prepared for the UNCTAD-ICTSD Project on IPRs and Sustainable Development, UNCTAD-ICTSD, Geneva.

Suthersanen, U., Dutfield, G. and Chow, K. B. (2007). *Innovation without Patents – Harnessing the Creative Spirit in a Diverse World*. Edward Elgar, Cheltenham and Northampton, United Kingdom and Mass.

Sykes, A.O. (2002). TRIPS, pharmaceuticals, developing countries and the Doha solution. University of Chicago Law and Economics, Online Working Paper No. 140, Chicago.

Teece, D.J. (1995). Firm organization, industrial structure and technological innovation. Consortium on Competitiveness and Cooperation. Working Paper No. 95–8, University of California, Berkeley.

Teece, D.J. (2005). Technology and technology transfer: Mansfieldian inspirations and subsequent developments. *Journal of Technology Transfer*, 30 (1/2): 17–33.

Teece, D.J. (2006). Reflections on "profiting from innovation". *Research Policy*, 35 (8): 1131–1146.

Thumm, N. (2004). Motives for patenting biotechnological inventions; an empirical investigation in Switzerland. *International Journal of Technology, Policy and Management*: 275–285.

Todo, Y. (2002). Foreign direct investment, licensing, and knowledge spillovers to developing countries: Theory and evidence. Tokyo Metropolitan University, Faculty of Economics, Tokyo.

UNCTAD (1996). The TRIPS Agreement and developing countries. United Nations publication, Geneva and New York.

UNCTAD (2006a). *The Digital Divide Report: ICT Diffusion Index 2005*. United Nations publications, Geneva and New York.

UNCTAD (2006b). *The Least Developed Countries Report 2006*. United Nations publication, sales no. E.06.II.D.9, Geneva.

UNCTAD (2006c). *Trade and Development Report: Global Partnership and National Policies for Development*. United Nations publication, sales no. E.06.II.D.6, Geneva.

UNCTAD and ICTSD (2002). Towards development-oriented IP policy: Setting an agenda for the next five years. Bellagio Series on Development and Intellectual Property Policy, the Rockefeller Foundation, 30 October–2 November, Bellagio.

UNCTAD and ICTSD (2003a). Intellectual property rights: Implications for development. Policy discussion paper for the project on IPRs and sustainable development, Geneva.

UNCTAD and ICTSD (2003b). Towards development-oriented IP policy: Advancing the reform agenda. The Second Bellagio Series on IPRs and Development, the Rockefeller Foundation, 18–21 September, Bellagio.

UNCTAD and ICTSD (2005). *Resource Book on TRIPS and Development, Project on IPRs and Sustainable Development*. Cambridge University Press, New York.

UNCTAD and ICTSD (2006). Intellectual property provisions of bilateral and regional trade Agreements in light of U.S. federal law. Issue Paper No. 12, Project on IPRs and Sustainable Development, Geneva.

UNESCO (2005). *Towards Knowledge Societies: UNESCO World Report*. United Nations Educational, Scientific and Cultural Organization, Paris.

UNIDO (2006). The role of intellectual property rights in technology transfer and economic growth: Theory and evidence. United Nations Industrial Development Organization, Vienna.

Von Hippel, E. (1981). Increasing innovators' returns from innovation. Sloan Working Paper No. 1192–81, Sloan School of Management, Massachusetts Institute of Technology, Cambridge, Mass.

Von Hippel, E. (2005). *Democratizing Innovation*. MIT Press, Cambridge, Mass.

Westphal, L. (2000). Industrialization meets globalization: Uncertain reflections on East Asian experience. Discussion Paper No. 8, UNU-INTECH, Maastricht. World Bank (2000). Bangladesh: A proposed rural development strategy. Bangladesh Development Series, World Bank, Dhaka.

World Bank (2001). *Global Economic Prospects and the Developing Countries 2002, Making Trade Work for the World's Poor*. World Bank, Washington, DC.

World Bank (2003). Private sector assessment for health nutrition and population in Bangladesh. World Bank, Dhaka.

World Bank (2006). Bangladesh country assistance strategy 2006-2009. World Bank, Dhaka and Washington, DC.

WIPO (2006). Patent report: Statistics on worldwide patent activities. World Intellectual Property Organization, Geneva.

WIPO (2007a). Provisional committee on proposals related to a WIPO Development Agenda (PCDA). Revised draft report, PCDA/3/3 Prov. 2, 19-23 February, World Intellectual Property Organization, Geneva.

WIPO (2007b). Provisional committee on proposals related to a WIPO development agenda (PCDA). Draft report from the 3rd session, 19–23 February, World Intellectual Property Organization, Geneva.

WTO (2001). TRIPS: Council discussion on access to medicines: Developing country group's paper. Paper prepared by group of developing countries, 20 June, World Trade Organization, Geneva.

Yang, G. and Maskus, K. (1998). Intellectual property rights and licensing: An econometric investigation. Working Paper, University of Colorado, Boulder.

Yang, G. and Maskus, K. (2005). Intellectual property rights and licensing: An econometric investigation. In Fink, C. and Maskus, K. (eds.), *Intellectual Property and Development: Lessons from Recent Economic Research*. World Bank and Oxford University Press, Washington, DC.

Yu, P.K. (2007). The international enclosure movement. *Indiana Law Journal, 82* (Winter).

Addressing the International Emigration of Skilled Persons

A. Introduction

The human capital endowment of an economy is a fundamental determinant of its long-term growth performance, of its absorptive capacity and of its performance in technological learning. It is an essential precondition for the development of domestic firms' technological effort. It is also a requirement for the effective working of trade, foreign direct investment, licensing and other channels as means of technology diffusion (Mayer, 2001; Kokko, 1994). Indeed, the movement of persons possessing a particular type of knowledge has traditionally been identified as a means of technology diffusion. It therefore appears alongside international flows of goods, investment and disembodied technology (analysed in chapter 1 of this Report) as a channel for technology transfer.

The movement of skilled persons may take place both within countries (e.g. among different firms) and internationally. The second case refers to both temporary movement of qualified persons (e.g. international technicians or consultants on short-term assignments) and permanent (or long-term) migration of skilled persons.[1] Those two forms of international flows are channels for the international transfer of knowledge, but are of different kinds. The short-term movement of professionals occurs mostly in the context of market-based transactions by firms seeking to acquire qualified services from other countries or to send them to other countries. Migration of skilled persons, by contrast, has different determinants, longer-term consequences and policy implications for countries of origin and for countries of destination. Countries may either gain or lose from those flows: international permanent (or long-term) immigration of skilled persons in principle contributes to building countries' skills endowment, while international permanent (or long-term) emigration of qualified persons entails (at least immediately) a loss in a country's stock of human capital. Those two processes are commonly referred to as "brain gain" and "brain drain" respectively. The circulation of qualified persons in any direction is termed "brain circulation". The most important issue for countries' long-term development is the net effect of migratory flows.

Least developed countries have a low skill endowment. Therefore, the international migration of skilled persons from and to those countries can have a strong impact on their human capital stock. This chapter discusses trends in international migration of skilled and professional workers from LDCs and endeavours to assess its consequences for those countries' brain drain and brain gain. It does not aim at an overall discussion of migration and its social and economic effects on LDCs. Rather, its main focus is to evaluate the impact of international migration of qualified professionals on the absorptive capacity of LDCs, so as to make policy recommendations regarding how to mitigate possible negative consequences of that type of migration or, possibly, how to make those flows contribute positively to the national knowledge system of LDCs.

The analysis is based on lifetime migration data for OECD countries. Skilled emigrants are proxied by the number of tertiary educated persons born in LDCs

Countries may either gain or lose from the movement of qualified people: international permanent immigration of skilled persons contributes to building countries' skills endowment, while international permanent emigration of qualified persons entails a loss in a country's stock of human capital.

LDCs have a low skill endowment. Therefore, the international migration of skilled persons from and to those countries can have a strong impact on their human capital stock.

and living in those developed countries. The skilled emigration rate is that figure as a share of the stock of tertiary educated persons in source countries in 1990 and 2000 (Manning, 2007). However, the increasing proportion of skilled workers migrating on temporary contract to developed and other developing countries is not covered here.[2] Furthermore, the discussion does not address South–South migration because it is less relevant for the migration of skilled persons. Although movements of persons among developing countries account for about half of all migration flows (Ratha and Shaw, 2007), they consist mostly of unskilled persons (except for Southern Africa and South-East Asia). By contrast, an estimated 90 per cent of international skilled migration flows were to OECD countries in the 1990s.

B. Causes and consequences of emigration

1. MAIN CAUSES

For many decades supply and demand forces in origin and destination countries have combined to increase the migration of skilled workers from LDCs to developed countries and higher-income developing countries. Slow economic growth and political instability, especially in parts of Africa, led to an increase in cross-border movements of professionals during the 1970s and 1980s, both to developed countries and to more rapidly growing neighbouring States (Russel, Jacobsen and Stanley, 1990). That migration supply pressure continued in subsequent years and into the new century, underpinned by economic, political and social conditions in source countries, as well as military conflicts in some cases. The economic situation of most LDCs has generally entailed limited employment opportunities for professionals and/or poor working conditions and career paths. Other factors are the low level of pay and the huge and widening gap between earnings in LDCs and those in developed countries or more advanced developing countries for the same careers. In contrast, economic growth and the creation of employment opportunities for educated manpower in LDCs appear to be closely associated with slower rates of brain drain (Lucas, 2004). Since that favourable situation has not been generalized in those countries, supply forces for emigration of skilled persons from many LDCs have remained strong in the past two decades.

At the same time, demand pressure for increased deployment of skilled migrants from developing countries (including LDCs) has increased in industrialized countries, despite their rapidly rising numbers of tertiary graduates. Opportunities for work among professionally qualified immigrants in developed countries have accelerated since the 1990s. More open policies were related to increasing shortages of skilled manpower, as a result of demographic and structural change. The major labour-importing economies, particularly the United States, the EU and its member States, Canada and Australia, have reacted in different ways to increase the supply of skilled manpower by attracting workers from abroad.[3]

While skill shortages have been experienced across the board in many increasingly technologically advanced developed countries, three sets of factors have been especially important in influencing renewed demand for skilled manpower. First, the ageing of developed country populations, especially in Europe and later in Japan, has contributed to slow growth in labour supply and increased demand for skill-intensive non-tradable services, particularly in health and old-age care. Second, the information technology revolution has greatly

For many decades supply and demand forces in origin and destination countries have combined to increase the migration of skilled workers from LDCs to developed countries and higher-income developing countries.

The economic situation of most LDCs has generally entailed limited employment opportunities for professionals and/or poor working conditions and career paths.

Demand pressure for increased deployment of skilled migrants from developing countries (including LDCs) has increased in industrialized countries.

increased the demand for skilled manpower in the production of computer software and the demand for computer and ICT engineers. Third, shortages of lower- to middle-level skilled manpower — technicians, electricians, plumbers, nurses and teachers — have been especially marked, as developed country workers shun difficult blue-collar and related jobs, and the output of their educational institutions has failed to keep pace with demand.

2. IMPACTS OF EMIGRATION ON DEVELOPMENT

The net impact of the migration of skilled persons in terms of the brain drain and brain gain of origin countries has not been clearly determined in the theoretical and empirical literature. A range of factors have been identified as important: the rate of economic growth and utilization of skilled persons back home, especially in certain skilled occupations (particularly relevant to the LDCs); the size of the brain drain relative to the domestic supply of skilled persons; the role of remittances; and the extent to which migration stimulates development of human capital in countries of origin (which is partly determined by the scale of out-migration and the role of the diasporas).

The net impact of the migration of skilled persons in terms of the brain drain and brain gain of origin countries has not been clearly determined in the theoretical and empirical literature.

Early theoretical studies focused on the short-run impact of a loss of human capital, the cost of which is mostly borne by domestic taxpayers, and the impact of the decrease in the supply of educated persons on national output (Grubel and Scott, 1966; Bhagwati and Hamada, 1974). Subsequent research regarding the impact of out-migration of skilled persons on countries of origin can be divided into two groups: the findings of the migration "optimists" and the findings of the migration "realists".

The short-run cost, a loss of human capital, is mostly borne by domestic taxpayers, and the impact of the decrease in the supply of educated persons is reflected in national output.

"Optimistic" models stress the dynamic effects of migration (e.g. Stark, 2004, and Mountford, 1997). They highlight the positive impact of remittances,[4] and the impact on human capital development in home countries, as a result of increased demand for and access to education among those left behind. The scope broadened to include technology and knowledge transfer and other benefits of brain circulation, and the potential benefits deriving from diaspora links. Docquier and Rapoport (2004: 27) summarize the main effects of the successful experience of migrants abroad: "successive cohorts adapt their education decisions, and the economy-wide average level of education partly... or totally catches up, with a possible net gain in the long run" and "the creation of migrants' networks that facilitate the movement of goods, factors and ideas between migrants' host and home countries". The diaspora reduces the costs of migration and risks in countries of destination, providing greater incentive and demand for migration-linked education at home (Kanbur and Rapoport, 2004, cited in Docquier and Rapoport, 2004). It must, however, be pointed out that the existence of a positive impact on countries of origin rests on the assumption that a significant number of graduates of new courses and new schools, who initially enrolled with the aim of going abroad, end up contributing to the provision of a higher value of goods and services to the domestic economy.

"Optimistic" models stress the dynamic effects of migration on remittances, technology and knowledge transfer and diaspora links.

At the same time, dynamic effects associated with brain circulation have received increasing attention. More attention in the empirical literature has been paid to the role of return migrants in raising skill levels, and promoting technology transfer and capital accumulation, especially in the successful growth cases of East and South Asia since the 1990s (Saxenian, Motoyama and Quan, 2002).[5]

The above-mentioned relationships are complicated, however, especially since theoretical models fail to take account of a number of factors: migration "realists" have focused on differences in the quality of out-migrants and return

Box 7. The importance of remittances

Remittances have increased dramatically in recent years, totalling an estimated $167 billion in 2005, according to World Bank estimates. They have grown faster than foreign direct investment and official development assistance over the past decade, doubling in several countries and increasing by close to 10 per cent per annum between 2001 and 2005 (World Bank, 2006). Their major role in receiving countries is to stimulate consumption and investment in those countries, help relax foreign exchange constraints and contribute to poverty alleviation (Adams, 2007). Their contribution to development depends on their macroeconomic impact and how they are used in receiving countries. There is evidence that they are more directed to consumption than investment, which perhaps explains why no link between them and long-term growth has been found (IMF, 2005: chapter 2).

Although remittances arise from both skilled and unskilled emigration, their effects just mentioned appear to be stronger in cases where unskilled migration predominates, as compared with situations where skilled migration predominates. Qualified emigrants have higher earnings abroad than unskilled ones, but are more likely to become permanent immigrants with weaker links to countries of origin; eventually, this leads to smaller remittances (Faini, 2006; Niimi and Ozden, 2006).

Box table 2 presents data on remittances over the period between 1990 and 2005 for a collection of LDCs for which data appear to be plausible.[1] On average, excluding a number of extreme values in the calculation of changes over time, remittances per capita appear to have increased quite significantly in LDCs in the 1990s and even more in 2000–2005. The mean value doubled from $284 million in 1990 to an estimated $621 million in 2005. Remittances are highly correlated with total rates of emigration to OECD countries and out-migration rates among skilled workers (for both there was a correlation coefficient of 0.79 between the value of remittances and migration rates in 2000).

Box table 2. Value of remittances and remittances per capita, least developed countries and selected countries with high rates of emigration, 1990–2005

Country group/Country	Value of Remittances (Current $ millions)			Remittances (% increase)		Value of Remittances (Per capita in current $)
	1990	2000	2005 (estimate)	1990–2000	2000–2005	2004
Africa and Haiti						
Sudan	62	641	1 403	934	119	43
Haiti	61	578	919	848	59	107
Senegal	142	233	511	64	119	45
Lesotho	428	252	355	-41	41	153
Uganda		238	291		22	11
Mali	107	73	154	-32	111	13
Togo	27	34	149	26	338	28
Benin	101	87	84	-14	-3	12
Asia						
Bangladesh	779	1 968	3 824	153	94	23
Yemen	1 498	1 288	1 315	-14	2	52
Nepal		111	785		607	34
Cambodia		121	138		14	10
Island States						
Cape Verde	59	87	92	47	6	197
Samoa	43	45	45	5	0	249
Comoros	10	12	12	20	0	20
Vanuatu	8	35	9	338	-74	43
Kiribati	5	7	7	40	0	76
Total						
Average	**284**	**366**	**621**	**29**	**70**	**53**
Average without outliers[a]				**12**	**64**	
India	2 384	12890	21 727	441	69	20
Mexico	3 098	7 525	18 955	143	152	175
Philippines	1 465	6 212	13 379	324	115	141
Colombia	495	1 610	3 668	225	128	70
Jamaica	229	892	1 398	290	57	528

Source: UNCTAD secretariat calculations based on Global Economic Prospects data set (World Bank), 2006, for remittances; and UNCTAD, GlobStat database for population.

a Sudan, Haiti and Vanuatu.

These figures are significant in terms of foreign exchange earnings for a large number of countries, apart from the major oil and mineral exporters, given that total merchandise exports were less the $500 million per year for the large majority of LDCs

Box 7 (contd.)

(UNCTAD, 2006: chart 1). For example, estimated remittances of nearly $4 billion in Bangladesh in 2005 were greater than the total value of merchandise exports of $1.4 billion in 2003–2004; among the smaller exporters — for example, Lesotho, Uganda and Senegal — an amount totalling approximately $200 million was equivalent to or greater than total exports in the same years. Among two very small countries — Cape Verde and Samoa — remittances of $92 million and $45 million, respectively, were the major source of foreign exchange. It is noteworthy that Senegal, Cape Verde and Samoa all had emigration rates of 20 per cent or more (69 per cent for Cape Verde) in 2000, and hence skilled out-migration probably played a major role in remittance incomes.

[1] The data need to be interpreted with care, given that the reliability of coverage appears to differ significantly for individual countries from year to year.

Box 8. Return migration

There is little quantitative information about the contribution of return migrants to skill formation and technology back home among LDCs. Nevertheless, limited studies in similar economies show that return migrants can make a difference in terms of the skills endowments of origin countries. Ammassari (2003: 2) concludes from a study of skilled returnees in Côte d'Ivoire and Ghana that they "fostered positive development effects in both private and public sectors". This differed across generations, with earlier return migrants assisting in "nation building", while the contribution of later cohorts was more directly related to entrepreneurship. Among the benefits which returnees themselves cited as most important, specialized technical expertise and communication skills ranked highest. Knowledge and skills were more important than work experience, although contributions to work morale and productivity in new jobs were also ranked quite high. In addition to technical expertise, returnees brought modest amounts of capital with them (reported to be less than $10,000 for over half of respondents in both countries), and mainly used them for housing and consumption of durable goods, although about one third also reported providing assistance to family members. Therefore, the main contribution of returnees in low-income countries seems to be their skills and human capital, rather than investment in the home country. It is likely that the same is the case in LDCs.

migrants, compared with their (potential) replacements back home and on the extent to which skilled migrants are employed in skilled occupations abroad (Docquier and Rapoport, 2004; Lucas, 2004). Several of those factors have been identified as reducing potential gains from brain circulation and remittances from skilled and professional persons in many LDCs.

Many studies have focused on the migration premium — a range of 2–10 times higher earnings among migrants compared with non-migrants in the same occupations, according to Docquier and Rapoport (2004) — while paying less attention to the costs of migration, both psychological and social, as newcomers seek to assimilate in new environments. One important finding about the jobs undertaken by educated migrants suggests that many work in less skilled jobs, and thus experience brain "waste". In such cases, the migration of educated persons is not necessarily a stimulus for education in countries of origin, or may be a stimulus for learning skills which do not replace those that are lost (for example, doctors retraining to become nurses in the Philippines).

Studies about the jobs undertaken by educated migrants suggests that many work in less skilled jobs, and thus experience brain "waste".

Impacts on human capital in places of origin are likely to be varied and larger in low-human-capital and low-migration contexts, either through return migration or remittances, than where an abundant supply of educated persons and substantial out-migration already exist (Docquier and Rapoport, 2004). Short-run brain drain effects are likely to be greater in countries with a narrow human capital base.

Short-run brain drain effects are likely to be greater in countries with a narrow human capital base.

Heterogeneity among migrants and non-migrants is also an important issue. Schiff (2006) has drawn attention to the fact that the more optimistic models of migration tend to ignore self-selection, which results in higher-quality persons going abroad. For those migrants there are not near-perfect substitutes among the remaining stock of skilled or potential persons. It has also been noted that the less successful skilled migrants tend to return home, and hence the brain gain is smaller than some of the theoretical models predict.

3. Implications for the LDCs

According to Docquier and Rapoport (2004: 34), while the optimal rate of skilled and professional out-migration "is likely to be positive", whether the "current rate is greater or lower than this optimum is an empirical question that must be addressed country by country". There appears to be huge variation in individual country experience with respect to brain drain, brain circulation and brain gain. One important factor is the size of the brain drain, which has both positive and negative effects: a large diaspora provides a cushion and a support for would-be skilled migrants, but at the same time may reduce the potential benefits to countries of origin over time. More settled migrants tend to have more tenuous links with home countries and their remittances tend to decrease in time.

More settled migrants tend to have more tenuous links with home countries and their remittances tend to decrease in time.

Industries that employ emigrants also play a part in determining the benefits. The out-migration of doctors and nurses in a largely non-tradable and heavily regulated industry (despite the internationalization of health care service provision in some countries) might be expected to have few benefits for home countries in terms of technology transfer, investment from abroad and, of course, trade. Benefits can be expected to be much more positive in a highly open, tradable industry such as ICT, where economic benefits provided by nationals working for private investors abroad can be substantial for technology, employment and investment in countries of origin.

Home country policies and growth prospects can play a major role in increasing brain gain and reducing the costs of brain drain. Rapidly growing middle-income countries that have passed the migration "hump"[6] are likely to be in a better position to utilize skilled persons from abroad and to invest in the human capital that is necessary for filling the gaps created by emigrants. But even at lower levels of per capita income, domestic policies appear to be important.

Data suggest that skilled out-migration from developing countries increased sharply in the 1990s and was the highest in LDCs.

C. Skilled emigration trends and developments

The latest data on the total number of skilled out-migrants are from the round of censuses conducted in 1990 and 2000 in OECD countries, which are host to a high proportion of all skilled migrants. The data suggest that skilled out-migration from developing countries increased sharply in the 1990s.[7] While the total OECD population expanded by less than 20 per cent in the 1990s, skilled immigration increased by some two thirds (12 to 20 million). The patterns are documented by Docquier and Marfouk (2006). Table 30 summarizes several of the main findings of that study:

The share of skilled migrants was negatively correlated with the level of development.

- Skilled out-migration rates were inversely related to country size.

- Rates of skilled out-migration were highest in LDCs (13 per cent). Nevertheless, LDCs accounted for only less than 5 per cent of all skilled migrants, while middle-income and high-income country groups accounted for close to 30 per cent each.

- The stock of skilled persons was positively related to the level of economic development, as might be expected. However, the share of skilled migrants was negatively correlated with the level of development.

Table 30. Rates of emigration for all workers and skilled workers among LDCs and other country groups, 2000
(Percentage)

	Rate of emigration		Share of skilled workers		Share of migrants
	Total	Skilled	Among residents	Among migrants	
By size					
Large (pop. >25 million)	1.3	4.1	11.3	36.4	60.6
Intermediate (pop. 15-<25 million)	3.1	8.8	11.0	33.2	15.8
Smaller (pop. 2.5-<15 million)	5.8	13.5	13.0	33.1	16.4
Small (pop. <2.5 million)	10.3	27.5	10.5	34.7	3.7
Total					96.5[a]
By income					
High-income	2.8	3.5	30.7	38.3	30.4
Upper-middle income	4.2	7.9	13.0	25.2	24.3
Lower-middle income	3.2	7.6	14.2	35.4	26.6
Low-Income	0.5	6.1	3.5	45.2	15.1
Total					96.4[a]
Least developed countries	**1.0**	**13.2**	**2.3**	**34.0**	**4.2**

Source: Docquier and Marfouk (2004, 2006).

a   Total sums to slightly less than one hundred because of rounding.

Out-migration is much higher in certain professions that are skill-intensive and where skills are relatively uniform internationally, such as medicine.

These data on skilled (tertiary educated) migration flows provide no breakdown by industry/occupation and level of schooling. Thus out-migration is much higher in certain professions that are skill-intensive and where skills are relatively uniform internationally, such as medicine. Moreover, migration of highly educated persons with more than basic tertiary training tends to be much greater than for the tertiary educated population as a whole. Lowell, Findlay and Stewart (2004) cite studies which suggest that as many as 30–50 per cent of the developing world's population trained in science and technology live in the developed world. This has a direct impact on those countries' skills base, on their absorptive capacity and on their technological catch-up possibilities.

Tables 30 and 31 provide information on the rates of emigration for all emigrants and tertiary educated emigrants, as well as on changes in those rates during the period 1990–2000 for all LDCs for which data are available.[8] To facilitate interpretation, the data are organized by regions.[9] Within regions, countries are ranked by total population size (table 31), which is correlated with the absolute number of emigrants, although not necessarily with migration rates.

Migration of highly educated persons with more than basic tertiary training tends to be much greater than for the tertiary educated population as a whole.

Three main patterns of skilled emigration and changes in emigration rates in the period 1990–2000 among the LDCs stand out. First, emigration rates were generally high among tertiary educated persons by international standards, with an unweighted mean for those countries of 21.4 per cent in 2000. That was much higher than for all lower-middle and low-income countries (7.6 and 6.1 per cent respectively in table 30), although the latter figure (weighted) is heavily influenced by quite low out-migration rates for China and India. There was considerable variation in the (unweighted) total rates of emigration among tertiary educated persons within and by country group among the LDCs. They were close to 25 per cent in the island LDCs, West Africa and East Africa, and lowest in the generally more populated Asian LDCs (6.4 per cent), with Central Africa falling in between (14.1 per cent).

As many as 30–50 per cent of the developing world's population trained in science and technology live in the developed world.

Second, these average rates of emigration of skilled persons across the main LDC regions conceal very substantial intraregional variations, with coefficients of variation close to 1 in all regions except East Africa. All regions, especially West and East Africa, show substantial variations in rates across countries in both 1990

Table 31. Brain drain from LDCs to OECD countries, 1990 and 2000
(Percentage)

Country group/ Country	Rate of out-migration				Increase in out-migration rate	
	1990		2000		1990–2000	
	Total	Tertiary educated	Total	Tertiary educated	Total	Tertiary educated
	(A)	(B)	(C)	(D)	(C-A)	(D-B)
Africa and Haiti						
Central (and North)						
Democratic Rep. of the Congo	0.3	8.3	0.3	7.9	0.0	-0.4
Sudan	0.1	5.0	0.2	5.6	0.1	0.6
Angola	2.7	7.1	2.7	25.6	0.0	18.5
Chad	0.1	8.7	0.1	6.9	0.0	-1.8
Central African Republic	0.2	4.4	0.2	4.7	0.0	0.3
Equatorial Guinea	0.2	4.3	4.1	34.1	3.9	29.8
Average	0.6	6.3	1.3	14.1	0.7	7.8
West (and Haiti)						
Burkina Faso	0.1	2.6	0.2	3.3	0.1	0.7
Mali	0.7	6.6	0.7	11.5	0.0	4.9
Niger	0.1	8.3	0.1	6.1	0.0	-2.2
Senegal	1.6	11.1	2.6	24.1	1.0	13.0
Guinea	0.3	5.1	0.5	11.1	0.2	6.0
Haiti	7.3	78.3	10.2	81.6	2.9	3.3
Benin	0.2	6.1	0.3	7.5	0.1	1.4
Sierra Leone	0.5	31	1.4	41	0.9	10.0
Togo	0.5	8.9	1.0	13.6	0.5	4.7
Liberia	1.1	27.7	2.6	37.4	1.5	9.7
Mauritania	0.6	3.5	1.4	23.1	0.8	19.6
Gambia	1.3	76	3.1	64.7	1.8	-11.3
Guinea-Bissau	0.8	5.9	1.8	29.4	1.0	23.5
Average	1.2	20.9	2.0	27.3	0.8	6.4
East (and South)						
Ethiopia	0.4	13.9	0.5	17.0	0.1	3.1
United Rep. of Tanzania	0.3	14.8	0.3	15.8	0.0	1.0
Uganda	0.4	29.9	0.5	21.6	0.1	-8.3
Mozambique	0.8	18.2	0.9	42.0	0.1	23.8
Madagascar	0.2	55.2	0.2	36.0	0.0	-19.2
Malawi	0.1	7.5	0.1	9.4	0.0	1.9
Zambia	0.2	12.2	0.3	10.0	0.1	-2.2
Somalia	14.2	48.9	14.6	58.6	0.4	9.7
Rwanda	0.1	9.4	0.2	19.0	0.1	9.6
Burundi	0.1	5.0	0.3	19.9	0.2	14.9
Eritrea	-	-	2.3	45.8		
Lesotho	0.1	6.2	0.0	2.4	-0.1	-3.8
Djibouti	0.3	9.4	0.5	17.8	0.2	8.4
Average	1.4	19.2	1.6	24.3	0.2	5.0
Average	1.2	17.4	1.7	23.6	0.5	6.2
Asia						
Bangladesh	0.1	2.3	0.3	4.7	0.2	2.4
Myanmar	0.1	3.3	0.2	3.4	0.1	0.1
Afghanistan	0.8	11.7	1.0	13.2	0.2	1.5
Nepal	0.0	1.9	0.1	2.7	0.1	0.8
Yemen	0.1	3.3	0.2	5.7	0.1	2.4
Cambodia	3.0	6.6	3.1	6.8	0.1	0.2
Lao PDR	6.7	14.9	7.1	13.8	0.4	-1.1
Bhutan	0.0	1.7	0.1	1.2	0.1	-0.5
Average	1.4	5.7	1.5	6.4	0.2	0.7
Islands						
Pacific Islands						
Solomon Islands	0.5	6.2	0.6	3.7	0.1	-2.5
Vanuatu	1.0	9.4	1.2	5.0	0.2	-4.4
Samoa	35.3	75.9	43.1	66.6	7.8	-9.3
Kiribati	3.9	26.8	5.1	24.9	1.2	-1.9
Average	10.2	29.6	12.5	25.1	2.3	-4.5
Other Islands						
Comoros	1.0	6.4	2.2	14.5	1.2	8.1
Cape Verde	23.8	54.4	23.5	69.1	-0.3	14.7
Maldives	0.1	2.3	0.2	2.2	0.1	-0.1
Sao Tome and Principe	6.2	9.7	5.6	35.6	-0.6	25.9
Average	7.8	18.2	7.9	30.4	0.1	12.2
Average	9.0	23.9	10.2	27.7	1.2	3.8
Mean	2.5	16.5	3.1	21.4	0.6	4.9
Standard deviation	6.4	20.3	7.2	20.0	0.8	-0.4

Source: Docquier and Marfouk (2004).

Note: Averages are unweighted arithmetic means.

and 2000. Out-migration rates were especially high in several of the very small island countries, in the South Pacific and elsewhere (Sao Tome and Principe, Cape Verde and Samoa), in countries that had experienced political instability in the 1980s and 1990s (Sudan, Liberia, Mozambique, Somalia and Eritrea) and in some of the poorest countries (e.g. Sierra Leone) (chart 11). The high emigration rates of LDCs were (weakly) inversely correlated with population size and the human development index, while GDP was positively correlated with out-migration among educated people (particularly in West Africa). These findings for LDCs are similar to patterns found for other developing countries (section A). Emigration rates were lowest in some of the larger countries (Democratic Republic of the Congo, Sudan, Niger and Malawi), and in all the more populous Asian countries (especially Nepal, Myanmar and Bangladesh) (chart 22).

Out-migration rates were especially high in several of the very small island countries, in countries that had experienced political instability and in some of the poorest countries.

Chart 11. Ten highest rates of out-migration (tertiary educated) among LDCs, 2000

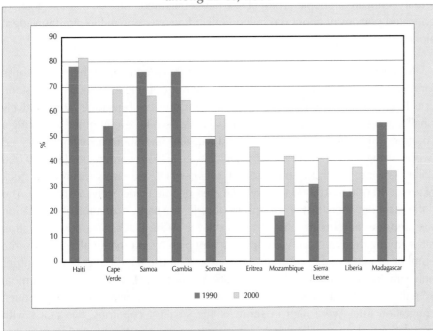

Source: Docquier and Marfouk (2004).

Chart 12. Ten lowest rates of out-migration (tertiary educated) among LDCs, 2000

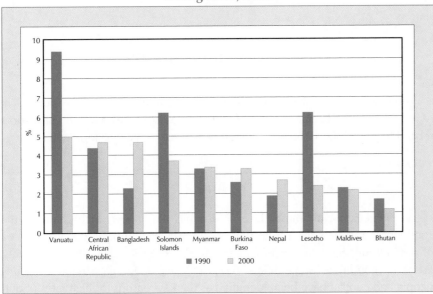

Source: Docquier and Marfouk (2004).

Third, increases in out-migration among the tertiary educated to OECD countries were quite substantial. The unweighted mean emigration rate rose from 16.5 per cent in 1990 to 21.4 per cent 10 years later. Such intensification of emigration among skilled persons was much stronger than among all emigrants from LDCs. The latter's emigration rate increased only moderately — from 2.5 per cent to 3.1 per cent over the same period. The major increases in emigration rates for skilled persons occurred in West Africa and in Central Africa. In five LDCs — Equatorial Guinea, Sao Tome and Principe, Mozambique, Guinea-Bissau and Mauritania — the emigration rate increased by 20 percentage points or more. In the Asian LDCs, by contrast, emigration rates were fairly constant between 1990 and 2000. In the Pacific islands they declined slightly, but were still high in 2000. The largest decreases in emigration rates (between 10 and 20 percentage points lower) were in Madagascar, Gambia and Samoa.

A projection based on figures in table 30 indicates that by 2004 one million tertiary educated people from LDCs had emigrated, out of a total stock of educated persons of about 6.6 million (including over one million in Bangladesh alone).

To put figures for LDCs in perspective, we have compared them with those for countries with the largest absolute number of out-migrants. Two points stand out. First, the absolute number of tertiary educated out-migrants was relatively small among all LDCs, viewed on a global scale. While several of the large origin countries (Philippines, India, China and Mexico) had about a million educated people living abroad in 2000, only Haiti among LDCs recorded close to 100,000 skilled emigrants. Most of the rest of the larger LDC exporters recorded a stock of about 20,000 to 40,000 tertiary educated people living overseas in 2000. The differences between the two groups of countries are partly a function of population size and low enrolment rates at tertiary level in the LDCs. Second, emigration rates among the educated were indeed very high by international standards in a number of LDCs. Table 32 indicates that among the large emigration countries only Jamaica recorded higher out-migration rates than Haiti, Cape Verde, Samoa, Somalia, Eritrea and Mozambique. This was not simply a matter of scale. Although emigration rates were high in some of the smallest countries, five LDCs with populations of four million or more ranked among the top 10 countries in the world in terms of emigration rates in 2000: Haiti, Somalia, Eritrea, Mozambique and Sierra Leone. Thus, even for a sample of larger countries, high emigration rates of qualified professionals are a feature of economic and social life in the LDCs.

D. Regional patterns

There are many similarities between countries in the main LDC regions — in Africa, Asia and the Pacific islands — but there are also some important differences related to geography, history, demography and economic development.

1. AFRICA

As the region with most LDCs, Africa has often been highlighted as the continent that suffers most from brain drain. The region has remained an area of net out-migration to the rest of the world, especially for skilled migrants. Economic conditions, wage differentials, rapid population growth among young people and conflict have been identified as the key reasons for high rates of out-migration (Lucas, 2006). In the African case, there is no clear resolution of the

---

By 2004 one million tertiary educated people from LDCs had emigrated, out of a total stock of educated persons of about 6.6 million.

Five LDCs with populations of four million or more ranked among the top 10 countries in the world in terms of emigration rates in 2000.

Africa is the continent that suffers most from brain drain due to economic conditions, wage differentials, rapid population growth among young people and conflict.

Table 32. Migration of skilled persons from developing countries and LDCs with highest emigration rates, 2000

Country	Total population	GDP per capita	No. of highly educated out-migrants	Emigration rate
	(Millions)	(PPP $)	(000)	(%)
	2005	2005	2000	2000
	(1)	(2)	(3)	(4)
Developing countries				
Philippines	84.2	4 923	1261	14.8
India	1 094.3	3 320	1022	4.2
China	1 307.6	7 198	906	4.2
Mexico	105.3	10 186	901	14.3
Viet Nam	83.2	3 025	447	39.0
Dem. People's Rep. of Korea	23.1[a]	1 800	423	5.3
Cuba	11.4[a]	3 900[b]	336	28.9
Iran (Islamic Rep. of)	69.5	7 980	283	13.1
Jamaica	2.7	4 381	261	82.5
Brazil	184.2	8 561	254	3.3
Colombia	46.0	7 326	233	11.0
Least developed countries				
Population > 4 million				
Haiti	8.3	1 791	92	81.6
Angola	11.1	2 813	38	25.6
Ethiopia	73.0	823	36	17.0
Mozambique	19.4	1 379	36	42.0
Uganda	27.2	1 501	32	21.6
United Republic of Tanzania	36.7	723	29	15.8
Madagascar	18.0	908	26	36.0
Senegal	11.1	1 759	24	24.1
Somalia	8.5	600[c]	16	58.6
Sierra Leone	6.0	903	14	41.0
Rwanda	8.4	1 380	5	19.0
Burundi	6.3	739	4	19.9
Eritrea	4.6	858	8	45.8
Population < 4 million				
Liberia	3.3	1 033	14	37.4
Samoa	0.2	6 344	7	66.6
Cape Verde	0.5	6 418	5	69.1

Source :   Docquier and Marfouk (2004) for out-migration; World Economic Outlook Database (IMF), 2006, for per capita GDP; and UNCTAD, GlobStat database for population.

a 2006 estimate; *b* 2005 estimate; *c* 2003–2004 estimate.

The underutilization of skilled persons at home, which is common in many countries, including the LDCs entails lower social costs of out-migration.

brain gain–brain drain debate. While out-migration of skilled persons can impose severe economic and social costs in sectors such as health (see box 9), a number of factors need to be taken into account before one can conclude that emigration is negative for national economies and communities. One consideration is the underutilization of skilled persons at home, which is common in many countries, including the LDCs. In such circumstances the social costs of out-migration are likely to be lower, at least in the short run. Furthermore, gains need to be evaluated carefully. Benefits from reverse capital flows, technology transfer and greater trade with countries of origin, such as identified in the case of India and the Philippines, are likely to be small in most African LDCs. Such benefits depend critically on economic conditions and the level of development of productive capacities in home countries.

Box 9. The case of health practitioners

The situation facing the health-care sector has been given particular attention in the literature on brain drain, especially with reference to the plight of Africa.[1] The main factors that have been identified as contributing to the brain drain among medical practitioners are very large wage differentials between countries of destination and origin,[2] poor working environments and poorly designed career paths, especially for nurses. Associated problems relate to the low efficiency of health-care systems, high risks for practitioners, especially those involved in HIV/AIDS programmes, and poorly designed social security programmes.

The emigration of doctors to the United States is a case in point (Hagopian et al., 2004). The proportion of Africans is small among the large number of doctors of foreign origin in the United States, and LDC Africans make up a tiny proportion of the total.[3] Nevertheless, these movements are significant in terms of the stock of doctors remaining at home. Box table 3 presents data on the number of physicians from four LDCs — Ethiopia, Uganda, Zambia and Liberia — residing in the United States. For these four countries, the percentage of doctors practising in the United States relative to the total stock of doctors back home ranged from 43 per cent (Liberia) to 10 per cent (Zambia). This might not be a problem if the stock of doctors remaining in their country of origin was sufficient to meet the needs of the population, but this is not the case. All four countries had very few doctors to serve their populations: even the country with the highest proportion — Zambia — had only seven doctors per 100,000 people. The percentage was low in all four countries, even compared with an African average of 13 per 100,000. Moreover, it was tiny compared with the United States level of close to 300. Thus, even though the absolute number of professionals from the poorest countries working abroad may be small, the impact on professional services back home can be severe. Moreover, the number of recent graduates leaving sub-Saharan Africa has been increasing in recent years (Hagopian et al., 2004).

Box table 3. Number of African trained physicians residing in the United States and Canada compared with number residing in countries of origin, 2002

Country	No. of African trained doctors residing in the United States or Canada (A)	No. of doctors residing in place of origin (B)	A/(A+B) (%)	Physicians per 100,000 population[a]
Ethiopia	266	1 564	15	2.0
Uganda	175	722	20	3.0
Zambia	74	676	10	6.9
Liberia	55	72	43	2.3
Sub-Saharan Africa	5 334	12 912	29	12.5[b]

Source: UNCTAD secretariat adaptation from Hagopian et al. (2004, tables 1 and 2).

a Physicians practicing in respective country or region.

b Data for all African countries.

Among South Asian LDCs, in Bangladesh and Nepal quite substantial early investment in the health sector and a supply of well-trained English-speaking medical practitioners have facilitated the brain drain. Adkoli (2006) notes, for example, that 65 per cent of all newly graduated Bangladeshi doctors seek jobs abroad and that the country loses 200 doctors from the government sector each year.

The emigration of health professionals is not the only cause of poor standards of health care in many LDCs and ODCs, particularly since many health-care workers are unemployed prior to departure. Lack of sufficient resources and insufficient (or inappropriate) training to meet the health-care needs of national populations have also been responsible for poor health systems. However, the emigration of health professionals aggravates the situation either in the short or medium term.

[1] For general surveys see for example Hardill and MacDonald (2000), and Martineau, Decker and Bundred (2004).

[2] The gap amounts to over 20 times in the case of Ghanaian nurses, compared with the United Kingdom and the United States, and it is likely to be similar or higher for LDCs.

[3] The large majority (some two thirds) of sub-Saharan African doctors working in the United States were from Nigeria and South Africa.

Lucas (2006) shows that in Africa tertiary enrolment and skilled emigration rates are strongly positively correlated, a fact that would seem to provide some support for the brain-drain hypothesis. Nevertheless, Lucas (p.41) warns that the interpretation of the finding for tertiary enrolments rates is not as simple as it might first appear ("whether a higher brain drain induces more students to enrol, or expanding the college education systems results in a larger exodus of the highly skilled, remain to be disentangled"), as it requires case studies covering long periods. An interpretation in favour of brain gain would be valid if emigration of tertiary graduates induces high levels of enrolment.

2. ASIA

Densely populated Asian LDCs (Bangladesh, Myanmar, Nepal, Bhutan and Cambodia) have experienced much lower levels of brain drain than the African or island LDCs, as mentioned earlier (chart 2).[10] Only the Lao People's Democratic Republic has emigration rates that approach the levels of other major LDCs. This is despite the fact that tertiary- level enrolments and the stock of tertiary educated are relatively high by LDC standards. For example, gross tertiary enrolment rates were estimated at 6.5 per cent in Bangladesh according to UNESCO (2006), higher than in any other LDC economy, with the possible exception of Samoa (for which more recent data are not reported).

On the demand side, relatively rapid economic growth in recent decades, in Bangladesh and Cambodia in particular, has almost certainly increased demand for skilled persons across a range of occupations. Nevertheless, brain drain issues have been important in development debates in the largest LDC economy — Bangladesh — especially with regard to the outflow of doctors to the United Kingdom (Dovlo, 2004). Loss of skilled persons abroad is also significant in Myanmar and the Lao People's Democratic Republic, both of which have experienced slow rates of economic growth in the last decade.[11] In the case of Myanmar, political conflict has also been a factor over several decades.

3. ISLANDS

The very small island State LDCs in the South Pacific — the Solomon Islands, Vanuatu, Samoa, Kiribati and Tuvalu — are characterized by relatively small populations, land abundance and dependence on Australia and nearby New Zealand in particular as migration havens. Consequently, emigration is intensive in some of those countries, and skilled out-migration and associated brain drain are an important policy issue across the region. The rate of emigration of professionals is particularly high in the case of Samoa and Kiribati (table 31), although it is considered a major policy issue throughout the region. Connell (2006) draws attention to some of the underlying factors contributing to movement overseas. Many of them are strikingly similar to those applying to many smaller African countries: slow economic growth and high youth (and educated) unemployment, especially in the main towns and cities; high rates of population growth; and close proximity to former colonial countries — in this case, Australia and New Zealand — both of which have experienced skill shortages in the past decade.

Although brain drain is an issue in countries such as Samoa and Kiribati, Governments are less concerned about its impact on development than in many other LDCs. They are more likely to be proactive in encouraging out-migration in order to support resident populations, many of which have few alternatives for developing gainful occupations. The Philippines has been taken as a model for the development of beneficial links through skilled migration in Samoa and Kiribati, with nurses and seafarers playing a major role in generating remittances (Connell, 2006). Diasporas play a major role in supporting communities back home, and remittances from some groups of skilled persons have remained high over several decades.[12] Unlike in Africa, however, brain gain in the form of return migration is not an issue: it is accepted that most skilled out-migrants will never return to work in their countries of origin, except perhaps to retire. The main policy issue appears to be the utilization of remittances and the skills of those abroad to greater advantage for community and national development (for example, through temporary return visits).

Benefits from reverse capital flows, technology transfer and greater trade with countries of origin, are likely to be small in most African LDCs. Such benefits depend critically on economic conditions and the level of development of productive capacities in home countries.

Densely populated Asian LDCs have experienced much lower levels of brain drain than the African or island LDCs.

Relatively rapid economic growth in recent decades, in Bangladesh and Cambodia in particular, has almost certainly increased demand for skilled persons across a range of occupations.

E. Conclusions and policy recommendations

1. IMPLICATIONS

Permanent emigration of skilled professionals entails a loss of human capital for the home country in the short run and hence a contraction in its absorptive capacity, including its capacity to make use of the major channels of international technology diffusion. This effect is particularly strong in LDCs, most of which are very poorly endowed with skills.

However, if emigrants are unemployed before leaving the country, the immediate loss for the latter is less great. Moreover, the costs of emigration can in principle be (partly) offset by other developments, including the eventual brain gain through the return of emigrants, brain circulation by means of temporary return, creation of business and knowledge linkages between emigrants and home countries (leading to technology flows, investment, etc.), higher enrolment in tertiary education and an increase in remittances. Many of those positive effects, however, occur only once countries have reached a certain level of development and income growth. That implies the existence of considerably improved economic conditions in home countries, which provide incentives for temporary or permanent return of emigrants and for the establishment of stronger knowledge and economic flows. Moreover, an improved domestic environment entails lower out-migration pressure.

That situation is obviously not the one prevailing in LDCs. Those countries are therefore most likely to suffer from brain drain, rather than benefiting from brain circulation, brain gain or the other positive effects possibly associated with emigration. The economic, social and political situation in LDCs means that the emigration rate of skilled persons in those countries is on average higher than in other groups of countries, being in some cases among the highest in the world. They are particularly high in African and island LDCs. By contrast, Asian LDCs have relatively low skilled emigration rates.

LDCs are more likely to have their accumulation of technological capabilities hampered by skilled out-migration. That situation requires policy action in order to minimize the costs of emigration and to maximize its benefits. The following subsections discuss policy alternatives that can be adopted at different levels. Some preliminary observations must be made, however. First, brain drain and the costs associated with out-migration of skilled workers are a consequence of dramatically different standards of living, wages and opportunities, widening in absolute terms, between LDCs and developed and even middle-income countries. It is not possible to halt those flows in the foreseeable future. It is therefore reasonable to suggest that policies in both sending and receiving countries should be targeted at reducing the flows that are shown to be most detrimental to national development, and at increasing the benefits from all types of skilled out-migration. Second, given the importance of circumstances in sending countries, the key to reducing the costs of brain drain, and increasing the benefits from brain gain, lies with economic and political conditions and related policies in countries of origin.

2. RECIPIENT COUNTRY POLICIES

Two broad and potentially conflicting policy objectives have emerged in recent years in countries of destination.[13] On the one hand, both rapid ageing of

---

In small island LDCs, the main policy issue appears to be the utilization of remittances and the skills of those abroad to greater advantage for community and national development.

Permanent emigration of skilled professionals entails a loss of human capital for the home country in the short run and hence a contraction in its absorptive capacity.

Many of those positive effects of emigration of qualified persons occur only once countries have reached a certain level of development and income growth.

LDCs are more likely to have their accumulation of technological capabilities hampered by skilled out-migration.

populations and rising living standards in developed countries have contributed to shortages of skilled persons. Governments in major developed countries have sought to fill those gaps by attracting qualified professionals from abroad through permanent (or long-term) immigration. On the other hand, there is growing recognition, especially in areas such as health care, that excessive brain drain can hurt developing economies and LDCs in particular. Several countries, led by the United Kingdom, have developed innovative policies to attempt to minimize the brain drain in certain sectors, especially from poor countries in Africa, but with mixed success.

The United Kingdom has been at the forefront of policies to reduce the impact of brain drain in the health sector in poorer countries (Lowell, Findlay and Stewart, 2004). Initiatives include banning National Health Service trusts from recruiting from South Africa and Caribbean countries, and the issuance by the Department of Health of guidelines on international recruitment for nurses, with a list of countries (including many in sub-Saharan Africa) from which recruitment is prohibited.[14]

Clearly, these are still limited objectives and might be extended to other areas where the social costs of migration are demonstrated to be high. Other European countries are still reluctant to introduce similar legislation, despite pressure from the United Kingdom. As a recent agreement between the EU and African countries indicates, developing a broader approach that slows the movement of skilled workers by seeking to dampen demand in developed countries is still a difficult task. The Joint Africa–EU Declaration on Migration and Development signed by foreign ministers on 23 November 2006 shied away from the sensitive issue of payments to African countries to compensate for the costs of skilled migration.[15] The EU rejected the African ministers' proposal that a special development fund, provided by the EU, be created to finance development in order to prevent young Africans from leaving for work in Europe. In essence, that fund would seek to have the similar effect, albeit in a different form, as the long-discussed migration tax proposed by Bhagwati in the 1970s (Bhagwati and Hamada, 1974). Nevertheless, progress was indicated by the joint decisions on "[p]romoting concrete and tailor-made policies and reforms to address skills shortages caused by brain drain" by supporting human resource and educational development and on "[s]upporting programmes which foster the mobility and temporary return of members of the diasporas with the necessary skills in their countries of origin". More proactive measures are required in order to enforce this commitment, however.

Development assistance is another, perhaps more effective, channel through which developed countries can help tackle the worst forms of brain drain. The case of the assistance provided to Malawi by the United Kingdom's Development for International Development (DFID) is instructive. Malawi has expanded the training of health professionals but has major problems in keeping staff in the country (Record and Mohiddin, 2006). DFID has developed a special programme of assistance for that country to increase training for both doctors and nurses, and to increase pay and job opportunities. DFID reports, moreover, that the programme has met with some initial success, with the enrolment of 450 new health workers, some 570 new staff members recruited to the Ministry of Health, recruitment of international volunteers and the establishment of new laboratories.[16]

While the United Kingdom has taken some important initiatives in the health-care sector, selective policies targeting professional and skilled workers is a major element in the country's immigration programme, regardless of country of origin (Nunn, 2005).[17] Professionals accounted for approximately 40 per cent of all migration into the United Kingdom from the mid-1990s, as an integral component of the medium-term economic growth programme. While North America and

Several developed countries have developed innovative policies to attempt to minimize the brain drain in certain sectors.

In the Joint Africa–EU Declaration on Migration and Development of 2006, progress was indicated by the joint decisions on "Promoting concrete and tailor-made policies and reforms to address skills shortages caused by brain drain".

Development assistance is another channel through which developed countries can help tackle the worst forms of brain drain.

the EU contributed the major share of foreign born academic staff, the number of African recruits totalled well over 1,000, including 100 from LDCs among lecturers and professors in the United Kingdom in 2002. In the light of a serious shortage of university staff in many African countries, Nunn recommends that the United Kingdom promote international protocols on recruitment similar to those developed by the National Health Services, in addition to efforts to improve the quality of teaching and the output of universities, and promote debate on compensatory mechanisms.

Incentives for emigrants to return home have been offered by some European countries.

Incentives for emigrants to return home have been offered by some European countries. For example, France, Italy and Germany have provided loans, training and technical assistance to migrants (World Bank, 2006). France has provided loans to emigrants from Mali and Senegal to establish businesses in their home countries. However, the small size of the programmes, lack of experience in undertaking business ventures (particularly among less educated migrants) and poor economic conditions at home are reported to have reduced the programmes' effectiveness. All those factors need to be taken into account if such programmes are to have a significant influence on the return of emigrants and on the impact of their return on local economies.

3. LDC POLICIES

The creation of employment opportunities for qualified professionals with increasing rates of pay is crucial for retaining locally trained human capital and for attracting returnees. This includes the successful development of technological capabilities in firms.

Brain retention and gain depend crucially on general economic and political developments in LDCs. The creation of employment opportunities for qualified professionals with increasing rates of pay is crucial for retaining locally trained human capital and for attracting returnees. That includes higher salaries, improved working conditions and career paths, and advances in governance, especially administrative and bureaucratic, in key public sector areas such as health and education. The successful development of technological capabilities in firms entails the creation of employment opportunities for a range of professionals, including engineers, technicians and researchers. The establishment of endowed professorships, through State, private, bilateral or multilateral partnerships, can help in retaining academic staff in LDCs (Tettey, 2003). However, targeted interventions can also be effective in the short to medium term.

Policies aimed at increasing the gains from return migration have some potential for LDCs. The benefits for LDCs are likely to be greater in the case of permanent return of former emigrants (as compared with temporary returns), particularly in terms of the skills endowment of countries of origin.[18] Policies to that end are, however, difficult to devise and implement, and there have been several cases of failure (see below). LDCs should therefore target short-term visits by skilled professionals, since that is where policy initiatives are most likely to succeed. They can involve teachers and professors giving crash courses, engineers providing specific inputs in sectors relevant to their field of expertise, doctors returning to assist with specific health-care campaigns, and so forth. Such actions can make a significant difference to specific development projects and programmes. Skilled persons selected from among the diaspora are likely to have the advantage over other international experts in terms of their understanding of local circumstances. Nationals living abroad who are interested in particular projects are likely to self-select if language ability and knowledge of local circumstances are important for effective application of higher-level skills in projects in LDCs. This is likely to obviate the need to apply "national preference" criteria in the selection of professionals based abroad.

LDCs should target short-term visits by skilled professionals, since that is where policy initiatives are most likely to succeed.

Programmes targeting emigrants can also produce longer-term "external" benefits by keeping them engaged with the environment and challenges of their home countries, and keeping open the possibility of return if conditions are favourable. Such programmes for return migration have been successfully applied by, for example, the Republic of Korea, Taiwan Province of China, Malaysia and, more recently, India and China.

One important initiative to ensure greater utilization of diaspora skills is the collection and tracking of information on the occupations and training of nationals working abroad. This requires that databases, which facilitate the establishment of networks of professionals, be established and maintained.

Countries of origin should also ensure that overseas nationals are able to retain their citizenship, even if they take up citizenship in destination countries. This means recognizing dual nationality, which may require special arrangements with countries of destination that do not allow dual citizenship, either in general or in specific cases (Aleinikoff and Klusmeyer, 2002). Other incentives involve revising regulations that discriminate against emigrants, such as eliminating restrictions on ownership of land and property.

In the health-care sector new initiatives are beginning to produce the desired effects in some countries (Dovlo, 2004). Measures taken include significant increases in salaries, especially those of nurses (Botswana); schemes to develop health-care cadres, particularly in rural areas (for example, Malawi and Zambia have clinical officers, and Mozambique has a similar category of health carer); and new programmes for management of migrant return, especially on a temporary basis. Other initiatives include extending the retirement age (for example, beyond 55, as is currently the practice in Malawi and Lesotho), using community-based curricula and strengthening training systems, especially those targeted at retaining skilled trainers. While some of those initiatives have met with resistance from the medical profession (such as substituting health cadres for trained professionals), they provide encouraging signs that targeted initiatives can have a positive impact in occupations badly affected by brain drain.

The policies described above replace unsuccessful initiatives utilized in the past. Such initiatives include programmes for the permanent return of migrants, and the use of bonds and financial sanctions. The latter have often failed because of poor administration and unrealistic restrictions placed on doctors and nurses, including long periods of placement in rural areas despite high wage differentials between those areas and urban areas, in addition to significant differentials between opportunities abroad and those at home (Dovlo, 2004).

Regional initiatives to increase the brain gain have been particularly important in Southern Africa through the South Africa Network of Skills Abroad (Mutume, 2003). Some 22,000 graduates from five countries were reported to be linked through its website to universities back home in a range of fields, including medicine, commerce, education and engineering. Brain gain consists in offers to train South African counterparts or help them conduct research, help transfer technology (for example, though the provision of computers and software) and facilitate business contacts. Initiatives of that kind could be extended to LDCs. The New Partnership for Africa's Development (NEPAD), has also addressed brain drain issues through discussion of conditions that help curb the brain drain, although concrete initiatives for LDCs in particular have not yet been addressed systematically.

Benefits deriving from programmes such as the ones outlined above are unlikely to be large in terms of overall national economic and social development, but they can assist in overcoming specific bottlenecks.

> *Programmes targeting emigrants can also produce longer-term "external" benefits by keeping them engaged with the environment and challenges of their home countries, and keeping open the possibility of return.*

> *One important initiative to ensure greater utilization of diaspora skills is the collection and tracking of information on the occupations and training of nationals working abroad.*

> *Countries of origin should also ensure that overseas nationals are able to retain their citizenship, even if they take up citizenship in destination countries. Other incentives involve revising regulations that discriminate against emigrants, such as eliminating restrictions on ownership of land and property.*

4. INTERNATIONAL PROGRAMMES

While discussions of recipient developed country programmes have centred on restricting inflows and on compensation, international agency policies have put greater emphasis on brain gain through returnees. The focus has been on maximizing brain gain by working with diasporas (either providing incentives for skilled migrants to return permanently or assisting in technology and skill transfer). The International Organization for Migration has been at the forefront of those efforts, which have had mixed success. In 1983 it established the Return of Qualified African Nationals (RQAN) programme with the main objective of "mobilising, and promoting the utilisation of highly qualified, qualified and skilled personnel in the development of African countries through voluntary programs" (Wickramasekera, 2002: 11–12). Over nearly two decades some 1,500 Africans were induced to return to their home countries before the programme was discontinued. The numbers may seem very small, although they are not insignificant in the context of the importance of highly trained returnees for certain LDC African countries. Nevertheless, the high unit cost of the programme, equity considerations (with regard to colleagues back home who did not migrate) and especially lack of ownership by recipient Governments were all identified as problems. However, there are indications that qualified return migrants are making a difference by occupying key positions in the public and private sectors (Ammassari, 2005).

In 2001 RQAN was replaced by the Migration and Development for Africa programme, which puts much greater emphasis on short-term visits and transfer of knowledge through the Internet and diaspora groups, rather than on the permanent return of skilled migrants.[19] The UN Development Fund for Women has launched a Digital Diaspora Initiative, which involves overseas professionals helping women in countries of origin use new information technologies (Mutume, 2003).

These shorter-term and more modest programmes appear to have greater chances of success, although they are not without their critics. Martin, Abella and Kuptsch (2006) note that only emigrants with permanent residence rights overseas are likely to return even for short visits, and the costs are still high by poor country standards.

Relaxing restrictions on trade in services can contribute to brain circulation of professionals from LDCs. The latter can benefit from temporary movement of professionals to technologically more advanced countries, where they can enhance their skills, learn new technologies and acquire more experience. That can be useful when professionals are working once again in their home countries. Temporary emigration rules should therefore be relaxed in order to benefit LDCs. In the case of services, this could be part of commitments by destination countries on temporary movement of persons (Mode 4) under the WTO's General Agreement on Trade in Services (Martin, Abella and Kuptsch, 2006). However, the political obstacles to temporary (contract) migration are much greater than for permanent movements. This fact is reflected in the stalled world trade negotiations of the Doha Round on those issues. Developed countries have not been prepared to remove many of the "economic needs" tests that inhibit the movements of skilled workers.[20]

International agreements on migration, or even the creation of an international body similar to the WTO (to establish rules and procedures for regulating international migration), appear to be difficult to achieve in the short to medium term.[21] However, regional agreements, often between LDCs and their more developed neighbours, may have greater prospects of success. For example, the ASEAN Framework Agreement on Services of the Association of Southeast Asian Nations — the regional equivalent of arrangements through GATS — has made some progress in facilitating the movement of architects, engineers, health-care workers (mainly nurses rather than doctors) from LDCs such as Myanmar, Cambodia and the Lao People's Democratic Republic to their better-off neighbours, particularly Singapore and Malaysia. However, actual migration under this programme is still limited; in practice, most movements between LDCs and the more developed countries in the ASEAN region have occurred as the result of unilateral policies that encourage the movement of skilled workers through the migration of "talents" and professionals on a contract basis for a period (with renewals) of up to six to seven years (Manning and Sidorenko, 2007).

Notes

1. In this chapter the terms "skilled", "qualified worker", "skilled professional" and "tertiary educated" are used interchangeably. The terms "out-migration" and "emigration" are also used interchangeably.
2. The numbers of professionals moving abroad on temporary contract are large, and are comparable in certain respects comparable with permanent movements. However, several of the issues for temporary migrants are somewhat different from those with respect to permanent out-migration, which was the consequence of the dominant mode of recruitment in most developed countries through to the 1980s and 1990s. Return migration is more predictable for many contract workers, although contracts are renewed in many cases, and highly valued contract workers may well become permanent. In destination countries, the brain gain related to those who do move is more immediate, but probably less substantial, and remittances are probably larger.
3. Both Canada and Australia have substantially liberalized their immigration regimes since 2000 with regard to skilled workers from abroad. Changes have occurred through programmes which allow graduates to stay on after completing their courses, and through the adoption of points systems that target specific skill groups in short supply. In Europe, the United Kingdom, France, Germany, Ireland and the Netherlands have also significantly relaxed restrictions on the employment of skilled persons through new legislation since the late 1990s (Mahroum, 2001).
4. See box 7.
5. See box 8 concerning the experience of low-income countries.
6. The migration "hump" refers to the process whereby the rate of (net) out-migration increases in the early stages of economic development until it reaches a peak, somewhere in the middle-income range of national GDP per capita, and then begins to decline.
7. More recent studies show that those patterns continued thereafter (Adams, 2003).
8. The main source of data is Docquier and Marfouk (2004), which was updated in Docquier and Marfouk (2006). While the earlier study contains data for a quite large number of countries, the revised version reports only the data for selected countries. The latter reports higher migration rates in 2000 for the Lao People's Democratic Republic (37 per cent compared with 14 per cent reported in the earlier version), Uganda (36 per cent compared with 22 per cent) and Angola (33 per cent compared with 26 per cent); at the same time, the rate is lower for Somalia (33 per cent versus 59 per cent earlier). For consistency, we have used only the data from the 2004 publication for the discussion of country trends in this chapter. While the absolute rates differ between the two studies, only the Lao People's Democratic Republic (which was already the highest out-migration country among LDCs in Asia according to the 2004 study) changes significantly in ranking among the high emigration countries.
9. The main sub-regions among LDCs in Africa are East, Central and West Africa. Sudan and Lesotho are included in Central and East Africa respectively. Haiti is included in West Africa.
10. Iguchi (2003) and Chalamwong (2004) provide general surveys of skilled migration from Asia.
11. In the case of Myanmar, official OECD data on out-migration are probably a significant underestimate, given substantial movements to other South and South-East Asian countries (such as the employment of Myanmar doctors in Malaysia). For a discussion of the migration of health care and IT professionals from those two countries within South-East Asia, see Manning and Sidorenko (2007).
12. Brown and Connell (2006) demonstrate that Samoan and Tongan nurses continued to remit considerable amounts back home 20–25 years after emigration, contrary to the pattern found elsewhere, whereby diaspora links with home countries and remittances tend to decline over time.
13. Lowell (2002), Lowell and Findlay (2002), Wickramasekera (2003) and Lowell, Findlay and Stewart (2004) provide general surveys of developed country policies.
14. www.dfid.gov.uk/news/files/world-health-day-2006.asp.
15. See www.euractiv.com/en/justice/eu-africa-talk-migration-brain-drain/article-159976.
16. www.dfid.gov.uk/news/files/world-health-day-2006.asp.
17. The three-tier programme launched in 2002 differentiates between the highly skilled (doctors, lawyers, engineers and academics), the skilled (nurses, teachers and administrators) and the low skilled.
18. See box 8.
19. Other international programmes include the Return for Qualified Afghans Programme (co-funded by the EU) and the Transfer of Knowledge Through Expatriate Nationals project run by the UNDP. The latter also stresses returns for shorter periods of three to six months (Lowell, Findlay and Stewart, 2004).

20. "Economic needs" tests require host employers to demonstrate that local workers with equivalent skills are not available.
21. Bhagwati (2003) has been in prominent in calling for the establishment of a world migration body equivalent to the WTO.

References

Adams, R.H. (2003). International migration, remittances and the brain drain: A study of 24 labor-exporting countries. Policy Research Working Paper No. 3069, World Bank, Washington, DC.

Adams, R.H. (2007). International remittances and the household: Analysis and review of global evidence. Policy Research Working Paper No. 4116, World Bank, Washington, DC.

Adkoli, B.V. (2006). Migration of health workers: Perspectives from Bangladesh, India, Nepal, Pakistan and Sri Lanka. *Regional Health Forum*, 10 (1): 49–58.

Aleinikoff, T.A. and Klusmeyer, D. (2002). *Citizenship Policies for an Age of Migration*. Carnegie Endowment for International Peace, Washington, DC.

Ammassari, S. (2003). From nation-building to entrepreneurship: The impact of elite return migrants in Côte D'Ivoire and Ghana. Paper presented at the International Workshop on Migration and Poverty in West Africa, 13–14 March, University of Sussex, UK.

Ammassari, S. (2005). Migration and development: New strategic outlooks and practical ways forward. The cases of Angola and Zambia. IOM Migration Research Series, No. 21, Geneva.

Bhagwati, J. (2003). Borders beyond control. *Foreign Affairs*, 82 (1): 98–104.

Bhagwati, J. and Hamada, K. (1974). The brain drain, international integration of markets for professionals and unemployment. *Journal of Development Economics*, 1 (1): 19–42.

Brown, R.P. and Connell, J. (2006). Occupation-specific analysis of migration and remittance behaviour: Pacific nurses in Australia and New Zealand. *Asia Pacific Viewpoint*, 47 (1): 135–150.

Chalamwong, Y. (2004). The migration of highly skilled Asian workers in OECD member countries and its effects on economic development in East Asia. Unpublished paper presented at an Experts Seminar, 10–11 June, OECD, Paris.

Connell, J. (2006). Migration, dependency and inequality in the Pacific: Old wine in bigger bottles. In Firth, S. (ed.), *Globalisation and Governance in the Pacific Islands*. Pandanus Press, Canberra.

Docquier, F. and Marfouk, A. (2004). Measuring the international mobility of skilled workers (1990–2000). Policy Research Working Paper No. 3381, World Bank, Washington, DC.

Docquier, F. and Marfouk, A. (2006). International migration by education attainment, 1990–2000. In Ozden, C. and Schiff, M. (eds.), *International Migration, Remittances and the Brain Drain*. World Bank and Palgrave Macmillan, Washington, DC and New York: 151–199.

Docquier, F. and Rapoport, H. (2004). Skilled migration: The perspective of developing countries. Policy Research Working Paper No. 3381, World Bank, Washington, DC.

Dovlo, D. (2004). The brain drain in Africa: An emerging challenge to health professionals' education. *Journal of Higher Education in Africa*, 2 (3): 1–18.

Faini, R. (2006). Remittances and brain drain. IZA Discussion Paper Series No. 214, Institute for the Study of Labour (IZA), Bonn.

Grubel H.B. and Scott, A.D. (1966). The international flow of human capital. *American Economic Review*, 56: 268–274.

Hagopian, A., Thompson, M.J., Fordyce, M., Johnson, K.E. and Hart, L.G. (2004). The migration of physicians from sub-Saharan Africa to the United States of America: Measures of African brain drain. *Human Resources for Health*, 2 (17): 2–10.

Hardill, I. and MacDonald, S. (2000). Skilled international migration: The experience of nurses in the United Kingdom. *Regional Studies*, 34 (7): 681–692.

Iguchi, Y. (2003). The movement of the highly-skilled in Asia: Present situation and future prospects. In OECD (ed.), *Migration and the Labour Market in Asia: Recent Trends and Policies*. Organisation for Economic Co-operation and Development, Paris.

IMF (2005). *World Economic Outlook*. International Monetary Fund, Washington, DC.

Kanbur, R. and Rapoport, H. (2004). Migration selectivity and the evolution of spatial inequality. Cornell University, Ithaca, NY, mimeo.

Kokko, A. (1994). Technology, market characteristics, and spillovers. *Journal of Development Economics*, 43: 279-293.

Lowell, B.L. (2002). Policy responses to the international mobility of skilled manpower. International Migration Paper No. 43, International Labour Organization, Geneva.

Lowell, B.L. and Findlay, A. (2002). Migration of highly skilled persons from developing countries: Impact and policy responses: Synthesis Report. International Migration Paper No. 44, International Labour Organization, Geneva.

Lowell, B. L., Findlay, A. and Stewart, E. (2004). Brain strain: Optimising highly skilled migration from developing countries. Asylum and Migration Working Paper No. 3, Institute for Public Policy Research, London.

Lucas, R.B. (2004). *International Migration and Economic Development: Lessons from Low-Income Countries*. Edward Elgar, Cheltenham, UK.

Lucas, R.B. (2006). Migration and economic development in Africa: A review of evidence. *Journal of African Economies*, 15 (2): 337–395.

Mahroum, S. (2001). Europe and immigration of highly skilled labour. *International Migration*, 39 (5): 27–43.

Manning, C. (2007). Brain drain and brain gain: A survey of issues, outcomes and policies in the least developed countries (LDCs). Study prepared for UNCTAD as a background paper for *The Least Developed Countries Report 2007*, UNCTAD, Geneva.

Manning, C. and Sidorenko, A. (2007). The regulation of professional migration in ASEAN: Insights from the health and IT sectors. Department Working Paper No. 2006-08, Division of Economics, Australian National University, Canberra.

Martin, P., Abella, M. and Kuptsch, C. (2006). *Managing Labor Migration in the Twenty-First Century*. Yale University Press, New Haven.

Mayer, J. (2001), Technology diffusion, human capital and economic growth in developing countries. UNCTAD Discussion Paper No. 154, UNCTAD, Geneva.

Martineau, T., Decker, K. and Bundred, P. (2004). "Brain drain" of health professionals: From rhetoric to responsible action. *Health Policy*, 70 (1): 1–10.

Mountford, A. (1997). Can brain drain be good for growth in the source economy? *Journal of Development Economics,* 53 (2): 287–303.

Mutume, G. (2003). Reversing Africa's "brain drain". *Africa Recovery*, 17 (2): 1–9.

Niimi, Y. and Ozden, C. (2006). Migration and remittances. Policy Research Working Paper No. 4087, World Bank, Washington, DC.

Nunn, A. (2005). The brain drain: Academic and skilled migration to the United Kingdom and its impact on Africa. Report prepared for the Association of Teachers and the College and Lecturers Union, Policy Research Institute, University of Leeds, United Kingdom.

Ratha, D. and Shaw, W. (2007). *South–South Migration and Remittances*. World Bank, Washington, DC.

Record, R. and Mohiddin, A. (2006). An economic perspective on Malawi's medical "brain drain". *Globalization and Health*, 2 (12): 1–8.

Russel, S.S., Jacobsen, K. and Stanley, W.D. (1990). International migration and development in sub-Saharan Africa. World Bank Discussion Paper No. 101, World Bank, Washington, DC.

Saxenian, A., Motoyama, Y. and Quan, X. (2002). *Local and Global Networks of Immigrant Professionals in Silicon Valley*. Public Policy Institute of California, San Francisco.

Schiff, M. (2006). Brain gain: Claims about its size and impact on welfare and growth are greatly exaggerated. In Ozden, C. and Schiff, M. (eds.), *International Migration, Remittances and Brain Drain*. World Bank and Palgrave Macmillan, Washington, DC and New York: 201–225.

Stark, O. (2004). Rethinking the brain drain. *World Development,* 32 (1): 15–22.

Tettey, W.J. (2003), Africa's options: Return, retention or diaspora? SciDecNet Policy Briefs (www.scidev.net).

UNCTAD (2006). *The Least Developed Countries Report 2006: Developing Productive Capacities*. United Nations publication, sales no. E.06.II.D.9, Geneva and New York.

UNESCO (2006). *Global Education Digest 2006: Comparing Education Statistics Across the World*. UNESCO, Paris.

Wickramasekera, P. (2003). Policy responses to skilled migration: Retention, return and circulation. Perspectives on Labour Migration, Report No. 5E, International Migration Programme, International Labour Office, Geneva.

World Bank (2006). *Global Economic Prospects 2006. Economic Implications of Remittances and Migration*. World Bank, Washington, DC.

Knowledge Aid

Chapter

5

A. Introduction

This chapter focuses on how foreign aid can be used to support enhanced use of science, technology and innovation (STI) for economic development and poverty reduction in the LDCs. The scale and the effectiveness of aid are critically important for those countries' economic development and the achievement of substantial poverty reduction. The justification for aid is usually articulated within a framework which stresses the limited ability of most LDCs to mobilize the domestic financial resources needed to meet a range of pressing economic, social and political objectives. But equally important, and actually even more fundamental, aid can help to build up the knowledge resources and knowledge systems of LDCs. This is particularly important for the LDCs because, as we have seen in chapter 1, knowledge accumulation and technological learning through international market linkages are currently weak in the LDCs. In that situation, there is a real danger of socio-economic marginalization for the now-open LDC economies as knowledge becomes increasingly important in global competition. Aid can play an important role in developing a minimum threshold level of competences and learning capacities which will enable LDCs to rectify that situation. Knowledge aid that strengthens the knowledge resources and knowledge systems of the LDCs is an essential component of aid which is not a hand-out, but rather a hand-up.

Knowledge aid that strengthens the knowledge resources and knowledge systems of the LDCs is an essential component of aid which is not a hand-out, but rather a hand-up.

Thinking about knowledge aid is particularly important for ensuring aid effectiveness. Towards the end of the 1990s, a strong consensus emerged that aid worked if the recipient country's policies and institutions were right. As discussed, in earlier LDC Reports, the econometric research underlying that position was flawed (see Hansen and Tarp, 2001; UNCTAD, 2002: box 19). Although it is clear that good domestic policies are necessary for effective aid, the precise nature of what constitutes the right policies is not as clear-cut as earlier thought. Moreover, by emphasizing the importance of recipients' policies, the role of donors' policies in the effectiveness of aid was left out of the picture. In effect there was a "one-eyed approach" to aid effectiveness (UNCTAD, 2000). With the Paris Declaration on donor alignment and the harmonization of aid practices, much more attention is now being paid to the role of donor practices in aid effectiveness. But there is still insufficient discussion of the impact of the composition of aid on aid effectiveness. This chapter is a contribution to the widening of the discussion. It is based on the belief that the provision of more knowledge aid could, if it is directed towards the right areas and through appropriate modalities, be the base for a radical break with past aid failures.

The provision of more knowledge aid could be the base for a radical break with past aid failures.

The chapter is organized into five major substantive sections. Section B defines knowledge aid and its relationship to aid for STI, and summarizes the findings of recent surveys on donor support for STI. Section C focuses on aid for STI in LDCs, identifying the scale and composition of STI-related ODA and also the types of projects and programmes towards which it is directed. From that analysis it is possible to identify a number of strategic weaknesses in knowledge aid for LDCs, and the next two sections make recommendations for improving aid for LDCs in building science, technology and innovation capacity, focusing firstly on agriculture (section D) and, secondly, on industry and infrastructure (section E). Section F looks at the current and potential role of aid for STI within Aid for Trade initiatives, and more specifically within the Integrated Framework for Trade-Related Technical Cooperation, and suggests how it may be possible to deepen trade preferences for LDCs through support for technological development. The conclusion summarizes the major message of the chapter.

B. Knowledge aid and aid for STI

By intensifying the knowledge content of their aid activities donors could increase aid effectiveness.

1. FORMS OF KNOWLEDGE AID

The idea that by intensifying the knowledge content of their aid activities donors could increase aid effectiveness has been recognized since the 1990s (King and McGrath, 2004). But there is no agreed definition of knowledge aid. In the present Report it will be defined as aid which supports knowledge accumulation in partner countries through the development of their knowledge resources and their domestic knowledge systems.

Chart 13 sets out different donor approaches to intensifying the use of knowledge for development to clarify the scope of knowledge aid. It distinguishes between approaches that are donor-centred and those that are partner-centred. The former approaches are designed to strengthen the knowledge base of

Chart 13. Donor approaches to intensifying the use of knowledge for development

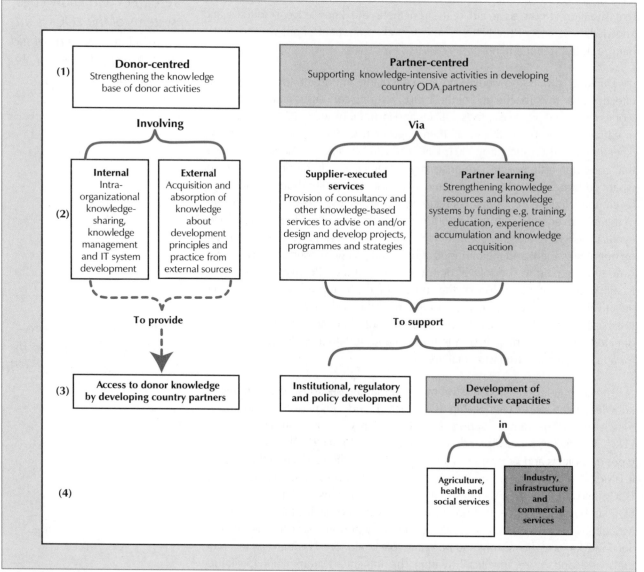

Source: Bell (2007).

the donors themselves: this can be done through internal reforms to increase intra-organizational knowledge-sharing, better knowledge management and IT system development. It is intended to increase the effectiveness of formulation and implementation of aid activities. It can also go further by providing partner countries with access to that donor knowledge — a notion that underlay the idea that the World Bank should act as a "knowledge bank". Partner-centred approaches, in contrast, are designed to support directly knowledge accumulation in partner countries. This can be done in two ways: either through supplier-executed services, where, for example, donors provide consultants who advise on, or design and develop, projects, programmes and strategies; or through strengthening the knowledge resources and knowledge systems of the partners themselves, a process which may be called partner learning. In either case, these activities might be designed to support better governance through increasing knowledge resources for institutional, regulatory and policy development, or to support the development of productive capacities through technological learning and innovation.

In this Report, knowledge aid is equated with partner-centred approaches. Aid for science, technology and innovation is a particular form of knowledge aid which is focused on building the science, technology and innovation capacity of partner countries. This can support innovation in productive sectors as well as social services such as health, and it can include enhancement of the capacity of policymakers to formulate and implement STI policy. The types of activities which have been traditionally supported as aid for S&T can include human capacity-building in relation to STI; support for other types of STI infrastructure, notably scientific research, technological R&D, and agricultural and industrial extension, and support for standards compliance and metrology. But aid for STI goes beyond this in supporting enterprise-based learning and innovation — for example, through enterprise-centred training activities, the development of domestic business linkages and the development of STI-related international linkages, including scientific cooperation and business-to-business links.

Aid for STI is a particularly important form of knowledge aid because developing innovation capacity within enterprises (both firms and farms) is the key to economic dynamism in the LDCs.

Technical cooperation grants are one mechanism for delivering knowledge aid. Technical cooperation is provided in two ways: firstly, as technical services required for the implementation of specific investment projects; and secondly, as free-standing technical cooperation, which is defined as "the provision of resources aimed at the transfer of technical and managerial skills or of technology for the purpose of building up general national capacity without reference to the implementation of any specific investment projects" (see OECD, 2006: 113). Some part of free-standing technical cooperation may be directed at building science, technology and innovation capacity within a country and as such would be part of aid for STI as defined here. But technical cooperation is not synonymous with aid for STI.

This chapter focuses on aid for STI as a form of knowledge aid. However, it is important to emphasize at the outset that donor approaches to intensifying the use of knowledge for development have generally been more donor-centred than partner-centred. King and McGrath (2004) demonstrate with respect to the experience of the World Bank and bilateral agencies in Sweden, the United Kingdom and Japan, that a very large part of the effort to mobilize knowledge for development has been concentrated on donor-centred activities. Moreover, even when this has ostensibly also been designed in a way that provides partner

Aid for science, technology and innovation (STI) is a particular form of knowledge aid that can support innovation in productive sectors as well as social services.

Aid for STI develops innovation capacity within enterprises (both firms and farms), which is key to economic dynamism in the LDCs.

countries with access to donor knowledge, the extent of such knowledge-sharing has been less effective than expected (King and McGrath, 2004).

Similarly, with respect to technical cooperation, the OECD's Development Co-operation Report 2005 distinguishes between technical cooperation which involves (a) "direct supply of skills from outside" and (b) "efforts to enhance the capacities of the local population" (OECD, 2006: 112), and noted that "In the past, donors have broadly assumed that they will promote capacity development, but reality has proved much more complex" (p. 111). A detailed case study of Cambodia shows how difficult it is to build domestic capacity in a situation in which there is chronic underfunding of government and very low salaries (Godfrey et al., 2002). Much technical assistance in that case actually served to facilitate donor resource flows rather than build domestic capacity, and the sustainability of donor projects and the effectiveness of government were undermined as key personnel were drawn out of the public sector to service a succession of donor projects.

In a situation in which there is chronic underfunding of government and very low salaries, much technical assistance served to facilitate donor resource flows rather than build domestic capacity.

2. AID FOR STI: EVIDENCE FROM RECENT SURVEYS

Various recent surveys enable the reconstruction of trends in aid for STI from multilateral and bilateral donors.

Crawford et al. (2006) survey World Bank lending for science and technology over the period 1980–2004. Their conclusion is stark: "Maybe with the exception of long-term support for agricultural research, the analysis of S&T projects over the last 25 years reveals no consistent approach or strategy on the part of the Bank toward developing S&T capacity in its client countries. In agriculture, sustained efforts have been put into supporting NARS [national agricultural research systems], much of which has been in the form of minor support undertaken in connection with other rural development activities. Regarding nonagricultural projects in general, the Bank's approach has been ad hoc, experimenting with different mechanisms for different circumstances as they occurred" (Crawford et al, 2006: 28–29). Quantifying the level of financing for S&T projects is difficult. But the study estimates (with quite a stringent definition of aid for S&T[1]) that:

The analysis of S&T projects over the last 25 years reveals no consistent approach or strategy on the part of the World Bank toward developing S&T capacity in its client countries.

- "Although 647 projects provided some support for science and technology, only 119 of the World Bank's 6,059 projects were dedicated primarily to promoting science and technology or contained a significant science and technology capacity building component" (p. 10).

- Over the last 25 years only 3.9 per cent of total World Bank lending has on average gone to S&T projects (p. 33).

- "Lending to science and technology in the last 5 years has declined significantly with respect to the previous 20 years" (p.14).

- Commitments to agricultural research projects have been declining since the 1990s, as part of a dramatic decline in World Bank lending to agriculture which began in the mid-1980s.

The geographical distribution of World Bank non-agricultural S&T lending during this period is also significant. The Republic of Korea was by far the largest borrower and other large borrowers were India, Indonesia, Brazil, Chile and Mexico. The only LDC in the list of countries with major non-agricultural S&T projects is Bangladesh. The overall focus has been on countries with a large population and on more advanced developing countries, with LDCs (other than Bangladesh) thus being effectively excluded.

Although S&T projects constituted a minor share of total World Bank lending and may have been "ad hoc", there was long-term involvement and continuity with a few countries. For non-agricultural projects, this focused on STI capacity-building blocks, namely the development of factor markets (for both technical skills and capital) and the development of public R&D and the general higher education system (Yammal and Casabonne, 2005). Table 33 summarizes some of the distinctive feature of this lending, differentiating between two major approaches — R&D system-centred capacity-building (exemplified by Brazil and Mexico) and firm-centred capacity-building (exemplified by India and the Republic of Korea). It seems that the latter approach was more effective.

Although S&T projects constituted a minor share of total World Bank lending and may have been "ad hoc", there was long-term involvement and continuity with a few countries.

With regard to bilateral lending, Watson, Crawford and Farley (2003) write: "Bilateral support has fluctuated enormously, with funding for research being one of the first activities to be cut when budgets are declining. This is especially damaging as continuity of support is vitally important to research and capability building. In general, only a small sub/group of donors have made systematic

Table 33. Different approaches to World Bank lending for STI: A cross-country comparison

	Brazil/Mexico	India/Republic of Korea
Content of lending		
Human capital	• Emphasis on the scientific PhD/Master's level • General tertiary education	• Emphasis on technical, vocational level and engineering • Mostly engineering at the tertiary level
Public R&D system	• Maintenance investment in public R&D infrastructure (almost no buildings) • Priority is given to cutting-edge research *- Centres of excellence*	• Expansive investment in R&D infrastructure (staff, and equipment intensive building) • Priority is given to developing technical skills • Support for technology diffusion (e.g. electronic projects in the Republic of Korea and India)
STI legal framework	• Sparse STI legislation linked to World Bank projects	• Dynamic legal reform, institutionalized incentive structure

Breadth of intervention	• Mostly horizontal
	  - Petrochemicals (Brazil)
		• Vertical and horizontal
		  - Electronics (India, Republic of Korea)
		  - Petrochemicals (India)
		  - Machinery (Republic of Korea)
		  - Cement (India), software (India)
		  - Pharmaceuticals (India)

Financial mechanisms	• Predominant use of matching grants in more recent projects • Very recent venture capital initiatives • Private sector as passive beneficiary • Industrial credit dispersed (in addition to banking reform, trade and export)	• Targeted credit for import and absorption of technology • Early efforts on venture capital • Private sector as co-investor and beneficiary • Focus on providing credit to industries
Methodology of lending		
Size of projects	• Fewer, larger projects (Mexico: 19; Brazil: 13)	• More, smaller projects (India: 37; Republic of Korea: 29)

Number of projects	• Fewer repeater projects (back to back or with minor gaps within a project series)
	  - 4 loans for industrial equipment fund (Mexico)
	  - 4 loans for small- and medium scale industrial development (Mexico)
	  - 3 loans for comprehensive STI (Brazil)
	  - 3 loans for development banking (Brazil)
		• Many repeater projects, overlapping; "holding hand" approach of Bank lending that enabled learning feedback
		  - 11 loans supporting ICICI (India)
		  - 9 loans for industrial import project (India)
		  - 4 loans for technology development (Republic of Korea)
		  - 3 loans for technology advancement (Republic of Korea)
		  - 5 loans for technical education (Republic of Korea)

Focus	• Comprehensive and multi-component ("omnibus" projects) • Sectoral budget support	• Highly focused and single-component

Intensity	• Low intensity: few concurrent projects
	  - Brazil and Mexico, 1980s: up to 4 concurrent projects
		• High intensity: many concurrent projects
		  - India, 1990s: up to 9 projects
		  - Republic of Korea, 1980s: up to 7 projects
		  - Republic of Korea, 1990s: up to 9 projects

Priorities	• R&D system-centered capacity-building	• Firm-centered capacity building
Timing (start of continued involvement)	• Mexico: 1972 (exc. 1950) • Brazil: 1976	• India: 1955 • Republic of Korea: 1969

Source: Yammal and Casabonne (2005).

attempts to: (i) give prominence to improving S&T capacity as an essential long-term development goal; (ii) approach S&T in an integral manner, emphasizing cross-sectoral connections; and (iii) reach out to smaller and poorer countries that have the greatest need and face the greatest challenges in improving S&T capacity. Success has been notable, although it has been on a small scale with modest resources" (p. 25–26).

Support to science, technology and knowledge for development is increasing across the donor community, but this support appears to be driven without a parallel increase in strategic guidance within donor institutions.

This situation is now changing. Farley (2005: 7), in a snapshot of the global landscape of support for science, technology and knowledge for development, found that: "Support to science, technology and knowledge for development, as defined by the institutions profiled, is increasing across the donor community and resulting in a wide array of activities and modalities for support". However, "this increase in support appears to be driven without a parallel increase in strategic guidance within donor institutions, or between them although their attention is now turning to this oversight".

Moreover, an updated and extended analysis of the pattern of donor support shows that some donors are beginning to develop a strategic approach to aid for STI (Farley, 2007). In particular:

- The International Development Research Centre (IDRC) has crystallized its vision for support to STI through its new Innovation, Technology and Society (ITS) Program Initiative with its 2006–2011 Prospectus.

- The United Kingdom's Department for International Development (DFID) has appointed a Chief Scientific Adviser and is formulating a science and innovation strategy.

- The Swedish International Development Agency's Development for Research Cooperation (SAREC) is completing a revised research strategy that will focus more on innovation systems research, climate, water, biodiversity and urban research.

Some donors are beginning to develop a strategic approach to aid for STI.

- A reorganization at the African Development Bank in 2006 has led to the creation of a new unit that focuses explicitly on higher education, science, and technology. This unit recently started a draft Strategy on Higher Education, Science and Technology and an accompanying Action Plan.

- The World Bank's new Science and Technology Coordinator has commissioned a number of studies that examine the Bank's approach to STI for development, which is being re-evaluated at present.[2]

Meanwhile, a number of other donors — the Netherlands, Denmark, Norway and the Canadian International Development Agency — are in the process of rethinking their strategies, which may change the proportion of aid they each devote to STI and the countries to which this aid is allocated.

C. Aid for STI in LDCs: Elements of the current situation

1. THE SCALE AND COMPOSITION OF AID FOR STI-RELATED HUMAN RESOURCES AND RESEARCH

One of the striking facts emerging from discussions with donors is that they cannot actually quantify how much aid they are giving for STI (Farley, 2005). This is indicative of the low priority given to the issue, as well as of the unclear conceptualization of the subject. There is no accepted definition of aid for STI, and thus this section uses the imperfect information which can be gathered from available OECD reporting codes to identify a number of features of the scale and composition of aid for STI in the LDCs.

It focuses on two categories of aid for STI that are identifiable:

- Aid for research, which includes agricultural, forestry and fishing research; technological research and development (essentially related to non-agricultural activities); education and medical research; and energy and environmental research;

- Aid for advanced and/or specific human skills, which includes vocational training, higher education, statistical capability-building, agricultural extension and various specific types of education and training related to social sectors, production sectors and trade.

Those categories (for which the Annex provides a complete list of the OECD Credit Reporting System Codes used in the analysis) are equivalent to a traditional view of aid for S&T which encompasses the development of human resources and building the institutional infrastructure for scientific research and technological development. The analysis examines reported aid disbursements and commitments.

Table 34 summarizes annual aid disbursements to LDCs for the two categories of aid for STI and their subcategories during the period 2003–2005. From the table, it is apparent that:

- Aid for STI is a low priority for donors. Annual disbursements for the development of advanced and specific skills and for research during the period 2003–2005 constituted $727.7 million, which was equivalent to only 3.6 per cent of total disbursements.

- Aid for advanced and/or specific skills is the major priority in aid for STI, constituting 90 per cent of the total disbursements during 2003–2005 as against only 10 per cent for research.

- Of aid for advanced and/or specific skills, 65 per cent was allocated to higher education. Without the latter, only 1 per cent of the total aid disbursements to LDCs in 2003–2005 was provided for developing advanced and/or specific skills. This included only $62.1 million per year for vocational training, only $12.4 million per year for agricultural education and training, and only $9.2 million per year for agricultural extension. This is equivalent to 8 cents per person for vocational training and 3 cents per agricultural worker for agricultural education and training and agricultural extension. Aid disbursements for advanced technical and managerial skills constituted only $17.6 million per year.

- During 2003–2005, 37 per cent of the total disbursements for aid for research was earmarked for medical research. Agricultural research received 30 per cent of total aid disbursements for research, equal to only $22.1 million per year during the period 2003–2005. This is equivalent to 0.03 per cent of agricultural GDP. Aid disbursements for industrial technological research and development in LDCs — a category which covers industrial standards, quality management, metrology, testing, accreditation and certification — received only $5.1 million per year during 2003–2005. This is equivalent to 2 cents per non-agricultural worker.

These aggregate numbers are stark. But there is also a geographical concentration of STI-related aid disbursements, and thus some LDCs did even

Aid for STI in LDCs is a low priority for donors.

Aid for advanced and/or specific skills is the major priority in STI-related aid, constituting 90 per cent of the total disbursements during 2003–2005 as against only 10 per cent for research.

Aid disbursements for industrial technological research and development in LDCs received only 2 cents per non-agricultural worker.

Table 34. Composition of STI-related aid to the LDCs, 2003–2005				
(Disbursements, average annual)				
	Total disbursements *(million, 2004 $)*	Share of total aid disbursements *(%)*	Sector share in total defined STI-related aid *(%)*	Subcategory share in each sector *(%)*
Research	**73.5**	**0.4**	**10.1**	**100.0**
Agricultural research	22.1	0.1	3.0	30.1
Medical research	27.5	0.1	3.8	37.4
Environmental research	13.5	0.1	1.9	18.4
Industrial technology R&D[a]	5.1	0.0	0.0	6.9
Other	5.3	0.0	0.7	7.2
Advanced and specific human skills	**654.2**	**3.2**	**89.9**	**100.0**
Higher education	425.23	2.1	58.5	65.0
Vocational training	62.1	0.3	8.5	9.5
Advanced technical and managerial training	17.6	0.1	2.4	2.7
Research institutions	30.1	0.1	4.1	4.6
Agricultural education and training	12.4	0.1	1.7	1.9
Agricultural extension	9.2	0.0	1.3	1.4
Other	109.97	0.5	15.1	16.8
Total	**727.7**	**3.6**	**100.0**	

Source: UNCTAD secretariat calculations based on OECD/CRS database; data extracted on 28 February 2007.

Notes: Data refer to disbursements from bilateral and multilateral agencies that report to OECD. For comparative purposes, the average annual real disbursements are as follows: ICT $28.7 million; road transport $894.9 million; primary education $580.8 million; and secondary education $29.3 million.

  a This relates to the CRS code 32182, Technological Research and Development.

African LDCs received 82 per cent of total aid for research for LDCs during the period 2003–2005, and Senegal alone accounts for a third of that aid.

worse than those figures indicate. African LDCs received 82 per cent of total aid for research for LDCs during the period 2003–2005, whilst Asian LDCs received 15 per cent. Senegal alone accounts for a third of STI-related aid disbursements going to African LDCs and for 28 per cent of total aid for research going to LDCs.[3] Similarly, over half of the aid disbursements for research to Asian LDCs go to Bangladesh alone. In value terms, however, Bangladesh received the equivalent of a fourth of aid for research going to Senegal. Similarly, African LDCs received more than 70 per cent, that is, $427.3 million, of the aid disbursements for advanced and/or specific skills for the period 2003–2005. As with research, Senegal is an important recipient. It received 11 per cent of aid disbursements for advanced and/or specific skills to LDCs during 2003–2005.

Disbursement data do not allow an over-time comparison to be drawn, as important donors started to report to the OECD's Creditor Reporting System (CRS) only from 2002. It is, however, possible to make a comparison with the recent past using aid commitments. The OECD's CRS aid database contains data on donors' commitments and donors' disbursements. Differences between the two series could be due to bottlenecks, administrative delays and unrealistic pledges by donors as well as limits to the recipients' absorptive capacity (Roodman, 2006).

African LDCs received more than 70 per cent of the aid disbursements for advanced and/or specific skills for the period 2003–2005.

Table 35 shows the level of STI-related aid commitments for LDCs during the periods 1998–2000 and 2003–2005. From the table, it is clear that there can be major divergences between aid commitments and aid disbursements during a particular period. However, the aid commitments indicate donors' intended priorities and in that regard a number of key trends are apparent:

- Aid commitments to LDCs for advanced and/or specific skills more than doubled between the periods 1998–2000 and 2003–2005. However, the major driving force behind this was an increase in commitments to higher education and, to a lesser extent to research institutions. Aid commitments for advanced technical and managerial training stagnated, and those for agricultural education and training and for agricultural extension actually fell between the period from 1998–2000 to 2003–2005.

- Aid commitments to LDCs for research remained at about the same level between 1998–2000 and 2003–2005. However, there was a major shift in the composition of aid commitments for research. Commitments for agricultural research halved to the benefit of medical and environmental research.

Those figures are indicative of the low level of importance that donors attach to STI and its role in strengthening productive sectors. There is, however, a major effort to strengthen universities. But the kinds of activities which can support innovation at the enterprise level — vocational training, advanced technical and managerial training, agricultural education and training, agricultural extension, and strengthening key technological support services such as industrial standards, quality management, metrology, testing, accreditation and certification — are all poorly funded. The last category, which is so important for developing enterprise competitiveness, received 0.02 per cent of total aid disbursements to LDCs during 2003–2005.

The kinds of activities which can support innovation at the enterprise level are all poorly funded.

It may be argued that those low levels of reported aid for STI reflect the insubstantial treatment of STI issues in PRSPs (see chapter 2). But in practice, for the one STI area which is emphasized in the PRSPs, namely agricultural research and extension, aid commitments to LDCs have actually fallen rather than risen

Table 35. Composition of STI-related aid to the LDCs, 1998–2000 and 2003–2005

(Commitments, average annual)

	Total commitments (million, 2004$)		Share of total aid commitments (%)		Sector share in total defined STI-related aid (%)		Subcategory share in each sector (%)	
	1998–2000	*2003–2005*	*1998–2000*	*2003–2005*	*1998–2000*	*2003–2005*	*1998–2000*	*2003–2005*
Research	**84.7**	**86.8**	**0.5**	**0.3**	**20.5**	**10.5**	**100.0**	**100.0**
Agricultural research	65.4	32.0	0.4	0.1	15.8	3.9	77.2	36.9
Medical research	5.4	26.1	0.0	0.1	1.3	3.2	6.3	30.1
Environmental research	1.2	16.1	0.0	0.1	0.3	1.9	1.4	18.6
Industrial technology R&D[a]	1.3	6.7	0.0	0.0	0.3	0.8	1.6	7.7
Other	11.5	5.9	0.1	0.0	2.8	0.7	13.5	6.8
Advanced and specific human skills	**329.4**	**740.4**	**1.8**	**2.4**	**79.5**	**89.5**	**100.0**	**100.0**
Higher education	141.3	427.5	0.8	1.4	34.1	51.7	42.9	57.7
Vocational training	67.3	99.0	0.4	0.3	16.3	12.0	20.4	13.4
Advanced technical and managerial training	15.5	16.3	0.1	0.1	3.8	2.0	4.7	2.2
Research institutions	9.6	37.2	0.1	0.1	2.3	4.5	2.9	5.0
Agricultural education and training	23.2	10.2	0.1	0.0	5.6	1.2	7.0	1.4
Agricultural extension	13.7	12.4	0.1	0.0	3.3	1.5	4.2	1.7
Other	58.7	137.9	0.3	0.4	14.2	16.7	17.8	18.6
Total	**414.1**	**827.3**	**2.3**	**2.7**	**100.0**	**100.0**		

Source: UNCTAD secretariat calculations based on OECD/CRS database; data extracted on 28 February 2007 and 22 April 2007.

Notes: Data refer to commitments from bilateral and multilateral agencies that report to OECD. For comparative purposes, the average annual real commitments for the period 2003–2005 are as follows: ICT $73.6 million; electricity production and distribution $363.1 million; road transport $2,044.6 million, primary education $1,162 million; and secondary education $227.7 million.

a   This relates to the CRS code 32182, Technological Research and Development.

since the late 1990s. It would thus seem that the low priority for STI reflects donors' practice rather than recipients' concerns.

2. STI PROJECTS AND PROGRAMMES

A more detailed picture of aid for STI in LDCs can be obtained by examining the types of projects and programmes that donors are supporting in LDCs. Farley (2007) analyzes 170 separate donors' initiatives undertaken in both the LDCs and other developing countries by eight bilateral donors (United Kingdom, Canada, Denmark, Norway, Sweden, Switzerland, United States and European Union), four multilateral donors (Asian Development Bank, Inter-American Development Bank, UNESCO and World Bank), and two foundations (Carnegie Corporation and Rockefeller Foundation). The analysis identifies some of the key characteristics of projects and programmes supported by donors in developing countries and how donor support in LDCs differs from that in other developing countries.

Farley (2007) identifies four major orientations for donor support for all developing countries (table 36). They are as follows:

Cluster 1 — global or regional public goods initiatives. These includes projects such as the International Aid Vaccine Initiative (IAVI) and the East Coast Fever Vaccine Project (see Chataway, Smith and Wield, 2005) or support for the CGIAR.

Cluster 2 — initiatives that deepen domestic STI capacity. These include projects for developing human resources, supporting domestic research institutes, improving universities or supporting the development of technological capabilities at the enterprise level.

Cluster 3 — international linkage initiatives. The emphasis of donor-funded activities, projects and programmes in this cluster is on the creation of capacity to link up with global and regional knowledge networks.

Cluster 4 — integrated initiatives. These initiatives seek to strengthen innovation systems or to integrate the multiple dimensions of STI capacity-building addressed in clusters 1, 2, and 3.

> *The low priority for STI reflects donors' practice rather than recipients' concerns.*

Table 36. Four major orientations of donor support to STI for development			
Cluster 1	**Cluster 2**	**Cluster 3**	**Cluster 4**
Global or regional public goods initiatives	*Initiatives that deepen domestic STI capacity (i.e. sectoral, subnational or national)*	*Linkage-based initiatives*	*Integrated initiatives*
• Support to research for global or regional public goods	• University development in STI-themed disciplines • Technical and vocation education and training • Sector-focused skill upgrading through graduate and post-graduate training • Productivity enhancement through technology and skills deepening in the private sector • Research and development • Centres of excellence • STI decision-making and priority-setting • Science and mathematics in primary and secondary schools, including teacher training • STI infrastructure and equipment • Information and communication technologies	• North–South linkage initiatives • South–South linkage initiatives • North–North–South linkages for policy alignment • Sectoral and cross-sectoral linkages initiatives • Linking individuals or institutions	• National innovation systems initiatives • Integrated innovation initiatives

Source: Farley (2007).

Of those four orientations, projects and programmes to deepen domestic STI capacity (cluster 2) are the most numerous for developing countries as a whole. They include the following types of programmes: development of S&T in universities; technical and vocational education; sector-focused graduate and postgraduate training; enterprise-based productivity enhancement; support for public R&D institutes; development of centres of excellence (research programmes within a university, a research institute or a centre operating independently); support for STI policy development and implementation; support for science and mathematics in secondary schools; support for STI equipment and buildings; and ICT infrastructure investments. Programmes to support international science and technology linkages (both North–South and South–South) are of increasing interest to donors. Integrated initiatives (cluster 4) are not a major approach for most donors, with the notable exception of the Inter-American Development Bank and the IDRC, with its Innovation, Policy and Science Programme, although many donors do have a few projects of this type.

Global and regional public goods initiatives (such as the CGIAR) are important for LDCs, but they do not appear to be sufficiently responsive to LDCs' research needs.

From this overall sample of projects and programmes, a number of clear patterns and concerns emerge with regard to the types of STI projects and activities that are supported for LDCs.

Firstly, global and regional public goods initiatives (such as the CGIAR) are important for LDCs. However, they do not appear to be sufficiently responsive to LDCs' research needs.

Secondly, programmes and projects to develop domestic STI capacity are the most numerous types of projects in LDCs, but they have a number of weaknesses:

The STI capacity building programmes in LDCs are disjointed and are neglecting the non-agricultural sector.

- They are disjointed and there is in general very weak coordination between STI human resource capacity projects and sector development projects. This is evident in both Uganda and Rwanda.

- There needs to be more projects to develop capacity for STI policy formulation and implementation. An important example is the World Bank initiative in Rwanda to support the articulation of an S&T action programme.

- The non-agricultural sector is neglected.

Thirdly, global linkage initiatives (cluster 3) are becoming an increasingly important aspect of donor support and they could be particularly important for LDCs. However, they tend to exclude LDCs because of the lack of a critical minimum level of capability for collaboration to take place. This is readily apparent in international science cooperation. But it is also apparent in technology cooperation. An example of this is NORAD's matchmaking project, which is currently benefiting some developing countries but has not started in the LDCs because lack of infrastructure and human skills is preventing potential investors from matching with suitable local companies (see box 10).

There needs to be a more systemic and strategic approach to supporting the development of STI capabilities in the LDCs.

Fourthly, with regard to systems initiatives (cluster 4), there are no national innovation system initiatives in LDCs. However, there are examples of integrated initiatives which combine elements of the previous three clusters. One example is the USAID-funded PEARL project and follow-on SPREAD project in Rwanda (see box 11).

To sum up, there needs to be a more systemic and strategic approach to supporting the development of STI capabilities in the LDCs. This should go beyond ad hoc projects to strengthen parts of public STI infrastructure, particularly unversities, and support innovation at the enterprise level by supporting the development of capabilities and knowledge systems. It should support firms as well as farms.

Box 10. An example of how technology transfer could work in the LDCs: The Norwegian Matchmaking Program

Originally started in 1994 in Sri Lanka, the Matchmaking Program (MMP) was later extended to South Africa and India. It is currently being extended until May 2009.

The MMP aims at enabling business links between local companies and Norwegian companies through technology transfers, and exchange of management and skills. Norwegian companies create business links with their local partner companies mostly through outsourcing and joint ventures, and, depending on country characteristics, through more flexible forms of cooperation such as subcontracting and licensing. The investing companies ensure that adequate technical competence, capacity and financial resources are available and included in long-term investment plans.

Furthermore, they have to meet financial requirements in order to qualify for the programme. The investing companies' areas of interest can be very diverse, ranging from sector-specific to product-specific activities.

Once the investing companies have been selected, the local contact point tries to find a potential partner. Although the companies have to pay a participation fee, financial support is provided by the Norwegian Agency for Development and Cooperation (NORAD) to enable them to visit the potential partners, and to support the start-up phase of outsourcing/joint ventures up to set levels. Matchmaking is successful when (i) it is commercially interesting for the investor and the local partner, (ii) the type of technology transfer is of interest to the local country, and (iii) there is enough capital to cover the risk.

The benefits of such a programme are multiple. They include unquantifiable benefits deriving from technology, and skills- and education-related transfers, as well as quantifiable ones deriving from the number of new joint ventures and new jobs created. For example, over the period 1994–2006, the programme has created 48 new joint ventures and some 3,000 news jobs in Sri Lanka. On average, 84 per cent of the Norwegian companies [that have joined the MMP] have been matched with one or more Sri Lankan profile.

Undoubtedly, similar projects would be very beneficial to the LDCs. However, the lack of suitable infrastructure and human skills, as well as weak capabilities, are regarded as being the major factors that discourage potential investors. LDCs have therefore not been included in this programme so far.

Source: Direct communication with NORAD.

Box 11. Coffee sector agribusiness development projects in Rwanda

In 2001, a USAID-funded project — Partnership for the Enhancement of Agribusiness in Rwanda (PEARL) — was started with the aim of improving rural livelihoods by reviving the coffee sector in Rwanda. PEARL has been successful in (i) improving-capacity building in the agricultural sector, (ii) improving agricultural quality, (iii) providing market diversification of export products, and (iv) empowering local farmers and building linkages with other actors in the private and public sectors.

In just six years the PEARL project has had a considerable impact. It introduced new practices for rural smallholder farmers, which increased the quality of the final product and made changes in local production, technology and supply-chain development. Two technological transformations that contributed to increased quality were (i) the introduction of new and improved washing stations, which enabled cleaning and sorting in accordance with qualitative standards, and (ii) training facilities to improve local washing techniques as well as tasting skills. The latter type of knowledge is necessary in order to enable sellers to negotiate a fair price for their coffee products. In 2006, for example, 60 individuals received training in testing, tasting and other quality-improving processes. The training, tasting and research facilities provided through the programme also facilitate the creation of a closed collaboration and linkages between farmers, sellers and researchers at the National University of Rwanda.

It is estimated that the technology and innovation programmes implemented through the PEARL project have increased the price for a kilo of unprocessed dried coffee — from $0.22 to roughly $2.00 — to the benefit of the local smallholder farmers. Furthermore, the number of farmers engaged in the cooperative increased from 400 in 2002 to 1,600 in 2006. The quality improvements brought about by the new washing facilities led to the creation of 75 stations throughout Rwanda.

Once the capacity to produce and sustain the production and export of high-quality products had been acquired, second-level agribusiness activities, such as coffee roasting and spin-off enterprises could be started. Building upon this improved capacity, a second project was launched as a follow-up to PEARL in 2007. The new programme — Sustaining Partnership to Enhance Rural Enterprise and Agribusiness Development SPREAD — aims at introducing the second-level activities as well as strengthening the linkages between development partners, including NGOs and universities. The SPREAD programme will increase linkages with technology extension agronomists and business development specialists to include health professionals, ICT experts and media programmes in a more integrated approach.

Source: Farley (2007).

3. THE ORIENTATIONS OF TECHNICAL COOPERATION

The current orientations of technical cooperation reinforce this picture. How statistics on technical cooperation are collected is now a subject that is being discussed, and it is therefore impossible to indicate where LDCs stand in detail in terms of modalities of technical cooperation.[4] However, table 37 shows the sectoral composition of technical cooperation disbursements to LDCs during the period 2003–2005 and technical cooperation commitments during 1998–2000 and 2003–2005. A number of very important patterns are apparent.

- Sixty-six per cent of total technical cooperation disbursements to LDCs during 2003–2005 were allocated to social infrastructure and services, with 20 per cent of total disbursements during that period going to governance (government and civil society), 18 per cent to education and 10 per cent to health.

- Only 22 per cent of total technical cooperation disbursements to LDCs during 2003–2005 were devoted to economic infrastructure and productive sectors (including multisector).

- Nine per cent of total technical cooperation disbursements in 2003–2005 went to emergency assistance and reconstruction.

- The share of total technical cooperation commitments to LDCs devoted for governance increased from 14 per cent during the period 1998–2000 to 25 per cent in 2003–2005.

- The share of technical cooperation commitment for economic infrastructure and productive sectors fell from 32 per cent during 1998–2000 to 25 per cent during 2003–2005.

Only 22 per cent of total technical cooperation disbursements to LDCs during 2003–2005 were devoted to economic infrastructure and productive sectors.

Table 37. Scale and composition of technical cooperation activities
(Disbursements and commitments, average annual)

	Disbursements			Commitments				
	Million, 2004 $	As % of total TC	As % of total aid	Million, 2004 $		% of total technical cooperation		% of total aid	
	2003–2005			1998–2000	2003–2005	1998–2000	2003–2005	1998–2000	2003–2005
Social infrastructure and services	2 308.1	65.8	11.2	1 579.3	3 452.5	62.1	66.0	8.8	11.3
of which:									
Education	626.2	17.9	3.0	577.3	794.9	22.7	15.2	3.2	2.6
Health	361.1	10.3	1.8	291.2	480.8	11.4	9.2	1.6	1.6
Population Programmes	343.7	9.8	1.7	189.0	509.7	7.4	9.7	1.1	1.7
Water Supply and sanitation	46.6	1.3	0.2	84.7	71.2	3.3	1.4	0.5	0.2
Government & civil society	684.5	19.5	3.3	343.2	1 299.4	13.5	24.8	1.9	4.2
Other social infrastructure	245.9	7.0	1.2	93.9	296.6	3.7	5.7	0.5	1.0
Economic infrastructure	198.5	5.7	1.0	170.6	354.0	6.7	6.8	1.0	1.2
Production sectors	269.9	7.7	1.3	366.9	379.9	14.4	7.3	2.0	1.2
Multisector	297.9	8.5	1.4	278.9	553.1	11.0	10.6	1.6	1.8
Commodity aid/ general programme assistance	103.3	2.9	0.5	23.2	96.2	0.9	1.8	0.1	0.3
Action relating to debt	1.5	0.0	0.0	3.0	2.3	0.1	0.0	0.0	0.0
Emergency assistance & reconstruction	306.8	8.8	1.5	58.0	366.6	2.3	7.0	0.3	1.2
Administrative costs of donors	2.4	0.1	0.0	18.1	1.2	0.7	0.0	0.1	0.0
Support to NGOs	3.0	0.1	0.0	0.9	3.6	0.0	0.1	0.0	0.0
Refugees in donor countries	0.5	0.0	0.0	1.3	0.5	0.1	0.0	0.0	0.0
Unallocated/unspecified	13.9	0.4	0.1	46.6	23.5	1.8	0.4	0.3	0.1
Total	3 505.5	100	17.0	2 546.7	5 233.5	100	100	14.2	17.1

Source: UNCTAD secretariat calcualtions based on OECD/CRS; data downloaded on 5 March 2007.

From this it is very clear that technical cooperation activities in LDCs are basically designed to improve public sector capabilities for governance and provision of services rather than private sector capabilities related to production. Donor priorities are starkly evident in the fact that annual technical cooperation commitments to improve governance (in the widest sense) in 2003–2005 were $1.3 billion, which may be compared with annual aid commitments of $12 million for agricultural extension during the same period.

A new approach to technical cooperation has been strongly advocated; it would be focused on "capacity development", which is defined as "the process whereby people, organizations and society unleash, strengthen, create adapt and maintain capacity over time" (OECD website), with capacity being broadly defined as "the ability to perform functions, solve problems and set and achieve objectives" (Fukuda-Parr, Lopes and Malik, 2002: 8). Similarly, the Commission for Africa (2005) defines capacity development as "investment in people, institutions and practices that will, together, enable a country to achieve its development objectives" (p. 389). This open-ended definition of capacity opens up the possibility that there can be greater use of technical cooperation to support technological learning and innovation at the firm level. But implementing this vision in the LDCs requires a change in the use of technical cooperation funds towards developing private sector capacities, and in particular STI capacities, rather than simply public sector capacities.

A change in the use of technical cooperation funds towards developing private sector capacities, and in particular STI capacities, is needed.

D. How donors can improve aid for STI in LDCs: Agriculture

This section and the next one consider how donors could improve aid for STI in LDCs in, firstly, agriculture, and secondly, industry and infrastructure. One of the important findings of the quantitative analysis of the scale and composition of aid for STI in LDCs is the very small scale of aid disbursements for agricultural research. This is particularly surprising, and not only because agricultural research is identified as an S&T priority in all the PRSPs analysed (see chapter 2, table 17). Empirical evidence suggests that there are "high rates of return from agricultural R&D investments, making agricultural research a cost-effective way for Governments to accelerate agricultural development" (Beintema and Stads, 2006: 1). The Bangladesh Rice Research Institute (BRRI), for example, has developed and released 31 modern varieties of rice (the main staple food) in the past two decades, and these now account for 65 per cent of total rice production. It is estimated that annual rice production doubled between 1970 and 2002 from 10.8 million metric tonnes to 24.3 million metric tonnes, but that without the BRRI's modern varieties, it would have increased by just 10 per cent over that period (UNESCO, 2005: 258).

The low level of donor support for agricultural research in LDCs makes it very difficult for LDCs' Governments to sustain sufficient public investment in agricultural research.

The low level of donor support for agricultural research in LDCs makes it very difficult for LDCs' Governments to sustain sufficient public investment in agricultural research.[5] An agricultural research intensity ratio is typically used to measure the agricultural research investment effort of a country or a group of countries. It is calculated as the percentage share of investment in agricultural research in agricultural output. The latest agricultural public research intensity ratio for the LDCs amounts to 0.47 per cent versus 1.7 per cent for the other developing countries.[6]

Chart 14 shows the average evolution of public agricultural research intensity for the LDCs and other developing countries from 1971 to 2003. It can clearly be

**Chart 14. Agricultural research intensity in the LDCs
and other developing countries (ODCs), 1971–2003**

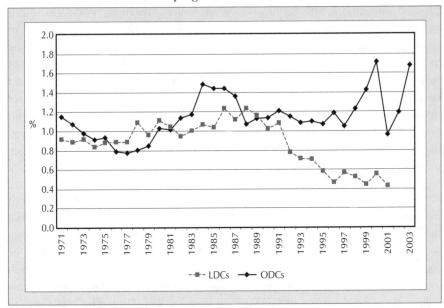

Source: UNCTAD secretariat calculations based on data extracted from the ASTI database on 5 May 2007.

seen that agricultural research intensity was at about the same level in each group of countries until 1991, when that of the LDCs dropped by more than half. If the slow increase in agricultural research intensity in the 1980s had continued in the 1990s, it would have resulted in a ratio equal to 1.4 by 2001, three times higher than the actual measured intensity ratio.

Although there is no official recommendation about preferred intensity ratios for agricultural R&D investments, the World Bank has suggested a 2 per cent target rate, while the Inter-Academy Council, focusing particularly on sub-Saharan Africa, recommends that an agricultural research intensity ratio of 1.5 be reached by 2015 (Beintema and Stads, 2004: 4). Raising the level of agricultural R&D expenditure even just to 1 per cent of agricultural GDP by 2015 will require a major increase in investment in the latter.

Part of that increase could come from the private sector. However, past patterns are not encouraging. Estimates suggest that only 2 per cent of total agricultural research expenditure in sub-Saharan Africa in 2000 came from the private sector (Beintema and Stads, 2006). It is extremely unlikely that the pattern is different in other LDCs. Pray and Umali-Deininger (1997: 1143) note that "profitability is the main determinant of private for-profit participation in agricultural research". Thus, they argue that private research can fill the gap created by stagnating or declining public research budgets in countries and industries with large markets for modern input and products for which returns on research are highly appropriable. But "products and sectors that may be of high social value, but command only a small market and exhibit a high degree of geographical and ecological specificity will most likely be ignored by the private for-profit sector. Because of their public good nature and their 'distance' from commercial application, basic and strategic research usually receive little attention by the private for-profit sector. This implies that the private for-profit sector will not always fill the gap and that alternative sources of research output, that is public and private non-profit sectors, have to be found to service socially beneficial but privately unprofitable 'orphan sectors' "(p. 1144).

Similarly, a study of ongoing attempts to privatize certain parts of agricultural research in seven African countries, including Ethiopia, Senegal, Uganda and the United Republic of Tanzania, warns of the possible emergence of a two-

Raising the level of agricultural R&D expenditure even just to 1 per cent of agricultural GDP will require a major increase in investment in the agricultural R&D.

Only 2 per cent of total agricultural research expenditure in sub-Saharan Africa in 2000 came from the private sector. It is extremely unlikely that the pattern is different in other LDCs.

track research system (Chema, Gilbert and Roseboom, 2003). Such a system may emerge if there is a large degree of privatization of research services and if farmers' associations, the agribusiness community (exporters, processors, input suppliers and commodity traders) and other beneficiaries are called upon to finance the research programme and researchers are paid incentives according to their proven contribution to farming profitability. In such a situation, peasant farmers who are engaged in low-value subsistence-oriented food production and keep livestock will be relatively neglected and there will be little incentive for researchers to work in those areas. Thus, the two-track research system could emerge "with a reduced number of researchers, drawing low salaries, conscripted to the war against poverty, while the best researchers work on those commodities for which there is private funding" (ibid.: 26).

Against that background, it would be wrong to believe that public research expenditure has been crowding out private sector investment in LDCs and that the latter will automatically increase as the former declines. Although the private sector can make a small contribution and there are certainly opportunities for some kinds of public–private partnerships, increasing the agricultural research intensity ratio in LDCs will require increased public R&D expenditure and this will, in turn, need increased ODA for agricultural R&D. Indeed, ODA flows to agricultural research for the LDCs must increase to levels much higher than the current ones.

There may be some reluctance to increase levels of and owing to disappointing results from past aid for agricultural R&D. However, there is an increased understanding of the weaknesses in national agricultural research systems (NARS). Those include imbalances in financing for research, extension and education, with Eicher (2001) pointing out the very low level of expenditure on agricultural education and Hayami and Ruttan (1985) the bias towards extension. Emphasis is now being placed on a systems approach to agricultural innovation (World Bank, 2006). Moreover, it is generally agreed that key elements for more effective NARS include a pluralistic institutional structure with many actors, including NGOs and the private sector; new competitive mechanisms for research funding; and management reforms to improve the efficiency and effectiveness of public research organizations (Byerlee, 1998). The African case studies referred to earlier also indicate that important reforms in NARS are taking place and include decentralization of agricultural research, greater stakeholder participation, a shift from block grants to competitive research funds, and the strengthening of system linkages.

Finally, global scientific linkages are important for increasing agricultural productivity in the LDCs. In that regard, recent research has identified worrying trends in global R&D in which "there is evidence of a large and sustained, if not growing gap, between a comparatively small group of scientific haves and a substantial group of scientific have-nots" (Pardey et al., 2006: 2). Those authors note that the rich countries' agricultural research agendas are shifting away from simple productivity concerns, and to high-technology inputs (such as precision farming technology), which are not as easily adopted and adapted by the developing countries as they were before and are particularly irrelevant for LDCs. They indicate that some fear that less developed countries will become "technological orphans".

Against the background of global shifts in agricultural R&D, the role of the network of international agricultural research centres known as the Consultative Group on International Agricultural Research (CGIAR) is particularly important in undertaking scientific research relevant for increasing agricultural productivity in the LDCs.[7] In the 1990s there was a broadening of the CGIAR's research agenda

---

Although the private sector can make a small contribution increasing the agricultural research intensity ratio in LDCs will require increased public R&D expenditure and this will, in turn, need increased ODA for agricultural R&D.

There is evidence of a large and sustained, if not growing gap, between a comparatively small group of scientific haves and a substantial group of scientific have-nots.

The role of the network of international agricultural research centres is particularly important in undertaking scientific research relevant for increasing agricultural productivity in the LDCs.

away from research on agricultural production of staple foods towards post-harvest handling, food processing and food safety and environmental issues, and this was accompanied by a stagnation of donors' financing. This change in goals reflects the developed countries' concern about environment and agriculture-related issues that are not strictly related to farming improvements, as well as the rise of new and powerful lobbying groups. Whilst issues related to post-harvest handling, environmental sustainability and food processing are certainly relevant, it is important that agricultural research continues to not reflect the reality of subsistence-oriented smallholder agriculture in LDCs. It has been estimated that in 2003 CGIAR spent only 10 per cent of the combined real spending by the African national agricultural research agencies on "African" issues (Beintema and Stads, 2006). Alston, Dehmer and Pardey (2006) argue that "Over time, the CGIAR has misplaced its original, well-defined sense of purpose and to some extent has degraded its capacity to meet its original objective: to stave off hunger by enhancing the capacity of the world's poor people to feed themselves, through research-induced improvements in agricultural productivity" (p. 348).

Thus, a second key priority for aid for STI in the agricultural sector is to ensure that CGIAR work remains LDC-relevant.

A priority for aid for STI in the agricultural sector is to ensure that CGIAR work remains LDC-relevant.

E. How donors can improve aid for STI in LDCs: Industry and infrastructure

Donors should not neglect aid to build STI capacity outside agriculture. There is at present very little aid that is supporting STI capacity in industry and economic infrastructure. Moreover, what is provided appears to be for supporting the development of human capacities and public S&T infrastructure. In contrast, very much less attention is given to enterprise-based STI activities and to strengthening the capacity to innovate.

There is at present very little aid that is supporting STI capacity in industry and infrastructure.

Against that background, Bell (2007) identifies three broad directions for an ODA strategy aimed at STI-related technological learning and capability development relating to industrial and physical infrastructure development:

- Supporting expanded activities and reoriented approaches to STI infrastructure development in LDCs;

- Developing new, modified or substantially expanded forms of ODA for fostering enterprise-based technological learning and capability building;

- Supporting policy development and implementation relating to industry and infrastructure-oriented activities.

With regard to STI infrastructure, the major objective should be to increase the scale of support for those activities and to reorient them so as to increase their relevance for industrial development and physical infrastructure development.

With regard to STI infrastructure, the major objective should be to increase the scale of support for those activities and to reorient them so as to increase their relevance for industrial development and physical infrastructure development, and to improve their effectiveness. Reorientation might involve, for example, increasing support for engineering in university education or re-examining the content of technical and vocational training. But beyond that, there is a need for a shift in the way in which technical and business support services away from providing services to enterprises towards supporting arrangements for strengthening capabilities in enterprises by embedding support services alongside commercial transactions in value chains. Such embedded business services are packaged within or bundled around commercial transactions between a buyer and a seller. An example of such an approach is the Local Industry Upgrading Programme set up in Singapore in 1986, which included the conclusion of cost-sharing contracts between the Government and subsidiaries of multinational corporations (MNCs) for enhancing local firms' learning and their linkages with the subsidiaries.

The second broad direction for ODA is the development of new approaches to support enterprise-based technological learning and capability-building. This requires novel forms of ODA which recognize that there is a need for investment in knowledge assets (particularly design and engineering capabilities) and that those assets must in large part be created through the training and learning activities of enterprises, because there are limits to what can be achieved through formal learning. Problems of non-appropriability, externalities and public goods mean that there is insufficient investment in those activities. Addressing that issue requires grants and soft loans for investment in the relevant types of knowledge assets. That could be achieved not by initiating totally new activities but by "stretching" existing donor activity to include STI capability-building. The following areas are particularly important:

- Value-chain development schemes;

- FDI complementation and linkage development;

- Industrial and infrastructure project funding, including through public–private partnerships;

- Promoting the role of the World Federation of Engineering Associations and NGOs dealing with engineering issues, including through fellowship funding;

- Facilitating South–South collaboration.

1. VALUE-CHAIN DEVELOPMENT SCHEMES

Some donor-funded projects to strengthen the technological capabilities of firms in the value chain and to foster knowledge-centred interactions between them are already in place. However, there is a need now to consider how to apply the principle of explicitly contracting with larger firms to augment the capabilities of value chain partners, and also the potential for such contracts with large importer organizations. Donors may be resisting the introduction of such projects because (i) it might appear that "subsidies" are being provided to large firms; (ii) there is limited funding; and (iii) limited analyses of the structure of the value chains prevent them from knowing the key actors and points for action. Those constraints should be actively addressed. Box 12 presents a successful value-chain development scheme in which business support services are embedded in commercial transactions along the value chain.

2. FDI COMPLEMENTATION AND LINKAGE DEVELOPMENT

Donors should consider cost-sharing partnerships with TNC subsidiaries investing in LDCs in order to forge new supply linkages with domestic firms and strengthen the capabilities of existing suppliers. The idea that TNC subsidiaries can be expected to engage in such efforts to build the capabilities of local suppliers without financial incentives is farfetched. However, evidence suggests that they are willing to collaborate in skills development activities if they are reimbursed for conducting expanded training activities. An example of this is the way in which SME linkages with the MOZAL aluminium smelter in Mozambique have been fostered by providing firms with packages of business and technical training and with access to finance, together with the development of local consultant support, partly funded by the International Finance Corporation.

New approaches are needed to support enterprise-based technological learning and capability-building.

There is a need now to consider how to apply the principle of explicitly contracting with larger firms to augment the capabilities of value chain partners.

Donor should consider cost-sharing partnerships with TNC subsidiaries investing in LDCs in order to forge new supply linkages with domestic firms and strengthen the capabilities of existing suppliers.

Box 12. Building Support Service Capabilities into Value Chains: Ghana's Craft Basket-making Industry

During the 1990s Ghana developed an export trade in craft products including woven baskets. This was based on a value chain that ran from small producers (many in rural areas) via export companies, some of which were also producers, to importers and wholesalers in advanced country markets. The Ghanaian exporters had played an important role in providing a range of services to their suppliers (independent producers and sub-contractors). These services fell into two roughly distinguishable categories: *market and management services* (e.g. shipping, market intelligence, financing) and *technological services* (e.g. product design, quality management).

By the early 2000s, it was evident that, although they were important, these services that were embedded in the transactions of the value chain were falling far short of achieving their full potential. In particular the more 'technology-centred' services were seriously constrained by a combination of limited skills in firms and limited incentives to invest in creating or hiring them - because of various forms of externality. This can be illustrated, for example, by the case of product design. Exporters sometimes passed on to their suppliers ideas about new product designs they received from importers. However this was a relatively 'passive' process. The importers seldom had the design skills or time required to work with exporters on more purposeful product development. Also, besides lacking design capabilities, the exporters were hesitant to invest in new product designs because these would be rapidly copied by competitors. There had been one or two cases in which aid donors had sponsored international design consultants to advise on design and production, but this service was much too expensive to be sustained by the industry on an ongoing basis beyond the one-off, donor-funded 'injections'.

To address this gap between potential and realised achievement, a project was implemented in 2002-2003 with donor support to strengthen the business service support system for the industry. This involved an integrated array of services, cutting across both 'technological' and others. It was distinguished from many such schemes by a simple principle: the aim was not to use specialised service suppliers to provide services for firms in the industry, but to strengthen the capabilities of firms in the value chain to provide services along the chain to other firms – focusing in particular on the capabilities of the Ghanaian exporters to provide support services to their upstream suppliers. Three *selected components* of the project can illustrate this principle in operation.

- Quality management (QM). Initially rejection rates by exporters were high and several had lost overseas clients because of poor quality. The project set up a two stage programme. The first involved several training workshops for teams of QM trainers. Each team brought together different actors in the value chain: technical officers from the exporters, co-ordinators of sub-contracted producers, and master weavers from producers. In the second step these teams provided training workshops for producers. Supported by a radio campaign, this resulted in reject rates falling to negligible levels, and key actors in the value chain had learned about organising QM development activities and about the gains they could derive from doing so.

- Market access. Exporters were supported in connecting to new international markets (e.g. via visits to trade fairs in the US and by training in ICT skills). This enhanced not only their own trade opportunities but also the opportunities for their suppliers to expand output and test-market new products.

- Product design and development. The design capabilities of exporters were enhanced by arranging firm-based internships for students from the College of Art at the Kumasi University of Science and Technology. This enabled the exporters to elaborate and test product design ideas they had not been able to fully develop. This formed the basis for securing large trial orders from importers and for providing new product specifications to producers. It also led to a critically important form of learning: "… a growing realization among the export companies that investment in new product development was the only way to remain competitive on the international market" (source, p. 42). This was linked to the demonstration of a mechanism for organising such in-house design activity on a sufficiently low-cost basis to be sustainable.

There were two important learning outcomes. One was the enhanced knowledge-base of the value chain firms (especially the exporters) that enabled them to provide key services to other value-chain members. The other was the exporters' learning that it was in their longer term interest to bear the short term costs of playing this role. Their trade volume increased, their costs fell and their margins widened - also their export market position was more sustainable relative to competition from Asian copiers of 'Ghanaian' craft products.

Source: Bell (2007).

---

3. INDUSTRIAL AND PHYSICAL INFRASTRUCTURE PROJECT FUNDING

This is the area where donors can have the greatest effect on STI development in the LDCs. What is required is that industrial and physical infrastructure investment projects are implemented in such a way that they incorporate substantial learning elements and are organized to generate knowledge spillovers. Donors should thus introduce STI capability components alongside core investment projects. Physical infrastructure development can be expected to provide a major contribution to the development of design and engineering skills in LDCs (see United Nations Millennium Project Task Force, 2005; Juma, 2006).

The basic constraints knowledge accumulation through industrial projects and physical infrastructure development are conceptual, namely (a) limited recognition by developing country clients and Governments (as well as aid donors) of the longer-term developmental significance of investing in engineering-centred knowledge assets as well as the physical assets of industrial and infrastructural facilities; (b) limited recognition of the importance of enterprise-based learning as a large part of the process of creating those assets; and (c) limited recognition of major investment projects as potentially important vehicles within which to embed such learning activities. However, it is clear that donor practices have also sometimes militated against local learning. For example, Marcelle, in her study of the wide variation in learning across a sample of investment projects for telecommunications facilities in four African countries, noted that "operating companies in Uganda and Tanzania, which relied on development assistance for network expansion programmes, reported the least satisfaction with the quality of the [learning] interface with suppliers" (Marcelle, 2004: 120). The limitations on learning arose from aspects of donor intervention that led, for example, to increased numbers of suppliers — resulting in poor long-term relationships with suppliers and lack of interoperability among equipment and network components. Larger operator companies in other countries that implemented network development programmes without such dependence on donors gained from the learning-intensive nature of long-term relationships with suppliers as well as from the ability to build up cumulatively deeper competence by standardizing equipment and network facilities across successive projects.

> *What is required is that industrial and physical infrastructure investment projects are implemented in such a way that they incorporate substantial learning elements and are organized to generate knowledge spillovers.*

Donors should explore innovative mechanisms for exploiting the learning potential of physical infrastructure investment projects with which they are already involved. Some of those mechanisms may be particularly promising in the context of donors' existing activities to foster public–private partnerships in infrastructure development.

4. ENGINEERING ASSOCIATIONS AND NGOS

Several engineering associations and NGOs, such as the World Federation of Engineering Organizations and Engineers without Borders, are active in pursuing development-related issues in the LDCs. Together with donors' support for engineering education activities and support for engineering volunteers to act in developing countries, those professional associations and NGOs constitute another way of pushing forward specific technical training and capacity development at the local level. Donors currently provide fellowship funding for collaborative research projects and technical training carried out at universities in the donor countries. Another way to strengthen STI capacity in LDCs would be to use the in-house training programmes of private engineering companies in developed countries. This would be an innovative way of involving the private sector through cost-sharing in building engineering capabilities in LDCs.

> *Another way to strengthen STI capacity in LDCs would be to use the in-house training programmes of private engineering companies in developed countries.*

5. FACILITATING SOUTH–SOUTH COLLABORATION

A particular problem in developing engineering capabilities in LDCs is the small size of the economies of those countries, the sporadic nature of investment projects and thus weak incentives to invest in creating engineering capabilities. That problem may be addressed if, in implementing the above proposals, donors foster greater South–South cooperation. In Africa, for example, this might involve a collaborative approach amongst neighbouring LDCs.

The third and final broad direction of policy that is required is greater donor support for STI policy formulation and implementation by LDC Governments.

F. Technological learning and Aid for Trade

1. Technological capability-building: The overlooked component of Aid for Trade

In response to the calls which were made by the G8 at the Gleneagles Summit in 2005 for reduction of the adjustment pressure that developing countries will face with the current round of trade negotiations, the Ministerial Declaration of the Hong Kong Ministerial Conference calls for an "Aid for Trade" (AfT) framework whose aim is:

> "to help developing countries, particularly LDCs, to build the supply-side capacity and trade-related infrastructure that they need to assist them to implement and benefit from WTO agreements and more broadly to expand their trade. Aid for Trade cannot be a substitute for the development benefits that will result from a successful conclusion to the DDA, particularly on market access" (Hong Kong Ministerial Declaration, 2005, para. 57, WT/MIN(05)/DEC).

Although the Ministerial Declaration called for AfT to build supply-side capacity and trade-related infrastructure, no definition of supply-side capacity was included, and thus the scope for AfT is rather flexible.

Although the Ministerial Declaration called for AfT to build supply-side capacity and trade-related infrastructure, no definition of supply-side capacity was included, and thus the scope for AfT is rather flexible. An informal understanding on the meaning of supply-side capacity exists, but it is equally vague as it defines supply-side constraints as "those that impede the efficient production of goods and services".

WTO (2006a: 2) — which is now the basic reference document on what constitutes Aid for Trade — states that "the scope of Aid for Trade should be defined in a way that is both broad enough to reflect the diverse trade needs identified by the countries, and clear enough to establish a border between Aid for Trade and other development assistance of which it is a part". It extends the categories of AfT to (a) trade policy and regulations, (b) trade development, (c) trade-related infrastructure, (d) building productive capacity, (e) trade-related adjustment, and (f) other trade-related needs. Along similar lines, the OECD (2006) proposes a definition of Aid for Trade that uses the objectives of the activity to be financed, rather than the type of activities it is supposed to finance, including (i) trade policy and regulations, (ii) economic infrastructure, and (iii) building productive capacity.[8]

One striking feature of this conceptual debate is that the role of technological capability-building and upgrading and its impact on export competitiveness and poverty reduction are currently marginal to the ongoing discussions.

One striking feature of this conceptual debate is that the role of technological capability-building and upgrading and its impact on export competitiveness and poverty reduction are currently marginal to the ongoing discussions. The importance of physical infrastructure is clearly recognized, but the development of technological capabilities is largely overlooked. This is a serious omission which must be rectified. Interestingly, the United Nations Conference on Financing for Development, which took place three years before the Hong Kong Ministerial Conference, provided a definition of supply-side constraints and asked donors to:

> "remove supply-side constraints, through improving trade infrastructure, diversifying export capacity and supporting an increase in the technological content of exports, strengthening institutional development and enhancing overall productivity and competitiveness" (United Nations, 2002: para. 36: 8).

The role of technological upgrading has been clearly demonstrated in a number of case studies on successful export development (Chandra and Kolavalli, 2006). There is thus an urgent need explicitly to integrate measures to promote technological development in the framework of AfT.

2. THE INTEGRATED FRAMEWORK (IF) FOR TRADE-RELATED TECHNICAL ASSISTANCE

Similar arguments can be applied for the IF. The IF is the major initiative through which donors, LDCs and agencies are seeking to improve the efficiency of trade capacity development within LDCs. Created in 1997, it was revamped in 2001 with the aim of including trade in the countries' poverty reduction strategies or development plans and assisting in the delivery of trade-related technical assistance. The Diagnostic Trade Integration Studies (DTIS), which are the main output under the first of the two funding "windows", contain an analysis of the constraints on trade competitiveness, and of policy responses and capacity-building strategies to overcome them. After discussion between Governments and stakeholders, the trade-capacity-building priorities should be integrated into the development plans, while concrete projects listed in the Action Matrix are financed under the second funding "window" (see UNCTAD, 2002 and 2004, for more details).

There is thus an urgent need explicitly to integrate measures to promote technological development in the framework of AfT.

Several evaluation exercises have been conducted recently to assess the efficacy of the IF. Their results highlighted weak country ownership, inadequate capacity-building support, and failure to integrate trade into the PRSP process and to finance the priorities identified in the action matrix (WTO, 2006a) The increased interest in the development dimension of trade to which the current round of trade negotiations has given rise led to the current and ongoing discussions on how to increase the effectiveness and timeliness of the IF (Hong Kong Ministerial Declaration, para. 48). The task force that was created to discuss the modalities for "enhancing" the IF "agreed that the scope of the IF should be broadened to support activities related to the analysis and prioritization of needs" (WTO, 2006a: 6). The DTIS template includes broader trade-related issues and response to needs emanating from the ongoing round of trade liberalization negotiations. Furthermore, the core areas eligible for intervention cover (i) institution-building to handle trade policy issues, (ii) strengthening of export supply capabilities, (iii) strengthening of trade support services, (iv) strengthening of trade facilitation capacity, (v) training and human resource development, and (vi) assistance in the creation of a supportive trade-related regulatory and policy framework to encourage trade and investment (WTO, 2006a).

Clearly, the current attempt to enhance the IF[9] fits into the broader discussions on how to strengthen the domestic (country-driven) approach of Aid for Trade. Specifically, the policies that would need to be implemented to achieve the DTIS core areas (ii) and (iv) include domestic technological upgrading and other structural transformation policies. At the current level of technological development, the LDCs have only a limited comparative advantage in exports other than primary commodities and low-skill manufactures.

An analysis of how science and technological upgrading is treated in the latest eight DTIS shows that, with some exceptions, S&T initiatives and considerations are included in the main body of the DTIS, but their relevance has not been fully recognized in the Action Matrices (table 38). In five out of eight DTIS, S&T matters are given only scant consideration in the Action Matrices. In those in which they are mentioned, the focus is related only on research (mostly agricultural-based) and training. The Action Matrices of Sierra Leone and the Lao People's

Democratic Republic refer only to the development of processing activities that could lead to higher-value products. Undoubtedly, new or improved processing techniques are an important, although not an exclusive, effect of the introduction of new technologies in the domestic production processes. Only the Action Matrix of Maldives contains specific projects aimed at fostering domestic technological improvements.

The scant consideration given to S&T matters in the Action Matrices does not reflect the way in which technological changes and improvements are treated in the main text of the DTIS. In the case of the Lao People's Democratic Republic, the DTIS states that "[...] the rapid pace of globalization and technological change threatens to bypass Laos and relegate its producers to relatively low rungs on the value chain unless action can be taken to adapt and adopt emerging technologies [...] (p. 124). The DTIS of Sierra Leone states that "efforts to export new products or to maintain competitiveness or exposure to imports, can lead to the introduction of new technology which results in higher productivity and lower costs per unit of output" and that "the most obvious way to use trade for poverty reduction is to expand output and employment. [.] A way to increase output and employment is through the introduction of better farming practices or new technologies, which improve farmer productivity and increases the range of options regarding production" (p. 19/20).

An analysis of how science and technological upgrading is treated in the latest DTIS shows that S&T initiatives and considerations are included in the main body of the DTIS, but their relevance has not been fully recognized in the Action Matrices.

The majority of the DTIS contain a specific paragraph or section covering and highlighting the importance of S&T issues. For most of the DTIS, trade policies include S&T initiatives, which are primarily linked with projects aimed at improving the technological content and capabilities of the domestic customs authorities through ASYCUDA and related technological improving projects. Surprisingly,

Table 38. How S&T is treated in the latest eight DTIS								
	Benin	Chad	Lao PDR	Maldives	Rwanda	Sao Tome & Principe	Sierra Leone	Zambia
	(Dec. 05)	(Oct. 06)	(Nov. 06)	(Nov. 06)	(Nov. 05)	(Mar 06)	(Oct. 06)	(Oct. 05)
In the main text of the DTIS:								
Is there a specific section/paragraph covering S&T issues?	N	N	Y	Y	Y	Y	Y	N
Do international trade policies include S&T initiatives?	N	N	Y	Y	Y	Y	Y	N
Are S&T issues treated at the level of								
- trade policies	N	N	Y	Y	Y	Y	Y	N
- FDIs	Y	N	Y	N	Y	N	N	Y
Are there technology-related infrastructure projects to improve								
- electricity	N	Y	N	N	Y	Y	N	N
- telecommunication	Y	N	Y	Y	Y	Y	Y	N
Are there projects aimed at increasing technological awareness through								
- vocational training	W	Y	Y	Y	Y	Y	Y	Y
- R&D activities	N	Y	Y	Y	N	Y	Y	N
Are there sector-specific technology extension programmes	N				N			
- in agriculture		Y		Y		Y	Y	
- other (tourism, mining)			Y					Y
Are S&T considerations included in the Action Matrix?	W	W	Y	Y	W	W	Y	W
Source: UNCTAD secretariat compilation based on IF, DTIS studies.								
Note: Y = yes; N = no; W = weak.								

The DTIS could be a key instrument for ensuring that the role of technological upgrading in trade development is fully recognized in Governments' and donors' policy agendas.

the technological implications arising from FDI inflows have not been accounted for in four DTIS. Although the development of technology-related infrastructure requires the expansion and improvement of electricity networks (necessary for the use of electrical machineries and devices) and of telecommunications (necessary for facilitating the flow of information and know-how), not all DTIS include them and they give priority to telecommunications. Virtually all DTIS recognize the importance of education, training and R&D activities for raising technological awareness. As in the PRSPs, vocational training is considered to be a critical instrument for the promotion of S&T development in the LDCs and for economic development in general, as the new skills can be directly applied to production processes. Furthermore, half of the DTIS include initiatives aimed at promoting and disseminating best practices in agriculture[10] and agriculture-related sectors (e.g. fisheries).

The DTISs have great potential since they could become the vehicle that could provide domestic Governments with an overall vision of where they are in terms of the technological upgrading policies for tradable activities, and what can be done to improve the domestic technological level on the basis of an ad hoc analysis of the countries' technological landscapes and policies. Furthermore, the DTIS could be a key instrument for ensuring that the role of technological upgrading in trade development is fully recognized in Governments' and donors' policy agendas. The DTIS Action Matrix is the means that Governments can utilize to present their policies on technological and human skills improvements for donors' financing. It has a dual role: (i) to summarize in single identifiable projects the analysis and recommendations contained in the main body of the DTIS, whether or not related to technology development, and (ii) to provide donors with clear projects in sectors and industries that are considered to be crucial for countries' development prospects and that require financing. The main text of the DTIS and the sector' studies are a useful tool that would enable Governments to identify the sectors and the industries with the greatest potential for expansion, whether it is for export-related purposes or not, and to indicate technological needs to ensure that export competitiveness is built up.

3. DEEPENING PREFERENTIAL MARKET ACCESS THROUGH A TECHNOLOGY FUND

For some LDCs market access preferences have supported the development of simple manufacturing activities, particularly garment manufacture. Those preferences enable exporters from the LDCs to pay lower tariffs or even enter markets quota- and duty-free. As discussed in past LDC Reports, the effectiveness of trade preferences can certainly be improved, particularly by widening the scope of product coverage and relaxing the rules of origin. However, some specialists have argued that they would be even more effective if they addressed supply-side constraints at the same time. In that regard, it has been suggested, for example, that trade preferences be linked to FDI.

If this issue is examined through the point of view of technological learning and innovation, it is apparent that trade preferences have succeeded in some countries — such as Bangladesh, Cambodia, Lesotho and Madagascar — in initiating the development of new sectors. But there has been limited diffusion of technological capabilities within domestic enterprises and little upgrading of production. This is particularly apparent in the case study of Cambodian ready-made garments discussed in chapter 1.

Against that background, it may be worthwhile to consider how a dedicated technology fund could be designed in such a way as to be linked to trade preferences. Its specific aim would be to increase the local learning impact of new economic activities stimulated by trade preferences. In particular, such a fund — which could be part of AfT provisions — should support local technological diffusion from foreign to domestic investors and also technological upgrading. Without such local learning effects, the benefits of market access preferences could be transitory. Enhanced technological learning is particularly important at the present time for the garments industry in LDCs as the transitional arrangements following the expiry of the Agreement on Textiles and Clothing themselves come to an end.

G. Conclusions

The main message of this chapter is that one of the most important insights regarding development in the last 25 years is that knowledge and learning are at the centre of the process of economic growth, and that most of the LDCs' development partners still need to translate this insight effectively into their programmes. Increasing knowledge aid which is directed to supporting knowledge accumulation in recipient countries by expanding their knowledge resources and supporting their knowledge systems could be the key to increasing aid effectiveness.

It is difficult to quantify the level of aid for STI in LDCs. But only 3 per cent of aid disbursements went to research and advanced and/or specialized training during the period 2003–2005. Moreover, aid for STI in LDCs is currently provided in a disjointed way with insufficient focus on systemic support for enterprise learning and innovation. The declining level of aid commitments for agricultural research, agricultural extension and agricultural education are particularly disturbing since agricultural research and extension are identified as priorities in LDCs' PRSPs. But it is equally important that donors support technological learning and innovation outside agriculture.

The Report makes a number of specific recommendations with regard to aid for STI in relation to agriculture, industry and trade. Firstly, there is a need for a rapid increase in ODA for agricultural R&D for the LDCs. Secondly, the effectiveness of ODA for non-agricultural technological learning and innovation has been severely compromised because donors do not prioritize that activity. It is recommended that donor-supported physical infrastructure projects all include components which use the construction process to develop domestic design and engineering capabilities. In addition, there is a need for public support for enterprise-based technological learning, which should be in the form of grants or soft loans for investment in the relevant types of knowledge assets. Such public support should be undertaken as a cost-sharing public–private partnership for creating public goods, particularly in relation to the development of design and engineering skills through enterprise-based practice. These STI capacity-building activities could be particularly useful if they are linked to value-chain development schemes, FDI linkage development and the facilitation of South–South cooperation.

Thirdly, it is important to integrate a technological development component into "Aid for Trade" and ensure that technological development issues are included in the Action Matrices of DTIS. Finally, there has been some discussion of ways in which trade preferences for LDCs could be enhanced not simply by extending their depth and coverage but also by linking them to supply-side support, for

One of the most important insights regarding development in the last 25 years is that knowledge and learning are at the centre of the process, and most of the LDCs' development partners still need to translate this insight effectively into their programmes.

There is a need for a rapid increase in ODA for agricultural R&D for the LDCs.

There is a need for public support for enterprise-based technological learning, which should be in the form of grants or soft loans for investment in the relevant types of knowledge assets.

Trade preferences for LDCs could be enhanced by linking them to supply-side support in the form of a technology fund which seeks to leverage the technological learning effects of the productive activities that are stimulated through such preferences, in particular through diffusion of best practices and encouragement of upgrading.

example through complementary measures to encourage FDI. From the point of view of technological assimilation, it is clear that trade preferences, particularly in relation to garments, have successfully stimulated the initial implementation of manufacturing activities in some LDCs. However, they do not explicitly facilitate the diffusion of best practices to domestic firms within a country and do not encourage technological upgrading. Against that background, it is worth examining whether trade preferences can be supplemented with a trade-preference-related technology fund which seeks to leverage the technological learning effects of the productive activities that are stimulated through such preferences, in particular through diffusion of best practices and encouragement of upgrading. Work should be done on the possible design for such a fund.

Notes

1   This includes (i) agricultural projects which involve investments in adaptive and applied research, the strengthening of national agricultural research systems (NARS) and human capital formation; and (ii) non-agricultural projects which were human resource development projects, including university-based research, projects to restructure public R&D institutes, technology development projects, health projects, environmental projects and comprehensive S&T projects which sought to link supply and demand for S&T services (Crawford et al, 2006: 8–9).

2   The Global STI Forum on "Building Science, Technology and Innovation Capacity for Sustainable Growth and Poverty Reduction", held in Washington, DC, from 13 to 15 February 2007, was an important aspect of that process.

3   Data in the OECD CRS database indicate that half of the aid for research going to Senegal is spent on medical research and a third on environmental research. France is the major donor.

4   For the latest thinking on measuring technical cooperation, see OECD (2007a).

5   For case studies within LDCs, see Ahmed and Karim (2006) and Elliott and Perrault (2006). The latter state that "the erosion of the current research capacity in Zambia" is a "quiet crisis" because it takes place against a positive chorus of achievements in liberalization and privatization while ignoring the simultaneous serious and perhaps permanent loss of institutional and human capacity" (p. 239).

6   Data are taken from the ASTI database and refer to 2001 for LDCs and 2003 for other developing countries. Available from the following URL: http://www.asti.cgiar.org/index. cfm. This database is not a full time-series database and covers only 19 LDCs, with data sparsely available through the period between 1971 and 2003. The implementing agencies considered include Governments, higher education and non-profit agencies. The private sector has been excluded as in Beintema and Stads (2006).

7   For discussion of agricultural research as a global public good, see Anderson (1998), Gardner and Lesser (2003) and Spielman (2007).

8   The OECD definition includes trade policy and regulations and trade development under trade-related technical assistance and capacity-building; transport and storage, communications and energy under economic infrastructure; and banking and financial services, business services, agriculture, forestry and fishing, industry and mining, and tourism under productive capacity (OECD, 2006: figure 5).

9   The objectives of the Enhanced Integrated Framework are to increase the volume and predictability of funding, strengthening of the in-country implementation capacity and improvement of the governance structure of the IF.

10   Specifically cocoa, rice, cotton, and palm oil.

References

Ahmed, R. and Karim, Z. (2006). Bangladesh: Uncertain prospects. In Pardey, P., Alston, J. and Piggott, R. (eds.), *Agricultural R&D in Developing World: Too Little, Too Late?* International Food Policy Research Institute, Washington, DC.

Alston, J., Pardey, P. and Piggott, R. (2006). Introduction and overview. In Pardey, P., Alston, J. and Piggott, R. (eds.), *Agricultural R&D in Developing World: Too Little, Too Late?* International Food Policy Research Institute, Washington, DC.

Alston, J., Dehmer, S. and Pardey, P. (2006). International initiatives in agricultural R&D: The changing fortunes of the CGIAR. In Pardey, P., Alston, J. and Piggott, R. (eds.), *Agricultural R&D in Developing World: Too Little, Too Late?* International Food Policy Research Institute, Washington, DC.

Anderson, J. (1998). Selected policy issues in international agricultural research: On striving for international public goods in an era of donor fatigue. *World Development*, 26 (6): 1149–1162.

Beintema, N. and Stads, G. (2004). Investing in sub-Saharan African agricultural research: Recent trends. 2020 Africa Conference Brief No. 8, International Food Policy Research Institute, Washington, DC.

Beintema, N. and Stads, G. (2006). Agricultural R&D in sub-Saharan Africa: An era of stagnation. Background Report for the ASTI Initiative, International Food Policy Research Institute, Washington, DC.

Bell, M. (2007). Technological learning and the development of production and innovative capacities in the industries and infrastructure sector of the LDCs: What role for ODA? Study prepared for UNCTAD as a background paper for *The Least Developed Countries Report 2007*, UNCTAD, Geneva.

Byerlee, D. (1998). The search for a new paradigm for the development of national agricultural research systems. *World Development*, 26 (6): 1049–1058.

Chandra, V. and Kolavalli, S. (2006). Technology, adaptation, and exports: How some developing countries got it right. In Chandra, V. (ed.), *Technology, Adaptation and Exports. How Some Developing Countries Got it Right*. World Bank, Washington, DC.

Chataway, J., Smith, J. and Wield, D. (2005). Partnerships for building science and technology capacity in Africa: Canadian and UK experience. Paper prepared for the Africa-Canada-UK Exploration: Building Science and Technology Capacity with African Partners, 30 January – 1 February, Canada House, London.

Chema, S., Gilbert, E. and Roseboom, J. (2003). A review of key issues and recent experiences in reforming agricultural research in Africa. ISNAR Research Report No. 24, Washington, DC.

Commission for Africa (2005). *Our Common Interest. Report of the Commission for Africa*. Penguin Books, New York.

Crawford, M.E., Yammal, C.C., Yang, H. and Brezenoff, R.L. (2006). Review of World Bank lending for science and technology, 1980–2004. Science, Technology, and Innovation Discussion Paper Series. Education Department, Human Development Network, Washington, DC.

Eicher, C.K. (2001). Africa's unfinished business: Building sustainable agricultural research systems. Staff Paper No. 2001–10, Michigan State University, East Lansing, Michigan.

Elliott, H. and Perrault, P. (2006). Zambia: A quiet crisis in African research and development. In Pardey, P., Alston, J. and Piggott, R. (eds.), *Agricultural R&D in Developing World: Too Little, Too Late?* International Food Policy Research Institute, Washington, DC.

Farley, S. (2005). Support to science, technology and knowledge for development: A snapshot of the global landscape (summary report). Paper prepared for the Africa-Canada-United Kingdom Exploration: Building Science and Technology Capacity with African Partners, 30 January – 1 February, Canada House, London.

Farley, S. (2007). Donor support for science, technology and innovation for development: Approaches to the LDCs. Study prepared for UNCTAD as a background paper for *The Least Developed Countries Report 2007*, UNCTAD, Geneva.

Fukuda-Parr, S., Lopes, C. and Malik, K. (2002). *Capacity for Development: New Solutions to Old Problems*. UNDP/Earthscan, New York and London.

Gardner, B. and Lesser, W. (2003). International agricultural research as a global public good. *American Journal of Agricultural Economics*, 85 (3): 692–697.

Godfrey, M., Sophal, C., Kato, T., Piseth, L.V., Dorina, D., Saravy, T., Savora, T. and Sovannarith, S. (2002). Technical assistance and capacity development in an aid-dependent economy: The experience of Cambodia. *World Development*, 30 (3): 355–373.

Hansen, B. and Tarp, F. (2001). Aid and growth regressions. *Journal of Development Economics*, 64 (2): 413–430.

Hayami, Y. and Ruttan, V. (1985). *Agricultural Development: International Perspective*. John Hopkins University Press: Baltimore, MD and London.

Juma, C. (2006). Redesigning African economies: The role of engineering in international development. The 2006 Hinton Lecture, Royal Academy of Engineering, London.

King, K. and McGrath, S. (2004). *Knowledge for Development. Comparing British, Japanese, Swedish and World Bank Aid*. Zed Books, London.

Marcelle, G. (2004). *Technological Learning. A Strategic Imperative for Firms in the Developing World*. Edward Elgar, Cheltenham.

OECD (2006). *The Development Dimension — Aid for Trade: Making It Effective*. Paris.

OECD (2007a). Disaggregating technical cooperation. DCD/DAC/STAT(2007)3, OECD, Paris.

OECD (2007b). Global monitoring of Aid for Trade flows. Joint meeting of the Development Assistance Committee and Working Party of the Trade Committee, COM/DCD/TAD(2007)1, OECD, Paris.

Pardey, P., Alston, J. and Beintema, N. (2006). Agricultural R&D spending at a critical crossroads. *Farm Policy Journal*, 3 (1): 1–9.

Pardey, P., Beintema, N., Dehmer, S. and Wood, S. (2006). Agricultural research: A growing global divide? International Food Policy Research Institute, Washington, DC.

Pray, C. and Umali-Deininger, D. (1998). The private sector in agricultural research systems: Will it fill the gap? *World Development*, 26 (6): 1127–1148.

Roodman, D. (2006). An index of donor performance. Working Paper No. 67, Center for Global Development, Washington, DC.

Spielman, D. (2007). Pro-poor agricultural biotechnology: Can the international research system deliver the goods? *Food Policy*, 32: 189–204.

UNCTAD (2000). *The Least Developed Countries Report 2000: Aid, Private Capital Flows and External Debt: The Challenge of Financing Debt in the LDCs*. United Nations publication, sales no. E.00.II.D.21, Geneva and New York.

UNCTAD (2002). *The Least Developed Countries Report 2002: Escaping the Poverty Trap*. United Nations publication, sales no. E.02.II.D.13, Geneva and New York.

UNCTAD (2006). *The Least Developed Countries Report 2006: Developing Productive Capacities*. United Nations publication, sales no. E.06.II.D.9, Geneva and New York.

UNESCO (2005). *UNESCO Science Report 2005*. United Nations Educational, Scientific and Cultural Organization, Paris.

United Nations (2002). Report on the International Conference on Financing for Development, A/CONF.198/11.

United Nations Millennium Project Task Force on Science, Technology, and Innovation. (2005). *Innovation: Applying Knowledge in Development*. Earthscan, London.

Watson, R., Crawford, M. and Farley, S. (2003). Strategic approaches to science and technology in development. Policy Research Working Paper No. 3026, World Bank, Washington, DC.

World Bank (2006). *Enhancing Agricultural Innovation: How to Go Beyond the Strengthening of Research Systems*. World Bank, Washington, DC.

WTO (2006a). Recommendations of the task force on Aid for Trade. Aid for Trade Task Force, WT/AFT/1, WTO, Geneva.

WTO (2006b). An enhanced Integrated Framework. WT/IFSC/W/15, WTO, Geneva.

Yammal, C. and Casabonne, U. (2005). Review of bank lending in science, technology and innovation capacity building: A cross-country comparison. Powerpoint presentation downloadable from 1089743700155/Yammal_Casabonne_SnT_Dec05.ppt.

Annex

OECD CRS Codes[a] used to define STI-related aid

CRS code	Description	Clarifications
1. Research		
11182	Educational research	Research and studies on education effectiveness, relevance and quality; systematic evaluation and monitoring
12182	Medical research	General medical research (excluding basic health research)
23082	Energy research	Including general inventories and surveys
31182	Agricultural research	Including plant breeding, physiology, genetic resources, ecology, taxonomy, disease control and agricultural bio-technology
31282	Forestry research	Including artificial regeneration, genetic improvement, production methods, fertilizer and harvesting
31382	Fishery research	Pilot fish culture; marine/freshwater biological research.
32182	Technological research and development	Including industrial standards, quality management, metrology, testing, accreditation, and certification
41082	Environmental research	Including establishment of databases, inventories/accounts of physical and natural resources, environmental profiles and impact studies if not sector-specific
2. Improvements of Human Skills		
11330	Vocational training	Elementary vocational training and secondary-level technical education, on-the job training, apprenticeships, including informal vocational training
11420	Higher education	Degree and diploma programmes at universities, colleges and polytechnics; scholarships
11430	Advanced technical and managerial training	Professional-level vocational training programmes and in-service training
12181	Medical education/training	Medical education and training for tertiary-level services
12261	Health education	Information, education and training of the population for improving health knowledge and practices; public health and awareness campaigns.
12281	Health personnel development	Training of health staff for basic health-care services
13081	Personnel development for population and reproductive health	Education and training of health staff for population and reproductive health care services
14081	Education and training in water supply and sanitation	
16062	Statistical capacity-building	In national statistical offices and any other government ministries
21081	Education and training in transport and storage	
23081	Energy education/training	Applies to all energy sub sectors; all levels of training
24081	Education/training in banking and financial services	
31181	Agricultural education/training	
31166	Agricultural extension	Non-formal training in agriculture
31281	Forestry education/training	
31381	Fishery education/training	
33181	Trade education/training	Human resources development in trade not included under any of the above codes. Includes university programmes in trade
41081	Environmental education/training	
43081	Multisector education/training	Including scholarships
43082	Research/scientific institutions	When sector cannot be identified

a   OECD CRS Codes available as of 2 February 2007.